ORGANIZATION DEVELOPMENT

A Publication in the Berrett-Koehler Organizational Performance Series
Richard A. Swanson and Barbara L. Swanson, Series Editors

ORGANIZATION
DEVELOPMENT

Principles ▪ Processes ▪ Performance

Gary N. McLean

BERRETT-KOEHLER PUBLISHERS, INC.
San Francisco

Berrett–Koehler Publishers, Inc.
235 Montgomery Street, Suite 650
San Francisco, CA 94104-2916
Tel: (415) 288-0260   Fax: (415) 362-2512   www.bkconnection.com

ORDERING INFORMATION

Quantity sales. Special discounts are available on quantity purchases by corporations, associations, and others. For details, contact the "Special Sales Department" at the Berrett-Koehler address above.

Individual sales. Berrett–Koehler publications are available through most bookstores. They can also be ordered direct from Berrett-Koehler: Tel: (800) 929-2929; Fax: (802) 864-7626; www.bkconnection.com

Orders for college textbook/course adoption use. Please contact Berrett-Koehler: Tel: (800) 929-2929; Fax: (802) 864-7626.

Orders by U.S. trade bookstores and wholesalers. Please contact Publishers Group West, 1700 Fourth Street, Berkeley, CA 94710. Tel: (510) 528-1444; Fax (510) 528-3444.

Production Management: Michael Bass Associates

Berrett-Koehler and the BK logo are registered trademarks of Berrett-Koehler Publishers, Inc.

Printed in the United States of America

Berrett-Koehler books are printed on long-lasting acid-free paper. When it is available, we choose paper that has been manufactured by environmentally responsible processes. These may include using trees grown in sustainable forests, incorporating recycled paper, minimizing chlorine in bleaching, or recycling the energy produced at the paper mill.

Library of Congress Cataloging-in-Publication Data
McLean, Gary N.
    Organization development: principles, processes, performance / Gary N. McLean.
        p.   cm.
    Includes bibliographical references and index.
    ISBN-10: 1-57675-313-1; ISBN-13: 978-1-57675-313-2
    1. Organizational change. 2. Organizational effectiveness. 3. Organizational
                                            Title.
                                                                    2006

                                                            2005050760

3   2   1

*T*hough not inclined to dedications, as I approach the culmination of my academic career at the University of Minnesota, I dedicate this book, first, to decades of students and clients who have helped me shape my thinking about OD.

The most important dedication is to my family for their love, support, challenges, and in-process laboratory: my wife, Lynn, and my adult children, their spouses, and my grandchildren: Katherine, Louis, and Amanda Taylor; Laird and Tina McLean with a child on the way; Melissa McLean; Paul and Laura McLean; Cynthia, Ron, Sophia, and Drew Lancaster; and Brian McLean.

I also want to dedicate this book to my parents, L. Neil and Robbie McLean; my father died during the writing of this book.

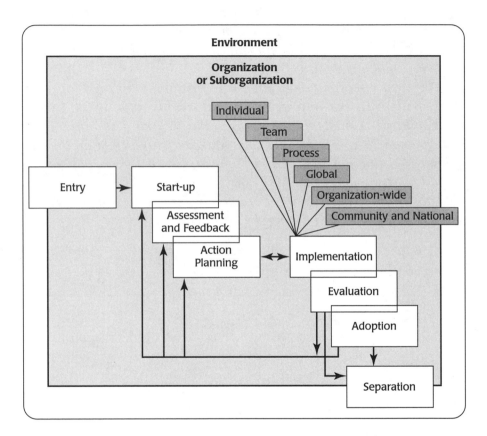

Organization Development Process Model

Contents

List of Figures

List of Tables

Preface

This book has been written as an introductory textbook in the field of organization development (OD). As such, it makes no claim for providing in-depth discussion of the many complex and dynamic issues surrounding the field. Nor does it claim to provide the reader with in-depth knowledge and skills about the specific aspects of organization development. A multitude of resources already exists providing detailed coverage of specific OD elements. In addition, it generally takes many years of working with a mentor to develop the skills essential for practicing organization development effectively.

Rather, the intent of this book is to offer readers an overview of the field to acquaint them with the vocabulary of OD and to provide some rudimentary processes to support them as they begin practicing in the field. (A quick note: when a Glossary term appears the first time in the text, we flag it by using *bold italic*.) It is my hope that some readers will develop a vision of themselves as organization development professionals and will pursue additional education, read specialized books, participate actively in the professional organizations that include an emphasis on OD, and find mentors from whom to learn the specific applications of the theories supporting the field.

I have long claimed that there are two foundational requirements for being an OD professional. The first is a deeper and richer understanding of the self. This might include extensive self-reflection and meditation, or it might require working with a professional therapist. The second foundational requirement is an acceptance of ambiguity. We live in a complex world that does not have black-and-white answers. I have developed a reputation for my inevitable response, "It depends," to almost any question that I am asked. Readers of this book will be reminded of the need to develop comfort with ambiguity, as I often suggest issues with which the field is struggling and seldom provide absolute answers. Simply stated, our profession is a reflection of our environment—changing and dynamic. Efforts seem to be going on continuously to find new ways to envision the field and to infuse it with new life.

Enjoy the book. Be creative as you continue to develop your understanding of yourself and of the field of OD. Expand your comfort level with ambiguity. And, as William Shakespeare said, "To thine own self be true!"

Acknowledgements

I would like to express my appreciation to two people in particular: Roland Sullivan and Richard (Dick) Swanson.

While Roland and I have chosen different paths and different approaches to the field of OD, it was Roland who, in 1979, as we were developing our graduate program in human resource development (then known as training and development), encouraged us to include OD in our programs. We did, and many of our students, especially those at the doctoral level, have gone on to make significant contributions to the field of OD in both theory and practice.

Dick and I were colleagues at the University of Minnesota for almost 30 years. We, too, see the world through different lenses. Fortunately, our friendship and professional collegiality have been strengthened as a result of respectfully challenging each other's ideas.

Thanks especially to my family for being a wonderful laboratory that continues to reward me on a daily basis. Special thanks to my wife, Lynn McLean; to Laird McLean and Cynthia McLean Lancaster, two of my children who have followed me in the OD field and are now part of our company, McLean Global Consulting, Inc.; and to Anne-Marie Kuiper, one of my doctoral students—all of whom provided very insightful feedback on early versions of the manuscript, helped me in putting together the pieces of the final manuscript, and generally helped ease the stress of creating a project like this. Thanks, too, to our son, Brian McLean, a graphic artist, who assisted in creating the core model for this book.

Gary N. McLean, RODC, Hon.BA, MA, MDiv, EdD
St. Paul, MN
June, 2005

1

What Is Organization Development?

CHAPTER OUTLINE

OVERVIEW   This chapter presents the definitional issues, the business case for OD, two primary models with their strengths and weaknesses (action research, appreciative inquiry), and the importance of organizational context. It also contains the historical roots of the field, as well as its values and principles. Concepts of organizational culture and change management are also explored briefly.

Welcome to the world of *organization development* (OD)! Every reader of this book comes with multiple experiences in organizations—from your family to your schools; churches, synagogues, temples, and mosques; workplaces; charitable organizations; government agencies; sports teams; social clubs; labor unions; and so on. Some of these experiences have probably been positive, while some have probably been negative. That's the nature of the world in which we live. In this book, you will learn some of the approaches that professionals in the field of OD use to turn negative experiences into positive ones, and how good OD practice that relies on solid OD theory can help organizations to be more productive, more satisfying, and more effective and efficient.

DEFINITIONS OF AN ORGANIZATION

The dictionary provides the following formal definition of an organization:

> a) the act or process of organizing; the state or manner of being organized: a high degree of organization; b) something that has been organized or made into an ordered whole; c) something made up of elements with varied functions that contribute to the whole and to collective functions; an organism; d) a group of persons organized for a particular purpose; an association: a benevolent organization; e) a structure through which individuals cooperate *systematically* to conduct business; the administrative personnel of such a structure. (*American Heritage Dictionary of the English Language*, 2000)

A more informal definition can include any situation in which two or more persons are involved in a common pursuit or objective. Given the broad-ranging and all-encompassing definitions of *organization*, it is easy to understand the complexity of OD and the large number of situations in which it can be applied.

Now, as you begin to think about your experience in past and current organizations, quickly jot down some of the positive and negative experiences you have encountered. Use two columns, with the positive in one and the negative in the other. By doing this, you are already using the early stages of one of the tools of OD, called a *force field analysis*. You'll hear more about this tool in a later chapter. An OD professional, along with others in the same organization, might use a list like this to determine how people in that organization feel about what is and what is not going well. This, too, is a part of the OD process of doing an *organizational analysis* or a *needs assessment*. The OD professional might use such lists to work with the organization in finding ways to build on the positives and to overcome the negatives.

The field of OD is not regulated, except through ethics statements developed by professional organizations (more on this later, too). As a result, anyone interested can practice what he or she might label as OD, even though the field might take exception to the accuracy of such a statement. But there is no recourse. Thus, one of the real challenges of the field is that some people who call themselves OD consultants or professionals (these terms are often used interchangeably and do not indicate whether the person is employed by the organization or is a self-employed person or a person employed by a consulting firm) is that they operate with a narrowly defined "toolbox"—a set of so-called solutions that they apply to every situation. Thus, we experience the "flavor of the month," a situation in which the latest fad is offered to organizations as *the* solution to all of their problems. Given the ambiguity of OD practice, having a strong theoretical background and functioning with proven models, therefore, become critical for successful and ethical OD practice.

DEFINING OD

As indicated earlier in this chapter, there is no standard definition of OD, and what may be considered as legitimate OD practice by some may equally be perceived by others, legitimately, as being outside the scope of OD. Here is your first challenge of *ambiguity*. How does the field continue to exist and thrive when we cannot agree on its definition?

What Can OD Address?

The field of OD is very large and complex; as such, OD professionals will find themselves in many different contexts using a wide range of methods and processes to bring about desired outcomes in organizations. This question will be answered more fully later in this chapter. For now, let me share a few situations in which I have been involved as an indication of the wide range in which one might practice OD.

. . . .

As our children were growing up, we used the tools of OD in our parenting. We held weekly family meetings with rotating facilitators (even the young children!) at which any grievances against each other or against parents could be voiced and (hopefully) managed, if not resolved. When it came to planning vacations, we used brainstorming to create a **Likert-type survey** to which everyone had equal input. The only differential role that we had as parents was in setting the budget. And whatever came out on top, that's what we did! With a family of six children (four are adopted Koreans), Lynn and I recognized how easy it would be for the individual child to be lost in the crowd. Thus, we created a system of providing each child with a "special day" once a month when each child could pick one parent and one activity that would be just for him or her. We used dialogue processes when there was conflict. We used storytelling to instill our values. Not only did OD serve us well as a family, but it also helped the children to develop some of the OD skills themselves.

. . . .

I have just finished a 3.5-year project sponsored by the U.S. State Department in which I worked with colleagues in Kyrgyzstan, a former soviet republic in Central Asia, to work on major initiatives to change the educational system by reinstituting free kindergarten, establishing graduate degrees for school administrators, instituting requirements for persons to become school administrators, establishing a professional organization for teachers, requiring transparency in the finances of schools and universities, and many other outcomes. One of my colleagues wrote to me shortly after the peaceful overthrow of the corrupt president indicating that the work we had done set the stage for the democratic processes that resulted in a peaceful transition of governments.

. . . .

I received an urgent telephone call from Saudi Arabia requesting my immediate assistance. There had been a serious refinery accident in which one person was killed and several other workers were injured. The company wanted me to do an assessment to determine why the accident had occurred and what changes the organization needed to make to reduce the risk of future problems in safety. This task required an exhaustive review of risk policies, safety training, the role of the corporate risk office in refineries, a review of the processes, and so on. Two of the major findings were that contract employees, who outnumbered regular employees 2:1, received no safety training, and the corporate risk office was viewed as an auditor rather than as a support system. No subsequent accidents have occurred since this project.

. . . .

Rather than going into detail on other projects, let me provide a sampling of others in which I have been involved:

- I have worked with a state agency to help it institute total quality management, with a specific goal of reducing roadside construction site accidents.
- I have worked as a coach to the CEO of a large consulting firm to provide him with feedback on his decision making and processes, and to serve as a foil for his ideas.
- I have worked with many organizations in helping approach a move into another part of the world.
- I have worked with several organizations immediately after a merger or acquisition to help create a common culture and to bring personnel, processes, and policies together.
- I assist organizations in conducting qualitative feedback to employees on their performance.
- I work with organizations to help them manage conflict when it has become destructive to the organization.
- I have provided support at the ministry level and research in the use of organization development principles and processes

> to improve the national situation in Kenya and the Republic of Korea. This emphasis is continuing and expanding globally.

....

This is not an exhaustive listing of the OD work that I do, and it is not even close to exhaustive of the work that can be done under the guise of organization development. I hope, however, that it will give the reader some sense of the scope and power of OD work.

Sample Definitions

Egan (2002) explored the range of definitions for OD. While not a comprehensive review, he did identify 27 definitions between 1969 and 2003. Providing all 27 definitions here probably serves no useful purpose. Thus, this section will present a few definitions that express considerably different perspectives. Change, whether planned or unplanned, is often associated with people's understanding of OD. Planned change was incorporated into what was perhaps the first formal definition for OD, that of Richard Beckhard (1969), though many such definitions emerged in that year. Beckhard defined OD as "an effort [that is] (1) planned, (2) organization-wide, and (3) managed from the top, to (4) increase organization effectiveness and health through (5) *planned interventions* in the organization's *processes*, using behavioral-science knowledge" (p. 9).

Some within the field are now critical of this definition, asserting that the world in which we live is too complex to plan change. Change, both positive and negative, imposes itself on us from many sources, most of which are beyond our control. Others argue that management from the top is hierarchical, a concept that is acceptable in some cultures but not in others, including, to some extent, the United States. On the other hand, if desired change is not supported by top management, can that change ever really occur or be sustained?

Another criticism of this definition is the use of a medical model and the reference to "health." At the same time, just as medical models are rapidly shifting from remediation to prevention, so also do we see this shift in OD. The final phrase of this definition, referencing the "behavioral sciences," underscores the multidisciplinary nature of the

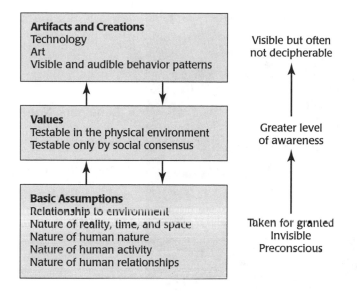

Figure 1.1 *Levels of Cultures and Their Interactions (adapted from Schein, 1980, p. 4)*

field. Many of the behavioral sciences are core to the practice of OD, including psychology, sociology, economics, and anthropology, among others.

Warren Bennis's (1969) definition positions OD as reactive to change, rather than proactive, as was the case in Beckhard's definition. Bennis also introduced the concept that is still core to our understanding of OD today—namely, organizational culture: "Organization development is a response to change, a complex educational strategy intended to change beliefs, attitudes, values, and structures of organizations so that they can better adapt to new technologies, markets, and challenges, and the dizzying rate of change itself" (p. 2). Bennis used four words that are seen today as key components of organizational culture: *beliefs, attitudes, values,* and *structures.* This view was later expanded by Edgar Schein (1980), who developed the idea of a ***cultural iceberg*** (see Figures 1.1 and 1.2).

These diagrams illustrate that change in an organization can occur at many levels. As behaviors and their associated artifacts are readily visible to others, OD can effect change in these relatively easily. However, when organizational change needs to penetrate the underlying

Photomontage by Uwe Kils

- Behaviors, Norms, Artifacts

- Stated Beliefs, Values

- Assumptions

Figure 1.2 *Schein's Cultural Iceberg*

beliefs, values, and, ultimately, the unconscious assumptions made in the organization, change is much more difficult. As illustrated in his metaphor of the iceberg, Schein indicated how difficult it is to "see" the assumptions that underlie our behaviors. Another metaphor used by Schein was the peeling of an onion. We can easily see the outside skin of the onion (behaviors), but, without peeling away the layers between the external skin and the core of the onion (the assumptions), we cannot really understand the onion (the people in the organization). This is the challenge that faces OD professionals—how do we peel away the layers of the onion or get to the bottom of the iceberg as we work in an organization? At the same time, because of its greater ease and efficient use of time, efforts to bring about change through OD should not attempt to go deeper than necessary to accomplish the objective (Harrison, 1970). If changes in behaviors or artifacts are sufficient (i.e., at the tip of the iceberg or the outer layer of the onion), then no further effort is necessary.

Moving forward, McLagan (1989), about whom you will hear more later in this chapter, also provided a definition:

> Organization development focuses on assuring healthy inter- and intra-unit relationships and helping groups initiate and manage change. Organization development's primary emphasis is on relationships and processes between and among individuals and groups. Its primary intervention is influence on the relationship of individuals and groups to effect an impact on the organization as a system. (p. 7)

Moving to a more current definition, Cummings and Worley (2005) proposed the following definition: "Organization development is a system wide application and transfer of behavioral science knowledge to the planned development, improvement, and reinforcement of strategies, structures, and processes that lead to organization effectiveness" (p. 1).

For the purposes of this book, I am proposing the following broad definition for *organization development,* based on a previous definition of *global human resource development* (McLean & McLean, 2001). The evolution of this definition is presented in Chapter 11.

> *Organization development* is any process or activity, based on the behavioral sciences, that, either initially or over the long term, has the potential to develop in an organizational setting enhanced knowledge, expertise, productivity, satisfaction, income, interpersonal relationships, and other desired outcomes, whether for personal or group/team gain, or for the benefit of an organization, community, nation, region, or, ultimately, the whole of humanity.

Egan (2002), using a card-sorting process based on the 27 OD definitions, identified 10 clusters of dependent variables (or desired outcomes) contained in the definitions:

- Advance organizational renewal
- Engage organization culture change
- Enhance profitability and competitiveness
- Ensure health and well-being of organizations and employees
- Facilitate learning and development
- Improve problem solving

- Increase effectiveness
- Initiate and/or manage change
- Strengthen system and process improvement
- Support adaptation to change (p. 67)

Such a broad set of desired outcomes adds to the complexity of the field of OD, impacting the expectations of OD by organizations and practitioners, which makes for a very challenging environment in which to do OD work.

A Separate Field or a Subset of Another Field?

Here is another piece of ambiguity: The answer to this question, as to much of OD work, itself, is "It depends!" The two professional organizations that exclusively represent OD professionals—OD Network and The OD Institute—have argued that OD is a field separate unto itself. Recently, however, the *Journal of Organization Development*, the journal of The OD Institute, has used OD along with the field of *human resource development (HRD)*. In addition, many other professional organizations see OD as a subset of that field:

- Academy of Human Resource Development (AHRD)
- Academy of Human Resource Development (India) (AHRD)
- Korean Academy of Human Resource Development (KAHRD)
- Academy of Management (AOM) (especially, the ODC—Organization Development and Change—Division)
- American Society for Training and Development (ASTD)
- Euresform
- Society for Human Resource Management (SHRM) (with several affiliated groups, such as the Arabian Society for HRM, the Japanese Society for HRM, etc.)
- Society for Industrial and Organizational Development (SIOP)
- University Forum of Human Resource Development (UFHRD)

It is interesting to note the number of global organizations that recognize OD as part of a larger field. Perhaps the most well-known of these inclusive models was developed by McLagan (1989) for ASTD.

Her research identified 11 functional areas within the larger field of human resources; this model is referred to as the *human resources wheel*, because it is often illustrated in a pie chart format. These functions were then grouped into two clusters: human resource development (HRD) and human resource management (HRM). Four of the 11 functions overlapped the two clusters, as shown in Table 1.1.

Note that OD is listed as one of three functions exclusively assigned to HRD. While McLagan has orally expressed some doubts about her model, this model is clearly embedded in the literature of HRD that is utilized around the world.

Exploring definitions of HRD globally led to the following definition:

> Human Resource Development is any process or activity that, either initially or over the long term, has the potential to develop . . . work-based knowledge, expertise, productivity and satisfaction, whether for personal or group/team gain, or for the benefit of an organization, community, nation, or ultimately, the whole of humanity. (McLean & McLean, 2001, p. 322)

It is easy to see from this definition, if accepted, how OD fits within the broader context of HRD globally.

TABLE 1.1   Assignment of 11 Human Resource Functions to HRD and HRM

HUMAN RESOURCE DEVELOPMENT (HRD)	HUMAN RESOURCE MANAGEMENT (HRM)
▪ **Training and development**	▪ **HR research and information systems**
▪ **Organization development**	▪ **Union/labor relations**
▪ **Career development**	▪ **Employee assistance**
▪ Organization/job design	▪ **Compensation/benefits**
▪ Human resource planning	▪ Organization/job design
▪ Performance management systems	▪ Human resource planning
▪ Selection and staffing	▪ Performance management systems
	▪ Selection and staffing

Note: Boldfaced items belong exclusively to that column. Nonboldfaced items are shared.

Source: Adapted from McLagan (1989).

Characteristics of OD

The American Society for Training and Development's OD Professional Practice Area attempted to provide a synthesis of the various definitions by providing the key points that it saw in the range of definitions available:

> We believe the practice of organization development:
> - must be in alignment with organization and business objectives;
> - is rooted in the behavioral sciences;
> - is long range and ongoing;
> - stresses a process orientation to achieve results;
> - is based on collaboration;
> - is a systems orientation.

The following conclusions can be drawn about the core characteristics of OD:

- OD is an interdisciplinary and primarily behavioral science approach that draws from such fields as organization behavior, management, business, psychology, sociology, anthropology, economics, education, counseling, and public administration.
- A primary, though not exclusive, goal of OD is to improve organizational effectiveness.
- The target of the change effort is the whole organization, departments, work groups, or individuals within the organization and, as mentioned earlier, may extend to include a community, nation, or region.
- OD recognizes the importance of top management's commitment, support, and involvement. It also affirms a bottom-up approach when the culture of the organization supports such efforts to improve an organization.
- It is a planned and long-range strategy for managing change, while also recognizing that the dynamic environment in which we live requires the ability to respond quickly to changing circumstances.
- The major focus of OD is on the total system and its interdependent parts.
- OD uses a collaborative approach that involves those affected by the change in the change process.

- It is an education-based program designed to develop values, attitudes, norms, and management practices that result in a healthy organization climate that rewards healthy behavior. OD is driven by humanistic values.

- It is a data-based approach to understanding and diagnosing organizations.

- It is guided by a *change agent*, *change team*, or *line management* whose primary role is that of facilitator, teacher, and coach rather than subject matter expert.

- It recognizes the need for planned follow-up to maintain changes.

- It involves planned interventions and improvements in an organization's processes and structures and requires skills in working with individuals, groups, and whole organizations. It is primarily driven by *action research (AR)* (which will be discussed soon).

Is OD the Same as Change Management?

In an effort to simplify an explanation of what OD is, some have suggested that OD and change management are the same. I disagree. There are times in the life of an organization where dramatic change is needed—change that does not and cannot rely on the use of OD. The marketplace sometimes requires that an organization take swift and unplanned actions in order to survive. It may require outsourcing domestically or to another country, downsizing, reductions in salaries, and increasing health care costs. Although all of these changes may be absolutely necessary for the survival of the organization, they do not necessarily follow the OD processes, principles, or values. An excellent distinction between OD change and change that does not follow OD principles is discussed in Beer and Nohria (2000). In essence, they argued that there is *E change* (economic value) and *O change* (organization's human capability), one of which is planned and follows OD principles (O), while the other (E) is market driven and does not follow OD principles; both can be included in what many people call change management. So, it is a mistake to equate OD with change management. The business benefits when *both* types of change are affirmed within an organization. While long-term, systemwide planning that results in change (the OD model) can be very beneficial for an organization and its bottom line, failure to act quickly and to make immediate decisions, even when those processes violate OD principles, may well result in the demise of the organization.

WHO IS AN OD PROFESSIONAL?

There are many ways to answer this question. We will answer it first by looking at where OD professionals are primarily employed, and then we will explore the qualifications for doing OD work. Finally, we will look at how OD consultants differ from management consultants or consultants in other fields of endeavor.

Internal versus External

OD professionals or consultants can be employed by the organization or can be hired on a contract basis. Regardless of whether they are internal or external to the organization, the term *consultant* is still commonly used. There is no right answer for whether an *internal consultant* is better than an *external consultant*, or vice versa (more ambiguity!). Table 1.2 outlines the advantages of each.

Because both internal and external OD consultants have advantages, it makes considerable sense for a partnership between an internal and an external consultant, so that the best of both can be available to the organization. For this same reason, it also makes sense to establish a partnership based on differences in demographics (e.g., gender, ethnicity, age) in order to capture fully the perspectives of varying views. What one might see, the other might not see or might see differently based on different socializing experiences. Thus, using a partnership approach can strengthen the ultimate outcomes from OD work.

OD work does not necessarily need to be performed by a professional serving in such a designated position. Increasingly, OD is performed by persons in other positions who have OD expertise. Thus, a line manager or a staff person in some other functional area who has been trained in OD can (and probably should) apply OD principles in his or her ongoing work. The more widely understood OD principles are in

TABLE 1.2   Advantages of Using Each Type of Consultant—Internal and External

INTERNAL	EXTERNAL
■ Already has familiarity with the organization and how it works ■ Knows the organizational culture better than any external can ever know it ■ Has relationships established that can get cooperation more quickly ■ Has a trust level already established ■ Lower cost by project because of organization's long-term commitment to employment ■ Organization takes less risk of confidential information being leaked ■ Less emphasis on getting the job done quickly as salary is already paid versus hourly pay for external ■ Greater accountability ■ Job security and less emphasis on marketing	■ Does not have preknowledge of the organizational culture, so does not enter the process with any preconceived notions ■ Often given more respect by insiders because he or she is not known except by reputation ■ More freedom to "say it like it is" because he or she has less at risk politically ■ Organization makes less long-term commitment for pay and no commitment for benefits, leading to lower overall costs. ■ Organizational members may be more willing to trust in confidentiality in sharing information with the consultant ■ Easier to be ethical; can refuse to do something that is deemed unethical ■ Can reject the project if there is a perceived lack of readiness for change in the organization ■ Usually has a broader set of experiences ■ Greater job variety ■ Can be separated from the organization quickly and easily if performance problems occur

an organization, the more likely it is that the organization will benefit from their use.

Qualifications for Doing OD Work

A subsequent chapter will focus extensively on the competencies needed by professionals doing OD work. This section will provide a very brief overview of the qualifications needed.

Given that OD work is based on the behavioral sciences, an OD professional would be expected to have an intensive and broad background in the behavioral sciences. Clearly, no one individual can be an expert in all of the behavioral sciences, so one would expect an OD professional to be involved in continuous study and lifelong learning in the profession. Furthermore, one would expect an OD professional to have advanced education specifically in OD, or in a field with a strong emphasis on the behavioral sciences in an organizational context (e.g., human resource development, industrial and organizational psychology, organizational behavior, etc.). At the same time, it should also be evident that no one can have complete knowledge of OD or of all of the behavioral sciences. So, do not be intimidated by what appears to be overwhelming content. At the same time, it should also be obvious that the field of OD is complex. A single course in OD, or in one or more of the behavioral sciences, is probably not sufficient to allow an individual to begin to practice OD.

Because there are no restrictions as to who can practice OD, trained professionals in the field have expressed concern that unqualified individuals can and do enter the field who may negatively affect the reputation of the OD field. This point leads to dialogue about whether there should be licensure, with the assumption that only qualified individuals will be licensed, thus protecting the practice of OD. Licensure is a legal requirement, usually enforced by a government entity. But licensure results in many problems. First, since we do not have a common definition of OD, how do we determine what competencies are necessary for licensure? Who will determine what is to be measured and how? Are the core competencies for OD even measurable? And what should be done with the thousands of OD professionals who are already in the field?

Another approach to becoming an OD professional, short of licensure, is to acquire appropriate credentials. The OD Institute is currently the only professional organization that provides specific certification in OD, though many universities may provide their own certification for students. The OD Institute has two levels of credentials: RODP (Registered Organization Development Professional) and RODC (Registered OD Consultant). Both certifications require ongoing membership in The OD Institute and an affirmation of the Code of Ethics of The Institute. In addition, to be an RODC (the higher level of certification) requires two letters of recommendation attesting to one's professional expertise and the passing of a multiple-choice examination. No identified research indicates that the work done by an RODP or an RODC is any better than that done by those without such credentials.

Finally, one can look at one's individual personality characteristics and one's level of knowledge and skill. An extensive list of competencies needed for OD professionals has been developed and will be explored in a later chapter. For now, it is important, again, to emphasize the importance of self-knowledge. When you work in an organization at the core of assumptions, beliefs, and values, it is easy to impose one's own assumptions, beliefs, and values on the organization, and to make judgments based on your own assumptions. It becomes critical, therefore, to understand fully what your own values, beliefs, and assumptions are to minimize the damage that may be done to the organization as a result of ignorance.

Another core expectation for an effective OD professional is basic knowledge of business and its language. Given that most OD work is done in a business environment, OD professionals need to understand that context. There are many skills and considerable knowledge that the OD professional must have that will be discussed in Chapter 16.

OD Consultants versus Traditional Consultants

A common and appropriate question is how OD consultants are different from traditional consultants, such as management consultants, information technology consultants, safety consultants, and almost every other field that employs consultants—and that means almost every field! While perhaps a biased perspective, Table 1.3 provides a

TABLE 1.3 Comparison of Traditional and OD Consultants

TRADITIONAL CONSULTANTS	OD CONSULTANTS
■ Are considered to be the subject matter expert	■ Function as facilitators rather than subject matter experts
■ Take more of a telling and directive mode with clients	■ Work/collaborate with clients and client members
■ Create dependency between the client and them	■ Create interdependency moving to independence for the client
■ Own and manage process and outcomes	■ Allow clients to own and manage process and outcomes
■ Transfer little or no skill to client organization	■ Transfer skill to client organization

comparison of traditional consultants and OD consultants—at least in the ideal world. Schein (1998 and earlier) referred to the OD consulting processes described in Table 1.3 as *process consultation*.

MODELS FOR DOING OD

This section contains an explanation of what a model is and how it is used in practice, followed by a basic presentation of the primary models in use for doing OD. This text is organized around the action research model. Although the action research model has been the dominant model in use in OD (and continues to be), it has been criticized, and alternate approaches have been suggested. All of the current alternative approaches, however, are still basically variations of the action research model.

The Use of Models in OD

A *model* is a representation of the real thing and is intended to provide general guidance and suggestions about how one might proceed. For example, a model airplane may look like the real thing in miniature, but it will be lacking some critical components, as it will not carry passengers or cargo and will not fly across the ocean. Yet it can be a very useful tool in aviation design and construction. A model plane used in a wind tunnel might well show engineers what design components are best equipped to deal with a variety of wind patterns. But no one loses sight of the fact that the model airplane is not the real plane.

The same is true of models utilized in the field of OD. Even though the model is not OD, an OD model has the capability to illustrate and lay the groundwork for the work to be done. Though it may be helpful in building our understanding of a certain phenomenon, a model cannot replicate a phenomenon, laying a foundation instead. Practitioners and even theoreticians sometimes lose sight of the difference between a model and reality. So, as you encounter models throughout this book, keep in mind that they are presented to help you understand a phenomenon, but not to describe it fully.

The Action Research Model

From early on in OD, the action research model (ARM) has been the organizing approach for doing OD. It remains deeply embedded within the practice of OD, and a form of it will be the organizer for the remainder of this book. Kurt Lewin, one of the widely recognized founders of the field of OD, is also credited with forwarding the ARM concept in the mid-1940s with his famous statement, "No research without action; no action without research."

A precursor to the ARM was Shewhart's PDCA cycle, developed in the 1920s as a model to explain the necessity for ongoing organizational improvement and a process through which such continuous improvement was to occur (see Figure 1.3).

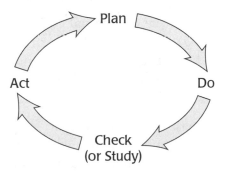

Figure 1.3 *Shewhart's PDCA Cycle*

At the Plan stage, decisions are made about what might be done to improve the organization and its processes, using a variety of decision-making tools. At the Do stage, those plans are carried out in a pilot or trial implementation. At the Check stage (W. Edwards Deming, well-known for his leadership in *total quality management*, later suggested that Study might be a better word here), measurements are taken to determine whether the pilot implementation did, in fact, result in the changes desired. At the Act stage, the process, if successful, is implemented. Whether successful or unsuccessful, the next stage is to begin the cycle all over again with a Plan stage. If successful, the new plans should explore what more can be done to improve the processes. If unsuccessful, new data may be gathered to determine what went wrong, and new plans are piloted to see whether they will improve the processes. The emphasis is on continuous improvement.

In many respects, the action research model reflects a similar commitment to continuous improvement. An earlier model (McLean & Sullivan, 1989) suggested a cyclical but sequential model, much like the PDCA model shown in Figure 1.3. This type of model, however, has been criticized on a number of counts. For example, even though the model appears to be cyclical, the unidirectional arrows still suggest a linear model. Furthermore, there is no indication of overlap between the phases, or any suggestion that there might be a back and forth movement among the phases. As a result, a modification of this model (see Figure 1.4) is used throughout this book, called the *organization development process (ODP) model*.

The ODP model consists of eight components or phases with inter-activity among the phases, each of which will become one (or more) chapters of this book. Each of these phases applies whether or not the OD professional is an internal or external consultant. Keeping in mind that OD can be applied at different levels of depth, some of these phases will be very brief and superficial, while more in-depth OD efforts will require more time, resources, and effort. Briefly, the purpose of each component is as follows:

> *Entry* – The first phase is when the OD professional ("consultant"), having done the requisite marketing, and a person representing the client organization (or part of an organization) ("client") meet to decide whether they will work together, assess the readiness of the organization to change, and agree on the conditions under which they will work together.

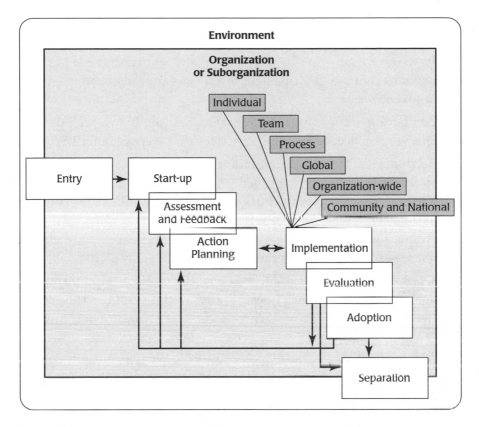

Figure 1.4 *Organization Development Process Model*

Start-up – The next phase occurs after an agreement has been reached to work together, and a basic infrastructure (such as a client team with whom the consultant will work) is put in place.

Assessment and Feedback – This phase is sometimes called *analysis* or *diagnosis*; in this phase, the consultant and client, together, determine the organizational culture, including its strengths and weaknesses, and give this information to the organizational members. The assessment can also focus on a specific area of interest to the organization that might, because of its lack of depth, require much less commitment of time and resources.

Action Plan – Based on what was determined in the previous step, plans are mutually developed as to how the organization wishes to move forward, in terms of both goals and objectives and how these will be accomplished.

Implementation – In this phase, the plans that were made in the previous step are implemented; in OD jargon, this is called an *intervention*.

Evaluation – This phase answers the question, "How well did our intervention accomplish the objectives that were planned?"

Adoption – If the evaluation indicates that the objectives of the intervention were accomplished, then the change that was implemented becomes institutionalized; that is, it becomes a part of the way in which business is done in the organization. If the evaluation indicates that desired objectives were not met, then this phase is skipped. In both cases, the process begins all over again.

Separation – At some point, the consultant will withdraw from the intervention process, having transferred his or her skills to the client organization (again, whether the OD professional is internal or external). This may occur because additional change is no longer a priority to the client organization, or that it is not ready for the next stage of change. It may be because OD skills are needed that the current OD consultant does not possess. It may be that the consultant has been co-opted by the organizational culture and is no longer able to maintain objectivity. For whatever reason, separation should occur intentionally and not by just letting it happen.

As can be seen by the model illustrated in Figure 1.4, the ideal, then, is that the process continues, with or without the consultant's involvement, with the objective of continuously improving the organization, no matter how well it is doing. Keep in mind the discussion earlier about the use of a model. Sometimes, phases need to be combined or even skipped because of the demands of the marketplace. This process should be done cautiously. Although the ARM/ODP process has served the field well, criticisms of its use do exist. Some claim that it takes too long to go through all of these phases and that the world is too dynamic to take the time to do a thorough job at each of these phases. A counterresponse to this criticism is to ask how much longer it takes when a step is skipped and the OD process fails because that step was skipped. As a result, the time and resources focused on improvement are wasted, requiring the OD practitioner to begin the process anew.

A second criticism of the model is that OD, using this traditional approach, has as its goal to find problems to be solved, thus leading to what has become known as the *appreciative inquiry (AI)* model. In contrast to ARM or ODP, AI looks solely for the positive in an organization. The counter to this argument, however, is that good OD, through the use of the ODP, is to find strengths in the organizational culture as well as problems. By focusing only on the positive, as AI does, neither the client nor the consultant has a systemwide view of the organizational culture. AI will be presented briefly in this section.

Appreciative Inquiry

Appreciative inquiry has come to be associated with Cooperrider (e.g., Cooperrider & Srivastva, 1987). It basically uses the same steps as the ODP with one major modification to one of the phases. Instead of exploring the full range of strengths and weaknesses of an organization's culture, the assessment stage uses a narrative approach to surface only positive aspects of the organization's culture. As identified by Egan and Lancaster (2005), however, consultants who use the AI approach have difficulty in convincing clients of its validity. *Anecdotal research* does, however, suggest that such an approach can be beneficial for an organization, especially if it has been traumatized in the recent past. For example, AI might be more effective than ODP when an organization has a long history of near bankruptcy, when an organization acquires another organization in a hostile takeover, or when severe downsizing has occurred.

Abbreviated Models of ARM/ODP

Many modifications to the ARM/ODP models have been proposed, though they consistently follow the components of the ARM/ODP, perhaps changing the wording or combining steps to produce fewer apparent steps. However, the essence of the model appears to be unchanged and continues to function as the normative approach to OD. Keeping in mind that no model is perfect and that every model is an imperfect representation of reality, given the history and usefulness of the ARM/ODP, we will use that model throughout the rest of this book.

ROOTS AND HISTORY OF OD

From the beginning of time, it is probable that humanity has tried consistently, though imperfectly and with notable exceptions, to improve the lot of life. There are many examples from religious literature of the use of consultants in making decisions. One common to many religious traditions is the consultation of Moses with his father-in-law, Jethro, to improve the organization of the large numbers of Israelites escaping from Egypt. Mohammed, also, had his consultants, and one could argue that the 12 disciples served as consultants to Jesus. So, as we look at the roots that led to the formation of OD, we have a limitless number of options from which to draw. Even when exploring the history of OD, one has difficulty, as with any history, in identifying exactly how the field emerged and developed. In a recent Web chat about the history and origins of the OD field with practitioners and theoreticians who had been around and involved when OD emerged, everyone had a different memory, including those who were in the same room at the same time! So it is difficult to argue that there is a single source of the field of OD. What is interesting to note is that almost everyone remembers OD as emerging—that no one set out to create a new field, but the important concepts and tools that were to make up the field of OD emerged as people were simply trying to do their jobs better.

Most of the early names associated with the field of OD were, not surprisingly, psychologists; as a result, our field has been heavily influenced by the psychological theories of Sigmund Freud, Carl Jung, Carl Rogers, and B. F. Skinner. Those influences are still present in management and the field of OD, in such theories as small group dynamics, reinforcement theories, the Myers-Briggs Type Indicator (MBTI), open-ended interviewing, and so on. Margaret Mead, Gert Hofstede, Fons Trompenaur, Edward and Mildred Hall, Edgar Schein, and others reflected efforts at describing cultures from an anthropological perspective. John Keynes, Thomas Malthus, and others have introduced economic theories. In the area of *quality management* and continuous improvement, names such as Joseph Juran, W. Edwards Deming, and Kaoru Ishikawa are considered primary contributors. In the area of systems theory, certainly biologist Ludwig von Bertalanffy must be included along with more recent contributors such as Peter Senge and Margaret Wheatley. We could easily fill pages and pages with names of people who have made contributions to the field of OD. What follows, in this section, are a few names selected out of my biases to reflect only some of the more significant factors that have contributed to the field of OD. Some of the ideas that follow are based on Alban and Scherer (2005).

Kurt Lewin (mid-1940s) – It is impossible in this brief paragraph to convey the significance of Lewin's contributions. Lewin worked with organizations to improve their productivity and through various consultancies created the concepts of force field analysis, *sensitivity training* (which led to team building), feedback, *change theory*, action research, and *self-managed work teams* (more about these as we move forward in this book).

Richard Beckhard (mid-1960s) – Most reports indicate that Beckhard was the first person to coin the phrase *organization development*.

W. Edwards Deming (1950s in Japan; 1980s in the United States) – Few would claim that Deming used the processes or language of OD. Nevertheless, at least in the United States, Deming, through his initial work in Japan, popularized the concept of continuous process improvement, with the emphasis on processes rather than results, arguing that the best processes lead to the best results—a good OD concept!

Wilfred Bion (late 1940s) – Bion was a key leader in London's Tavistock Institute (in the UK), where discoveries were being made about group processes at about the same time as *T-groups (training groups)* were emerging in the United States. The two concepts eventually came together as there were interactions across the ocean.

Eric Trist (1950s) – Also working in the UK, Trist is credited with the development of the *sociotechnical system (STS)* in his work in the coal mines of England. STS focuses on the interface among people, machines, and their environment.

Other important names will surface as specific OD concepts and tools are presented throughout the remaining chapters of this book.

WHEN AND WHY SHOULD AN ORGANIZATION USE OD?

The field of OD is extremely broad—one of the problems in communicating clearly what the field entails. OD is not a technique or a group of tools, though some OD professionals practice as if it were. Rather, OD can be applied any time an organization wants to make planned improvements using the OD values. OD might be used in any of the following situations:

- To develop or enhance the organization's *mission statement* (statement of purpose) or *vision statement* for what it wants to be
- To help align *functional structures* in an organization so they are working together for a common purpose
- To create a *strategic plan* for how the organization is going to make decisions about its future and achieving that future
- To manage conflict that exists among individuals, groups, functions, sites, and so on, when such conflicts disrupt the ability of the organization to function in a healthy way
- To put in place processes that will help improve the ongoing operations of the organization on a continuous basis
- To create a collaborative environment that helps the organization be more effective and efficient
- To create reward systems that are compatible with the goals of the organization
- To assist in the development of policies and procedures that will improve the ongoing operation of the organization
- To assess the working environment, to identify strengths on which to build and areas in which change and improvement are needed
- To provide help and support for employees, especially those in senior positions, who need an opportunity to be coached in how to do their jobs better
- To assist in creating systems for providing feedback on individual performance and, on occasion, conducting studies to give individuals feedback and coaching to help them in their individual development

This is not an exhaustive list—it is suggestive only. But it will give you some idea of the range of activities for which OD professionals might be called on to assist an organization.

OD as a field has thrived because of the value-added concepts and tools that it has brought to organizations and its *stakeholders* (those concerned with how the organization operates), including customers, stockholders, employees, management, the community, and even the nation. If an OD professional can be helpful in bringing about desired change with a process that uses the values described in the next section, everyone benefits. *Organization Development* (1991) suggested the following benefits to the use of OD (as opposed to other types of consulting or using individuals within the organization who do not have OD skills):

> An atmosphere can be established which will support more innovation and creativity, increase job satisfaction, develop more positive interpersonal relationships and foster greater participation in creating plans and defining organizational goals. Systems can help to establish this kind of atmosphere. (p. 2)

All of this will create a more effective and efficient organization that will, consequently, provide higher-quality goods and services at a reasonable price, increase profitability, improve stock values, improve the work environment, and support management in its leadership role.

A VALUES-BASED FIELD

In the characteristics section of this chapter, I mentioned that OD is a value-driven, humanistic field. An entire chapter of this book has been devoted to the ethical processes by which OD consultants are expected to act. In this chapter, as a concluding section, two statements are provided to illustrate the values base of the field. The first is the mission statement of the Academy of Management's Organization Development and Change Division (2005):

> The Organization Development and Change division represents scholar/practitioners committed to individual and organization success and to the fulfillment of humanity's spirit and potential. It encourages efforts that create, develop, and disseminate

knowledge or extend the practice of constructive change management and organization development.

The division affirms the importance of a triple bottom line in organization effectiveness (human-social, financial, and environmental); justice, dignity, and trust; and shared accomplishment resulting in positive, meaningful contributions to the global society. The division acknowledges and accepts the responsibility for contributing in a significant way to the creation and enhancement of an ethical and humane global community. (www.aom.pace.edu/odc/draftofvm.html; reprinted by permission)

Second, a portion of the statement of principles of practice being promulgated by the OD Network (2003) reads as follows:

OD Principles of Practice
Organization Development is a planned and systemic change effort using organization theory and behavioral science, knowledge and skills to help the organization or a unit within an organization become more vital and sustainable.

The practice of OD is grounded in a distinctive set of core values and principles that guide practitioner behavior and actions (called *interventions*).

Values Based. Key values include:
- Respect and inclusion—to equally value the perspectives and opinions of everyone.
- Collaboration—to build win-win relationships in the organization.
- Authenticity—to help people behave congruent with their espoused values.
- Self-awareness—committed to developing self-awareness and inter-personal skills within the organization.
- Empowerment—to focus on helping everyone in the client organization increase their individual level of autonomy and sense of personal power and courage in order to enhance productivity and elevate employee morale.
- Democracy and social justice—the belief that people will support those things for which they have had a hand in shaping; that human spirit is elevated by pursuing democratic principles.

Supported by Theory

OD's strength is that it draws from multiple disciplines that inform an understanding of human systems, including the applied behavioral and physical sciences.

Systems Focused

It is grounded in open systems theory and approaches to understand communities and organizations. Change in one area of a system always results in changes in other areas and change in one area cannot be sustained without supporting changes in other areas of the system.

Action Research

A distinguishing OD feature, contrary to empirical research, that posits things change by simply looking at them. Therefore, the results from planned action must be continuously examined and change strategies revised as interventions unfold.

Process Focused

The emphasis is on the way things happen, more than the content of things, per se. Management consultants are more concerned with the what versus the why.

Informed by Data

Involves the active inquiry and assessment of the internal and external environment in order to discover valid data and create a compelling rationale for change and commitment to the achievement of a desired future organization state.

Client Centered

OD Practitioners maintain focus on the needs of the client, continually promoting client ownership of all phases of the work and supporting the client's ability to sustain change after the consultant engagement ends. (Organization Development Network, 71 Valley Street, Suite 301, South Orange, NJ 07079-2825; [973] 763-7337—voice, [973] 763-7488; www.odnetwork.org; reprinted by permission)

An interesting dilemma concerns the way in which values of OD practitioners and authors think about how they do OD. Bradford (2005) captured this dilemma succinctly:

OD is confused about its values. On the one hand, OD claims that it is firmly based in the applied behavioral sciences. But on the other hand, it stresses its humanistic roots. What happens when the latter is not supported by the former? Unfortunately for many OD consultants, it is the humanistic values, not the applied behavioral sciences, that dominate. . . . What OD has lost is its commitment to rigorous, objective analysis of what truly is effective and instead has replaced that with a view of what it thinks the world should be. (p. xxvi; italics in original)

It is my hope and intent that I have been successful in this book of providing a balanced approach, one that is not either/or but, in the spirit of accepting ambiguity, both/and. We do not always have clear answers from research about what the appropriate behavioral science response should be in a consultancy. And, while we cannot and should not leave our values behind, we must proceed in a thoughtful and aware way. I am a humanist, and I am a behavioral scientist. That is an ambiguity I have had to accept in my life. I hope you are able to find a balance in your own life as you read this book.

CHAPTER SUMMARY

From the many definitions of organization development that exist, a few were presented to give the reader a sense of how the broad field of OD has evolved. Detail was provided in support of the action research model, the core approach to OD, modified in this text as the organization development process model, with an explanation of each of its eight phases or dimensions: Entry, Start-up, Assessment and Feedback, Action Planning, Implementation, Evaluation, Adoption, and Separation. Brief mention was also made of the appreciative inquiry approach to doing OD. The organizational context is an essential factor influencing how OD is done in that organization. Generally, reference to this is to organizational culture. The components of culture were explored, with a recognition of the difficulty of determining the assumptions that reside within organizational members. Some of the major historical roots of OD were explored. Clearly, as with almost every topic in this book, such coverage is not comprehensive as whole books exist on the topic. The positive impact of doing OD work on an organization's performance was then explored. Finally, the values espoused by the OD Network and others were presented in support of the concept of OD being a value-based process with a bias toward humanistic values in creating an open system designed to meet the needs of its stakeholders.

QUESTIONS FOR DISCUSSION OR SELF-REFLECTION

1. Is the list you made of positive experiences in your selected organization while reading this chapter longer than the negative experiences, or vice versa? What is there about that organization that leads to this outcome?

2. Which definition of OD do you prefer? Why?

3. Do you think it makes a difference if OD is viewed as a stand-alone field or as a subset of another field? Why?

4. Describe an example of change in an organization that does not follow OD principles. What is it about that example that is not consistent with OD principles?

5. Pick an organization of which you are a member. Would you rather work with an internal or an external OD consultant? Why?

6. From your perspective, is it important to have recognized credentials for OD consultants? Why?

7. Why do you think there are so few credentialing organizations? Why is the existing credentialing process not more rigorous?

8. Why do you think that appreciative inquiry consultants might have a difficult time in selling the concept to clients? What arguments might be used to make the concept acceptable?

9. How do you think the OD Principles of Practice would influence how an OD consultant does his or her job? Discuss whether you believe that following the OD Principles of Practice statement will add business value to an organization.

2

Entry: Marketing and Contracting

CHAPTER OUTLINE

Marketing
The First Meeting with a Prospective Client
Contracts
Chapter Summary
Questions for Discussion or Self-Reflection

OVERVIEW   In this chapter, we explore how OD professionals obtain work (both internally and externally), the contracting process (again, both internally and externally), determining the readiness of the client to change, and establishing collaborative networks.

Obviously, before organization development work can begin, there must be a place in which to begin this work. This requires the OD professional to interact with potential clients, whether as an internal or as an external OD professional, and reach agreement on the work to be done, the processes to be followed, and the allocation of work responsibilities among all parties. Using the organization development process model, as shown in Figure 2.1, we are at the beginning of the cycle in phase 1: *Entry*.

MARKETING

Innumerable books, chapters, and articles have been written on marketing and how and when to utilize different marketing strategies. However, the purpose of this section is not to provide a detailed account of marketing initiatives but, rather, to provide the basics of a few aspects of identifying and building a client list, as well as attaining new projects, both internally and externally. Advantages and disadvantages of each marketing approach for external consultants are summarized in Table 2.1. Marketing should not be viewed as a point-in-time experience but as an ongoing process. Reliance on one or a few clients can be a disaster if that client should decide to discontinue the relationship. For this reason, most OD professionals must constantly market their skills and services to ensure that work is always available. Not surprisingly, therefore, one of the main challenges for every OD professional is to find a balance between the work itself and marketing so that there is always close to the desired level of work available, without having either too much work or too little work.

Identifying Potential Projects or Clients Externally

External OD consultants have many ways to identify and build a client portfolio or start new projects. Suggestions are described here, with their possible strengths and weaknesses.

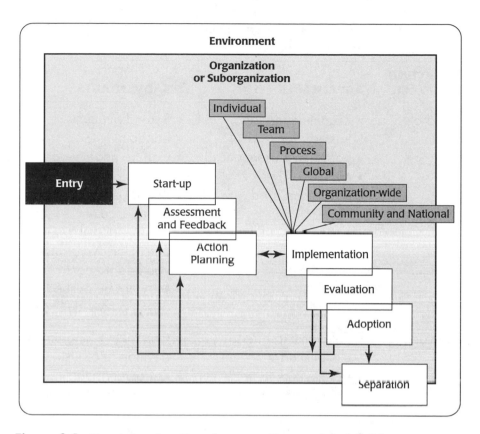

Figure 2.1 *Organization Development Process Model, Phase 1: Entry*

Word of Mouth.   Recommendations from clients is, by far, the most frequently used and most successful approach to getting new clients. People trust the unsolicited recommendations of their business colleagues and, naturally, will want to replicate the success of your present or former clients. Thus, outstanding work as an OD professional can often lead to establishing new clients through word-of-mouth. When an OD professional identifies a market niche based on industry, geography, level, function, type of work, or some other characteristic, word of mouth can become even more effective because the scope of work is much more focused. This approach can be low-cost and effective, leading to projects with known processes.

However, word of mouth also has the potential to negatively impact your business when news begins to circulate that a project you managed

TABLE 2.1 Summary of Possible Advantages and Disadvantages of Each Marketing Approach for External Consultants

MARKETING APPROACH	ADVANTAGES	DISADVANTAGES
Word of mouth	■ Recommendation trusted ■ Based on performance ■ Most effective ■ Most often used	■ Serendipitous ■ Random ■ Can be negative as well as positive ■ Based on most recent experience ■ Held responsible for outcomes over which you had no control ■ May not be pushed to develop new skill sets
Networking	■ Relationship already established ■ Develops skills while doing something you enjoy ■ Is established while doing something you enjoy ■ Can also accomplish something good for the community	■ Can take a long time to develop into business ■ Restricted to those geographic and subject areas in which you are involved ■ Can be seen as insincere and manipulative
Prior employers	■ Already have a trusted relationship ■ Work perhaps already under way ■ Eliminates gap between employment and consulting	■ Limited in number ■ Can create dependencies

TABLE 2.1 *(continued)*

MARKETING APPROACH	ADVANTAGES	DISADVANTAGES
Web sites	■ Expected in techno-logical era ■ Readily available to almost anyone in the world ■ Easily updated	■ Passive contact ■ Expensive to develop with quality ■ Needs ongoing maintenance (time and cost) ■ Can be read only where there Is access to the Internet
Printed materials	■ Proactive contact ■ Can be read anywhere (once put into people's hands)	■ Expensive ■ Difficult to distribute ■ Less frequently used in technological era ■ Difficult and expensive to update
Request for proposals (RFPs)	■ Know work already exists ■ Know what is expected by the client	■ Time-consuming to develop proposals ■ Often, considerable competition ■ No return for time spent on developing if project not won ■ Possible that insufficient funds are allocated to the project or are bid low simply to win the bid ■ Possible that client uses your work without compensating you

(continued)

TABLE 2.1 *(continued)*

MARKETING APPROACH	ADVANTAGES	DISADVANTAGES
Referrals from or work with associates	■ Benefit from associates' reputation ■ Trusted recommendation ■ Work with others ■ Know work already exists	■ Negatively influenced by associates' reputation ■ May not enjoy working with associates or these particular associates
Previous clients	■ Relationships already established ■ Corporate culture already known	■ May not have had successful experiences ■ May not develop new skill sets ■ May lead to dependencies ■ Over time, may become more difficult to speak the truth
Visibility (publications, presentations, teaching)	■ May be rewarded with work for doing something you enjoy ■ Can be financially rewarding in itself for a select few	■ Requires skill at writing and presenting ■ Takes a lot of work without guaranteed rewards ■ Is difficult to succeed in writing or presenting ■ May be a long time before the investment begins to pay off ■ Can be a low correlation between doing OD work and writing or presenting

TABLE 2.1   *(continued)*

MARKETING APPROACH	ADVANTAGES	DISADVANTAGES
Contract agencies	■ Provides some stability ■ Marketed by someone else ■ Allows you to continue marketing while earning a stable income	■ Lower pay ■ Less choice in the type of work ■ Less choice in the type of organization ■ Does less to build reputation
Pro bono (or reduced-fee) work	■ Reflects ethical practice ■ Provides an opportunity to serve the community ■ Provides a platform to showcase your expertise to potential clients ■ Demonstrates the value of OD work to potential clients	■ Competes with time to work with other clients ■ Creates possibility that people don't value what they don't pay for ■ May foster image that working in nonbusiness settings means that you don't work in business ■ May lead to realization that processes that work in business settings don't work well in nonbusiness settings ■ May require special expertise to work in some settings that might be clients of pro bono work

failed. Once this happens, you may experience difficulty in obtaining referrals. In addition to the negative effect this approach may have when a project fails (which may have occurred because the organization was not ready to commit to an OD effort), the word-of-mouth approach is serendipitous and random and, thus, outside your control. For this reason, many consultants have a guarantee built into their contract. If the client is unhappy with the process, the fee can be negotiated down or even waived to avoid bad word of mouth. Furthermore, such an approach is unlikely to push you into developing new competencies in different areas.

Networking.   In most cultures, business is conducted at least in part through existing relationships. In some cultures, preference is given to people who come from the same place, who graduated from the same school, or who belong to the same religious community. In other cultures, benefits are given to those who are personally known. This might be because of former connections, but steps can be taken to increase one's present and future opportunities for connections. Networks can be developed through participating in professional organizations (at both national and local levels, such as the OD Network, The OD Institute, or the ODC Division of the Academy of Management), in community organizations (e.g., boards, religious groups, volunteer work), or community professional organizations (e.g., Kiwanis, Rotary Club, Chamber of Commerce). This approach also allows you not only to contribute to your community or professional organization but also to create relationships that can lead to future business. Furthermore, participating in professional organizations facilitates the development of new skills that could be useful in your OD work.

On the negative side, some people may see this approach as manipulative and insincere. For this reason, it is particularly important to be sincere, honest, and committed to the group with which you are networking. Networking also provides no sure business outcome.

Prior Employers.   When an individual decides to become an external consultant, that person's previous employer often becomes the first client. Clearly, there are advantages to both parties in this situation. When a person leaves an employer, undone work often remains, and, occasionally, there is also a gap between the time a person leaves until the time he or she is replaced. The employer knows the quality of work that the person does, and, if that former employee was competent enough to become an external OD professional, the quality of that work was presumably high. This can also be a bridging experience for the OD professional, allowing the professional to begin earning a fee immediately, without having to wait until the effects of other marketing approaches fall into place.

Because most people have worked for a limited number of employers, this approach is also limited and cannot usually be counted on for an extended period of time. Other disadvantages include the professional developing an overreliance on this single client and not creating enough of a mix of clients, and the continuing dependence of the client on the OD professional, continuing to treat the professional as an employee rather than as an external professional.

Web Sites. In today's technological era, it is almost impossible to be an external OD professional without having a Web site. The challenge, however, is to get potential clients to go to your site. Because Web sites are rather passive, you need to take action to attract potential clients to your Web site. Inviting people in your networks to visit your site (perhaps through listservs) may increase your hit rate. Many of the other approaches suggested here, such as writing a book, can increase the number of visitors to your Web site.

It should also go without saying that your Web site needs to be informative, effective, and professional, providing the needed information for interested and potential clients. If your Web site does not tell people what they want to know, visitors might conclude that an unprofessional site is a reflection of your work. It is worth investing in creating a Web site that will do what you need it to do; do not try to cut expenses by not investing in a high-quality site. Web sites also need to be kept up-to-date, requiring time and costs for ongoing maintenance.

Information that you might want to have on your Web site includes:

- your organization's mission, vision, and values;
- key personnel within your organization—names, qualifications, photos;
- the kind of work that you do;
- a list of previous clients (but *only* with their permission);
- a brief description of cases on which your organization has worked;
- publications that personnel in your organization have authored—this can be a list with links, if available, or there might even be the full publication in pdf format (using Adobe Acrobat to post a generally unchangeable copy);
- an opinion piece (often called a *white paper*) that lends a dynamic character to the Web site and will give people a reason to return;
- any products that you have for sale;

- information on how you can be reached—e-mail, phone numbers, fax numbers, address;
- testimonies from previous clients.

Printed Materials.   With increasing reliance on the computer for advertising, archiving and conveying information, communicating, and billing, the importance of printed materials has diminished. Your business card and your stationery must communicate professionally and contain all of the necessary contact information. They can communicate who you are and be a means of proactively inviting people to your Web site. Expensive published brochures, however, in most marketplaces, may no longer be cost-effective. It is difficult and costly to determine who potential clients might be and then to get the brochures in the right hands. It is also difficult and costly to make changes in them. Something that is simpler and less expensive may be more cost-effective in today's world.

Requests for Proposals (RFPs).   Sometimes organizations, especially government agencies, will issue a call for proposals or a *request for proposals (RFP)*. In these situations, the organization has already determined the work it wants done and perhaps even the processes that it wishes to follow. An RFP is an attempt to find the best-qualified individual, often at the lowest cost or at least within a predetermined cost, to do the desired work. RFPs may be distributed to listservs, posted on Web sites, or printed as official notices in newspapers or listed in government publications. The client's goal is usually to distribute the RFP widely to get many responses and proposals from which to choose.

OD professionals who write a proposal in response to an RFP must pay close attention to the requirements listed in the RFP. Failure to follow an RFP's specifications will usually lead to a proposal's immediate disqualification. The advantage of responding to an RFP is that the OD professional knows that work is available and that a contract will be issued. On the downside, there is no way of knowing how many responses the RFP will generate, and the OD professional may invest many, many hours in writing proposals that are never selected. While unethical, it is not unknown for a receiving organization to use the ideas included in a proposal without ever hiring or paying the individual who presented the ideas. Furthermore, the amount of money that is available for the project may not be sufficient to do a quality job.

Referrals from or Work with Associates.   Many OD professionals who are working as independent consultants will ask colleagues or professional friends to work with them on projects that are too large for them to handle alone. Such associates are then in an ideal position to know the quality of the work done by these associates. When a consultant has too much work, and another project presents itself, it is often the case that your name will be recommended to the organization looking for a consultant.

Likewise, if you have included an associate in a project that is too large for you, it is expected that that person will include you when he or she has a project too large for that person. One potential problem with such an approach is that the quality of the work done by the colleague may be associated with you. If that quality is not as high as your own work, it can have a detrimental effect. On the other hand, if the work quality is better than yours, you also have the opportunity to learn from the experience, and the reputation of that associate may rub off on you.

Previous Clients.   Don't forget former clients. Sometimes, as you move on, you tend to forget about clients with whom you have worked in the past, and they may forget about you as well. Create a *tickler file* of all of your clients to remind you, periodically, to make contact with them, even if it is just a phone call to stay in touch or to have lunch together. Not only might this approach generate new business with the previous client, but it will also create goodwill that might result in a referral to other potential clients. A potential downside of continuing to work with previous clients is that you both may create unhealthy dependencies.

Visibility (Publications, Presentations, Teaching).   There are many examples of consultants who have gone from relative obscurity to national visibility because they have written a best-selling book (e.g., Peter Senge [1990], Margaret Wheatley [2001], and many others) or published an article in the *Harvard Business Review*. Establishing yourself as an expert by writing books or articles or making presentations can result in new business—and higher rates! Publications can be useful as handouts to leave with participants in workshops or presentations. Such approaches require that you have a niche to fill with an idea that attracts attention, and it also involves a considerable amount of upfront time. In addition, very few people are able to write a book or article that will attract this kind of attention.

Presentations might be made at the local level (e.g., to a Rotary Club) or at national or international conferences. If your goal is to develop clients, however, the audience for such presentations must consist of people who are likely to be potential clients. Presenting to an audience of academics or people not in a position to make a hiring decision, for example, is not likely to generate much, if any, new work, especially in the short term.

Teaching is another way of creating potential clients, especially if the students are already employed (e.g., those in an executive MBA program). Over a longer term, teaching students who are not yet employed can still be effective, as they move into positions in which they will be making decisions about hiring consultants.

Contract Agencies.   Some agencies work specifically to place people with organizations that are looking for temporary employment. A consultant might want to use this approach when a tight market has made it difficult to get a sufficient number of clients. One can work for a company for 3 to 4 months while developing new competencies and continuing to market in order to begin work with new clients once the short-term assignment has been completed.

Doing Pro Bono Work.   Most ethical OD consultants will do occasional pro bono (free), or at least reduced-fee, work for organizations with which the consultant shares a common value. Over the years, I have worked with a number of such organizations, and, given my value system, these have been churches, organizations focusing on immigration issues, international organizations, grassroots charitable groups, and many others. While the intent is to return a service to the community, it can also serve as a marketing tool. Many members of these organizations are also individuals who work in organizations that need OD consulting. Having observed your work, they see your expertise as well as possibilities for applying that expertise in their organizations.

As summarized in Table 2.1, there is no one answer to the question of which marketing approach to use. As mentioned earlier, "It depends" is a common answer in doing OD work. Much of the work done in OD is ambiguous; that is, there are no clear right or wrong answers. This table is a good illustration of that principle.

Identifying Potential Projects or Clients Internally

Just as an external OD professional needs to identify potential projects or clients, so, too, does an internal OD professional. The emphasis for the internal professional is, of course, not on finding the organization but, rather, on finding the points of focus within the employing organization. In this situation, all of the following approaches can be useful.

Know the Business Well, and Speak the Organization's Language.   An internal OD professional needs to know the business in which he or she is working and its personnel well. He or she needs to know where process improvements are possible and where the potential for growth exists, the corporate culture, the organization's history and potential, and anything else that would help identify where and how the OD professional can help contribute to the success of the organization. To do this effectively, the OD professional must be able to speak the language of the organization, understand what its processes and functions are, know the mission and vision of the organization, and align her or his efforts with the strategic direction of the organization. All of this will help the organization see how the OD professional can add value.

Share What You Are Working On.   Many (probably most) people within the organization will not understand what an OD professional does and how they can use such expertise in helping them do their jobs better. When people begin to see what you are doing and how you are helping others in the organization, they will begin to trust your expertise and see how you might be able to work with them. This exposure will then often result in their contacting you to do work with them.

Share Your Successes.   This recommendation is similar to the preceding point: success breeds success. Take advantage of opportunities to provide information about your successes in employee meetings, annual meetings, newsletters, Web sites, and other sources of information.

Be Visible, Especially at Decision-Making Tables.   Too often, OD professionals feel ignored because they are not consulted or involved when strategic decisions are being made. Knowing the business and making concrete, value-added contributions to the organization will increase your visibility and encourage others to invite you to participate in their part of the organization. The details of how this is done may vary across cultures.

Have a Mentor or Sponsor Who Is Well Respected in the Organization. Having a champion from within the organization, especially someone near or at the top of the organization who is well respected, can help position you to make concrete contributions to the organization. This assistance might come by way of advice (e.g., from a mentor or coach), or it might come through the sharing of your expertise or recommendations to specific parts of the organization to take advantage of your know-how.

Foster Word of Mouth.   As with external OD professionals, internal OD professionals also benefit (or suffer from) word of mouth. Managers and executives talk with each other about what is going on in their part of the organization. When you have been particularly successful in one part of the organization, others are likely to talk about your successes with their colleagues, generating more opportunities for you to contribute to the organization. Conversely, colleagues will also talk if things do not go well.

Walk Around.   To enhance your knowledge of the business and its processes, walk around the organization. Talk with people about how things are going, and observe the processes that are in place. During this process, you will learn where potential work is and make connections with those who will make the decision to invite you into their business.

THE FIRST MEETING WITH A PROSPECTIVE CLIENT

Once you have identified a potential project or client, whether as an internal or an external OD professional, the next step in the Entry process is to meet with the prospective client to determine whether there is, in fact, work to be done in that organization or in a subpart of the organization, whether you are the right person to take on the project, and what resources you might need to complete the project successfully.

Once you have identified a potential project or client, a number of things still need to be done before either party decides that you are the right person to handle the task. Before your first meeting with the client, you need to do your homework. You should review as much information as you can prior to the first meeting. If you are an external professional, you can review the background of most organizations on the Web. If the organization is a public corporation, you can also, usually, find its annual report in the business section of most public or university libraries, as well as online resources. If you are an internal professional, you can usually find internal documents that would give you a good background and insight into the specific part of the organization you are targeting.

The steps outlined in this section might well be made in an on-site meeting, during a breakfast or lunch, or over a series of meetings. It is often helpful to meet in the client's place of business because this setting may provide the OD professional with additional information on the client's culture (e.g., interactions with customers, noise and activity levels, conservative or modern furnishings, employee interactions, etc.). The Entry phase is not completed until a contract is developed and agreed on, or the decision is made not to work together.

Determine Whether You Can Work Together

Whether internal or external, if you and the potential client have never met, this first meeting is an opportunity for you to meet each other, with the ultimate goal of determining whether you are a good match to work together. Such decisions are often made within the first few minutes of meeting each other. The opening conversation will often consist of small talk—information not necessarily relevant to the potential contract. Such conversation, however, can be very insightful in helping determine whether a working relationship is possible by revealing the following:

- What is the other person's general demeanor—serious or relaxed, open or closed, positive or negative, and so on? And what might this mean in working together?
- The client will be asking him- or herself, What impact is this person likely to make in my organization?
- The client will also be wondering, What do I think the chances are that this person will be able to accomplish what we need to have accomplished?

- You might be asking yourself of the client, Does this person have the power base to support me in the work that I need to do in this organization?

- You might also be thinking, How committed does this person seem to be about making change in the organization?

- How comfortable are you with each other's choice of dress style? (This might seem to be a minor point, but I know of an external consultant who lost a job because he was wearing Hush Puppy shoes. The CEO of this Fortune 50 company did not believe that Hush Puppies were sufficiently professional.)

These are, obviously, not questions that are asked directly, at least in the opening stages, of the other person. And the answers will invariably be based on imperfect and limited information. Nevertheless, this is the process that does go on, and you may want to try to limit and, more important, be aware of your judgments until you have more information. However, as first impressions do count and occur frequently, you are not in a position to keep the client from making rash judgments.

Determine Presenting Problems

There is a reason why the client is willing to meet with you. On the most optimistic side, the client may simply want to know how well they are doing as an organization so they can continue to build on their strengths. Truly progressive organizations will recognize the need for continuous improvement. Unfortunately, however, organizations are most likely to call you in to assist when they think they have a problem that needs fixing. And it is not unusual for the client to think that the organization knows not only what the problem is but also what it will take to fix it. This is called the *presenting problem*.

As an example, I was contacted and asked to conduct a workshop on conflict management because a potential client had determined that department managers were not working well together and were constantly disagreeing. The potential client had determined that the presenting problem was conflict and that the solution to this problem was to conduct a workshop.

Conduct a Miniassessment

Once the presenting problem is on the table, you need to ask questions and trust your intuition and previous experience to help you determine the accuracy of the client's diagnosis. In my experience, it is seldom the case that the presenting problem is the actual problem.

In the situation just described regarding perceived conflict, I began to ask questions about what the department managers disagreed on and how it was manifest in the organization. It became apparent, rather quickly, that major problems existed with the systems that were in place that caused the managers to disagree with each other. They were forced to compete for resources, which put them in a position where they had to compete with each other, causing the conflict to exist. To conduct a workshop and leave the systems unchanged had no chance of positively changing anything and, in fact, would likely increase the extent of tension and conflict within the group.

Determine the Organization's Readiness to Change

The next step is to attempt to determine how ready the organization is to do what is necessary for the changes to occur. From an ethical perspective, you do not want to use the organization's resources if there is little chance of success, nor do you want to put your reputation in jeopardy when the intervention does not succeed. I find the following questions useful in helping determine the chances that the organization is ready to change:

- Have you worked with an OD professional before? How successful was it? What were the outcomes?
- How do people within the organization feel about the situation that is the presenting problem?
- How ready are people to change?
- Where does the organization fit in its market?
- How well is the organization doing?

- What resources (financial and personnel) have been dedicated to this project?
- How accurately do the mission and vision of the organization reflect what is actually done in the organization?
- How long has the problem existed?
- What is motivating the change now? What is different? What has changed?

Many years ago, Pfeiffer and Jones (1978) created a questionnaire to determine, mathematically, how ready an organization is to change. The intent of the instrument is to provide an objective measure, based on 15 variables weighted according to their importance. Some people feel more comfortable with a measure that they believe to be objective, even if the numbers are determined subjectively. While the concept of readiness for change is important, reaching a numerical measure may be misleading and consume too much time to get an accurate measure.

In the case previously described, I asked whether the organization was prepared to change its processes if it was determined that the source of the conflict was not the individuals but the system that was in place. The representatives of the organization responded that this shift was not in their plans and that they were not open to it. This reply demonstrated, quite quickly, that they were not ready for change, and I subsequently decided to decline the contract.

Establish Your Credibility

Once you have a sense of where the project might go and are certain that the organization is ready for change, the next step is to establish your *credibility* for doing the project with the client. The client has probably already reviewed your Web site and knows a considerable amount about you and the work that you do. Word of mouth may also have informed him or her about how you work and what your areas of expertise are.

You may want to bring with you a copy of your Web site materials, a brochure that you have published for this purpose, or a résumé that contains this information. You may also want to share with the client your experiences working in similar industries or on similar projects and what the outcomes of those experiences have been. Copies of publications might also be useful, if you have them. The client will certainly have some questions as well. You should be prepared to provide the client with references, but only with the approval of the previous clients. If you are an internal OD professional, you can share names of others within the organization with whom you have worked. If you are an external consultant, with the permission of previous clients, you can share names of clients with whom you have worked on similar projects. Almost always, the client will want an estimate of how long you think the project will take and an estimate of the costs. These figures are not something that you need to provide in detail at the first meeting, but they are likely to be something that you will want to provide in your follow-up contact with the client.

Before ending the meeting, you and the client need to decide what the next steps are, what additional information you both might need, and when a decision will be made by both parties about moving forward. Once both parties have decided to work together, the next step is to establish a contract.

CONTRACTS

Once the client and the OD professional, whether internal or external, decide that they want to work together, an agreement about the conditions, either oral or written, should be articulated. It is usually wise for external professionals to use a written contract (also referred to as a *letter of agreement* or a *memorandum of understanding*). It may be useful to think of the contracting process in phases. One contract might apply for the analysis phase, with a subsequent contract for the implementation phase. A sample of a written contract is shown in the appendix of this chapter. Some of the items that you will want to include in the agreement (or contract) follow, with explanations.

Who Will Do What?

Both parties—the client and the OD professional—will have roles to play during the project. Although it will not necessarily be clear in the beginning exactly who will do what, it is helpful to articulate these roles in the agreement or contract as clearly as possible. As additional information regarding roles becomes available, the contract can be amended, either formally in writing or orally, though, of course, there are huge risks in any oral contract.

What Are the Desired Outcomes?

This aspect of the agreement is intended to let both parties confirm their understanding of what outcomes will be deemed as acceptable, often indicating, too, when the project will be completed. Including this item in the contract enforces the inclusion of an evaluation component right from the beginning. The first outcome may be an analysis of the organization (if the ODP model is being followed). A second contract (known as *scope of the project*, which might include deliverables, focus, boundaries, etc.) may need to be developed once the analysis is completed if there is additional work for the OD professional following this phase.

What Is the Desired Time Line?

This aspect of the agreement answers the question of when the project is to be completed. You need to be careful in including this information, especially if there is a *penalty clause for nonperformance*. Because the work of the OD professional relies on the cooperation of personnel from within the client organization, control over the time line is not solely in the hands of the OD professional. Further information about when the OD professional will work, when he or she can be contacted, and other factors are related to timely completion of the project.

What Aspects of the Project Are Confidential and for How Long?

This is a particularly tricky question for an internal OD professional. Can you share with others in your organization what you determine with the client? With whom can you share it? For the external OD professional, the details of any project will almost always be confidential, but for how long? Usually, two years is a sufficient period, as anything you learn during this time will have changed within two years, given the dynamic nature of business. This is also an appropriate time to ask whether you can list the client on your Web site or résumé.

What Personnel Resources Will Be Needed?

The client will want to know how many personnel from the consultant organizations will be needed; who they are, along with their qualifications; and the percentage of time they will allocate to the project. The client will also want to know how many of the client organization's personnel will be needed.

Fees

The contract will specify the fees to be paid, as well as what expenses will be reimbursed, the process to be used for billing and reimbursement, and when payments are due. Determining the fees to charge is a very difficult process. First, you need to decide whether you are going to charge an hourly rate or on a project basis. Charging an hourly rate requires a level of trust that you will not take advantage of this billing arrangement. On the other hand, charging on a project basis requires a near-perfect prediction of the amount of time that a project will take—an almost impossible task given the nature of OD work. If you overestimate the time it will take, the client will pay more than necessary for the project. If you underestimate the time, then you will not be reimbursed for the hours you have worked. Furthermore, almost every case entails additional steps to be done that were not anticipated in the beginning of the project. This situation often leads to conflict over whether the extra time should be included in the project fee or if it should be added to the project fee. A *supplementary contract*, also referred to as a *change order*, can be used to ensure that there is no misunderstanding. Another option is to be employed on a retainer. The client organization makes a regular payment throughout the year, and, for that payment, the client organization may call on the consultant as work is needed. This approach has advantages to both parties, but it does make it difficult for the consultant to plan his or her work.

The second question is how much to charge. Clearly, part of this decision should be based on your experience and level of expertise. Talking with others in your community about their charges and researching online is almost essential so you can decide where you want to position yourself relative to the market. You may also want to use a sliding scale, charging one rate for for-profit businesses and a different rate for nonprofits. You might also give a discounted rate to long-term clients. However, it is important to be consistent in your fee structure. Client organizations usually know who is charging what for each type of service.

Another approach to determining your charges is to develop a personal budget worksheet to determine what income you need to cover your income and benefits needs, as well as your expenses. A shorthand approach that is sometimes used to determine annual income needs is known as the *3X approach*, in which you simply multiple your annual salary by 3. Although this is a good approach for the individual consultant, it is not necessarily going to make you competitive in the marketplace.

Internal consultants have an even more difficult time in determining charges. In some organizations, it may not be necessary to charge a client part of the organization. In other organizations, OD might be a profit center, with the expectation that the OD service will at minimum recover its costs. But then there is the question about what costs to include that must be recovered. The financial function of the organization will often be helpful in determining internal budget allocations for the provision of OD services internally.

Deliverables

Another item to be included in the contract is what will be delivered by the consultant to the client organization. When will reports be delivered? To whom will they be delivered? Will the reports be oral or written? Will there be a public presentation? Will results of analyses be presented in aggregated form (combined so no individual respondent can be identified)? What level of *anonymity* or *confidentiality* will apply? While detail is probably not possible or necessary in the contract, responses to these questions should be addressed.

What Recourse Do the Parties Have for Nonperformance?

For an external OD professional, it is helpful to have a clause indicating agreement of both parties to use mediation rather than the courts if disagreement arises about any aspect of the contract. However, the popularity of including this phrase in a contract seems to be diminishing, recognizing that it is always an option to use mediation if both parties agree, even if not stipulated in the contract.

Internal professionals usually work under more pressure than external professionals. They may well have their jobs on the line, not only if they do not perform according to the contract, but also if they refuse to take on a project.

CHAPTER SUMMARY

The Entry phase is extremely important for the OD professional because it begins the organization development process model. It is through the Entry phase, with its focus on marketing, that work is identified (whether internally or externally). Many approaches can be used for marketing one's expertise, there is no single best approach, though word of mouth is clearly of great importance in the field. And, with increasing reliance on technology, every OD professional will probably want to have a Web site.

During the opening dialogue that takes place between the OD professional and the representative of the client organization, both parties will be assessing the other person (or persons) to determine compatibility in a working environment. The client organization will also present the reason why it wishes to work with the OD professional. If the client wants to address a specific matter, this is called the presenting problem. The difficulty for the OD professional, however, is that this problem might be a symptom of the real or root cause. Thus, the OD professional will want to do a miniassessment to determine the likelihood that the presenting problem is the real problem. Then the OD professional can make a quick judgment about his or her competence to do the OD work that is being requested. Finally, the components of an OD contract were presented in this chapter, along with a sample contract.

QUESTIONS FOR DISCUSSION OR SELF-REFLECTION

1. With which of the marketing methods do you feel most comfortable? Why?

2. With which of the marketing methods do you feel the least comfortable? Why?

3. What do you think you could do to overcome your lack of comfort with the methods identified in question 2?

4. Why is it important for an internal OD professional to market him- or herself?

5. Why do you think it is important to determine the client's readiness for change before entering into a contract?

6. What are some of the factors that you think would discourage a client from entering into a contract with a potential OD professional?

7. What are some of the factors that you think would discourage an OD professional from entering into a contract with a potential client?

8. What are the advantages and disadvantages of each of oral and written agreements?

9. Other than the items included in this chapter, what are other factors that might be included in a contract?

10. Is it important for an internal OD professional to have an agreement with the internal client? Why?

APPENDIX 2.1
SAMPLE CONTRACT

CONSULTING AGREEMENT BETWEEN XYZ ORGANIZATION AND McLEAN GLOBAL CONSULTING, INC.

By this contract, XYZ Organization and McLean Global Consulting, Inc. (MGC), an independent consulting firm, acknowledge and agree to the following:

1. All materials and information furnished during the course of this consultancy, including brochures, reports, correspondence, etc., are for the exclusive use of MGC in support of this contract. MGC agrees to use such materials only for purposes consistent with the objectives of XYZ Organization. All materials remain the property of XYZ Organization, to be returned at its request or upon termination of this contract.

2. MGC agrees that, upon termination, no materials or property belonging to XYZ Organization will be taken, including but not limited to the originals or copies of any correspondence, memos, manuals, or any other documents or records, and that MGC will return whatever may be in his possession at that time, except as agreed on and specified in writing. All products developed under the provisions of this contract are the proprietary rights of XYZ Organization and may not be used by MGC for any further financial gain. However, notes taken that might violate confidences if returned to the client will be destroyed by MGC. One copy of all materials developed will be given to MGC for its files or may be retained in its computer files.

3. All information gained during the contract, including but not limited to clients, procedures, etc., shall be considered confidential information. Such information shall not be shared with any person, agency, or corporation, directly or indirectly, at any time, either prior to or subsequent to termination of this contract. This provision will expire three years after termination of the consultation.

4. During the course of this contract, MGC will not undertake any other consulting relationship that will be detrimental to the contracted obligations to XYZ Organization.

5. MGC's hourly pay is to be $300 and includes travel time. An invoice will be submitted at the end of each month. Payment will be made within two weeks of receipt of invoice. Expenses to be reimbursed include mileage at $0.415 per mile; meals during consultation time; other transportation and lodging, as required; and supplies necessary for carrying out the contract (e.g., duplicated materials, etc.). Only time actually used will be billed.

6. This contract will remain in force until canceled by either party in writing, without advance notice being required.

7. XYZ Organization will provide all facilities for the proposed activities, as needed.

8. MGC will provide facilitation to XYZ Organization to support a quality management transformation. This activity might include, but not be limited to, coaching of senior management in the implementation of a quality management process, providing feedback during management and employee meetings designed to improve processes, assisting in identifying processes for statistical process control, and so on. Additional organization development activities would also fit under the purview of this contract as mutually agreed upon.

9. MGC agrees that it will not attempt to induce clients, members or employees of XYZ Organization or its successors away from XYZ Organization, either during the contract or after its termination. It will not canvass, solicit, take away, or interfere with any business, clients, or trade of XYZ Organization.

10. In the event of any violations of this agreement, any fees, costs, or expenses incurred by the injured party in seeking compliance will be borne by the other party, assuming that reasonable efforts have been made to reach satisfactory compliance through means other than the courts.

This agreement was signed on the 8th day of January, 2006.

_____   _____

Gary N. McLean, President   Ann Johnson
McLean Global Consulting, Inc.   Chief Executive Officer
                                                          XYZ Organization

3

Start-up and Systems Theory

CHAPTER OUTLINE

Establish the Infrastructure

Set Project Management in Place

Establish the Team with Which You Will Be Working

Determine the Assessment Processes to Be Used

Identify Those to Be Involved in the Assessment

Develop a Time Line for the Assessment and Feedback Process

Get Confirmation of the Feedback Process to Be Used and
Who Will Receive It

Systems Theory

Chapter Summary

Questions for Discussion or Self-Reflection

OVERVIEW   What are the first steps that an OD professional carries out in entering an organization or a subpart of an organization? A critical component is setting project management in place. Establishing partnerships within the organization is also critical to the ultimate success of the project. How this is done, and with whom, will be explored in this chapter. Determining when it is time to move on to the next phase will be discussed as well. The entire OD process must be set in the context of systems thinking. A brief overview of systems theory is also presented in this chapter.

You have been successful in connecting with a client, and you now have a contract in hand. What happens next? The Start-up phase is important in establishing an *infrastructure*, including project management, that will support the work being done in the organization or subpart of the organization, though in some cases parts of this stage might have been addressed in the contracting component of the Entry phase, illustrating that there is not a clear distinction between phases of the ODP model. Start-up is also important in preparing for the next phase of the cycle—conducting the organizational assessment and providing feedback. See Figure 3.1 for how this phase connects the Entry phase to the Assessment and Feedback phase.

ESTABLISH THE INFRASTRUCTURE

To do your job effectively, it is important to set your infrastructure within the client organization in place. Obviously, if you are an internal OD professional, the infrastructure will already be established. But, if you are an outside consultant, you need to establish whether you will have an office equipped with a computer and other necessary supplies or whether you will use your laptop and have a mobile office. Where will interviews be held? Preferably, this space will be a room that provides privacy and is away from the mainstream of foot traffic so it is not obvious as to whom you are meeting. Where will you be meeting with people? Where will team meetings be held? Will you have a company phone number, or will you need to use your cell phone? Do you need a security pass? What level of accessibility will you have? These are questions that need to be answered at the beginning of the process.

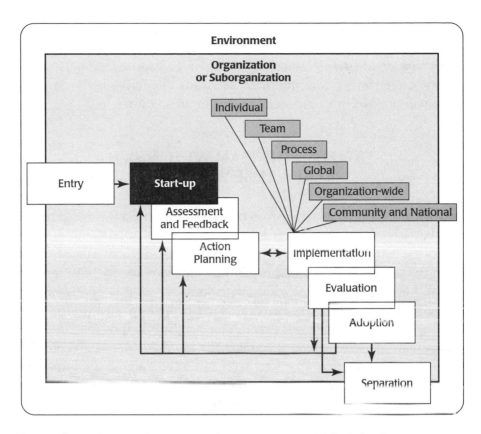

Figure 3.1 *Organization Development Process Model, Phase 2: Start up*

SET PROJECT MANAGEMENT IN PLACE

It will be your responsibility to put a *project management system* in place so you can track what is to be done, by whom, and when. This need not be a sophisticated system, depending on your expertise and the complexity of the project on which you are working. A simple project management tool is suggested in Chapter 5 on action planning that can well be used at this beginning stage to ensure that the appropriate tasks have been accomplished in preparation for moving on with the Assessment and Feedback phase.

Another aspect of project management is a *status reporting process.* This could include the vehicle used for communicating with all parties involved (hard copy vs. e-mail vs. oral; formal vs. informal), the audience for the communications (internal OD professional, *steering team, executive committee*), and frequency of communication (weekly, monthly, quarterly). Making these decisions explicitly at the Start-up stage will prevent misunderstandings from arising later.

ESTABLISH THE TEAM WITH WHICH YOU WILL BE WORKING

Usually, the most successful projects are those that establish a partnership between the client's organization and the OD professional's organization, whether internal or external. First, you need to identify your point person within the client organization, often another OD professional. I have found that working with someone who is opposite from me helps broaden the perspectives that are brought to bear in the project. So, as a white male, well past middle age, it is helpful if I can work with a minority female who is younger than I am. Generational, gender, ethnic, and many other characteristics can have a significant impact on how one views the world. Thus, working with a partner or partners with different characteristics can help incorporate a range of viewpoints during the process.

Second, you will likely be working with a team within the client organization. This might be the executive committee consisting of senior managers. Or, you may find it more helpful to establish a *project steering committee* to work with a cross section of people with various demographics and representing a range of areas from within the client organization. You will want to be sure that this team includes experts in the area on which you will be focusing during the project.

Third, you will want to have access to top management within the organization if your project is to have real impact. If you are not working with the executive committee as your team, you will want assurances that you can meet at almost any time with the organization's chief executive officer (CEO) or the senior manager in the area of the organization in which you will be working. Since change almost always requires at least the support of the person or people at the top, such access often becomes critical for the project's success.

DETERMINE THE ASSESSMENT PROCESSES TO BE USED

As will be discussed in the next chapter on assessment and feedback, many approaches can be used to conduct an organizational assessment. It is during the Start-up phase that the decision is made as to which assessment approach will be used.

This is usually a decision that you will make in consultation with your organizational point person or, even better, with the steering team with which you are working from within the organization. You can help the team understand the strengths and weaknesses of each, and the various costs associated with each. The team can then make an informed decision as to which approach to use.

IDENTIFY THOSE TO BE INVOLVED IN THE ASSESSMENT

Another decision that can be made in consultation with the steering committee is who to involve in the assessment. In a large organization, it is not necessary to involve everyone. In fact, depending on the approach that has been chosen for the assessment (e.g., interviewing), it may be impossible to incorporate everyone in the assessment phase. *Sampling*—in which a subset of the employee base is selected—provides *efficiency* (the greatest value at the least effort) and may even add to *effectiveness* (doing the appropriate thing).

Sampling

There are many ways to sample from the organization. In the ideal setting, *random sampling* is performed. In random sampling, every member of the organization has an equal chance of being selected. A list of employees can be obtained from the human resource (HR) department, and a number assigned to each employee (if the organizational system does not already have numbers assigned). Then, using a table of random numbers, you select which employees to include (a free Web site, www.randomizer.org, makes this process very easy).

If you wish to have employees represented proportionate to their presence in the organization, *proportional random sampling* could be done. Let's assume that, in an organization of 1,000 employees, you wish to sample 100 (or 10%). You determine that 600 men and 400 women work in the organization. You would then include 10% of each (60 men and 40 women) in the sample. These men and women would be selected at random using the Web site referenced earlier. *Random selection* does not mean asking supervisors to pick who they want to be included in the sample, nor does it mean standing at the door to the cafeteria and picking out who you want to include in the sample.

Occasionally, however, you may want to do *purposive sampling*. With purposive sampling, you select employees because they fit pre-specified criteria. For example, you may wish to interview the top 10 salespeople and the bottom 10 salespeople to determine whether identifiable characteristics distinguish them.

However, there are costs to not including everyone. Depending on whether you are doing a general assessment or whether you are doing the assessment because problems have been identified, a trust issue could exist in the organization. People who are not included in the assessment may not trust the results. This could be particularly the case if the random sampling yields significantly more representation from one group in the organization than from another—for example, union members versus exempt employees, employees from one geographic part of the organization or from one function, or employees overrepresenting one demographic group. Especially if you have chosen to use a questionnaire approach, it may be worth the extra costs to include everyone and avoid political rejection of the assessment results. These issues will be discussed in greater detail in the next chapter.

DEVELOP A TIME LINE FOR THE ASSESSMENT AND FEEDBACK PROCESS

As part of the project management plan, and as decisions are made regarding the assessment processes, a *time line* can be developed along with calendar targets for completing various aspects of the assessment process.

GET CONFIRMATION OF THE FEEDBACK PROCESS TO BE USED AND WHO WILL RECEIVE IT

A few of the difficult questions that must be tackled before moving on to the Assessment and Feedback phase is who is to receive the feedback, who will deliver it, and how it will be delivered. The steering team will need to establish the feedback process to be used and who will receive it, with confirmation from top management, before the assessment is begun. If agreement is not reached prior to the assessment, it may become a source of discontent or conflict that could negatively affect the project's outcome.

SYSTEMS THEORY

In the process of considering the infrastructure and how the work will be done in the organization, the OD professional and members of the organization's team must take fully into account the implications of *systems theory* and *systems thinking*. This concept has its origins in the biological sciences; it has also had a relatively long-standing importance in the field of OD. However, the concept was popularized for many people in business with the publication of Senge's (1990) *The Fifth Discipline*.

Stated very generally, a *system* is defined by a boundary that contains many subsystems and that also separates the system from its environment (see Figure 3.2).

Within any system or subsystem, we will find inputs, being acted on by processes, producing outputs, with a continuous feedback loop to the inputs, as depicted in Figure 3.3.

Interdependency is the condition that prevails in a system when what happens in any one subsystem has varying degrees of impact on some or all of the other subsystems.

Cause and effect is what, in our positivistic world, we often would like to discover yet, according to systems theory, is impossible to find. Change in any of the subsystems is almost certain to impact the system, but, likewise, the nature of change is impossible to predict. *Chaos theory*, popularized in the business literature by Wheatley (2001), is an explanation for why this happens. As much as we want to control the outputs of our systems, and as much as we think we are doing so, the

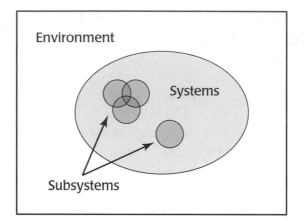

Figure 3.2 *Visual Depiction of a System*

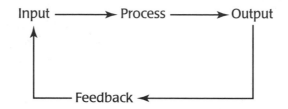

Figure 3.3 *Components of a System or a Subsystem*

systems themselves have a regenerating capability that takes the power away from individuals. This is a great frustration for people in business and for OD professionals because we want to have planned change, as indicated by the definitions reviewed in Chapter 1.

Open and Closed Systems

Understanding the impact on organizations of *open* and *closed systems* is another important aspect of systems thinking for OD professionals. Systems may be open-in, open-out, open both ways, or closed both ways, as illustrated in Figure 3.4.

Following are some examples of each type of system, recognizing that no organization fits one of these models perfectly. An *open-in system* might be a country's intelligence service—they want all of the information they can get (open-in), but they are not prepared to share it (closed-

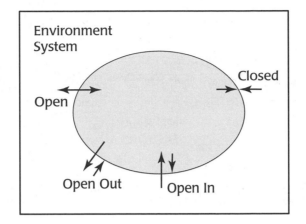

Figure 3.4 *Open and Closed Systems*

out). An ***open-out system*** might be an evangelical group that wants to influence other people (open-out) but is not seeking to be influenced (closed-in). An open system, theoretically, is a university, where the desire is to gain knowledge (open-in) and then to share it widely (open-out). Finally, a closed system might be the Amish, who seek neither to be influenced (closed-in) nor to influence (closed-out). Figure 3.5 depicts some of the factors that might influence an organization, both internally and externally.

According to Senge (1990), systems thinking is one of five areas (he called them "*disciplines*") critical for organizational success. Senge described systems thinking through an analogy; it is a framework for seeing interrelationships rather than things—seeing the forest *and* the trees. As depicted in Figure 3.5, systems thinking requires recognizing and taking into account all of the factors in the environment (external) as well as all of the factors inside the organization (internal).

Systems theory is complex. The following statements may be simplistic, but they are important aspects of systems that affect everything that we do in OD:

- Everything is connected to everything else; nothing is truly isolated.
- There is no "away"; you cannot escape some system.
- There is no such thing as a free lunch; everything that you do costs something.
- Nature knows best and always wins.

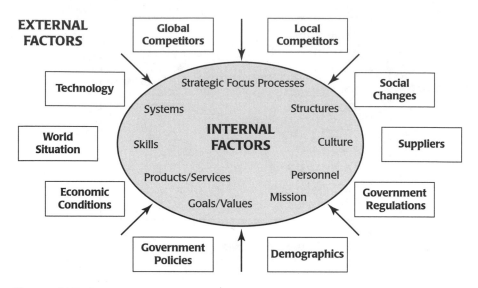

Figure 3.5 *Systems Components of a Business Organization*

- It is not what you do not know that will hurt you; it is what you think you know that is wrong.
- Obvious solutions do more harm than good; they result in tampering. *Tampering* is an attempt to change a system without understanding the system or the effects of the system change, thus resulting in making the system worse.
- Nothing grows forever (we cannot have an unending growth in revenues, profits, etc.).
- Do not resist positive feedback, and support negative feedback.
- Do not try to control the players; change the rules.
- Eighty percent of your problems are in your system, not in the people. (Deming [1986], however, estimated this figure at 94%.)
- There are no final answers.
- Every solution creates new problems.
- Do not be fooled by *system cycles*; a point-in-time measure may simply reflect the reality of the cycle, not a real change or improvement.
- Attempts to optimize one part of the system results in sub-optimizing another part of the system.

A friend of mine was working for an appliance manufacturing company. The company was looking for ways to save money on the manufacture of its refrigerator doors. It created an incentive program by which members of the purchasing department would receive a bonus based on the amount of money that it could save on the purchase of parts for the manufacture of refrigerators.

The department researched alternative sources for parts and found that they could purchase door hinges at a price considerably below the current price. They were able to save a few dollars on each door through reduced hinge prices. The members of the department had optimized the prices paid for door hinges, and they enjoyed a nice bonus.

Very soon, however, the company began to receive phone calls indicating that refrigerator doors were falling off because the hinges would not hold. The company had to set up service centers all over the world to replace the hinges on the refrigerator door, costing the company millions of dollars. Optimizing one part of the systen resulted in suboptimizing another part of the system. Failure to exercise systems thinking cost this company millions of dollars, not to mention a loss in reputation.

Systems Thinking versus Traditional Thinking

Systems thinking requires a very different perspective of the organization from traditional thinking. These differences are outlined in Table 3.1.

CHAPTER SUMMARY

The Start-up phase is critical to a successful project. The infrastructure needs to be established, project management needs to be in place, and the internal team with which the OD professional will be working needs to be assembled. At this stage, it is necessary to determine the assessment process to be used, who will be involved in the assessment process, and a time line for the assessment process. Missing or skipping any of these steps may jeopardize the success of the project. Once an agreement of how to proceed in the Start-up phase is in place, it is time to move forward with the Assessment and Feedback phase, which we

TABLE 3.1 Systems Thinking Compared with Traditional Thinking

HOW WE TEND TO THINK	COMPLEX SYSTEMS
Connections between problems and causes are obvious and easy to trace.	Such relationships are indirect and not obvious.
Others are to blame for our problems and they must change.	We unintentionally create our own problems; we solve them by changing our behavior.
Short-term policies assure long-term success.	Quick fixes make no difference or make things worse in long term.
To optimize the whole, we must optimize the parts.	To optimize the whole, improve relationships among parts.
To implement change, tackle many independent initiatives simultaneously.	Only a few key coordinated changes sustained over time will produce large systems change.

explore in Chapter 4. All of this must be done in the context of systems thinking.

QUESTIONS FOR DISCUSSION OR SELF-REFLECTION

1. Why is it important to work with a steering committee rather than simply moving forward in doing the work for which you have been professionally trained?

2. What are the advantages and disadvantages of working with an internal person who is different in demographics from you as an OD professional?

3. What things do you think need to be done in the start-up phase other than those things suggested in this chapter?

4. How might systems thinking affect the actions taken during the Start-up phase?

5. Share an example from your organizational experience about when systems thinking was ignored. What was the impact on the organization?

4

Organizational Assessment and Feedback

CHAPTER OUTLINE

Risks and Benefits in Conducting Needs Assessment

Psychometrics

Assessment Approaches

Analyzing and Reporting on Needs Assessments

Providing Feedback

Relationship between Assessment and Evaluation Phases

Chapter Summary

Questions/Activities for Discussion or Self-Reflection

OVERVIEW   Assessment is carried out in four ways, either singularly or in combination: observation, secondary data, interview, and survey. The pros and cons of each approach will be presented, along with specifics on how to make each one most useful. We will consider differences between the organization development process model and the appreciative inquiry model. Issues related to triangulation, customized versus standardized instruments, and psychometrics will be included. Finally, a keystone of OD is providing feedback on the outcome of assessment, so we will consider a rationale for feedback. Deciding to whom feedback should be provided, by whom, and in what format will also be discussed.

Once the Entry and Start-up phases are complete, or nearly so, you are then ready to conduct an organizational assessment—also called *diagnosis, check-up, cultural survey, employee survey*, and many other terms. See Figure 4.1 to see where the Assessment and Feedback phase fits into the organization development process model cycle.

One of the concerns in selecting a term for this task is to communicate that the process is looking not just for problems but equally for strengths and weaknesses of the organization's culture. Appreciative inquiry, which will be discussed later in this chapter, focuses solely on what is going well in the organization. Keep in mind that *organization*, depending on what was agreed on in the Entry phase, may refer to a department, a division, a site, a business unit, a function, a work team, or some other subsystem within the larger organization, or it can refer to the whole organization.

RISKS AND BENEFITS IN CONDUCTING NEEDS ASSESSMENT

While the ODP model stipulates that an assessment of the organization is to be done, it is not always the case that the benefits outweigh the risks for the organization in conducting an assessment. Risks in doing an assessment are almost always present to some extent.

Risks

Let's consider briefly some of the risks in conducting an assessment of the organization.

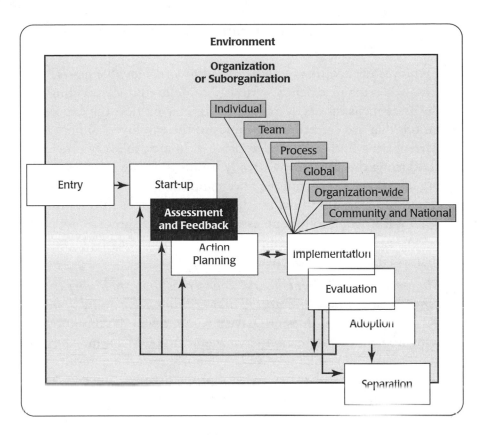

Figure 4.1 *Organization Development Process Model, Phase 3: Assessment and Feedback*

Employees believe that management will not take results seriously. Sometimes they are concerned that the assessment process is simply an exercise to make a show of management's desire for employee input, without any intent to utilize employee feedback. As a result, employees then feel as if they have been manipulated and will not participate freely or fully in the process.

Employees believe, perhaps correctly, that nothing will be done in response to findings. It is extremely difficult for an OD professional to go into an organization where previous assessments have been ignored. If there has been a history of ignoring such assessments, employees will simply not participate in the process, anticipating that past behavior predicts the future. I have heard of many situations where assessment reports have been filed and never heard of again.

Employee expectations will be raised to unachievable levels. Even when management is seriously committed to responding to the assessment results, it may be impossible to meet the expectations that are created in the minds of the employees simply from participating in the assessment process. In fact, the very process of conducting the assessment already begins to create changes in the organization as expectations affect employee behavior. In many situations, no matter how much management does to respond to what it learned, a follow-up assessment usually shows a less positive assessment, because employee expectations may be higher than what could ever be met.

Management will "benchmark" low scores that are higher than other organizations and decide that nothing needs to be done. When management does not have a commitment to continuous improvement or total quality management (TQM), it may be more concerned with results relative to other organizations' results (benchmarking) rather than ways that the organization can continue to improve on the factors being assessed. Communication is almost always an area where employees believe that management is not doing as well as they would like it to do. In many cases, I have seen management be satisfied with a score because it is better than the average, even if the score is low relative to other areas rated by employees in the organization. Rather than using this preference of some managers as an excuse not to respond to this assessment result, the OD professional can regard it as an opportunity to educate management in the importance of continuous improvement. Although benchmarking of processes has some value (see Chapter 8 on process interventions), benchmarking of numbers only has little value for an organization, especially if it is done without exploring the context in which the benchmarking numbers were produced.

Individual managers or employees will be scapegoated. Even though anonymity is promised in the process of conducting an assessment, there is always the concern that individuals may be identified and held responsible for outcomes that management deems to be negative, rather than looking at the whole system of the organization. The OD professional must do everything possible to avoid this situation.

Management will use the results for its own purposes, rather than for the good of the organization. Sometimes an OD professional is called in to deflect difficult decisions that management does not want employees to know have already been made. Management may have a hidden agenda for the process and may not have any intention of using the process to help the organization or its employees.

In each of these situations, it becomes the responsibility of the OD professional to do everything possible to avoid or at least minimize these risks and to maximize the benefits. After we consider the benefits of needs assessment, we will explore some suggestions for offsetting the risks with the benefits.

Benefits

Of course, there are many reasons for doing an assessment, leading to the following benefits:

Assessment will confirm or reject the presenting problem. As identified during the Entry phase, a presenting problem is often the perspective of a limited number of people, and they tend to be those at the top of the organization—who may be very much out of touch with the greatest part of the organization or most distant from the work that is being done in the organization. The OD professional's task is made easier if the problems and strengths within the organization are perceived to be real by most of the organization. This does not mean that OD professionals do not use management's input in the assessment process. It is possible, of course, for management to see something within the system that the bulk of employees do not see. It is also possible that inappropriate behaviors have become ingrained in the culture. This is one of the reasons why demographics, including job title, are often gathered in an assessment process. It then becomes possible to identify varying perceptions of those at different levels of the organization and to explore why these differences exist.

The right priorities will be emphasized, leading to greater efficiency and effectiveness. Even if the presenting problem is confirmed, it may not be the most important area to address in the beginning of the process. Other areas might well yield greater benefit to the organization. Thus, an assessment will allow the organization to prioritize areas that have the potential for improving the organization.

Greater synergy *will occur.* The assessment process, depending on which process is selected, may bring together people from across the entire organization. By tapping into the expertise and understanding of all members of the organization, assessment can bring greater synergy into the processes to be used for continuous improvement.

Management will be pressured to respond. Especially when the results of an assessment are shared throughout the organization (as will be argued later), it becomes very difficult to ignore the results. Management may well feel as if it must make an overt and clear response to whatever results emerge from the assessment process.

Measurement of improvements will motivate management and employees. The assessment can provide a starting point (or benchmark) that will make easier a later evaluation of whatever processes are planned in response to the assessment. Both management and employees may be motivated by the ability to track improvement over time when the same assessment process is used on a periodic basis.

Data will assist management in understanding the organizational system. Many management approaches recognize the importance of managing on the basis of data. An assessment may provide the information necessary to help management in making data-driven decisions.

Employees' morale will increase through a sense of empowerment. Asking employees for their opinions about how things are going in the organization provides them with considerable power and influence, especially when they see action being taken as a result of their input (see the discussion on the Action Planning phase in the next chapter). Answering questions about the organization's culture will give everyone a sense of ownership in the OD process and in the organization itself.

Offsetting Risks with Benefits

Determining whether the benefits will outweigh the risks is a key *competence* of a good OD professional. During the Entry and Start-up phases, the OD professional needs to be making ongoing assessment of the willingness of management to take the input seriously and to take action based on the input provided.

Another competence of importance in this process is an educational one. Both management and employees need to understand the role of unreasonable expectations in the process of responding to assessment feedback. Involving employees in the Action Planning phase can also go a long ways in sending signals to employees that their input is being taken seriously.

If the decision is that the benefits outweigh the risks—and good OD work should have that outcome—then the decision must be made about how to do the assessment. Before exploring specific approaches, it is necessary to explore general requirements for any measurement system, known as *psychometrics*.

PSYCHOMETRICS

Every quantifiable measure must be both reliable and valid, concepts that will be described briefly in this section. *Qualitative data* (as in interviews or focus groups) must be accurate and respond to the questions posed. These factors will be discussed in the section on interviews.

Reliability

Stated simply, *reliability* is an indicator of the consistency of the results obtained. Gathering information under similar conditions and ensuring the clarity of directions will help increase reliability. Most statistical software packages contain reliability measures. Cronbach's alpha, for example, is one of the most commonly used measures, details of which are outside the scope of this book.

Validity

Validity means that you are measuring what you want to measure, all of what you want to measure, and nothing but what you want to measure. There are many approaches to validity, but the first requirement for a valid measure is that it must be reliable. A reliable measure is not necessarily valid, but a valid measure must be reliable.

Of the many types of validity, two are of particular relevance in conducting an assessment. *Concurrent validity* requires that the instrument provide the same results as some other, proven instrument. Later in this chapter we discuss triangulation, a process that might be helpful in establishing concurrent validity. *Face validity* is another popular approach to establishing validity. Given that you are working with an internal team (based on the process used in the Start-up phase), this team can review the instrument to determine its face validity by confirming its clarity and appropriateness for obtaining the desired information.

ASSESSMENT APPROACHES

Four basic approaches may be used in conducting an assessment, with some variations:

- Observation
- Secondary data
- Interview—individual and group
- Questionnaire/survey

Observation

Observations begin from the first time the OD professional encounters a representative from the client organization and continue as the OD professional enters the client organization to begin work. So many questions can be asked and answered in this process. How busy are the employees? Do they seem stressed? Do they appear to be happy, angry, or sad? How do they interact with each other? How do they interact with customers? What is the work environment like—clean, dirty, messy, crowded, spacious? How large are the offices? Where are the

TABLE 4.1   Advantages and Disadvantages of Observation as an Assessment Tool

ADVANTAGES	DISADVANTAGES
■ Involves no intervening party between you and what is being observed ■ Allows a real situation to be observed without anyone putting on a show or trying to hide facts ■ Provides a context for other forms of assessment ■ Can be done from the beginning, to assist in miniassessment as well as full assessment ■ Can generally be done quickly and at low cost	■ Provides information at a point in time only; may miss important factors that are not continuously occurring ■ Gets filtered through your perspective and assumptions ■ Is limited in scope and geography, thus limiting the ability to generalize ■ May encourage people to act in a way to mislead if they are aware of the observer's presence and purpose ■ Is time-consuming if some of the above points are to be mitigated (e.g., wide geographic distribution, many time periods) ■ The very act of being present to observe changes what is happening.

offices located? Who occupies what kind of office? And on and on the list could go.

You often can get such questions answered before you even begin to work officially on the contract. And you can gather such information in a nonintrusive way. No one needs even to know that you are gathering the information that comes about from the observation. Keep in mind, however, that you always observe through the lenses of your experiences and assumptions. As with the entire assessment process, there is no such thing as a truly objective measure, but all measures are interpreted by those viewing the information. Table 4.1 cites some of the advantages and disadvantages of observation as a tool for assessment.

Secondary Data

Secondary data entail anything that preexists entry into the organization. This might include things like annual reports, Web sites, meeting minutes, reports from other consultations, statistical data (attendance, separations, voluntary turnover, grievances, safety records, percentage of minority employees, comparative pay scales by gender, etc.), memos and letters, customer complaints, shoppers' reports, policy manuals, training materials, and so on. One of my clients had a library of videotapes of the CEO making quarterly presentations to employees; that archive proved to be a useful resource. Clearly, what you examine will depend on the focus of the intervention into the organization. There is always much more secondary data than can possibly be reviewed in a reasonable amount of time.

See Table 4.2 for a list of the advantages and disadvantages of using secondary data as an assessment tool. As with observation, this is an assessment approach that is almost always included, to some degree, in any assessment process.

Individual Interview

Interviewing individuals, either face-to-face or by telephone, is the most popular approach to assessment, for several possible reasons. First, you have an opportunity to establish a trust level between yourself and the interviewee, which might result in better data being collected (though in some cultures interviewees will reveal less in an interview than in a survey). Second, interviews result in much richer stories. Stories often set a context for the less personal data that result from surveys. Third, while planning and preparation for conducting interviews are important, these steps are still much less time-consuming than they are with surveys. Furthermore, interviews are conducted in private. Thus, in contrast with a mistake on a survey that everyone sees, interviews can be prepared for quickly, and, if a mistake is made, few see it. Table 4.3 provides some of the advantages and disadvantages of using individual interviews as an assessment tool.

When interviews are conducted, interviewees are often assured that the information they share will be confidential. Clearly, that is a misuse of the word *confidential*. If it were indeed confidential, then the infor-

TABLE 4.2 Advantages and Disadvantages of Secondary Data as an Assessment Tool

ADVANTAGES	DISADVANTAGES
■ Involves no intervening party between you and what is being observed ■ Reviews historical situation without anyone putting on a show or trying to hide facts ■ Provides a historical context for other forms of assessment ■ Makes a wide range of perspectives possible ■ Contributes to developing trends as information is often comparable over time	■ Gets filtered through your perspective and assumptions ■ May represent only a slice of the organization, depending on what is reviewed ■ Is biased by the person developing data ■ Relies on records that may not be well maintained or readily available ■ Can be time-consuming, depending on how many records are reviewed ■ Involves possibility that client perceives some secondary data as sensitive, resulting in a selective review of secondary data only ■ Runs the risk that data easy to get may not be the most important data for the client's needs

mation could never be shared, defeating the purpose of the assessment process. Instead, what is typically intended is that we are assuring employees of anonymity. In other words, we assure them that, although their information will be included in an aggregated report, the source of the information will not be revealed, whether through name, title, department, or any stories that would give this information away, even if not stated explicitly. We need to be precise in what we are committing ourselves to with interviewees. Other ways of ensuring anonymity include not collecting identifying information (though this may reduce

TABLE 4.3   Advantages and Disadvantages of the Individual Interview as an Assessment Tool

ADVANTAGES	DISADVANTAGES
■ Is quickly developed ■ Is easier than other approaches in establishing rapport and trust ■ Can give extra assurance of anonymity to interviewees, encouraging greater depth in information provided ■ Results in high response rate ■ Is conducted behind closed doors, so errors not so obvious ■ Allows employees to feel ownership in outcomes because they feel that they have had real input into the process ■ Is flexible, as probing questions can be asked and clarification given, if needed	■ Is time-consuming to gather data and analyze; therefore expensive ■ Is difficult to analyze ■ Gets filtered through interviewer's perspective and assumptions ■ Involves inconsistency of interviewers (if multiple interviewers are used) ■ Adds costs with interviewer training (with multiple interviewers) ■ Is time-consuming and expensive to transcribe tapes if the interviewer uses audiotaping (with permission of the interviewees) ■ Is challenging to conduct many interviews daily and for many days

the meaningfulness of the information collected) or destroying such information immediately after it has been collected.

To illustrate, I was once conducting interviews as part of an organizational assessment for a chain of fast-food restaurants. The interviews were being held at a centralized off-site location. Each interviewee was given assurances of anonymity in the interviews. About 15 minutes into one interview, the interviewee asked me whether she could share something with me confidentially. I agreed, put my laptop away, and just listened. She shared a number of stories of sexual harassment that had occurred in her store with her manager that affected both her and her coworkers. As I had agreed to her condition of confidentiality, I needed to find out from her more specifically what she meant by *confidentially*. She agreed that I could share with upper management that there was a serious problem with sexual harassment in one of its stores, but I could not indicate where or at what level, which really would have fit into my assurance of anonymity. Nevertheless, I assured her that this would be the case. Rather than wait for the interviews to be completed, since management did not know whom I was interviewing or when, I immediately reported to management that they had a serious problem with sexual harassment in one of its stores. Management's response was that they knew where it was and would take immediate action. I never did figure out why they needed me to tell them something that they already knew and that they realized put them in a potential litigious situation, but the situation was resolved almost immediately, without violating anonymity. Clearly, however, it was important for me to verify what the interviewee meant by confidentiality, because sharing anything about the situation would have violated confidentiality

This example illustrates another very important point regarding interviews. Unlike some of the helping professions (e.g., lawyers and, under some circumstances, therapists, clergy, and physicians), OD professionals do not have client privilege or protected communications. Under court order, an OD professional would need to reveal anything that was learned in a consultation. Failure to report knowledge of a criminal activity could also, conceivably, result in charges of complicity in the act.

Core Interview Questions.　After greeting the interviewee, introduce yourself briefly, review the purpose of the interview, and reassure the interviewee, again, of the commitment to maintain anonymity in the interview and subsequent reporting process. Then, in most OD assessments, there are four key, or core, questions that you are likely to ask:

- In what areas do you see the organization (department, unit, team) as having particular strengths? Why do you see these as strengths?

- In what areas do you see the organization (department, unit, team) as having particular needs for change, growth, and improvement? Why do you see these as areas to develop?
- What specific recommendations for change, growth, and improvement would you make to the organization (department, unit, team)?
- What else would you like me to hear about the organization (department, unit, team)?

More questions might be asked when the OD professional is brought in for a specific and limited focus (e.g., to conduct multirater feedback). Or, more questions might be asked to explore more fully what was perceived in the presenting problem. Care must be taken, however, to not bias responses by asking questions that are so narrow and explicit that respondents are not able to provide the broader context of the organization, or are not able to provide evidence that the problem (if there is one) is something other than that contained in the presenting problem.

From an Appreciative Inquiry perspective, only positive perspectives are sought, and these are, preferably, embedded in stories. Given AI's positive perspective, an AI OD person might ask the following questions:

- Think about something that you really liked that happened (or is happening) in your organization. Can you tell me a story about that time?
- Can you share other examples with me?

In any interview, one of the challenges for the interviewer is to ask follow-up and probing questions without revealing to interviewees your perspectives about the organization, or the answers they have already provided. You do not want to bias the results of the interviews.

Characteristics of an Effective Interviewer.   An effective interview is not easy to conduct. It requires an interviewer with skills developed through experience and observation. An effective interviewer is likely to have most, if not all, of the following characteristics:

- Is aware of his or her own biases and can control for them; does not use leading questions or make leading statements
- Is an effective note taker; ideally, he or she has excellent keyboarding skills so interviews can be taken almost verbatim, eliminating the need for subsequent transcription, while allowing the interviewee to maintain eye contact with the interviewee most of the time. Personally, I avoid tape recording. Some interviewees refuse to allow tape recording, most are nervous about it to some degree, and it requires extra time and, therefore, cost to transcribe the interview.
- Is prepared with initial and follow-up questions; open and probing
- Maintains standardization by asking the same core questions
- Creates a sense of trust and rapport easily
- Listens attentively, maintaining good eye contact and using appropriate body language to encourage continued conversation (nodding, smiling)
- Does not interrupt
- Talks only to ask questions, not to make statements (after the introductory comments)
- Clarifies interviewee statements that are not understood by the interviewer
- Clarifies interviewer questions that are not understood by the interviewee
- Is aware of good time management, without rushing the interviewee, but also keeping the interviewee on track

Working with an experienced, skilled interviewer as a mentor or coach can confirm whether you have these skills and what you may need to do to develop them further.

Group Interview

Sometimes, because of cost or time constraints, or because you think that the group can benefit from building on each other's ideas, you may choose to conduct a group interview rather than individual interviews.

TABLE 4.4 Advantages and Disadvantages of a Group Interview as an Assessment Tool

ADVANTAGES	DISADVANTAGES
■ Permits lots of information to be gathered in a short time	■ Can lead to groupthink in which people start to agree with dominant personalities
■ Is easy to develop	
■ Is easy to establish rapport and trust	■ Invariably includes dominant personalities who may not allow for broad participation without strong facilitation skills
■ Allows participants to build on one another's ideas	
■ Lets employees feel ownership from the empowerment of their involvement	■ Can't guarantee anonymity because so many people hear what has been said
■ Is flexible, allowing probing and clarifying questions	■ Can't guarantee anonymity, so participants may be reluctant to reveal the most important information
	■ Gets filtered through facilitator's perspective and assumptions
	■ Is difficult and time-consuming to analyze
	■ Entails unknown reliability
	■ Will last longer than an individual interview so participants are required to give up more of their workday time

These are two very different processes requiring very different skill sets. Some of the skills needed for group interviews and processes to be used are presented in Table 4.4, which outlines the advantages and disadvantages of group interviews.

Guidelines for Facilitating Group Interviews. Although the same kinds of questions can be used for group interviews as for individual interviews, the process itself is quite different. The following guidelines should be helpful in conducting a group interview:

- Record all input so everyone in the group can see the responses. While one person facilitates the interview, a second person may record on a flipchart or with a computer with projected images.
- Maintain approximately equal participation from all group members; invite nonparticipants to share; suggest that overly active participants let others participate more.
- Encourage moving on to another theme if the group seems to be stuck on one theme. Once it's recorded, that's all that's needed; discussion is not necessary.
- Ask for clarification if a comment is not clear.
- Check with participants periodically to ensure that comments are being recorded accurately
- Start on time and end on time. End earlier if the group has no further input.
- Be willing to go back to an earlier question if someone thinks of something that fits.
- Don't let things drag. When the group is struggling for new items, move on to the next question.
- Don't put words in participants' mouths. Everything recorded should come only from the group at participants' own initiative.
- Don't ask any questions other than those provided in your interview guide, except for clarification; don't go fishing.
- Don't let anyone give a speech; if necessary, interrupt kindly and encourage shorter input.
- Thank group members for their participation.

Questionnaire/Survey

While a questionnaire can contain open-ended questions (similar to an interview, only the respondent writes his or her responses; most respondents are reluctant to write much, so such an approach is not likely to yield much information). This section focuses specifically on a written instrument that contains questions with a range of responses from which respondents can select, used to glean *quantitative data*. (In this section, *questionnaire* and *survey* are used as synonymous terms; Table 4.5

TABLE 4.5 Advantages and Disadvantages of a Questionnaire/Survey as an Assessment Tool

ADVANTAGES	DISADVANTAGES
■ Statistically establishes reliability and validity	■ Is difficult and time-consuming to develop
■ Is easy and fast to analyze	■ Makes getting an acceptable response rate difficult
■ Uses the same language for all respondents	■ Uses the same words that may be interpreted differently by respondents
■ Can be repeated for benchmarking, with others or over time	■ Is difficult to establish rapport and trust
■ Lets organizational members feel ownership; because of its ease in administration and analysis, allows all employees to be involved	■ Is harder to convince respondents of anonymity because of lack of personal contact
■ Is efficient to administer once developed; only involves costs of duplication, postage, and analysis, which might be avoided or mini-mized if using the Web for input and analysis (though there may be costs for development and hosting of the instrument and creating the analysis process)	■ May be used inappro-priately to make compari-sons between departments or organizations (though there may be times when such comparisons are appropriate)
■ Is easy to customize to fit an organi-zation's vocabulary and needs for specific information	■ Provides results that tend to lack depth
■ Results in quantification that lends credibility to process	■ Usually collects only objective, countable data, lacking in stories or explanation
■ Can be used in written, Web, or telephone format	■ Provides no opportunity to probe
■ May encourage organizational members to reveal more in-depth information or more accurate infor-mation because they are not sharing the information face-to-face	■ May encourage respon-dents to provide socially desirable responses rather than accurate responses
■ Can assure anonymity, which is es-pecially important when gathering sensitive information	■ Is difficult to develop a sound, clear survey

Note: Some of these items were adapted from suggestions in Patten (2001).

TABLE 4.6   Advantages of Standardized and Customized Surveys

STANDARDIZED	CUSTOMIZED
▪ Is available immediately, so development time is not needed ▪ Should have appropriate psychometrics already established, not requiring such expertise in the organization ▪ Has analysis systems already in place, so expertise and development time are not needed ▪ May appear more professional ▪ Does not change from year to year so improvements can be tracked over time ▪ Does not require expertise in developing surveys within the organization	▪ Is cheaper than a standardized instrument if time is not considered ▪ Uses the language/vocabulary of the organization ▪ Focuses on the areas of greatest interest to the organization ▪ Keeps the focus on the organization rather than worrying about benchmarking with other organizations ▪ Creates greater ownership among those who create the survey ▪ Can be modified from year to year to respond to emerging issues ▪ Entails questions with which employees can identify more readily

describes pros and cons to this form of assessment.) Gathering the same information using such a structured instrument via telephone or on the Web is also possible. There is always the option, too, of purchasing a *standardized* instrument that has been developed professionally, rather than developing a *customized* survey. The advantages of each type are shown in Table 4.6.

Criteria for a Good Survey.   In addition to reliability and validity, several other criteria are necessary to produce an acceptable, quality survey:

▪ All items must be clear and understandable, as must be the directions.

- All targeted organization members must have an equal chance of being selected and participating.

- A high response rate is required, preferably over 90%. There are a number of ways to increase the response rate. First, the survey should be easy to complete. Second, respondents must believe that the survey is important and will affect their futures. Third, if mailed, use a commemorative stamp and provide a stamped return envelope. Fourth, sometimes incentives are used. One of the most useful approaches I have used is to allow respondents to select from a list of charities to which the company will make donations if the survey is returned. This approach does not violate anonymity and appeals to human instincts to help others. Fifth, allow employees to complete the survey during work time, even in a reserved location away from the workstation.

- Keep the survey short, no more than 10 minutes. Don't go fishing—ask only the essential questions. Tell respondents, based on a pilot test, how long the survey will take.

- Randomly reverse the polarity of the items to attain individual item discrimination. This criterion requires that some items be stated positively and some negatively. While some respondents find this approach confusing, it also ensures that respondents must read each item. Be sure to account for reversing these items in the analysis phase.

- Randomly distribute items in the survey (i.e., no blocking of items by category) to avoiding creating a halo effect where respondents respond to every item in the category the same way because of how they feel about the category in general.

- Make sure that the survey is easy to read (featuring large font size, plenty of white space, clear color contrasts—no white on light blue, e.g., or purple on black or red).

- Label each response option.

- Be sure that each item contains one, and only one, concept. Watch for the word *and* as it usually signals that two concepts are involved, such as "My supervisor is fair and available." How does someone respond if the supervisor is fair but not available, or available but not fair?

Questions to Be Answered in Designing a Survey. Some questions may need to be answered in a survey that do not have preset suggestions. These are based on individual preferences and what the survey designer is attempting to do with the assessment. Such questions, with factors to consider, include the following:

- *Should the response options have an even or odd number?* If there is an even number, then respondents must make a choice, a forced choice. In contrast, if there is an odd number, then respondents can choose the middle number, a neutral response.

- *How many response options should there be?* Too many responses can be confusing but can increase discrimination and reliability. Most surveys settle on five or seven options (if an odd number is being offered), or four and six (if an even number). Some OD professionals collapse the number of categories into only three for reporting purposes; if that's all the discrimination that is needed, then that's the number of response options that should be provided in the survey. It makes no sense to use seven response options and report them as if there are only three.

- *Should neutral responses be allowed (as mentioned in the first bullet), and, if so, how should they be allowed?* One option is to provide a middle point (an odd number of responses), which should then be included in the analysis. Another option is to allow for a "Not Applicable" (N/A), which, then, is not included in the analysis.

Conducting an Affinity Diagram to Create Items and Determine Survey Categories. Most surveys explore a variety of themes, and it is often desirable to report results by category, in addition to individual items. Statistically, but after the fact, the categories identified can be confirmed (or rejected) with the use of factor analysis, a statistical tool. In an attempt to create the best categories possible a priori (before the fact), consider conducting an *affinity diagram* with the organizational team formed during the Start-up phase. An affinity diagram is used to reduce a large number of items into a few categories. Use the following process with the team:

1. Ask the team to develop a clear statement about why the survey is being conducted.

2. Give the team 5 minutes or so to make an individual list, *or* the group can begin to brainstorm a list of items to include; each note should consist of a phrase of no more than three to four words.

3. As one option for getting ideas posted, each respondent can write and place his or her own items. Use a marker pen to write each idea on a 3 × 3 or 3 × 5 sticky note. I also find it useful to affix to the wall with masking tape a large piece of fabric that has been prepared in advance with spraying artists' glue (e.g., 3M Spray Mount Artist's Adhesive™) on it (the kind of glue that allows for easy removal of paper with adhesive backing from whatever it is attached to). In this case, plain paper can be used for the notes.

4. Alternatively, select two or three recorders. Go around the room, one participant at a time, getting *one* idea at a time from each participant. This idea should be written by a recorder and placed on a sheet of flipchart paper in the center of a large table or on the prepared sheet of fabric. The notes should be placed at random, without any attempt to categorize the responses at this point. People can pass when they no longer have suggestions to make.

5. Continue this process until no one has any new ideas to add. Participants may pass and then offer new items at a later time. No discussion about the items should occur during the brainstorming (see Chapter 7). Items should be accepted even if they are close in concept to other items. Discard items only if they repeat an item that has already been submitted.

6. Without any discussion or talking, participants then arrange the notes in clusters. No explicit reason for including an item in a cluster is needed (or permitted) at this point. Participants are free to move an item from one cluster to another if they wish. Clusters may not be formed so high that some participants cannot reach them. This process continues until no participant is moving a note.

7. The facilitator focuses on one cluster at a time to label that cluster: "What is there about the items in this cluster that brings them together?" In the process, participants can decide

whether items are duplicated, in which case one of the two items is discarded with consensus. The group may also decide that an item does not belong in the cluster. That item can be moved to another cluster, or it can be set aside to see whether it forms the nucleus of another cluster. It is also appropriate to discuss whether a given item is desirable and should be included at all. Items may also be reworded, with consensus.

8. When there is consensus, the title of that cluster is written on a larger (or different-colored) note and placed above that cluster. The title should clearly communicate the items in that cluster without having to see the cluster items. This process continues until all notes have been included in a cluster and labeled. Clusters of one are not acceptable. This process usually results in six to eight categories being identified.

9. The results are then typed in preparation for the next meeting with the cluster label and the individual items within that cluster. At the next meeting, the list is reviewed to be sure that there is still consensus around the items included in the list, as well as in their assignment to a specific cluster. Modifications should be made as agreed on.

10. The survey is then written using the clusters and the items under each cluster label.

Criteria for Good Survey Items.   Unfortunately, there is a great lack of understanding about how difficult it is to write a good survey item. Just because someone is a good writer does not mean that this person is able to write good survey items. It is critical that a survey be written well, without any typographical or grammatical errors, because everyone in the organization is going to see the results of this part of the process. Here are some tips for composing good survey items:

- Ensure that each item contains one and only one idea; remember to watch for *and* as a red flag. Consider, for example, "The trainer was prepared and clear." How should the respondent answer if the trainer was prepared but not clear, or clear but not prepared?
- Keep items as simple and short as possible.

- Use unambiguous words. Avoid *successful, sometimes, usually,* and the like.
- Use simple vocabulary.
- Use the jargon, titles, descriptions, and other terms that are familiar to the respondents.
- Use parallel construction (e.g., start every item with a verb).
- Proofread, proofread, proofread, and then proofread. (Do not rely on spell checking, but use it!) Have others read the items as others can sometimes catch errors that the author will never catch no matter how frequently reviewed.
- Use the team formed at Start-up to review the final survey before implementing.

ANALYZING AND REPORTING ON NEEDS ASSESSMENTS

Once the assessment instrument or process has been determined and implemented, the next step is to analyze the results and report them to the respondent group. The following bullets—segmented into general suggestions, suggestions for quantitative data, and suggestions for qualitative data—suggest rather simple steps that everyone can take in doing an analysis and reporting the results. Those interested in greater detail should refer to Patten (2001) and the American Psychological Association (2001) handbook.

General Suggestions for Analysis
- Determine the experience level of those who will be reading the results, and adjust the details of the results and analysis to match that level.
- Protect respondent anonymity. Use groups of at least five when you are reporting results by demographic groups (e.g., department, gender, title, etc.).
- Double-check for accuracy. Results are very important to the organization; if it finds an error, your reputation will be in jeopardy.

Suggestions for Analysis of Quantitative Data
- Distinguish between levels of information that have been obtained as this affects the type of analysis that can be done. Briefly, these are as follows:

- □ *Nominal.* This type simply names something, such as position (manager, supervisor, employee), gender, marital status, and so on.
- □ *Ordinal.* Ordinal levels of information put items in order, but there is no way to know whether the differences between two points are the same as between two other points. For example, on a response scale from 1 to 5, there is no way to know whether the difference between 4 and 5 is the same as that between 2 and 3. Similarly, on a forced-order ranking on performance appraisals, the difference between the top- and second-ranked employees is likely to be different from the difference between the second- and third-ranked employees.
- □ *Interval.* Although the difference between all points is identical, there is no absolute zero (e.g., 0 degrees in temperature does not mean that there is no temperature).
- □ *Ratio.* The differences between all points is identical, and there is an absolute zero base (e.g., salary, age, years of employment, etc.).

- ■ Descriptive statistics are generally sufficient. *Means* and *standard deviations* are generally expected at a minimum for data that are interval or ratio. Most people will usually accept these statistics for ordinal data with a scale (e.g., 1 to 5). For other ordinal data and for nominal data, frequencies and percentages are usually shown. Never show percentages without also showing frequencies.
- ■ *Modes* are also useful if the results are highly skewed (most results are positive or negative) or if the responses are simply a description of a category rather than having continuous data. Consider using bar charts and line graphs.
- ■ Avoid reentering data, if possible (e.g., analyze directly from Web input, use bubble sheets, etc. that can be scanned), to minimize errors.

Suggestions for Analysis of Qualitative Data
- ■ Read through the transcripts several times, highlighting phrases related to the same theme with different colors of highlighters (e.g., all phrases related to supervision in yellow, all references to strategies in red, etc.).

- Report the dominant themes with sample quotes related to that theme. Be sure that your sample quotes do not reveal the identity of the respondent in any way.

Triangulation

It should be obvious from the previous discussion that each approach to assessment is likely to result in a different type of information. Is it also *consistent* information? This is an important question in determining how many of the five approaches need to be used. Collecting data using two or more methods—an approach known as *triangulation*—can be very helpful in determining whether the data are the same regardless of method used. If they are, then we have a form of reliability.

However, we should not expect the data to be consistent. Surveys are designed to gather quantitative data; interviews are designed to provide qualitative stories. They should support each other rather than provide the same information. Some have argued that difficulty arises when the methods produce different results. Instead, while one should expect that there is not contradictory information, each approach has its own richness and helps broaden the perspective that one has of the situation within the organization. Triangulation is a reason why organizations will almost always want to use more than one approach to assessment. Invariably, I want to include secondary data and observation, along with at least one of the other three modes of assessment.

PROVIDING FEEDBACK

When the assessment is completed, this phase of the organization development process model also requires that the results of the assessment be fed back to the organization. Feedback is provided for two primary reasons: to ensure validity of interpretation and to increase ownership among the members of the organization.

. . . .

As one example of the positive results of offering feedback to an organization, a survey identified a concern by the employees that they worked in noisy spaces. Their offices were modular, with walls reaching only part way to the ceiling. It was a noisy place—phones were ringing, you could hear conversations over the walls, people talked with each other by shouting over the walls, and you could hear laughing and general office noises easily. We were anticipating that we would need to do something about improving the situation with the walls so that such noise would not carry across the modular walls—a relatively expensive undertaking. During the feedback session, however, the employees reacted quite negatively when this interpretation was offered. They saw the current modular walls as a way in which they could still interact with each other easily and regularly. It turned out that the problem was that noisy fans hung above each desk area. The building engineers made some quick adjustments, and, within an hour, everyone was satisfied with the noise level, a process that cost the organization almost nothing!

Feeding back the results of the assessment process raises four questions (at least) that need to be answered: Who should receive the feedback? Who should provide the feedback? What format should be used in providing the feedback? What should be included in the feedback?

Who Should Receive the Feedback?

A basic value of OD is that ownership of the data belongs with those who provided the data. With this value in mind, the feedback of the outcome of the assessment process belongs to all of those who participated in the assessment process. Managers are sometimes uneasy with this approach, because they believe that the results may cause a decline in employee morale if the results are negative, and they will be made to look bad. The response to this concern is that the employees provided the information, so there is nothing that they are going to be hearing that will be new to them—they already know it!

The only time when this basic principle might be set aside is if there is information that might truly have a negative impact on the stock market or on competitive advantage. However, this possibility should be acknowledged ahead of time and planned for in the instructions that accompany whatever assessment process is used. So, unless unusual extenuating circumstances exist, the basic rule is that the feedback belongs to everyone involved, and this point should be stipulated in the contract.

Who Should Provide the Feedback?

Ownership of the data by management is more likely to occur if management provides the feedback, though this also leads to the risk that employees will not trust the feedback. Cascading the results from the top layers of management to lower levels can get the information out quickly and send the message that management is taking the results of the assessment process very seriously. The risk in having the management team do this is that the team may be tempted to comment on the data and be defensive about any feedback from employees that they perceive to be negative. They can also send a message that they are not open to any questions or comments from the audience during the feedback sessions. If management is to provide the feedback, the OD professional will likely want to spend time with top management personnel, coaching and training them on how to provide the feedback. He or she may even wish to be in the audience during the feedback session.

In What Format Should the Feedback Be Given?

When feasible, face-to-face feedback is most powerful. Questions that relate to the data or to the planned response to the results can be answered immediately and directly for the entire audience. Be sure, however, to provide enough time in the feedback session for questions. In a large organization-wide survey, on the other hand, this allowance may not be feasible, though the cascading approach by management, as described previously, may make this viable. With the ready availability of computer technology for the projection of slides, a very nice, mostly consistent presentation can be made across the organization. However, the presenter may not be prepared to answer questions if he or she is not directly involved in the project. Careful consideration must be given to whether handouts are desirable, given the ease with which printed data could be shared with competitors, either intentionally or accidentally.

Concern about the confidentiality of the data is also a factor that may influence the decision not to share the information in writing with the whole organization. Written feedback, however, may be the only means that works well in some organizations. If some information is deemed too sensitive to put into writing for such widespread dissemination, a note to that effect should be included in the distributed information.

Whatever approach is used, reporting with multiple formats is better than singular formats. Some people are more visual and will prefer graphs, whereas others are more data oriented and will prefer tables of numbers.

What Should Be Included in the Feedback?

Recipients of the feedback should expect to see the following information: how the information was gathered, a summary of the information gathered, management's intent for using the data, steps that have already been taken to address the priorities identified in the data, and some means for providing feedback about either the process or the results. If previous studies have been conducted, then historical data will also be useful in giving employees the opportunity to see past and current organizational progress or even failure. Be careful, however, not to overwhelm the audiences with too much information. A lot of information typically comes from an assessment process, and audiences can easily be overwhelmed.

In the final stages of the feedback sessions, it is helpful to involve attendees in beginning to brainstorm in small groups appropriate responses to the concerns that have surfaced to begin the Action Planning process, the next phase in the ODP model.

RELATIONSHIP BETWEEN ASSESSMENT AND EVALUATION PHASES

Looking ahead in the organization development process model, you will find that Evaluation follows the Implementation phase. Ideally, if the Action Planning stage is based on a high-quality assessment, then the processes used to create the feedback may be the best way to meet the Evaluation phase needs. Therefore, it might be useful to begin reminding people as the Assessment phase begins that they will be asked to repeat the process in the Evaluation phase. This step might prevent frustration from occurring when the evaluation phase begins. There will be more about the issues of repeating the Assessment processes in the Evaluation phase chapter.

CHAPTER SUMMARY

This chapter has explored in detail the processes to use and the advantages and disadvantages of the primary forms of assessment—observation, secondary data (preexisting information), individual interviews, group interviews, and questionnaires/surveys. Using two or more approaches, or triangulation, enables the OD professional to determine whether there is consistency in the results or whether the different approaches surface different information. Reliability (consistency) and validity (measuring what is intended) are two basic psychometric characteristics that must occur in any assessment approach. Finally, feedback is essential as a means of confirming the accuracy of the information gathered and beginning the process of mutual Action Planning, the next phase in the organization development process model.

QUESTIONS/ACTIVITIES FOR DISCUSSION OR SELF-REFLECTION

1. Conduct an interview role play conducted in pairs based on real working situations.
2. Form a small group and conduct an affinity diagram process for a survey to determine the culture of a class or a workplace.
3. Write several survey items, and then critique them with a partner.
4. Add additional advantages and disadvantages to the tables provided in this chapter.
5. Describe how a triangulation process might work for you in an assessment process.
6. Discuss the advantages and disadvantages of providing feedback to all members of the participant group rather than just to the Start-up team and senior management.

5

Action Planning and Introduction to Interventions

CHAPTER OUTLINE

Distinguishing between Training and OD Needs

Creating an Action Plan

Interventions Available to OD Professionals

Chapter Summary

Questions for Discussion or Self-Reflection

OVERVIEW   Based on the findings of the assessment, an action plan must be created. What goals and objectives will the organization establish, and what will the organization do as a result of the assessment and feedback? This chapter includes a form to assist practitioners in the process of doing action planning as a collaborative group, relying heavily on the use of the affinity diagram process described in the previous chapter. An overview of implementation options will be included in this chapter to suggest approaches that might be included in action plans.

With the assessment and feedback completed, and with the input of those receiving the feedback, the steering team can now begin the process of deciding what to do in response to the assessment. This step, the Action Planning phase, is shown in Figure 5.1.

A wide range of interventions is available to OD professionals. (An *intervention* is an activity designed to help achieve the goals and objectives established in the Action Planning phase.) What follows in this chapter is, first, a discussion of a process for separating training needs from other types of OD needs. This will be followed by a description of one approach to creating an action plan, followed by a brief overview of the range of implementation interventions available.

DISTINGUISHING BETWEEN TRAINING
AND OD NEEDS

Many organizations suffer from something of a "training can fix everything" syndrome. Because several organizations are not familiar with the tools used by OD professionals, organizations may feel that they have a limited range of interventions from which to choose. While training is considered to be an OD intervention by most, it is, by far, not the only OD intervention available. So the question facing organizations and OD professionals working with the organization is, How can we know whether this situation requires a training solution or some other type of OD approach?

There is, of course, no magic way to determine when training will be helpful and when some other type of intervention will be more helpful. But some processes can assist in making this determination. It is

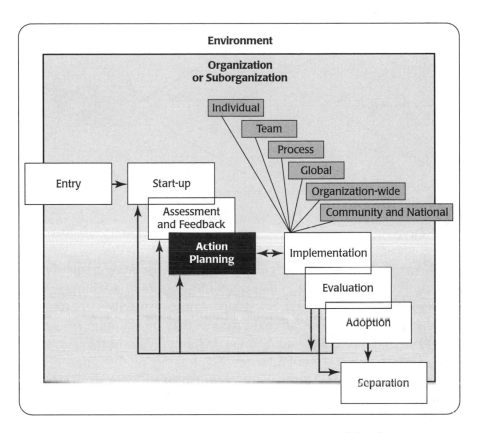

Figure 5.1 *Organization Development Process Model, Phase 4: Action Planning*

important to keep a systems perspective in trying to sort out what the cause of any problems identified might be and the solutions that might be tried to overcome them. When a problem appears to originate in a lack of expertise or knowledge, then it is probably a problem that can be addressed through training. If, on the other hand, the problem is a matter of policy or process, then there is likely to be a nontraining OD response. If the question is yes to "If it were a matter of life and death, could the individual perform this task?" then the problem is probably not a training problem.

Keep in mind, in addressing this question, the expertise of the person who is making the recommendation. Unfortunately, because there are no requirements that must be met before someone can claim to be

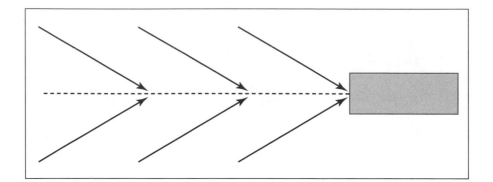

Figure 5.2 *Cause-Effect Diagram (Blank)*

an OD professional, people with limited expertise may be involved in making recommendations. This sometimes results in a whatever-is-in-the-toolkit approach to OD. So, if a person is primarily a trainer, then the answer to any organizational problem may be training. If that person is certified to use a certain process or tool, the use of that process or tool is often the recommendation. So, having or developing more knowledge about OD can help an organization become a better consumer of OD processes. It can also help avoid the problem of using a process to address findings of an assessment with the wrong intervention. Organizations, as consumers of OD, must understand what OD is and what it can and cannot do.

The total quality management (TQM) movement has contributed a tool that can be extremely useful in determining the true (or root) cause of a problem. A *cause-effect diagram*, also known as a *fishbone diagram*, because of its appearance, or an *Ishikawa diagram*, named for the Japanese consultant who popularized it, is designed to identify all of the causes of a specified problem and then, from these possible causes, determine the one that is most likely to be the root cause. Figure 5.2 shows a blank cause-effect diagram; directions for completing one are provided in the next section.

How to Use a Cause-Effect Diagram

Determining the real or root cause of a problem is critical in planning action in response to an organizational assessment. Using the diagram in Figure 5.2, follow these steps:

1. At the right side of the diagram, in the box, write the problem that the organization faces.

2. Brainstorm possible causes of the problem. Place each major cause on one of the primary "bones" coming off of the spine (or main bone). If you are not sure where to begin, a common approach is to label the "ribs" as Materials, People, Methods, Machines, and Environment.

3. As additional causes are brainstormed, the decision needs to be made regarding whether the suggestion is a main cause or a subcause of a major cause that has already been written on the diagram. If it is a main cause, it should be written on a primary bone. If it is a subcause, a line (a minor bone) should be drawn off the primary bone and the subcause written on that line. Subcauses of subcauses can also occur.

4. This process continues until there are no additional causes, subcauses, or sub-subcauses identified.

5. Once all ideas have been placed on the diagram (see Figure 5.3), encourage facilitated discussion about the root causes, what each alleged root cause means, and how likely it is that this is the most important cause of the problem.

6. None of these primary "ribs" is detailed enough to be a root cause. The next step is to develop each rib into two or three sublevels. For example, "Improved Competition" might have a number of first-level items: more stores opened, more companies, competitors more innovative, competitors provide better

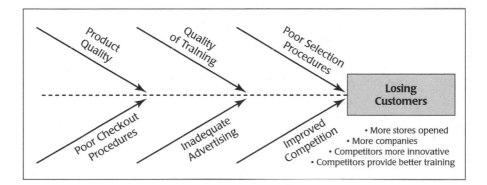

Figure 5.3 *Cause-Effect Diagram (Completed)*

training, and so on. A next level might also be explored for each of these; for example, for "competitors provide better training," another series of ribs might mention "on-site sales training every month," "OD consultants brought in to help HR," and the like. If these points in turn can be developed further, they should be.

7. Once everyone understands all of the causes to the deepest level possible and has adequately discussed the most likely root cause of the problem, participants then vote on what they believe the root cause to be. This can be done by having each person put a check mark opposite the cause believed to be the root cause, or each person could be given three (for example) sticky colored dots to place directly on the diagram.

8. The cause that gets the most votes is tentatively identified as the possible root cause. An action plan is then developed to address that root cause.

CREATING AN ACTION PLAN

Whenever any team is working on a process or a task to be done that is not documented or recorded somewhere, has not become routine, and involves a complexity that exceeds just a few steps, an action plan can be a helpful way to organize and complete the process or task within a timely manner. Thus, an action plan can be used to address the root causes identified through the use of cause-effect diagrams or problems that are identified in some other way. Keep in mind as you proceed that an intervention has a greater probability of being successful if it builds on strengths that exist within an organization.

The following steps describe how to create an action plan. Use the form shown in the Appendix 5.1 as a template for creating action plans. A completed sample action plan is also included at the end of this chapter, in Appendix 5.2.

1. Write a clear goal statement that everyone on the team understands and accepts. Add strategy, outcomes, and team leader for that particular action plan.

2. Brainstorm a list of all of the steps that will need to be accomplished for the successful accomplishment of the outcomes

desired; each item should be written on a large sheet of paper and posted on the prepared sticky fabric (see the previous chapter for details on doing an affinity diagram).

3. Review all sheets (as would normally be done with brainstorming). Remove all sheets with items that do not have agreement; write new notes if clarification is needed or if sheets/points are to be combined.

4. Put the sheets in chronological order, preferably on the left side of the sticky fabric so the arrangement matches that which will ultimately be transferred to the action planning form (see Appendix 5.1). The team members move the notes around without discussion. If disagreement occurs about the placement of a sheet/point, another team member can move the sheet back to where it was or to another place. This process continues until no one moves another note. Another possible way to accomplish this phase is to have the team members discuss where the sheets should go, with the facilitator moving the sheets as consensus emerges. If there appears to be considerable disagreement (e.g., the participants continue moving the sheets around without consensus emerging), discussion may be a more effective way to proceed.

5. When the group agrees on the order, they next attach a name (or names or a team) to each step to show who will be responsible for it, along with a date signifying when that step should be done. Budgets should be estimated for each step that will encounter costs.

6. This information is then prepared in the appropriate format, as per the action planning form in the chapter appendix. Having a blank copy of this form in a computer file (a template) ensures that everyone will be using the same format, and a format does not need to be created each time it is needed. When completed, the form should be reviewed at the next meeting and necessary changes made.

7. Review the action plan at each team meeting. *The action plan should be considered flexible.* Update as necessary by completing the "Revised Date" and "Revision Number" columns, as well as the "Date Completed" column when the step is completed. The responsible team may find it necessary to shift or

change any factor on the form. Whether they need approval or not depends on the extent of the change and how the change might influence other decisions. As money is spent, fill in the "Actual Spent" column. Modify the action plan as necessary.

8. Periodically, review the "Revision Number" column to determine where the planning process did or did not work well. Try to determine why so many revisions were needed, if that situation applies, or why no revisions were needed, if that situation applies. Compare "Budget" and "Actual Spent" columns; determine why gaps exist, if they do. The intent is to learn from the process so that future action plans will be improved.

INTERVENTIONS AVAILABLE TO OD PROFESSIONALS

One of the important roles for an OD professional in the Action Planning phase is to help an organization understand what options are available in terms of addressing concerns that emerge from an assessment process. Because OD can influence an organization at many levels, interventions that are implemented in OD can be targeted at the individual, the team or work group (both within the group and with other groups), the process, the global components of an organization, or the whole organization level. Some of the interventions available at each of these levels will be briefly described in this section. Subsequent chapters will describe these interventions in more detail and, briefly, how each can be used. Also, because OD efforts are not limited to the organization but can also impact communities, nations, and regions, another chapter will focus on these emerging perspectives for OD.

The statement of OD Principles of the OD Network, referenced in Chapter 1, contains a list of 51 "Organization Development Methodology, Technology and Tools." And that list is not even close to being a comprehensive list of all of the interventions and approaches used in OD. Likewise, this book cannot contain all of the interventions and approaches used in OD and the new approaches that surface regularly.

One of the problems with the OD field, however, is that we have not done a good job of doing the research necessary to determine which approaches seem to work best and when and which approaches seem not to work at all. Therefore, we are left with many fads or "flavors of the month"—someone's idea of what is the latest and best tool for the field. We need to discriminate carefully when new approaches are put forward and be willing to review both the old and the new approaches critically to determine whether they add value to our work as OD professionals.

Individual Interventions

Some have found it strange to think about OD as having concern for the individual, given that "organization" is part of organization development. Yet, if we recognize that an organization consists of many subparts (also known as *subsystems*) and that every organization is made up of many individuals (who are each a subpart of the organization), then it should not be surprising that we do focus on the individual as one aspect of the work of an OD professional.

Laboratory Training Groups.   *Laboratory training groups*, or *T-groups*, emerged in the 1960s and were very popular for a while, but they are less popular today because many people believe that they have too much risk associated with them. A small group meets over 2 to 3 days with the intent of providing in-depth feedback to each other as to how each individual is perceived within the group. The purpose of this process is to increase self-awareness, especially related to how one interacts in a group.

Coaching.   *Coaching* is defined as "the process of equipping people with the tools, knowledge, and opportunities they need to develop themselves and become more effective" (Peterson & Hicks, 1996, p. 14). Coaching can occur at any level of the organization, though it is more likely to be available to senior managers and executives. Coaching is almost always offered by external resources.

Mentoring.   In contrast with coaching, *mentoring* is often offered internally. OD becomes involved when formal mentoring systems are put in place. The objective of mentoring is to help individuals take advantage of opportunities for career and personal enhancement. To avoid conflict of interest, it is often offered by someone who is at least two levels higher than the person being mentored.

Mentoring of some sort almost always occurs informally. When formal mentoring is put in place, individuals identified as high potentials for promotion, or those from protected classes (women, minorities) but who tend not to have others from the same class available to mentor them, are usually the recipients of mentoring.

Self-Awareness Tools.   Many self-awareness tools are available. One of the most popular, referenced in Chapter 1, is the Myers-Briggs Type Indicator (MBTI), which purports to help individuals understand four aspects of their personality. While such instruments can be very useful in generating conversation, their validity is often lacking or even undetermined.

Reflection.   Schön (1983) popularized the concept that practitioners improve through reflection on their work, their interactions, their successes, and their failures. This self-assessment process is intended to occur regularly. The role of the OD professional in this process is to pass on ways that might be useful (meditation, journaling) in helping employees with this self-assessment.

Training, Education, and Development.   Much training, education, and development occur outside the realm of OD, yet OD professionals also need to understand the role that these three concepts have in contributing to excellence in an organization. In 1970, Len Nadler (Nadler & Nadler, 1989) first laid out his model for defining human resource development—a concept in which he included training (with direct and immediate application to the person's work), education (with long-term application to the person's work), and development (for individual purposes).

Leadership Development.   A very popular concept, though very difficult to define, is development of leaders for the organization. Such programs often fail to distinguish clearly between management development, executive development, and leadership development. The first two (management and executive) are position-specific, whereas leadership development, by definition but not always in practice, applies across the organization and across levels.

Multirater (360-Degree) Feedback. *Multirater feedback*, also called *360-degree feedback*, is "the process of receiving perceptions of one's performance from a variety of sources, typically supervisor(s), peers, direct reports, self, and even customers" (McLean, Sytsma, & Kerwin-Ryberg, 1995, p. 1 in Section 4:4). Input to the process can be provided through interviews or surveys. Research (McLean, 1997) suggests both problems with its use as a performance appraisal process but also potential when used solely for developmental purposes.

Job Design. Examining the components of a job may lead to the conclusion that greater (or less) variety may enhance the job for most people. The challenge for the OD professional is to find the balance between work efficiency and job satisfaction.

Job Descriptions. Identifying the tasks included in a specific job leads to a job description. Whether to construct a job description is somewhat controversial. In some work environments, job descriptions lead to rigidity by assigning people to specific tasks in their work, rather than being able to assign people to the highest-priority tasks at any given time. On the other hand, job descriptions can help ensure that all tasks that must be performed are assigned.

Responsibility Charting. *Responsibility charting* is a formal process of clarifying ambiguous areas of responsibility in complex relationship situations in order to eliminate overlapping responsibilities and to ensure that there are no uncovered areas of responsibility.

Policies Manual. To avoid confusion about what organizational policies are and to help individuals know what their responsibilities are as employees, most organizations have a policies manual. This handbook may contain a wide range of topics, including vacations, holidays, benefits, pay periods, promotion processes, grievance procedures, sexual harassment, diversity, and so on. An OD person may be responsible for determining what policies the organization wishes to include, writing the policies, and then facilitating meetings to have the policies approved. A good policies manual also provides the organization with legal protection and employees with clear expectations and workplace guidelines.

Values Clarification and Values Integration. Often people do not give conscious thought to what their values are. Yet, much of our behavior emerges out of our values. *Values clarification* exercises help individuals determine what their values are.

While research indicates that there is no clear connection between one's values and one's behaviors (McKenzie-Mohr & Smith, 1999), identifying the barriers that exist between values and behaviors can help in the integration process. *Values integration* is a process that helps individuals compare and align their values with those needed in the job and in their personal life. This process may lead to making changes in their jobs and their personal lives, or actually moving to a new job or into new personal lives.

Conflict Management. Historically, in both business and society, reference was made to *conflict resolution*, a phrase seldom seen in the OD field as the desirable outcome of working with conflict in an organization. *Conflict* implies a difference of opinion, and it is only through some level of conflict that innovation and creativity can flourish. Thus, we do not want to resolve conflict, in the sense of removing it from the environment. Instead, we want to be able to ensure that healthy conflict is nourished and unhealthy conflict is banished. Unhealthy conflict occurs when the focus of the differences is not on the idea but on the individual. Any abusive conflict is to be avoided, and, when it occurs, it must be addressed and eliminated. Thus, the preferred term used by OD professionals is *conflict management*.

Action Learning. *Action learning* is an approach to working with and developing people that uses work on an actual project or problem as the way to learn. Participants work in small groups to take action to solve their problem and learn how to learn from that action. Often a learning coach works with the group in order to help the members learn how to balance their work with the learning from that work (York, O'Neil, & Marsick, 1999, p. 3).

Team/Work Group Interventions

The next group of interventions are those that focus on the work group or teams within the organization. The ultimate goal is to improve the effectiveness and efficiency of the groups, and much of the focus is based on research that has been done to improve group dynamics.

Dialogue Sessions.   A *dialogue session* is a structured conversation designed to explore a topic that has potential for being conflictual, with the desired outcome resulting from a deeper understanding rather than from persuasion. Previously unacknowledged assumptions of the persons present are explored through reflection among everyone, with all participants being considered equal within the conversation. Developed within religious communities, this process has now migrated to other types of organizations (Lindahl, 1996).

Team Building.   Team building is a broad category of interventions that can include a multitude of approaches. Originally, these activities often included artificial tasks, sometimes called *ice breakers*, or games designed to help people learn about each other within a team context. Recently, however, there has been a trend toward doing team building in the context of real activities. Beckhard (1969) suggested the following objectives of team building, in order:

1. Establish and/or clarify goals and objectives.
2. Determine and/or clarify roles and responsibilities.
3. Establish and/or clarify policies and procedures.
4. Improve interpersonal relations.

Team Development/Effectiveness.   The objective of team building is to improve the way in which teams function, to increase their effectiveness. The primary role of the OD professional is to serve as a mirror to team members so that they can see better how they interact and perform.

Meeting Facilitation.   Effective functioning of a team includes some skill-based concepts, such as role identification and description, development of timed agendas, and determination that the appropriate individuals are in the meeting. The OD professional needs to model appropriate facilitation, provide feedback, and train team participants.

Conflict Management/Confrontation Meetings.   Just as healthy conflict is affirmed between individuals, so, too, is healthy conflict affirmed between teams. In fact, sometimes conflict needs to be surfaced because it has been suppressed. Many approaches can be used to manage inter-team conflict, as well as to help teams surface and confront their conflicts.

Fishbowls.   When individuals are not aware of the impact of their inter-actions on team functioning, a *fishbowl* approach can be used. In a fish-bowl, roles might be assigned, or individuals can be allowed to interact as they normally would in a team setting. A small group is placed in the center, acting roles or interacting normally, with others circling the small group that is "in the fishbowl." The outer circle provides the inner circle with feedback on the interactions that occur.

Strategic Alignment Assessment.   According to Semler (2000), *organizational alignment* is "a measurement of how well the behavior of peo-ple and systems in organizations work together to support the goals and visions. It represents the essential agreement and cooperation be-tween the organization's vision, strategy, culture, and systems" (p. 757). The focus of **strategic alignment assessment** is to determine how well a team is aligned within itself and in relation to the organization's strate-gic positioning. Semler has created an instrument that will help measure the extent of alignment.

Process Interventions

The first two intervention categories have focused on people. This sec-tion summarizes *process interventions* that are useful in improving organizational processes:

- *Six sigma* – According to Chowdhury (2001), *six sigma* is both a statistical tool for improving productivity and a management phi-losophy. It is an outgrowth of the TQM movement (see next item).
- *Continuous process improvement/TQM* – Popularized in Japan after World War II and then around the world in the 1980s, the contributions of Deming and Juran, in particular, are still im-pacting the business world. Deming (1986) developed 14 management points, primarily emphasizing management by data through statistical process control.
- *Process reengineering* – Hammer and Champy (1993) pro-moted the concept of business *process reengineering* (BPR), a

concept popularized in the 1990s but then fell into disrepute because of its association with downsizing and what was perceived as its inhumane approach. Basically, BPR focuses on radical redesign of business processes (which means getting rid of existing processes and replacing them with new ones), yielding dramatic improvements in productivity and performance.

- *Benchmarking* – Many organizations like to compare themselves with other organizations as one means of determining how well they are doing. There are two ways to benchmark: (1) compare outcomes (often obtained from consortia of similar organizations in the same industry), and (2) compare processes (difficult because organizations with similar processes are likely to be competitors). My perspective is that we have much to learn from comparing processes, with the goal of process improvement, *if* cooperation can be gained from organizations using similar processes. Comparing outcomes is often what organizations prefer to do, but little can be done with such information, given that there is no way to know what processes, equipment, raw materials, and so on, were used.

- *Sociotechnical systems (STSs)* – Popularized by Eric Trist in the coal mines of the United Kingdom, STS is designed to create processes that integrate and balance the people needs (*socio-*) with the tools and equipment (*-technical*) in an organization.

Global Interventions

As organizations move from domestic to international to global organizations, OD professionals need to be increasingly aware of how to work across many cultures, integrating the best from all of the cultures. In an era of globalization, organizations are being forced to become more global in their outlook and functions (see Friedman, 2005, for an excellent discussion of this issue). The following are some of the *global interventions* that might be used in helping organizations adopt such a perspective.

Virtual Teams and Virtual Team Building.   As organizations/people interact with other organizations/people around the world, much of this interaction will occur online, leading to the formation of *virtual teams*. Learning to interact with others when you have never met them face-to-face, and likely never will, requires special skills. It is easy enough to be misunderstood in the same culture when interacting online; doing so across cultures increases the possibility of such mis-communications. The OD professional may need to develop new ways to implement what occurs relatively easily in a face-to-face context.

Cross-cultural Teams and Cross-cultural Team Building.   Similar to virtual team building, developing *cross-cultural teams* is also important in building trust and honest feedback across cultures. The difference in the two approaches is that one is face-to-face and the other must be done at a distance across cyberspace.

Cultural Self-Awareness.   One of the first steps in cross-cultural team building, a variation of values clarification, is cultural self-awareness. It is virtually impossible to understand another's culture without first understanding your own. Most people understand their own culture implicitly only; they cannot explain it explicitly to others or even to themselves. An OD professional, using appropriate techniques, can help individuals learn their own culture and then describe it to others.

Cross-cultural Training.   There are many approaches to providing cross-cultural training. Landis and Bhagat (1996) ranked the following ones from least to most effective:

- Cognitive (knowledge)
- Behavior modification (providing feedback to change individual behaviors)
- Experiential (which might include simulations or actual experiences in another culture)
- Cultural self-awareness
- Interaction (which could occur in a training setting, in an area of the city where groups of individuals from other countries might settle, college or university settings, etc.)
- Attribution (culture assimilator) (scenarios are presented with options from which to choose the best response)
- Integrated (a combination of two or more of the approaches)

Storytelling/Sharing.   Many cultures share those cultures through the telling of stories. Narration is often one of the areas of expertise for OD professionals. Combining the expertise of the OD professionals with the cultural bias toward storytelling can be an effective partnership for preparing an organization for becoming more global.

Joint Ventures.   Increasingly, organizations develop expertise for working in other cultures by creating joint ventures with organizations located in the geographic location to which the organization wishes to expand. The problem, of course, is that the cross-cultural learning becomes a form of on-the-job training, and many cultural misunderstandings can emerge in the process of creating and implementing the joint venture.

International Diversity.   Increasingly, organizations will need to hire people from countries around the world. Heenan and Perlmutter (1979) created a very useful model for determining who will be hired and who will be promoted, based on the stage of global maturity of the organization.

Job Assignments.   As organizations respond to global competition, it becomes almost mandatory for those wishing to move up in the organization to have experience working in a country other than the one in which they live. This does not mean just sending people from the home country to another country (expatriates) but also bringing employees from other countries to the home country (inpatriates), as well as moving people between other countries.

Blending.   OD professionals are increasingly observing a *blending* movement in which organizational cultures combine the best of local culture (indigenous) with specific elements from other cultures, thus enhancing their original culture. A case where U.S. practices were blended with Japanese practices (McLean, Kaneko, & van Dijk, 2003) is described in detail in Chapter 9.

Organizational Interventions

The next level of intervention is focused on those interventions that are intended to affect the whole organization, though it must be recognized that, within systems theory, all of the preceding levels also impact the whole organization in some way.

Organization Design.   This intervention is often what people think of when they are unfamiliar with the comprehensive nature of OD. It involves a structural approach to change in an organization and, simplistically, is reflected in an organizational chart that reflects who reports to whom. This approach is also referred to as *organizational development*, as opposed to the field of organization development (note that the term describing the field does *not* include -al at the end of *organization*).

Company-wide Survey.   As indicated in Chapter 4, one approach to conducting an assessment is to do a company-wide survey. Once the survey is undertaken, change will already begin to surface, because of changing employee expectations.

Learning Organization.   A *learning organization*, a concept popularized by Senge (1990), is "an organization that has woven a continuous and enhanced capacity to learn, adapt and change into its culture. Its values, policies, practices, systems and structures support and accelerate learning for all employees" (Nevis, DeBella, & Gould, 1995, p. 73).

Organizational Learning.   *Organizational learning* is the process whereby an organization becomes a learning organization. It requires that an organization be prepared to learn from both failures and successes; rather than being a blaming organization, it becomes one that celebrates and learns.

Culture Change.   In almost every aspect, every intervention described in this chapter is designed to bring about an improvement in the organization's culture. According to Uttal (1983), *corporate culture* is "a system of shared values (what is important) and beliefs (how things work) that interact with a company's people, organizational structures and control systems to produce behavioral norms (how we do things around here)" (p. 66).

Accountability and Reward Systems.   Organizations spend a lot of time and a lot of resources trying to create accountability and reward systems that they believe are necessary to motivate employees. Once their basic needs are met, however, most employees are more likely to feel rewarded from intrinsic satisfaction. While this area may primarily be the responsibility of human resource management, OD professionals can help HRM personnel understand how the policies and practices put in place for accountability and rewards impact the whole system.

Succession Planning.   *Succession planning* has taken on heightened importance in most organizations today due to the demographics confronting most of the industrialized world. We are facing a rapidly aging population, with too few younger workers coming into the workplace. As a result, most organizations are likely to be challenged by a dramatic loss of senior leaders. Because of the shortage of younger workers available, many companies will need to develop a retire-rehire policy, to take advantage of the intellectual capital possessed by those who have retired. They will also need to develop a thoughtful and planful approach to putting senior managers and executives in place who have the capability of providing leadership to the organization and who can help younger, less experienced leaders who will need time to acquire the intellectual capital from those leaving the organization (McLean, 2004).

Valuing Differences/Diversity.   *Diversity* exists in every workplace to some degree, based on gender, age, ethnicity, race, religion, nationality, sexual orientation, geographic origin, and even ideas, politics, and ideologies. In an organizational context, diversity has the potential of fostering new ideas and approaches, enhancing customer bases, and generally offering the potential of innovation and creativity. However, a climate for seeing such diversity in positive ways often must be created so that the organization can benefit from its existing diversity. Diversity must be valued, not just accepted, in order to maximize its benefits.

Moving an organization in this direction is not easy. Experiential exposure, self-reflection, small-group interactions, and to some extent training can all be beneficial in creating a positive environment so that the potentials of diversity can be fully realized.

Strategic Planning, Including Environmental Scanning and Scenario Planning.   *Strategic planning* runs the gamut from the rather mechanical 1-, 3-, and 5-year strategic plans using decision trees, to the classic *SWOT* (strengths, weaknesses, opportunities, threats) approach, to *environmental scanning* (determining the marketplace competition and factors that are likely to impact the business). Another approach is *PEST* (political, economic, social, technological) factors affecting the organization. The problem with this approach, however, is that it is time-consuming and relatively static. The dynamism of the marketplace requires an intervention that allows for rapid strategic response to change.

Another approach, one that has been around for a while, is receiving renewed emphasis: *scenario planning* (Chermack, 2004). Under this approach, all possible changes in the environment are considered, and strategic responses are developed before there is any way to know how the environment will actually change.

Mission, Vision, and Values Development. Perhaps one of the most important interventions that an OD professional can bring is facilitating the development of the organization's mission, its vision for the future, and the values it will use to accomplish that vision. There is no common acceptance of the meaning of *mission* and *vision*, and the terms may be used in opposite ways. Basically, as I use it, *mission* refers to the organization's reason for being.

Large-Scale Interactive Events (LSIEs). A *large-scale interactive event*, as described by Dannemiller and Jacobs (1992), involves getting the whole organization together in one place (ranging from 100 to several thousand) and using small groups with vertical and lateral representation to interact on issues of importance to the entire organization, often to focus on mission and vision. The intent is to get widespread ownership and to communicate to everyone in the organization quickly, rather than the slow quality that usually accompanies a cascading process.

Open Systems Mapping. The objective of *open systems mapping* is to identify changes that are needed within the system. It uses systems theory, with an understanding that a system, such as an organization, interacts with its environment and is, therefore, an open system that is always changing. Mapping where the system currently is and what we want the system to be in the future will help determine the steps needed to close the gap between what is and that which is desired. Closing the gap is accomplished through exploring those factors that influence the system, the nature of the relationship, and the feelings about the relationship (Heap, n.d.).

Future Search. Weisbord and Janoff (2000) developed the concept of *future search* in which a cross section of members of a system come together in a large group planning meeting to explore the past, present, and future related to a specific, focused task. The outcome is commitment to an action plan based on the values of those involved in the process.

Open Space Technology Meetings. Based on the dialogue concept, *open space technology meetings* are used to address a wide range of issues within organizations, including strategic ones. After identifying issues to be considered, participants post each issue on the wall, with an agenda and time specified to meet to address the issue. People decide which issues meeting(s) they choose to attend, and dialogue technology is used. Ideas are then captured on flipcharts and are posted on a results wall. People have the freedom to address any issue they want, as well as to express any opinion they wish about that issue.

CHAPTER SUMMARY

This chapter explored processes to use in Action Planning, along with a blank form and a sample plan to be used in providing accountability in carrying out the action plan. The action plan should emerge from the Assessment and Feedback phase, and the process may actually begin during the feedback sessions as employees suggest next steps in addressing the assessment's findings. This chapter also described interventions at the individual, team or work group, global, process, and organization levels.

The following five chapters deal with each of these levels of intervention with the sample intervention processes explained in detail. A chapter on the emerging application of OD at the community and national levels is also included.

QUESTIONS FOR DISCUSSION OR SELF-REFLECTION

1. Who should be involved in the action planning process and why?

2. Select a task that fits the criteria for when a formal action plan should be used, and complete an action plan, using the processes described in this chapter.

3. Given the extensive list of interventions included in this chapter, and recognizing that they are simply a sample of the interventions available to OD professionals, what do you think might be necessary for you to become effective in the use of these interventions? How might you make your own action plan to acquire these skills?

4. While included in one level of intervention or another, several of the interventions could actually fit more than one level. Which interventions do you think could have been included in a different level of intervention and why?

5. With which interventions are you most familiar? Which have you actually experienced? Which are the least familiar to you?

6. What preexisting bias do you have about any of the interventions mentioned, and how did you acquire this bias?

ACTION PLAN

Goal: _____

Strategy: _____

Tactic (or Outcome): _____

_____

Team Leader: _____

STEP NO.	STEP	RESPONSIBLE	DATE DUE	REVISION DATE	REVISION NO.	DATE COMPLETED	BUDGET	ACTUAL COSTS
1								
2								
3								
4								
5								
6								
7								

ACTION PLAN

Goal: _____

Strategy: _____

Tactic (or Outcome): _____

_____

Team Leader: _____

STEP NO.	STEP	RESPONSIBLE	DATE DUE	REVISION DATE	REVISION NO.	DATE COMPLETED	BUDGET	ACTUAL COSTS
8								
9								
10								
11								
12								
13								
14								
15								

ACTION PLAN

Goal: To increase revenues by 20% this year

Strategy: Improve customer service

Tactic (or Outcome): Identify problems with customer service and
develop new action plan to respond to findings

Team Leader: Mary Mitchell

STEP NO.	STEP	RESPONSIBLE	DATE DUE	REVISION DATE	REVISION NO.	DATE COMPLETED	BUDGET	ACTUAL COSTS
1	Brainstorm possible problems.	Team	7/31					
2	Construct survey for all employees who have direct contact with customer	Mary, John, Miguel	8/31					
3	Review survey	Team	8/31					
4	Post to Web site and send e-mail to employees inviting their participation	Sophia in IT, Mary	9/15					
5	Send out reminder	Sophia in IT, Mary	9/30					
6	Analyze results of survey	Mary, John, Miguel	10/15					
7	Create fishbone diagram and identify probable root cause	Mary, Team	10/15					

ACTION PLAN

Goal: _____

Strategy: _____

Tactic (or Outcome): _____

_____

Team Leader: _____

STEP NO.	STEP	RESPONSIBLE	DATE DUE	REVISION DATE	REVISION NO.	DATE COMPLETED	BUDGET	ACTUAL COSTS
8	Use affinity process to write new action plan to respond to identified root cause	Team	11/01					
9								
10								
11								
12								
13								
14								
15								

6

Implementation: Individual Level

CHAPTER OUTLINE

Laboratory Training Groups (T-Groups)

Coaching

Mentoring

Self-Awareness Tools

Reflection

Training, Education, and Development

Leadership Development

Multirater (360-Degree) Feedback

Job Design

Job Descriptions

Responsibility Charting

Policies Manual

Values Clarification and Values Integration

Conflict Management

Action Learning

Connecting Assessment Results to Specific Interventions

Chapter Summary

Questions for Discussion or Self-Reflection

OVERVIEW   The individual-level OD interventions provided in Chapter 5 are the subject of this chapter. Whereas Chapter 5 provided a brief description of each of the individual interventions, this chapter focuses on the process of implementation, along with strengths and weaknesses of each approach where appropriate. The interventions described in this section include T-groups; coaching; mentoring; self-awareness tools; reflection; training, education, and development; leadership development; multirater (360-degree) feedback; job design; job descriptions; responsibility charting; policies manual; values clarification and values integration; conflict management; and action learning.

OD interventions at the individual level are perhaps the most challenging for OD professionals because they are asked to be aware of their boundaries of competence. Many of the interventions discussed in this chapter have the potential to raise serious issues related to mental health for the targeted individuals that go beyond the competence of most OD professionals. The role of the OD professional in such a situation must be to recognize that such a problem exists and to refer the individual(s) involved to appropriate professionals (therapists, psychologists, psychiatrists, social workers, etc.). This concern is explored in much more detail in Chapter 15, "Ethics and Values Driving OD."

What follows in this chapter is not an exhaustive list of individual interventions. It does, however, give the reader a sense of the wide range of interventions available to the OD professional for addressing individual-level concerns in organizations. Readers are reminded that individual-level issues are of interest to the OD professional because they have the potential to influence the well-being of the organization. If individuals within an organization, especially those in leadership roles, can be strengthened, then the organization will be stronger, too.

Figure 6.1 shows the organization development process model with individual interventions following the Action Planning phase.

LABORATORY TRAINING GROUPS (T-GROUPS)

A T-group, a term shortened from *training group*, is a process used to help individuals reflect on who they are and how they are perceived by

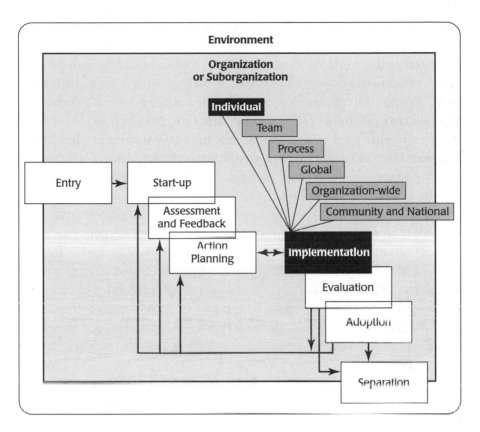

Figure 6.1 *Organization Development Process Model, Phase 5: Individual Intervention*

others. T-groups have lost much of their popularity since their heyday in the 1960s and 1970s. In part, this decline is because such activities have migrated out of the organization due to the difficulty of having individuals work with the same people after having revealed themselves deeply in the T-group setting. Such a scenario often led to a sense of embarrassment and discomfort with boundaries having been crossed. This situation in turn made it difficult to function with each other afterward on a daily basis. Another major problem was that many T-groups often were run by individuals who were not qualified. As a result, individuals received incorrect feedback so that appropriate interactions with others were compromised even further.

Nevertheless, T-groups remain a potentially valuable process in the hands of the right facilitators and with the right people involved in the group. Thus, organizations still can find T-groups useful for individuals who need to develop deeper insight into themselves and how they are perceived by others. However, instead of conducting groups internally, as occurred during the early days of T-groups, organizations now usually send individuals to well-established sources of such opportunities, such as National Training Laboratories (NTL) in Bethel, Maine, where well-qualified facilitators work with nonassociated individuals in a group. No OD professional should attempt to run a T-group until gaining extensive experience as a T-group member and until becoming certified to lead such groups.

A modification of the T-group process that provides a little more control than one finds in a T-group is in the *Power Lab* process created by the Tavistock Institute in the United Kingdom. The Power Lab differs from the T-group in that individuals are seeded into the group with assigned roles. While there is still no set agenda, it is clearer to participants that the outcome of the Power Lab is to determine how people react to different leadership types, what leadership styles individuals prefer for themselves, and how others respond to various leadership styles.

Currently, the historical emphasis of the Tavistock Institute continues, with the following description of some components of its present work:

> [G]roup, organisational and social dynamics; the exercise of authority and power; the interplay between tradition, innovation and change; and the relationship of an organisation to its social, political and economic environment. Participants can expect to develop their capacity to:
> - manage themselves in the multiple roles needed for contemporary leadership,
> - use their emotional literacy to inform their actions,
> - understand and overcome resistance to change in themselves and others,
> - and exercise formal and informal leadership roles. (Tavistock Institute, 2004)

Because the Tavistock Institute process is less self-revealing, it requires individuals to take fewer risks, but it also limits the extent of self-discovery.

COACHING

Coaching has been defined as "the process of equipping people with the tools, knowledge, and opportunities they need to develop themselves and become more effective" (Peterson & Hicks, 1996, p. 14). In recent years, coaching has become a very popular process, offered by internal and external professionals, not all of whom are OD professionals or qualified professionals. While there is no set way of coaching others, one expectation is that there be a match in understanding of expectations between the person doing the coaching and the person being coached. A number of instruments have been developed to help match coach to participant in terms of expectations for how they will function with each other. One such instrument is Coaching for the Gold (Tolbert, Larkin, & McLean, 2002; sample items are shown on the Web site listed in the References). The point of such instruments is to maximize the benefits of coaching by ensuring that the coach functions in a way that the person to be coached wants the process to operate. It can also be used to improve coaching and to provide feedback to a coach about his or her coaching performance.

A movement toward manager as coach is under way, and such instruments can help managers develop themselves as coaches (e.g., Sussman & Finnegan, 1998). A quick search of the Web will identify many organizations prepared to offer certification in organizational coaching.

Figure 6.2 shows that any coaching activity involves a relationship among three factors: the coach, people, and task. An effective coach values people over tasks, works with the coachee to accomplish the task, communicates openly, and accepts the ambiguous nature of the workplace. All of these factors must be included in any effort to develop coaches in a workplace setting. They also serve as useful self-assessment processes for OD professionals who wish to use coaching as one of their intervention approaches.

Coaching, although primarily focused on individuals, can also be a useful team-based intervention. As individuals function on teams, coaching of the individuals can make them better team members. Coaching is an intervention that can also be applied to team building, a concept developed more fully in the next chapter.

According to Evered and Selman (1989), 10 essential elements or characteristics of coaching not only define coaching as distinct from other techniques but also express the core of coaching:

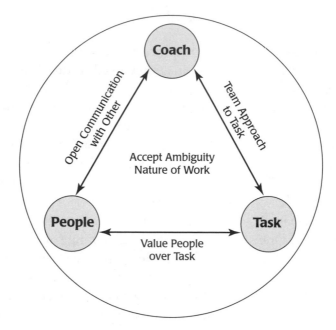

Figure 6.2 *Interactions among Parties Involved in Coaching (from McLean, Yang, Kuo, Tolbert, and Larkin, 2005; used with permission)*

- Developing a partnership
- A commitment to produce a result and enact a vision
- Compassion and acceptance
- Speaking and listening for action
- A responsiveness to employees
- Honoring the uniqueness of employees
- Practice and preparation
- A willingness to coach and be coached
- A sensitivity to individuals as well as to groups
- A willingness to go beyond what has already been achieved

There are, however, reasons why coaching is not more widely accepted as part of the role of managers:

Time constraints and changes in managers' attitudes are two perspectives from managers as to why coaching is neglected. . . .

Many organizational climates are not conducive to coaching, and managers are not rewarded for developing employees. As a result, managers are not motivated to initiate the new role of coach. In other words, without a management style that emphasizes coaching organizationwide, managers may not recognize the benefits of coaching to themselves nor to their subordinates. (McLean et al., 2005, p. 160)

Managers may fear that they will lose the ability to influence or control employees. They may also fear their ability to make the shift from traditional order-and-control managers to managers who can support and coach.

Training is essential in preparing managers to become coaches. Furthermore, being a coach to the coaches can also provide managers with immediate feedback that has the potential of developing their coaching skills. As for the time constraint, it may be possible to shift the managers' focus from coaching all employees to coaching only those who show high potential for development and advancement and those who are having problems.

Coaching offered by a qualified OD professional, either internally or externally, uses a process similar to that used by managers, except that the role ambiguity (between coaching and managing) is dramatically reduced. The OD professional does not have a management role; his or her sole role is to listen, to reflect, to question, and to probe so that the person being coached clarifies what his or her issues are and what needs to be done to overcome problems or to strengthen one's abilities to problem solve and move forward.

MENTORING

Mentoring often happens informally, simply because one person who is in a position of some influence wants to help someone else grow and develop professionally. This section, however, focuses on deliberate attempts to establish mentoring as a formal process within an organization. Formal mentoring typically entails a relationship between a person who wishes to develop professionally in specific ways related to his or her career (*mentee*) and a person with significant experience (mentor) who is assigned to work with the mentee to provide advice, feedback, and opportunities that might not otherwise be available to the mentee. Mutual benefits occur through the transfer of experiences and the sharing of different perspectives.

As a side note, although the term *mentee* has become widely used in the literature, some people object to its use, preferring *protégé*, though this word also has negative connotations for some, as being male-oriented with suggestions of dominance and subservience, which is definitely contrary to the concept of mentoring. *Mentee* will be used in this text.

Sometimes, the intent may be to establish a mentor for a specific individual who has been identified as a high-potential employee. Sometimes, it might be to assist those who are often overlooked or excluded in development opportunities, such as women and minorities. Other times, the intent is to establish mentoring for anyone who requests it. Unlike coaching, the focus of mentoring is directed mostly toward career development, rather than to improvement of performance in the workplace, which is the primary goal of coaching.

To be effective as a mentor, individuals need to

- maintain regular and proactive contact with the mentee,
- be on time for scheduled meetings,
- be honest in providing the mentee with feedback about goals and expectations,
- realize that you as a mentor do not have all the answers,
- respect confidentiality, and
- keep trying—think of new ways to work together.

Strategies that an OD professional needs to put in place to ensure effective mentoring include the following (this list is adapted from a project overview developed by the Human Resource Development Department of the University of Minnesota for a pilot project for mentoring students, 2003):

A positive attitude – Encourage the mentee to be enthusiastic and accepting of self and others in the development of goals and objectives.

Valuing – Encourage the mentee to examine his or her beliefs and ideals to establish personal values and goals.

Open-mindedness – Encourage the mentee to keep an open mind to ideas offered.

Interrelations – Make the interactions between mentor and mentee situations of sharing, caring, and empathizing.

Creative problem solving – Encourage the mentee to use a creative problem-solving process.

Effective communication – Encourage the mentee to be an attentive listener and an assertive questioner.

Discovery – Encourage the mentee to be an independent thinker.

Strengths and uniqueness – Encourage the mentee to recognize individual strengths and uniqueness and to build on them.

Confidence – Assist the mentee in developing self-confidence.

Awareness – Stress the environment and being intuitive, problem sensitive, and ready to make the most of opportunities.

Risk taking – Encourage being a risk taker and an active participant, not a spectator.

Flexibility – Share the importance of being flexible and adaptable in attitudes and action, looking for alternatives, and seeing situations/persons from different perspectives.

SELF-AWARENESS TOOLS

Just as T-groups are designed to improve self-awareness, thousands of self-awareness tools are available that also intend to increase self-awareness. A long-standing model, called the *Johari window*, named after the first names of the developers of the concept (Luft & Ingham, 1955), is useful in understanding the importance of self-awareness, receiving feedback and information from others, and improving communications (see Figure 6.3).

The idea behind the Johari window is that there are things we know about ourselves that others do not see (Facade, lower left), while, at the same time, there are things others know about us that we do not see in ourselves (Blind Spot, upper right). There is information about us that others know and that is shared with us (Arena, upper left). That leaves the Unknown or Unconscious (lower right) that neither others nor we know about ourselves. A change in any one of the quadrants means that all other quadrants will also change. Communication improves as the upper left quadrant gets larger. The goal of self-awareness

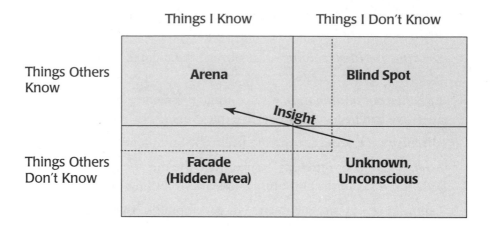

Figure 6.3 *Johari Window*

is to gain insight about ourselves, which, at minimum, would reduce the blind spots (upper right); even more desirable is to reduce the Facade and Unknown areas (lower left and lower right).

In addition to gaining feedback from others, self-assessment tools are also widely used to reduce the Blind Spots and Unknown quadrants. A problem common to most of them is that they are lacking in reliability and validity, and many of them have categories that are a priori (before-the-fact) conclusions by the authors, rather than being confirmed through appropriate statistical analysis (e.g., factor analysis). Using instruments that do not have appropriate psychometric criteria can lead individuals to see themselves inaccurately. Organizations can also misuse such instruments by requiring individuals within the organization to participate, even when they are not ready for such self-understanding and when appropriately trained facilitators and follow-up professional support are not provided. When instruments have been developed according to appropriate psychometric criteria and are taken freely, and appropriate personnel are available to assist in interpretation and follow-up support, they can be very useful in helping individuals understand themselves.

Two self-assessment tools have become very popular: the *Myers-Briggs Type Indicator® (MBTI)* and *DiSC®*.

MBTI

First developed in 1943, the MBTI has gone through considerable change and development since that time. It is purported to be based on the psychology of Carl Jung. The instrument identifies a person's personality type on four dichotomies: Extroversion-Introversion (E-I), Sensing-Intuitive (S-N), Thinking-Feeling (T-F), and Judging-Perceiving (J-P). Each of these characteristics is described in Table 6.1.

TABLE 6.1 Characteristics Described by the Four Dichotomies of the MBTI

EXTROVERTED CHARACTERISTICS	INTROVERTED CHARACTERISTICS
■ Act first, think/reflect later ■ Feel deprived when cut off from interaction with the outside world ■ Usually are open to and motivated by outside world of people and things ■ Enjoy wide variety and change in people relationships	■ Think/reflect first, then act ■ Regularly require an amount of private time to recharge batteries ■ Motivated internally, mind is sometimes so active it is "closed" to outside world ■ Prefer one-to-one communication and relationships

SENSING CHARACTERISTICS	INTUITIVE CHARACTERISTICS
■ Mentally live in the now, attending to present opportunities ■ Use common sense and create practical solutions is automatic-instinctual ■ Have memory recall that is rich in detail of facts and past events ■ Best improvise from past experience ■ Like clear and concrete information; dislike guessing when facts are fuzzy	■ Mentally live in the future, attending to future possibilities ■ Use imagination and create/inventing new possibilities is automatic-instinctual ■ Have memory recall that emphasizes patterns, contexts, and connections ■ Best improvise from theoretical understanding ■ Are comfortable with ambiguous, fuzzy data and with guessing its meaning

(continued)

TABLE 6.1 *(continued)*

THINKING CHARACTERISTICS	FEELING CHARACTERISTICS
■ Instinctively search for facts and logic in a decision situation ■ Naturally notice tasks and work to be accomplished ■ Easily able to provide an objective and critical analysis ■ Accept conflict as a natural, normal part of relationships with people	■ Instinctively employ personal feelings and impact on people in decision situations ■ Are naturally sensitive to people needs and reactions ■ Naturally seek consensus and popular opinions ■ Are unsettled by conflict; have almost a toxic reaction to disharmony

JUDGING CHARACTERISTICS	PERCEIVING CHARACTERISTICS
■ Plan many of the details in advance before moving into action ■ Focus on task-related action; complete meaningful segments before moving on ■ Work best and avoid stress when keep ahead of deadlines ■ Naturally use targets, dates, and standard routines to manage life	■ Are comfortable moving into action without a plan; plan on the go ■ Like to multitask, have variety, mix work and play ■ Are naturally tolerant of time pressure; work best close to the deadlines ■ Instinctively avoid commitments that interfere with flexibility, freedom and variety

Source: Used by permission of C. Ross Reinhold, PersonalityPathways.com.

This instrument yields an individual profile based on one's preferences in each of the four areas. There are 16 personality type profiles based on the various combinations of the four variables—more detail than can be provided in this chapter. Keep in mind that this instrument is copyrighted by the Myers-Briggs Type Indicator Trust and tightly controlled by the instrument publisher, CPP, Inc. (formerly Consulting Psychologists Press). Facilitators are not allowed to use the instrument unless they are qualified to provide interpretation and follow-up for participants through certification by CPP.

DiSC

Originally developed in 1972, this instrument was extensively revised and researched in 1994 to provide evidence of its meeting psychometric criteria (Inscape Publishing, 1996). DiSC was designed, using a forced-choice format, to increase self-awareness and also awareness of others with whom individuals work. The letters of the instrument stand for Dominance, Influence, Steadiness, and Conscientiousness. Individuals who are dominant in one of these scales are described by the publisher (Inscape Publishing, n.d.) as follows:

Dominance (Direct and Decisive)
D's are strong-willed, strong-minded people who like accepting challenges, taking action, and getting immediate results.

Influence (Optimistic and Outgoing)
I's are "people people" who like participating on teams, sharing ideas, and energizing and entertaining others.

Steadiness (Sympathetic and Cooperative)
S's are helpful people who like working behind the scenes, performing in consistent and predictable ways, and being good listeners.

Conscientiousness (Concerned and Correct)
C's are sticklers for quality who like planning ahead, employing systematic approaches, and checking and rechecking for accuracy.

REFLECTION

Reflection is another way to reduce the Blind Spots and the Unknown quadrants of the Johari window, discussed earlier. Schön (1987) described the steps to be used in doing reflection in action:

It involves a surprise, a response to surprise by thought turning back on itself, thinking what we're doing as we do it, setting the problem of the situation anew, conducting an action experiment on the spot by which we seek to solve the new problems we've set, an experiment in which we test both our new way of seeing the situation, and also try to change that situation for the better.

Schön (1987) clarified that it is not necessary to verbalize this reflection or even to make it explicit. Reflection often requires space away from distractions and time for it to occur, but it is largely intuitive. It is also important to reflect on the reflections to inform future reflection in action.

While OD professionals can remind people to reflect on their reflections in action, consistent with Schön, other things can also be done. One way to reflect on both successes and failures is to keep a journal. By writing their reflections, people make explicit their thoughts about why something worked or why something did not work, hopefully reinforcing a culture of learning rather than a culture of blaming. Meditation can also be effective as a reflection tool. This practice is regularly built into the routine of some Indian organizations based on Hindu traditions. It is also easy for mentors and coaches to encourage reflection.

TRAINING, EDUCATION, AND DEVELOPMENT

A whole literature is dedicated to training, education, and development. Whereas some see training and development (T&D) as an OD intervention, others see it as a field separate from organization development. As a result, reference here is restricted to only a few classics that might be useful for readers interested in more information about T&D: Goldstein (1993), Stolovitch and Keeps (1992), and Swanson (1994).

These three functions—training, education, and development—were included in Nadler's 1970 definition of human resource development (Nadler & Nadler, 1989). In this context, training was viewed as acquiring knowledge and skills to be applied directly and immediately to the job; education was seen as more long-term in application at some time in the future but still applied to the job; and development was seen as more personal than job related. As can be seen by some of the terms used in the next paragraph, *development* is often used in the same sense as *training* or *education* might have been used by Nadler.

Training can be focused on specific areas, such as sales training, technical training, computer training, customer service training, supervisory development, management development, executive development, and, as suggested in the following section, leadership development. Training is offered in thousands of specific content areas, including diversity, sexual harassment, safety, new product, new employee orientation, and on and on.

LEADERSHIP DEVELOPMENT

Almost every organization has some form of leadership development, though most organizations have difficulty in defining what outcome is actually desired. Thousands of vendors exist for leadership development, with one of the most popular being the Center for Creative Leadership. Because there are so many approaches to leadership development, it is almost impossible to define a common approach. How leadership development is presented will depend on the level of the individual within the organization, the experience of the participant, the desired goals and outcomes, the level of support that exists within the workplace, the expectations of others for the development activities, and so on. The OD professional who is interested in offering leadership development must be clear that there is widespread disagreement as to what is expected in such an intervention. Many such programs are based on other interventions described in this chapter, primarily self-assessment tools and multirater feedback.

Key references for those interested in pursuing this topic further include Bass (1990); Carter, Giber, Goldsmith, and Bennis (2000); McCauley and van Velsor (2003); and Shtogren (1999).

MULTIRATER (360-DEGREE) FEEDBACK

Multirater or *multisource feedback* refers to any situation in which more than two people provide input into a feedback process to an individual employee. When a 360-degree approach is taken, a full circle of feedback is implied that includes self, peers, subordinates, supervisors, and customers. Any combination of these sources of feedback might be used, through a customized or standardized instrument, e-mail input, or in-person interviews. The richness of narratives argues for interviews, though this approach can be more expensive and take longer to complete.

Multirater feedback can be used for many purposes: to make "general personnel decisions, such as promotions and terminations" (Hedge & Borman, 1995, p. 453); to "identify training and development needs, pinpointing employee skills and competencies that are currently inadequate but for which programs can be developed" and to be used "as a criterion against which selection and development programs are validated" (Hedge & Borman, 1995, p. 453); to contribute to worker satisfaction because they believe that their opinions are being heard (Bernardin & Beatty, 1987); and to improve organizational culture or climate.

Its use for promotions and compensation decisions has been called into question because of the lack of agreement among the several sources of feedback. McLean, Sytsma, and Kerwin-Ryberg (1995), for example, found that none of the correlations among the various sources of feedback (self, supervisors, peers, and subordinates) is high enough to warrant making major personnel decisions within the organization. With a general expectation of .70 as a reasonable correlations, the correlations found are shown in Table 6.2.

The process for conducting 360-degree feedback, according to Noe, Hollenbeck, Gerhart, and Wright, (1997), focuses on development as the reason for using multirater feedback:

> Managers are presented the results, which show how self-evaluations differ from the other raters. Typically, managers are asked to review their results, seek clarification from the raters, and engage in action planning designed to set specific development goals, based on the strengths and weaknesses identified. (p. 393)

Regardless of the purpose, the following suggestions might improve the use of multirater feedback (McLean, 1997):

- Be clear about the purpose for which multirater feedback is to be used, and communicate it to everyone involved in the process.

- Involvement in multirater feedback must be voluntary on the part of raters and ratees, and the source of specific feedback

TABLE 6.2 Highest Correlation within Each Ratings Group: Comparison at Time 1 and Time 2

GROUP	SELF	PEER	SUBORDINATE
Peer	.24/.08		
Subordinate	.40/.29	−.23/.12	
Supervisor	.36/−.15	.28/.21	.22/.20

must be kept anonymous. (Although some may object to the use of the word *ratee*, it, like *mentee*, is now widely used in the literature.)

- The organization must provide consistent, continuous, and nonwavering support to ratees throughout the process, including a guarantee that competent support personnel will be available, as needed, throughout and following the process, including clinical psychologists. It is possible that the feedback received from time to time will so impair an individuals' self-concept that support at the clinical level may be needed.

- Raters, ratees, and third parties must be well trained in their roles.

- Instruments must be psychometrically sound—that is, valid and highly reliable. Except in very unusual organizations, this characteristic probably requires the use of instruments that have been commercially developed by expert psychometricians. Hastily constructed, in-house instruments are likely to cause more damage than good.

- Be aware of other factors occurring in the organization at the time of the administration of the questionnaires. Systems thinking is critical in understanding the factors that affect both the feedback provided and the ways in which the feedback is received.

- Do not rely on the multirater feedback instrument alone to accomplish its purpose. Again, a systemic perspective is necessary. Dialogue—both one-on-one and group—has been identified as one useful adjunct to the instrument, itself. Another useful supplement is documentation (e.g., statistical process control, artifacts). These add-ons become processes for triangulation.

As many have recognized (see, e.g., McLean, Damme, & Swanson, 1990), individual performance is heavily influenced by the systems in which one performs, whereas typical performance appraisals make the assumption that one's performance is heavily influenced by the individual. See McLean (1997) for a detailed literature review on multirater feedback and detailed discussion about the four purposes for which it is usually used.

JOB DESIGN

According to the Canadian Centre for Occupational Health and Safety (2002), *job design* refers to the way that a set of tasks, or an entire job, is organized. Depending on its objectives, job design could be seen as a process intervention. It is included in this chapter on individual interventions because job design is often used to enhance an individual's satisfaction with his or her job.

Job design helps determine

- what tasks are done,
- how the tasks are done,
- how many tasks are done, and
- in what order the tasks are done.

Taking into account all factors that affect the work, job design organizes the content and tasks so that the whole job is less likely to be a risk to the employee (e.g., minimizing repetitive hand movements) and also provides rewards to both the organization and the employee. It might involve

- job rotation,
- job enlargement,
- task/machine pacing,
- work breaks, and
- working hours.

Modern approaches to job design take a systems perspective. Thus, the focus is greater than the individual job, to look at how jobs, people, equipment, processes, work environments, reward systems, and so on, all interact (see "Sociotechnical Systems" in Chapter 8 on process interventions). Generally, the purely mechanical approach that predominated in the scientific management era so simplified jobs that it led to worker boredom.

The current approach to job design incorporates employee input into the design of the job. High quality of work life must be present along with effectiveness and efficiency. Subsystems must support the job (and vice versa). While one goal is to reduce variation, other goals include quality and continuous improvement, as well as worker autonomy. Job design applies to all types of jobs—manufacturing, service, office, management, and so on.

This emerging approach to job design does have its limitations, however. First, not every organization is prepared to give employees autonomy, and not every worker is prepared to accept autonomy. Second, if successful, this type of job design reduces the need for supervisors and managers. Third, as a result, many supervisors and managers are unclear about their new roles under the new job design. Finally, putting the new job designs in place can be time-consuming and thus expensive.

To conduct a job design, the Canadian Centre for Occupational Health and Safety (2002) outlined the following steps:

Do an assessment of current work practices.
Is job design needed or feasible? Discuss the process with the employees and supervisors involved and be clear about the process or any changes or training that will be involved.

Do a task analysis.
Examine the job and determine exactly the job tasks. Consider what equipment and workstation features are important for completing the tasks. Identify problem areas.

Design the job.
Identify the methods for doing the work, work/rest schedules, training requirements, equipment needed and workplace changes. Coordinate the different tasks so each one varies mental activities and body position. Be careful not to include too little or too much in the job.

Implement the new job design gradually.
You may want to start on a small scale or with a pilot project. Train employees in the new procedures and use of equipment. Allow for an adjustment period and time to gain experience with the new job design.

Re-evaluate job design on a continual basis.
Make any necessary adjustments. You may also want to establish a committee to represent the various groups involved. Job design should involve employees, unions, the health and safety committee, and managers during the entire process. Participation of all parties increases communication and understanding.

Be clear that the purpose of the job design is to strengthen the operations and its workforce, not to eliminate jobs or sets of skills (used with permission).

JOB DESCRIPTIONS

A job description impacts directly on the work that an individual in an organization performs. And how and what an individual performs are both extremely important to an organization. Thus, while some might argue that job descriptions are the responsibility of the HR department, OD professionals also have great interest in the process of developing job descriptions. This task provides a great opportunity for collaboration between HR and OD.

If the decision is made to develop job descriptions, given some of the concerns expressed earlier about their use introducing rigidity into the workplace, the job design process outlined earlier will provide an excellent first step in creating the job description. Especially important is the task analysis, which should identify all of the pieces of an individual's job. To build in the flexibility desired in a job description, it is normal to add "Other tasks as assigned" or "Other tasks as mutually agreed upon."

A number of templates are available to help you with your task of building job descriptions, including templates for a wide variety of occupations (see, e.g., www.acinet.org/acinet/jobwrite_search.asp). Typically, a job description will include, at minimum, the following components:

- Job title
- Position start date
- Job location
- Contact information
- Number of positions available
- Number of hours per week
- Required years of experience
- Required degree or formal education
- Required license, certificate, or registration

- Starting salary
- Benefits

RESPONSIBILITY CHARTING

When concerns arise about where accountability lies for decisions that need to be made, responsibility charting may be an appropriate process to use.

I was working with an acquisition that brought together three dairy companies located in diverse geographic locations under a cooperative parent organization that had acquired the merged company, which also had its own parent organization. Confused? Yes, and so were they. There were five groups of managers and executives, many of whom had similar jobs and responsibilities. It was not clear who was responsible for what tasks moving forward, or who was to be kept informed about what actions had been taken. Tasks were going undone, while several people were trying to do the same things in other areas. Needless to say, this situation was confusing and not very efficient or effective. It was decided to get all of the players together for a two-day retreat to work through these issues. Responsibility charting was the primary tool that was used. One page of the output of the retreat is shown in Appendix 6.1 at the end of this chapter ("Sample of Responsibility Charting").

In responsibility charting, a small group of 8 to 12 people complete a matrix to indicate what level of responsibility each person who touches each task has in seeing that the task is completed or a decision is made. The steps to follow in creating a responsibility chart are as follows:

1. Create a form, on computer for projecting, on a flipchart, or, if many people are involved, on butcher paper that is taped to the wall. The left column is headed "Decision"; to the right of this column is a separate column for each person who has some level of responsibility in the organization headed by that per-

son's name or title. Then, fill in the first column by listing all of the decisions that are currently of concern.

2. Agree on codes to be used. These can be whatever works best for the organization, but they might look something like these:
S—sign off
C—consulted
R—responsible
I—informed

3. Have each participant complete the first row on his or her own without consultation. This should reflect what is, not what should be. There are options here. The entire form could be completed, turned in, and compiled for the next meeting. Or, each decision could be processed by the group one decision at a time.

4. Compare responses and discuss. If there are discrepancies, discuss until consensus emerges. Be prepared for conflict. If the decisions listed are at the right level of complexity (this process would not be done for simple decisions), there will be conflict.

5. Review the chart by looking at each decision maker's column. Does an individual have too much or too little to do at too high or too low a level of decision making? Can the level be reduced? Make changes as seem appropriate.

6. Review the chart by looking at each decision. Does someone have responsibility, or is that a gap? Are there too many sign-offs required? Does everyone really need to be informed? Adjust as appropriate.

POLICIES MANUAL

Another opportunity for collaboration between HR and OD occurs in the development and updating of policies manuals. Because organizational policies have a direct impact on organizational culture, the development and maintenance of policies manuals are of significant importance to OD professionals.

Most organizations already have policies manuals (also known as *employee handbooks*), unless the organization is in start-up. Many sample manuals are available on the Web or in software packages, providing good templates from which to begin developing a manual. Once a manual has been developed, however, it needs frequent review to ensure that it is still meeting the needs of individuals and the organization. The OD professional should not work on a manual alone but will need to partner with the HR and legal departments. OD professionals are frequently involved in such development and maintenance, however, because policies affect the quality of work life and, through systems theory, every aspect of the organization.

A sample table of contents of a policies manual, from Johns Hopkins University (http://hrnt.jhu.edu/elr/pol-man/), follows:

Sections
1. Purpose and Purview
2. General Policies
3. Recruiting and Employment
4. Transfers, Promotions, Demotions and Reclassifications
5. Salary Administration Program
6. Position Categories
7. Hours of Work and Overtime
8. Grievances
9. Standards of Conduct and Performance
10. Termination
11. Vacation
12. Holidays
13. Absences
14. Sick Leave
15. Family and Medical Leave Policy
16. Employment Related Accident or Illness (ERA/I)
17. Leave of Absence Without Pay
18. Military Leave

Appendices
A. Equal Opportunity Policy
B. Policy on Accommodation for Disabled Persons
C. Sexual Harassment Prevention and Resolution
D. Policy on Sexual Assault Procedure
E. Policy on Alcohol and Drug Abuse and Drug-free Environment
F. Possession of Firearms on University Premises
G. Faculty and Staff Assistance Program

H. Organizational Development Services
I. Smoke-free Policy
J. University Closings
K. Adoption Assistance Plan
L. Policy on Software Duplication
M. Management and Staff Training Policy
N. Termination and Leave of Absence Codes
O. Personnel Benefits
P. Position Classification Number System
Q. Personnel Time Record Electronic 210
R. Policy Addressing Campus Violence

VALUES CLARIFICATION AND VALUES INTEGRATION

Many exercises can be used to help individuals clarify their values and then integrate their behaviors, statements of values, beliefs, and, if possible, assumptions. One of the exercises that I find useful is to ask individuals to complete the form in Appendix 6.2, "Values Clarification Worksheet," and then form a small group to discuss their responses. Depending on the level of values clarification desired, participants can be provided with difficult case studies to discuss in small groups or a set of difficult values questions to answer and discuss. This can be a challenging and painful process for some who think that they have strong beliefs in a certain area and then find through discussion that a lack of alignment exists among their values, beliefs, assumptions, and behaviors. The OD professional running such exercises should be prepared to address such misalignments, not to create shared values, beliefs, assumptions, and behaviors but to help people understand their differences and why there are differences.

CONFLICT MANAGEMENT

Within this chapter, with its focus on the individual, conflict management becomes an intervention designed to help remove or at least reduce unhealthy conflict between two individuals. The goal is to help individuals find mutuality of interests in a solution that relies on collab-

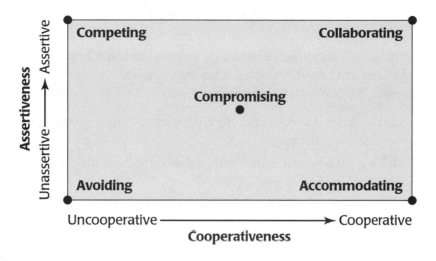

Figure 6.4 *Approaches to Conflict (used with permission of Marvin Dunnette, copyright holder)*

oration, rather than avoidance, aggressive domination, compromise, or giving in, measured with the Thomas-Kilmann Conflict Mode Instrument (TKI). See Figure 6.4 for a graphic depiction of these various approaches to conflict.

Conflict between two individuals has its roots in differing needs, perceptions, emotions and feelings, power, and values. Thus, one role of the OD professional is to help clarify what these are in the conflict situation. Another OD role is to help those in conflict understand their conflict style, as is possible using the TKI. Then, I like to interview the two individuals separately to get an idea of what is happening for them, and, when I think I have a good idea about what is happening for each person, I get them together in the same room to have a moderated conversation or dialogue (see more about dialogue in the next chapter). This process will not always go smoothly. Unless all parties to an unhealthy conflict are resolved to address the conflict, no one, including a skilled OD professional, can force people to address their conflictual behaviors. The concept of emotional intelligence, as promulgated by Goleman (1995), may also prove useful in addressing conflict, including the instruments that Goleman and others have developed.

ACTION LEARNING

A definition of *action learning* (AL) was provided in Chapter 5. Basically, AL uses real-world problems for learning and cooperative problem solving. AL is used appropriately when

- no one knows the solution to a problem or the way out of a complex situation;
- there is no obvious solution to try or nobody is prepared to come up with one; and
- the organization and its senior management are committed to the technique and prepared to consider implementing the proffered solution.

Action learning should *not* be used when

- an answer to the "problem" already exists—this is a puzzle, not a problem;
- a traditional "programmed learning" type of approach will produce a solution;
- systematic analysis will give you a solution; or
- senior management will do exactly as they want, regardless.

The processes typically used in conducting action learning, though there are variations, include the following:

- Traditionally, a small group (8 to 10 individuals) from across organizations with different projects and problems work together, usually with a coach. Competitive organizations should not be included in the same group.
- Currently, AL often takes place within one organization; it is not unusual for a team to consist of people with a common task or problem, with or without a facilitator.
- The focus of the group is on *both* programmed or planned knowledge or learning *and* group attention on real-world problems that each person brings to the group. The intent is not just to provide optional approaches to solving the problems but also to learn from the process.

Benefits of an action learning program, some of which are specified by Smith and Peters (1997), are many:

- It is designed to suit the organization.
- The brightest people are challenged to solve critical problems.
- The resulting contributions are visible, practical, and active.
- The process emphasizes getting things done.
- Leadership is naturally developed.
- New hires and seasoned individuals develop together.
- Mentoring and nurturing skills develop instinctively.
- A network of current and future leaders is matured.
- Diversity is addressed naturally.
- Capability/career assessment is based on real results.
- Development is rapid.
- Whole person development results.
- Defined and accidental learning occur.

CONNECTING ASSESSMENT RESULTS TO SPECIFIC INTERVENTIONS

It is not a simple task to move from assessment results to picking a specific intervention, which is one of the reasons why widespread input into the development of the action plan is useful, and why an experienced OD professional is helpful in this process. Many in management would like to see a perfect "If . . . then" correlation between assessment results and interventions; that is, "If we find x, then we should do y." The ambiguity and systems view of OD that have been discussed many times earlier in this book make this outcome impossible.

If a fishbone diagram points to the root cause of a problem being at the individual level, then it is likely that one of the interventions included in this chapter is going to be helpful in moving the organization forward in the desired direction. If, on the other hand, such an analysis points to the root cause being at the team, process, global, or organization-wide level, then interventions described in subsequent chapters are likely to be more appropriate.

CHAPTER SUMMARY

This chapter explored a sample of interventions that can be applied at the individual level. It is important to reiterate that this is not an all-inclusive list of such interventions but, rather, a fairly comprehensive sample of such interventions. For each intervention, basic processes for implementation were underscored, and factors to consider when using each intervention were also noted. Some other reminders include the realization that there is no perfect intervention, nor is there any one solution to a particular type of problem. The context will affect how these decisions are made. In addition, the expertise of the OD professional must be considered in selecting interventions to be used within the organization.

QUESTIONS FOR DISCUSSION OR SELF-REFLECTION

1. Which interventions do you think are most likely to have an impact on the whole organization? Why?

2. Which interventions do you think are least likely to have an impact on the whole organization? Why?

3. Which of the interventions do you believe would be the easiest for you to facilitate at this time? Why?

4. Which of the interventions do you believe would be the most difficult for you to facilitate at this time? Why? What steps might you take to change this?

5. Discuss why you believe each intervention is appropriate for an OD professional to facilitate rather than some other type of consultant.

6. Identify one intervention from among those presented in this chapter that you would like to know more about, and explore it more fully on the Web. Share your findings with a partner or with the class.

APPENDIX 6.1
SAMPLE OF RESPONSIBILITY CHARTING

TASK	T.P.	K.C. L.G. D.T.	D.S.	P.G.	T.M.	J.S.	B.H.
Pricing—Local, general market	I	CCP	I	C	I	I	I
Pricing—Local, specific account	I (Maj.)	PII		I		I	
Pricing—Regional slotted warehouse, commodity		C	C	P		I	
Pricing—Regional slotted warehouse, value added		I	P	C		I	
Pricing—New markets			P	I		I	
Pricing—Cross-areas		C/P		P/C			
Report on margins	I	I	I	I	I	P	I
Sales*—Local	I	P	C	C	I		
Sales*—Slotted warehouse	I	C	C	P	C		
Sales*—New markets			P(LOL)		I		
Sales*—Cross-areas	I	C/P	C	P/C	I		
Serve on functional new account sales team	I	P		P	I		
Serve on functional sales team		Pt	Pt	Ptl			
Develop local/ competitive promotion	I	P	C	C/P	I		

(continued)

APPENDIX 6.1
(continued)

TASK	T.P.	K.C. L.G. D.T.	D.S.	P.G.	T.M.	J.S.	B.H.
Develop major/ cross-areas promotions	I	C	P	C	I		
Provide sales process training		C		P			C
Develop category management	I	Pt	Ptl	Pt?			
Develop product assortment process	I	C	P	C	C		

Code: P = primary responsibility; C = to be consulted; I = to be informed;
* = defined on a separate sheet; t = team; l = Leader. People's initials are cited
in the top columns.

APPENDIX 6.2
VALUES CLARIFICATION WORKSHEET

In the blank cells provided, write what you understand the values of the respective cultures are for each row.

FACTOR	VALUE OF THE DOMINANT CULTURE IN THE COUNTRY IN WHICH YOU CURRENTLY LIVE	VALUE OF A SUBCULTURE IN THE COUNTRY IN WHICH YOU CURRENTLY LIVE	YOUR VALUE
Time			
Technology			
Work Ethic			
Religion			
Ethical behavior			
Role of politics in business			
Role of women			
Role of men			
Ethnocentrism, global perspective			
Class			

(continued)

APPENDIX 6.2
(continued)

In the blank cells provided, write what you understand the values of the respective cultures are for each row.

FACTOR	VALUE OF THE DOMINANT CULTURE IN THE COUNTRY IN WHICH YOU CURRENTLY LIVE	VALUE OF A SUBCULTURE IN THE COUNTRY IN WHICH YOU CURRENTLY LIVE	YOUR VALUE
Equality			
Power, control			
Education			
Friendship			
Entertainment			
Sports			
Older people			
Children			
Marriage			
Competition			

APPENDIX 6.2
(continued)

In the blank cells provided, write what you understand the values of the respective cultures are for each row.

FACTOR	VALUE OF THE DOMINANT CULTURE IN THE COUNTRY IN WHICH YOU CURRENTLY LIVE	VALUE OF A SUBCULTURE IN THE COUNTRY IN WHICH YOU CURRENTLY LIVE	YOUR VALUE
Teachers			
Managers			
Workers			
Politicians			
Money			
Cooperation			
Racial diversity			
Quality			

Implementation:
Team and Interteam Levels

CHAPTER OUTLINE

Dialogue Sessions

Team Building

Process Consultation

Meeting Facilitation

Fishbowls

Brainstorming

Interteam Conflict Management

Strategic Alignment Assessment

Chapter Summary

Questions for Discussion or Self-Reflection

OVERVIEW   This level of intervention includes interventions to strengthen teams or formal groups and improve the relationships between teams or groups. These interventions include dialogue sessions, team building (the most common OD intervention), process consultation, team effectiveness, meeting facilitation, fishbowls, brainstorming, interteam conflict management, and strategic alignment assessment.

K atzenbach and Smith (1993) suggested that a *team* is a group of interdependent people sharing a common purpose, having common work methods, and holding each other accountable. This chapter focuses on the teams that exist in organizations. Team/work group and interteam interventions are part of the Implementation phase shown in Figure 7.1.

The number of intervention types focused on the team or group level is almost endless. This chapter will expand on a few of them in some detail as examples of what an OD professional might find appropriate in helping improve team or group functioning. The OD professional needs to be sure to use team interventions only when there is a need for people to work together interdependently. Using the intervention for the sake of having an intervention, rather than for the purpose of transforming the team, is neither effective nor productive. Many of the basic definitions of the interventions presented here were covered in Chapter 5.

When working with teams, Cummings and Worley's (2005) advice about the factors affecting the outcome of team interventions is important: "the length of time allocated to the activity, the team's willingness to look at its processes, the length of time the team has been working together and the team's permanence" are all critical (p. 232).

DIALOGUE SESSIONS

As stated in Chapter 5, a dialogue session is a structured conversation designed to explore a topic with the potential for being conflictual, with the desired outcome resulting from a deeper understanding rather than from persuasion (Lindahl, 1996). This intervention appears to be growing in popularity and is often used for confronting conflict that exists within a group.

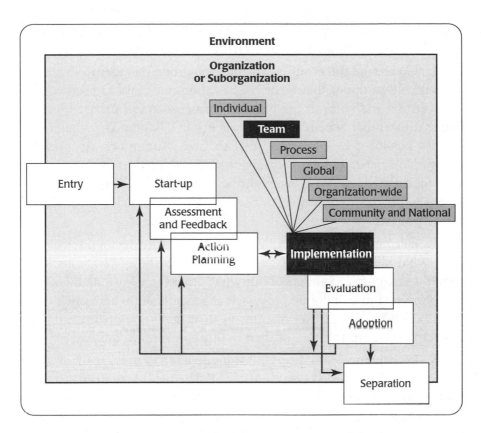

Figure 7.1 *Organization Development Process Model, Phase 5: Implementation at the Team and Interteam Levels*

As with most OD interventions, there is no one way to do dialogue. When I have used this process, I have generally used the following steps with a small group of 8 to 12:

1. Identify and clarify what the issue is that is to be the focus of the dialogue process.

2. Reinforce to the group that all members of the group are equal and that any outside authority associated with group members does not apply in the dialogue process.

3. Reiterate, as in all group activities, the importance of confidentiality or anonymity. The group needs to decide on which to apply. As always applies, names should not be repeated outside the group. The group will need to decide whether the dialogue remains in the group or

whether it can be shared. Setting boundaries allows participants to share their feelings and thoughts more openly without fear of repercussions.

4. Go around the group, allowing each group member to express the basic assumptions that he or she has about the issue. Do so without interruption and without questions. Because assumptions are buried deeply (remember Schein's cultural iceberg in Chapter 1), it may not even be possible for participants to state their assumptions. As a result, this step may also include participant stories related to the issue, one way that buried assumptions might be identified. The purpose of this step is to get the assumptions out so they can be set aside for the rest of the process.

5. During this process, individuals should note, to themselves only, what their reaction is to each member's sharing. We are accustomed to making judgments about what others say, but judgment is not permitted in a dialogue process. But recognizing where one's emotions become strong, either in agreement or in disagreement, can help participants get to the core of their assumptions more quickly.

6. Participants should use "I" statements to express their response to what they've heard ("I feel that . . ."). The facilitator needs to pay particular attention to any statement that sounds like a "should" statement for others ("You should really consider . . . ") or statements that represent a group's response ("We in production think that . . .").

7. Ask the group to listen to what others have to say for the sole purpose of trying to understand them. During the listening process, participants truly listen. They do not argue, or interrupt, or persuade. While clarifying questions are allowed, indirect statements in the form of questions are not permitted.

8. It is not the goal of a dialogue process to reach a solution or agreement; the dialogue has been successful if members of the group understand each other's positions better. Thus, the final step might be to close the session by going around the group one last time, asking each participant to state one new understanding that has emerged from the session.

. . . .

I was working in a large multinational corporation with minority support groups representing different protected classes. While the members of each group had experienced some form of discrimination in either their workplace or their personal lives, it became evident that the rest of the groups were uncomfortable with the **GLBT** (gay-lesbian-bisexual-transsexual) group. Many in these underrepresented groups believed that the existence of the GLBT group detracted from their own important agendas. Their belief came from the negative view they believed other organization members had of the GLBT group, which mirrored their own view. Dialogue groups with representatives from all of the underrepresented groups were organized to focus on feelings about sexual orientation. At the conclusion of the process, it was clear that the comfort level with sexual orientation had become much higher.

TEAM BUILDING

Team building has long been a core intervention for OD and continues to be widely used. Yet, the term covers such a broad range of activities that the phrase itself does not communicate clearly what the intervention in a team might look like. As stated in Chapter 5, Beckhard (1969) suggested the following objectives of team building, in order:

1. Establish and/or clarify goals and objectives.
2. Determine and/or clarify roles and responsibilities.
3. Establish and/or clarify policies and procedures.
4. Improve interpersonal relations.

In spite of this ordering, however, many, many commercial resources are available to "do" team building that focus on the fourth, and least important, objective. Several of these activities, classified broadly as icebreakers, are designed for groups that are forming so individuals get to know each other, often at a level a little deeper than the superficial. For example, some OD facilitators have worksheets that they use for team members to complete and then share their answers with a partner, who then introduces the partner to the group. Some of the questions may be simple, descriptive questions ("What is your favorite food?" "What do you do on vacations?"); some can be more symbolic ("If you were a tree, what kind of tree would you be?"). Other approaches include playing games, drawing a personal coat of arms (with each section responding to a specific question), and doing anything that will put people at ease but still help them share personal information about themselves. Although some of these approaches can be fun and useful in early stages of team development, adults often feel uncomfortable with the non-business-related content of such activities. It may be useful to break down that resistance to get team members thinking outside the box. However, the OD professional needs to be sensitive to the responses of the group and move on to other activities in a timely way when appropriate.

All of the objectives established by Beckhard (1969) can be accomplished while the team is doing its work. For example, when the team comes together, it is essential that it decide why it has been formed. To do this, the team must develop its goals and objectives, clarify its roles and responsibilities, and determine its policies and procedures. With appropriate facilitation, in the process of accomplishing all of these objectives, the team members can also get to know each other better and develop relationships (objective 4). And it is essential for a team to function effectively so that each of these objectives can be accomplished. However, Beckhard was clear that a team should focus on only one objective at a time; otherwise, individuals set their own priorities. Thus, following Beckhard's advice, each of these objectives should be addressed in the order of priorities listed previously.

A long-standing but somewhat controversial set of stages of team formation was developed by Tuckman (1965): Forming, Storming, Norming, and Performing. During the Forming stage, all of the questions from the last paragraph, and all of the objectives indicated by Beckhard (1969) need to be addressed. As forming is often characterized by a lack of clarity, good team building helps the team get some clarity about its purpose. During the process, however, chaos and conflict often surface, leading to the Storming phase. Not only is there conflict over the purpose of the team, but there is also jockeying for leadership of the team. As some sense of direction and leadership emerges, norms are established (the roles, responsibilities, policies, and procedures) outlined in the objectives. Some teams move more quickly to the Norming stage by creating ground rules (described in the next paragraph). Finally, the team moves to the Performing stage. Tuckman's stages and Beckhard's objectives are closely related.

Ground rules can be established by a team early in the forming process. These are often put on flipchart paper and posted whenever the team meets. The group decides on how it wants to function, brainstorming a list of behavioral expectations. The list that follows is much too long for any one team to use, but I have found it useful in providing suggestions from which teams can choose:

Sample Ground Rules

1. Come prepared.
2. Begin on time, and do not go beyond scheduled ending time, except occasionally by consensus.
3. End meeting when the business is over, even if before scheduled end time.
4. Use an agenda with times for each item. Normally, an item will not exceed 30 minutes; exceed times only with consensus.
5. Review the agenda at the beginning of each meeting; modify by consensus.
6. Distribute agenda with the purpose of the meeting, supporting documents, and expected outcomes at an agreed upon time prior to meeting.
7. Take minutes of all meetings to record actions taken.
8. Use personal statements such as "I think," "I feel," "I want," and so forth.
9. Wait until others are finished before speaking (no interruptions).
10. Acknowledge what others have contributed (no "plops"). (A *plop* occurs when a statement is made or a question is asked that is ignored.)
11. Present reasons for disagreement, not attributions (no discounting; no personal attacks).
12. Be open about your personal agenda; ask early for what you want and need.
13. Listen to what is being said; paraphrase what you think the person said if you're not sure.
14. Share personal feelings, even if (*especially* if) they might lead to conflict; confront with "I" statements rather than "blaming" ones.
15. Use the names of other participants.
16. Provide feedback on your sense of the group's processes as they occur.

17. Share participation (no dominance or avoidance).

18. Keep discussion contributions on target.

19. Pass if there is nothing to add.

20. Take risks; risk taking is to be applauded.

21. Avoid distractions (taking phone calls during meeting, opening mail, using sidebars— private conversations—etc.).

22. Use a consensual model for decision making.

23. Qualify attendees; invite guest speakers if they will be helpful in accomplishing the task.

24. Expect strong facilitation around these ground rules. Select a monitor.

25. Add to this list as issues emerge, and delete from this list as issues no longer apply.

26. If a team member is absent because of an emergency, a person who is present will be assigned to bring that person up-to-date.

The responsibility for enforcing these ground rules does not reside solely with the OD professional. Each member of the team takes responsibility for identifying behaviors that the team has decided not to use.

Team building does not have a beginning and an ending point. So long as the team is continuing to meet, the process of building and rebuilding that team will occur. Whenever a new member comes on the team, for example, the team may need to return to the forming stage as the new member is incorporated into the team. The critical piece to keep in mind is that team building is not based on artificial activities but emerges from the ongoing work of the team.

PROCESS CONSULTATION

Process consultation is also a keystone of the OD profession. Its primary purpose, also consistent with the objectives of team building, is to improve team effectiveness. As indicated in Chapter 5, the primary role of the OD professional in process consultation is to serve as a mirror to team members so they can see better how they interact and perform. There are many ways to do this.

Periodically, the OD professional may wish to call the attention of the team members to the agreed-on ground rules, reminding the members of their mutual responsibilities to enforce them. He or she may also periodically use observed behavior as a learning opportunity to feed back to the team members what has been noticed and help them learn alternative ways to deal with the situation.

Some tools also can be used to give explicit feedback. A *sociogram* can be used to provide specific feedback on the way in which the team communication is occurring. For example, are there dominant participants, people who are not involved (*isolates*), or pairs who talk only to each other? The OD professional (and others can easily be trained to use these tools, too) draws a diagram with a circle for each participant on the team. This diagram is not shared publicly at this time; only the completed diagram is shared. (When I am performing this task, I often stand behind a flipchart so participants cannot see what I am doing.) Draw a line from the circle of the person who begins the conversation to the next person who speaks. The marker stays on the paper and is moved to each subsequent speaker's circle in turn. This process can continue for 10 to 15 minutes. The diagram can then be shown to the participants for their discussion.

In Figure 7.2, participant D, the isolate, did not participate at all in the conversation. Participant B connects with everyone except D, which suggests that B may be the leader. The dominant conversation occurs between A and B. Perhaps this outcome is driven by the content and the expertise of the participants. But perhaps it is representative of the team's interactions. The team would then need to discuss why this is the pattern and whether it makes sense. The second part of the sociogram is a tally of the amount of time that is being taken by individuals. In

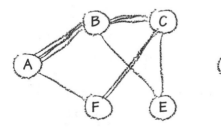

A ⱵⱵⱵⱵ Ⱶ
B ⱵⱵⱵ ‖
C ‖‖‖
D
E |
F ‖

Figure 7.2 *Sociogram Results for Discussion*

this case, these tallies are consistent with the sociogram, but it could be different. Participant E made only one comment, but it could have been a monologue that lasted for several minutes, compared with participant A, whose contributions may all have been one- or two-word responses. If there are problems with participants interrupting each other during the team session, interruptions can also be inserted into the sociograms indicating who was interrupting whom to see whether there is a pattern of men interrupting women, or one participant regularly interrupting another participant, and so on. I indicate interruptions by adding an arrow from the circle of the person interrupting to the circle of the participant being interrupted.

Other ways to give feedback to team participants could be through periodic process discussion by team members, brief surveys in which participants can give feedback to each other in an anonymous way, one-on-one coaching from the process consultant (OD professional), and other suggestions that might arise from the team members themselves.

MEETING FACILITATION

Reference has already been made to some tools to improve the effective functioning of a team. First, it must be clear why the team is meeting. What do you expect to accomplish? Second, the right people need to be invited. Are guests needed to provide their expertise? Third, the agenda should be developed by inviting all team members to contribute to the agenda—it might even be set before the previous meeting is adjourned. Fourth, an estimated time is assigned to each agenda item. The appendix to this chapter displays a sample agenda containing these components (Appendix 7.1).

Another process that can be used to improve effectiveness is to identify ongoing role identification and description. A sample document of how role identification and descriptions might appear, based on the PDCA model (see Chapter 1), appears in Appendix 7.2 at the end of this chapter. There is no expectation that these roles will appear in all teams, but something similar to this document will help improve the effectiveness of team meetings. The OD professional needs to model appropriate facilitation, provide feedback, and train team participants.

FISHBOWLS

Another way that an OD professional can help team members understand their own dynamics is to use a *fishbowl*. This approach works best with a large team. A subset of the team is selected to sit in a circle, with the rest of the team sitting around this subgroup. I typically have five people in the inner circle, with five different roles described on a sheet of paper; each participant chooses a slip of paper blindly and then discusses some topic of interest playing the role described. The outer circle provides the inner circle with feedback on the interactions that occur, identifying the role that each person played. As the next subgroup takes the center, I insert one or two role descriptions that say, "Act as you normally would in a team setting." Finally, all of the slips of paper for the inner subgroup indicate that participants should act as they normally would. This gives the outer circle permission to give honest feedback to the inner circle participants.

BRAINSTORMING

A very common process used in teams to generate ideas is *brainstorming*. Reference to brainstorming was made in Chapter 4, as brainstorming is an integral component of affinity diagrams, a process described in that chapter. Traditionally, it is difficult to get a team to think creatively, to think in directions that they have not considered before. Thus, brainstorming is a means to generate as many ideas as possible on a specific problem or issue in a group setting. Some "rules" and process for conducting a brainstorm follow:

Brainstorming Rules
1. Everyone participates in generating ideas.
2. Spontaneous, freewheeling responses are encouraged. Be creative!
3. Build on others' ideas.
4. Quantity, not quality, is desired.
5. No discussion or critique of ideas is allowed until all ideas are listed.
6. Negative nonverbal responses are discouraged.
7. All responses are written down on the flipchart by the facilitator.

How to Conduct

1. Choose a specific problem or issue. (This information might be sent to group members in advance of the meeting, although this step is not necessary.)

2. Communicate the rules to group members. Post the rules so they are visible to everyone. Clarify any rules that seem unclear.

3. Have members spontaneously call out ideas. (If the group is large, have people raise their hand so they do not interrupt each other.)

4. Record all ideas as they are stated on a flipchart, board, computer, or overhead so that everyone can see them.

5. Be prepared to throw out a few idea starters if the group has trouble getting started or gets stuck.

6. End the brainstorming when it appears that the group has run out of ideas. But be patient—just because the group is silent does not mean that all the ideas have been communicated. Some people may need more time to think.

Modifications

1. A few minutes before beginning the brainstorm, give the group time to jot down ideas. Some people think better in silence than when the group is responding.

2. If some individuals are not participating, modify the process by going around the group person to person. It's OK for someone to pass. When everyone passes, the process should end. (This process is known as *nominal group technique [NGT].*)

INTERTEAM CONFLICT MANAGEMENT

At times, unhealthy conflict can arise between task forces, functional areas, or teams. If these groups need to work together, the unhealthy conflict can interfere with productivity and creativity. The OD professional might work with the teams in ways similar to those used in addressing conflict between individuals (see Chapter 6). Another approach is the *mirroring process*, described next.

Mirroring Process

Objectives

1. To develop better mutual relationships between teams
2. To explore the perceptions teams or work groups have of each other
3. To develop plans for improving the relationships

Steps

1. The large group develops a list of ground rules to support openness in feedback and discussion.
2. Each group is assigned to a separate room, with a flipchart and markers. An OD professional moves between the two groups.
3. Each group is to answer the following questions as completely and honestly as possible on the flipchart paper:
   - "What qualities or attributes best describe our group?"
   - "What qualities or attributes best describe the other group?"
   - "How do we think the other group will describe us?"
4. The two groups are brought together with their flipchart pages. *One* person from each group presents the results. Those from the other group can ask questions for clarification only. They cannot justify, accuse, defend, or make any other kind of statement.
5. The two groups then return to their own rooms. At this point, a number of misunderstandings or discrepancies should have surfaced.
6. The two groups then analyze and review reasons for differences. The emphasis is on solving the problems and reducing the misunderstandings. The groups are not to ask whether the perception is right or wrong but, rather, "How did these perceptions occur? What actions on our part have contributed to these perceptions?" The group then works on what they can do now to close the gap.
7. The two groups get together again and share their analyses and possible solutions. Free, open discussion is encouraged, focusing on the development of a list of remaining areas of friction or disagreement.

8. The two groups work together then to develop specific action steps to solve specific problems and to improve relationships.

9. A follow-up meeting is scheduled to report on actions implemented, identify further problems, and formulate additional action steps.

Expected Outcomes

1. Improved understandings of the other group will occur.

2. Misunderstandings and miscommunications will be diminished.

3. Specific action steps for improving relationships will be identified.

4. In the long run, unhealthy conflict will be reduced and the opportunity for healthy conflict increased (because it will be safer for everyone).

. . . .

I have found the mirroring process to be especially useful following a merger or acquisition. In one instance, a colleague and I were helping facilitate an acquisition of three companies that occurred simultaneously by the parent (acquiring) company. The cultures of all four companies were very different, yet, following the merger, members of all four organizations were assigned to major teams within the acquiring organization. It became apparent fairly quickly that people were resisting the efforts to move toward a common culture. At a subsequent annual meeting of the senior executives of the four organizations, the mirroring process was used. It was a rather complicated application of the process as there were four groups involved rather than two, as suggested in the text earlier.

Some of the feedback was very difficult for the previously separate companies to hear from the other companies. Fortunately, there were two of us as facilitators, and we had the opportunity each to spend time with two of the groups and to support them as they struggled through the feedback that they had received. The commitment to improve relationships was very strong, leading, ultimately, to a positive outcome. Action plans were put in place to address the areas where systems and processes were creating some ongoing conflict. Over the period of a year following the annual meeting and the mirroring exercise, teams were coming together in much more positive ways, and the unhealthy conflict among the companies was considerably diminished.

Some OD professionals also use instruments, such as the MBTI or DiSC, to identify personality differences that might exist among team members—differences that might explain why conflict exists on the team. So long as the results are used for the purpose of discussion about differences, rather than seeing the instruments as perfect descriptors of the individuals involved, such use can be beneficial for the team.

STRATEGIC ALIGNMENT ASSESSMENT

According to Semler (2000), any part of an organization must be aligned (consistent with) the organization itself to be effective. Thus, any team must share with the organization certain components. Semler suggested that these components are vision, values, and purpose; strategy; culture; rewards; structure; practices; systems; and behaviors. Thus, the task of the OD professional is to work with the team to determine any discrepancies in any of these areas between the team and the organization—in other words, to conduct a *strategic alignment assessment*. This analysis might well call for adjustments in the components of the team that are not in sync with those components in the organization. Of course, it is possible that the team is out ahead of the organization, and alignment might well call for adjustments in these components of the organization, to bring it into alignment with the team. Gaps could well be identified through the assessment process (Chapter 4), if analysis of the data is done in such a way as to identify these components within teams.

CHAPTER SUMMARY

Much of the work in today's organizations is done by teams or work groups. The more effectively teams operate together, the more they can contribute to the objectives of the organization. Many processes/interventions can be used to improve team functioning in an organization.

Though not an exhaustive discussion, this chapter described and provided some processes that support teams and improve their effectiveness. From the broad array available, this chapter discussed dialogue sessions, team building (the most common OD intervention), process consultation, team effectiveness, meeting facilitation, fishbowls, brainstorming, interteam conflict management, and strategic alignment assessment.

QUESTIONS FOR DISCUSSION
OR SELF-REFLECTION

1. Pair up with another member of your class. Identify a topic that has the potential for developing an emotional response and that might lead to differences between the two of you. Conduct a dialogue discourse. Discuss your reactions to the process.

2. Have a class member conduct a sociogram for a brief period of classroom time. Discuss its implications.

3. Discuss the strengths and weaknesses of each of the team interventions presented in this chapter.

4. Identify a need that a team has of which you are a part. Select one of the interventions suggested in this chapter, and discuss how it might be implemented to address that specific team's need.

5. State a problem that needs solution in your personal life. Brainstorm ways in which you might resolve that problem.

6. Discuss experiences you have had with teams (either in the workplace or in the classroom). How effective did you find the team's processes? How might a team-based intervention have helped improve the experience?

APPENDIX 7.1

TENTATIVE AGENDA FOR QUALITY TRANSFORMATION TEAM MEETING

1:00 P.M.   Review agenda and modify, as needed.

Identify scribe and process coach.

Define expected outcome (EO): consensus on meeting activities.

1:05 A.M.   Review minutes of previous meeting; modify, if necessary.

EO: Agreement on minutes

1:10 P.M.   Informational updating and sharing

EO: Shared knowledge

1:30 P.M.   Present ideal state—drafts of what's going well and barriers

EO: Sufficient feedback to each presenter to allow a second draft to be developed

3:00 P.M.   Break

3:15 P.M.   Continue sharing of first drafts.

4:45 P.M.   Determine next steps/set agenda for next meeting.

EO: Clear expectations for steering team members

4:55 P.M.   Evaluate meeting.

EO: Areas of needed improvement identified

5:00 P.M.   Adjourn.

APPENDIX 7.2

TEAM/MEETING PROCESS ROLES AND RESPONSIBILITIES

Role: Team/Meeting Leader

The leader manages the team and meeting process. This role does not rotate, providing a constant contact. This appointment will be reviewed every 6 months.

Plan: Before the Meeting

- Decide that a meeting is necessary based on the agenda items received.
- Ensure that a date, time, and place are decided and secured by the team/group.
- Develop the agenda with times based on input received.
- Distribute agenda with supporting materials prior to the meeting as requested by the team
- Consult with the process coach.
- Notify members as soon as possible if a meeting is to be canceled.
- Determine tools to be used.

Do: During the Meeting

- Post ground rules.
- Keep track of time.
- Help keep the team on track, focused on the agenda.
- Support the presenters: summarize after each item, clarify, maintain balanced participation, be tactful and diplomatic, and help the team select appropriate tools to use.
- Be a full-fledged member of the team.
- Make sure that responsibilities are taken for action items.

Check: End of the Meeting

- Summarize topics.
- Help identify next meeting agenda items.
- Ensure that the meeting process gets evaluated.

Act: After the Meeting

- Attend to improvements identified by meeting evaluation.
- Add new agenda items.
- Consult with process coach.
- Maintain master file.

Role: Process Coach

The *process coach* acts as a consultant to the team and meeting process. He or she helps supply the team/meeting with tools, methods, and feedback to improve the team/meeting process. This position rotates from meeting to meeting.

Plan: Before the Meeting

- Help the team leader plan methods to collect data on the team and group interactions, and help with methods to implement agenda items.
- Locate resources as necessary/requested.
- Determine methods to provide the team with feedback following the meeting.

Do: During the Meeting

- With assistance of the team, the process coach takes primary responsibility to do the following:
- Suggest alternate ways to deal with a situation, especially when the team is "stuck."
- Challenge the team to deal with uncomfortable issues.
- Be supportive of all team members.
- Use the concepts of quality, especially related to the philosophy of Deming, and remind the team of this philosophy when necessary.
- Listen to and observe the team/meeting process.
- Remind the team when a ground rule has been violated.
- Assist team members in using data and the PDCA cycle.
- Suggest tools for meeting process.
- Monitor the appropriate use of data.
- Be a full-fledged member of the team.

Check: End of the Meeting

- Help the team evaluate its process.
- Summarize observed behaviors.
- Help the team identify improvements.

Act: After the Meeting

- Assist with the improvement of the team/meeting process.
- Analyze feedback data.
- Assist in planning next agenda.

Role: Scribe

The *scribe* is responsible for documenting activities at team meetings. This role usually rotates for teams and meetings.

Plan: Before the Meeting

- Bring necessary equipment to meeting (e.g., paper and pens, flipcharts, laptop computer, etc.).

Do: During the Meeting

- Note decisions.
- Summarize conclusions and discussions; ask for clarification if unclear.
- Record action items—who took responsibility to do what and when.
- Assist leader in summarizing after each agenda item.
- Identify agenda items not covered; make sure these are on next meeting's agenda.
- Keep track of topics brought up during the meeting that are future agenda items.
- Be a full-fledged member of the team.

Check: During the Meeting

- Ask for clarification on issues to document.
- Improve minutes with feedback from members about last meeting.

Act: After the Meeting

- Prepare and distribute meeting minutes within 2 days.

Role: Team Member

Plan: Before the Meeting

- Read previous meeting minutes, noting changes needed.
- Review agenda for upcoming meeting.
- Complete any action items.
- Notify leader if you cannot attend.
- Provide leader with any agenda items, with time needed and support documentation.

Do: During the Meeting

- Bring materials as needed.
- Practice good team skills according to the ground rules.
- Focus comments on fact rather than opinion, whenever possible.

- Assist leader and process coach throughout the meeting as needed.
- Act as leader when presenting a topic.
- Be a full-fledged member of the team.

Check: During and End of the Meeting
- Monitor your behaviors according to ground rules.

Assist in evaluating the meeting process.

Act: After the Meeting
- Follow through with assignments.
- Follow through with items identified to improve the meeting process.

Role: Champion

The *champion* oversees and supports the activities of the team. Usually, the champion has authority to provide resources and make changes in the process being studied. This role does not rotate but is constant.

Plan: Before the Meeting
- Seek clarification and direction, as appropriate, from parent company steering team.
- Invite employees to become team members.
- Meet with individual members of the implementation team to ensure that they have understood and carried out their assignments.
- Meet with the team leader to help in the development of the agenda.

Do: During the Meeting
- Provide information needed by the team when known by the champion.
- Provide ongoing encouragement.
- Be a full-fledged member of the team.

Check: End of the Meeting
- Determine what the team's expectations are for the champion prior to the next meeting.

Act: After the Meeting
- Provide regular feedback to parent company steering team about progress being made by the team.
- Obtain resources needed by the implementation team.

- Meet with the manager(s) of the process, the people who perform the process, and those who control the resources used within the process, where necessary, to gain cooperation.
- Meet with team members to determine and provide whatever assistance they need to carry out their assignments.
- Provide whatever support is needed by the team leader.

8

Implementation: Process Level

CHAPTER OUTLINE

Continuous Process Improvement/Total Quality Management
Six Sigma
Business Process Reengineering
Benchmarking/Best Practices
Sociotechnical Systems (STS)
Chapter Summary
Questions for Discussion or Self-Reflection

OVERVIEW   The process level focuses on organizational processes, including many concepts associated with quality improvement, including continuous process improvement/total quality management, six sigma, business process reengineering, benchmarking/best practices, and sociotechnical systems.

The term *process* is used in many ways. In fact, most of this book is about processes—how we relate to others, how we create and support culture change in organizations, how we work across cultures, and so on. The focus of this chapter is not about the processes that we use as OD professionals but, rather, about the processes used by the organization to produce its products or deliver its services. As with all of the categories used to structure this book, this is a somewhat artificial distinction, as some products and services are delivered by teams, but those processes are covered in Chapter 7, while Chapters 6, 9, 10, and 11 focus largely on people processes. This chapter considers interventions that are useful in improving organizational processes. Process interventions are part of the Implementation phase shown in Figure 8.1.

Entire books have been written about process improvement, and each of the interventions in this phase also have books dedicated solely to them. The purpose of this chapter, therefore, is to provide a brief overview of the intervention and show how it can be implemented in an organization.

CONTINUOUS PROCESS IMPROVEMENT/ TOTAL QUALITY MANAGEMENT

Though often treated as a fad in the United States, total quality management (TQM) has a long life, having been implemented first in Japan during its reconstruction after World War II, based on the work of Deming (1986), Juran (Juran & Godfrey, 1998), and others. TQM, also known as *continuous process improvement (CPI)* or *continuous quality improvement (CQI)*, is both a philosophy and a set of tools and techniques that enable managers to manage with data. The tools and techniques are very detailed and are presented in an excellent and relatively easy-to-understand way in Scholtes (1988).

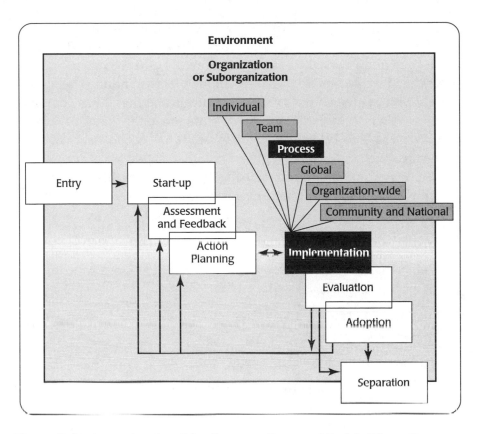

Figure 8.1 *Organization Development Process Model, Phase 5: Implementation at the Process Level*

Although many U.S. companies claimed to have committed themselves to TQM, I heard Deming say repeatedly that only 5% of U.S. companies actually took TQM seriously and could effectively implement it. Management became frustrated over the evolutionary process of change demanded by TQM and the length of time that it took to embed the philosophy of quality into the organization. As a result, these organizations gave up. Those companies that really understood the implications of TQM—that it was a company-wide effort that demanded extensive training and education of all employees, that managers and supervisors had to change the way in which they interacted with employees, that statistical process control had to be implemented, and that cherished management practices, such as annual performance reviews and management by objectives (MBOs), would have to be discontinued—continued to focus on the philosophy and the tools. Today, these companies typically have incorporated TQM into their management thought and practices. Thus, although less attention is being paid to TQM today than in the 1980s, I am suggesting that it has continued in a less visible way, perhaps moving from above the water of Schein's cultural iceberg to below the water, where it has become a basic value of managers.

A common model for doing TQM is to use a seven-step approach to bring about continuous improvement of processes:

1. Define the system and the problem focus.
2. Assess the current situation.
3. Analyze the root causes.
4. Try out improvement theory.
5. Study the results.
6. Standardize improvements.
7. Plan continuous improvement.

It is obvious that this approach relies heavily on Shewhart's PDCA cycle (as described in Chapter 1).

One controversy that surfaces frequently in my TQM consulting experience has been the apparent conflict between the emphasis in TQM on process rather than on results, with *results* being a buzzword that managers need to see in order to support the TQM approach. The managers' assumption often is that results do not occur unless they are the specific focus of the work. TQM, however, argues that focusing on results cannot bring about results, because it is only in having the right processes in place that results can occur.

Schaffer and Thomson (1992) underscored the concern of many companies that quality efforts do not move along quickly enough. Reluctant companies want to be sure that business results occur and that the inefficiency that is perceived to be associated with many CQI efforts is eliminated. Detractors pointed to the high level of failure among quality endeavors as measured by bottom-line results. This evidence, however, fails to note the fact that surveys consistently have pointed to "success" *if* companies stay with the process past 3 years. They then set up a dichotomy between "activity-centered programs" and "results-driven programs." Skeptics argue against the former and for the latter. It is interesting to note that, after criticizing most quality improvement efforts because of a lack of a strong empirical database of successes, these detractors offer as cause for rejecting them just two brief case studies!

All of the examples included in Schaffer and Thomson (1992), such as the 30% reduction in defects within 2 months on a work line, are totally within Juran's breakthrough sequence concept—that there are many early opportunities to make improvements with TQM, but such improvements quickly plateau unless mechanisms are in place to improve processes on a continuous basis.

The Schaffer and Thomson article suggests setting arbitrary goals to arrive at results,, yet most quality professionals would argue against such goals. According to Persico and McLean (1994), goals, within a quality context, must be "valid"; that is, they must meet the following criteria:

- Data must be derived from a system in a state of statistical control.
- Valid methodology must be used.
- Employees must be able to meet the goal.

The second point with which quality professionals would take issue is Schaffer and Thomson's observation that "the mood is one of impatience. Management wants to see results now, even though the change process is a long-term commitment" (p. 83). In addition to the double-talk that may be seen as part of this point, this statement is an example of Deming's (1986) "Deadly Disease 2": emphasis on short-term profits.

The distinction between the two approaches is an artificial one suggesting an either/or perspective. Deming (1986), Juran (1988), Imai (1986), and Crosby (1984) were all explicit in their condemnation of existing business practices that emphasized a results rather than a process focus, resulting in a lack of quality. This does not mean that any one of these authors supported activities that did not ultimately point to improved results. Likewise, every one of them *was* interested in results; in fact, they recognized that, over the long term, the only way results could be improved was through a process orientation.

While pointing to the tension in which TQM finds itself between the **Newtonian paradigm** (linear) and the **complexity paradigm** (or chaos paradigm), Dooley, Johnson, and Bush (n.d.) have raised concern about results-based thinking:

> The way to avoid [entropy] is for every organization to experiment with TQM practice and develop their [*sic*] own theory. There is a tendency, however, because of impatience for quick results, to look for "cook-book" answers—a canned list of steps that will solve everything. Again, this type of thinking is based on determinism. (p. 15)

Table 8.1 captures some of the contrasting concepts between what has typically been associated with *immediate* results-oriented approaches and process-oriented approaches.

What's the bottom line? Of course, organizations want (and must demand) results. The critical question is how they get them. An organization can choose to focus on short-term results (as proposed by Schaffer & Thomson, 1992) and, without care and attention to processes, end up with *tampering*. Or an organization can choose to focus on processes, without understanding why, and end up with *entropy*. Or, finally, an organization can choose synergy, integrating the appropriate activities into its culture to lead to long-term, continuous improvement that must show results within the mission and vision of the organization. Without such results, no organization will be able to continue in the "new economic age" (Deming, 1986) in which the world finds itself.

This dichotomy is, thus, an artificial one—results are needed, and we get them by focusing on the improvement of processes.

SIX SIGMA

Six sigma is an outgrowth of the TQM movement and uses the seven-step process listed in the previous section. Six sigma is a way to manage with data (in contrast to intuition or tradition) in a process of continuous improvement. Existing systems use an extensive set of titles to track expertise in the system, such as Green Belt, Yellow Belt, Black Belt, and Master Black Belt. As one acquires more knowledge about six sigma, one moves up the list from *Green Belt* (a part-time position) to *Master Black Belt* (a full-time position with responsibility for teaching others).

Sigma is a statistical term that refers to the variation that exists within a system. By identifying the number of defects in a system, the expectation is that the system will come closer to producing no defects.

TABLE 8.1   Results versus Process Approach

RESULTS APPROACH (R ORGANIZATION)	PROCESS APPROACH (P ORGANIZATION)
Short-term	Long-term
Quick fix	Continuous improvement
Isolated view	Systems perspective
Taylor	Deming, Juran, Imai, Crosby
Predetermined outcomes	Continuous improvement
"Carrot and stick" rewards and	determined by the system
punishment	Management support
Individual performance evaluation	Group support and team
Dramatic change	focused
Erratic	Gradual, undramatic change
Consistent	Management responsible
Worker responsible for system	for system
Decisions based on hunches	Decisions based on fact
Unrealistic perspective of system	Realistic view of system
simplicity	complexity
Lack of awareness of process	Acknowledgment of process
variation	variation
Behavior + Attitudes = Results	Processes + Systems + Behavior
"Just do it!"	+ Attitudes + Culture
	= Quality (Result)
	"How can we improve how we
	do it?"

There is, of course, no such thing as "no defects"; as improvement occurs in the system, expectations increase. Variation is reduced, but the goal of continuous improvement means that the organization is never satisfied with its level of quality. To reach the level of six sigma, a process must produce fewer than 3.4 defects per million opportunities to create a defect. A *defect* in this context is anything that does not meet a customer's expectations.

The section on TQM discussed valid goals. Six sigma, just like a valid goal, depends on determining process capability, which means what the process is able to deliver. Another factor for a valid goal was stability. This concept, too, is important in six sigma; a process needs to provide a consistent, predictable process. Thus, six sigma focuses first on reducing process variation to produce a stable process; after that, the emphasis is on process improvement.

Chowdhury (2001) used an interesting example about a pizza store. The store found that it was losing customers. As a first step, it sat down with customers and asked them what they wanted that the store was not producing, expecting that they would say more toppings, different varieties, and so on. Surprisingly, the customers indicated that their concern was burnt crusts. This was a surprise because the store already recognized that there was a problem, as three to four pizzas per hundred were thrown out because the cheese had browned or the crust was totally blackened. Customers, however, said that "burnt" meant *any* signs of blackness on the crust. Reviewing their records, the store found that it had 12 to 15 pizzas burned a day under this criterion. Using a six sigma process would indicate that the store had to listen to its customers, first, and then had to figure out how to improve the process to reduce its defects, as defined by the customers. The company would need to strive to get the number down to within six sigma, or 3.4 pizzas "burnt" per million!

BUSINESS PROCESS REENGINEERING

In spite of the huge popularity of Hammer and Champy's (1993) book on *business process reengineering (BPR)*, the book was also the subject of many criticisms because of the perception, later supported by Champy (2002), that "the efficiencies created by the first round of reengineering primarily benefited the shareholders at the expense of customers and employees" (p. 2). Both the original book and public presentations by Hammer that I heard ("Carry the wounded, but shoot the stragglers!") showed little regard for employees and often resulted in downsizing of the very people who made the radical changes possible. Davenport (1995) went even further, concluding that BPR had become "a code word for mindless bloodshed" (p. 70). It is no surprise to me that it fell into disrepute.

In spite of this ill repute, however, interest in BPR continues by some managers. However, as Champy (1995) observed, managers often left themselves out of the reengineering process while many of the inefficiencies of the business were centered on management processes. This is another reason, according to Champy, why BPR was not more successful. Having reviewed the many reasons why BPR failed, Davenport (1995) concluded that the one positive of BPR was that it focused on business processes, because processes are at the core of how people work.

To achieve such radical redesign, Hammer and Champy (1993) suggested seven steps to be followed:

1. Organize around outcomes, not tasks.
2. Identify all the processes in an organization and prioritize them in order of redesign urgency.
3. Integrate information-processing work into the real work that produces the information.
4. Treat geographically dispersed resources as though they were centralized.
5. Link parallel activities in the work flow instead of just integrating their results.
6. Put the decision point where the work is performed, and build control into the process.
7. Capture information once and at the source.

The research that exists on reengineering success does not find the kind of success rate that one would hope with the billions of dollars spent on reengineering projects. Cummings and Worley's (2005) summary of a half dozen reports suggests that the failure rate, in which there were no gains in productivity or gains that were too small to offset costs, ranged from 60% to 80%.

As Davenport (1995) noted, the focus on processes in BPR is commendable, but the lack of concern for people and the expectations created of massive cost savings have created enough concern that BPR is unlikely to become a major force in business again. Other approaches, reviewed in this chapter, also focus on processes but without the negative components of BPR.

BENCHMARKING/BEST PRACTICES

Benchmarking and *best practices* are terms often used synonymously or at least in the same breath. To determine how well an organization is doing, it is often deemed appropriate to compare one organization's results with another's or with a set of companies. The problem with this approach is that you may well find out the how much, but not the how. And because every organization is different and has different processes, infrastructures, suppliers, customers, and so on, knowing how much is often not very useful. Many industries have industry groups that collect extensive information anonymously from member companies to assist them in the benchmarking process. However, to maintain that anonymity, it is never possible to tie the results (the output variables) to the conditions (the input variables).

. . . .

I once worked with an oil refinery in the Middle East that was part of a 150-refinery consortium. Every year, extensive statistics were gathered anonymously by an outside firm and published in a book under condition of anonymity. The particular refinery I was working with was considerably overstaffed according to the benchmarks gathered by the outside firm. The parent company then told the refinery that it had to lay off enough workers to reduce the head count to the number that had been benchmarked.

But this approach posed problems. First, the refinery was much older than the average age of refineries benchmarked, and much of its technology was less efficient and required more personnel to operate. Second, the raw material being refined was not consistent across the benchmarked companies. Finally, although the finished products were similar, there were differences in the mix of product produced. None of these factors was built into the benchmarks. So, a decision to reduce personnel solely on the basis of the benchmarks made no sense and reflected a lack of understanding about processes and the value of benchmarks.

. . . .

I believe that benchmarking processes is much more valuable than benchmarking results. However, problems arise with trying to do so. First, the best organization to benchmark processes with is a competitor. Yet, how many competitors are anxious to open up their processes to a competitor? Not many! And then there are legal concerns: any discussion about costs or pricing could well land both parties in court for price fixing. There is still value in looking, for example, at marketing in a company that is not a competitor; however, finding a company that is good enough to learn from and that is willing to give the extensive time that is required will be difficult.

Of course, other sources of information may be available other than going directly to another company. Perhaps information easily accessible in the literature or on the Web would help. But it is unlikely that these sources will provide sufficient information.

"Best practices" is clearly a better approach than simply a benchmarked result. But any "best" is set in the context of the industry, the product, the customers, the suppliers, the infrastructure, and so forth, as suggested earlier. What is best practice for Company A may not be the best practice for Company B. I do not believe that there can be transfer from one company to another unless the systems in the two organizations are identical—which can never happen. Clearly, I am not a champion of best practices or of benchmarking with external parties.

An organization may potentially benchmark itself. This task can be done in a couple of ways. Probably the most useful is the process built into continuous process improvement—with the same process over time. As performance within a system is tracked, using statistical process control, it is possible to determine whether that process is performing better over time, with *better* being defined as more stable and with fewer defects. It might also be possible to benchmark within an organization across locations, assuming that the processes in the two parts of the organization are roughly the same. There should not be a problem with cooperation given that all organizations involved in the benchmarking process are a part of the same company.

So, benchmarking's greatest value is when it is done internally and when it is done historically. I have not seen benefit from looking at best practices that are produced in other contexts, and the concept of "best" may contradict the basic premise of continuous improvement.

SOCIOTECHNICAL SYSTEMS (STS)

One of the problems of the business process reengineering movement was that it forgot the basic importance of viewing systems from a sociotechnical perspective. Any system must create processes, and thus design jobs, that integrate and balance the people needs (*socio-*) with the tools and equipment (*-technical*) in an organization.

According to Berniker (1992), the basic premise of STS is that work is best done in autonomous groups to accomplish the desired synthesis. As such, STS also supports the use of multidisciplinary teams to do the job design work. Ideally, these teams are self-regulating and continue to redesign work as needed. The bias of STS is that people are the source of solutions, not problems, and that, whenever possible, letting people at the source make decisions is likely to lead to the best outcomes. Berniker (1992) concluded that "the philosophy and values of STS practice argue that effective action takes precedence over administrative control."

The principles of sociotechnical systems are still very much in place in the workplace today. Self-directed work teams, projects on the quality of work life, and telecommuting are all examples of the application of STS principles. There is no set of proscriptions to be followed in implementing STS; rather, as with the philosophical underpinning of all of the successful uses of the process interventions, successful application of STS principles requires a commitment to the core principles.

CHAPTER SUMMARY

This chapter focused on interventions designed to improve the processes that produce the goods and services offered by organizations. Each has a philosophical underpinning that requires that management make a sincere commitment to the intervention over a period of time for it to succeed. When such commitment is not present, the intervention becomes a fad that has the potential for doing more harm than good and that wastes organizational resources. When used appropriately, with commitment and with appropriate resources, and applying a sociotechnical system concern for *both* people and technology, the interventions stand a good chance of success.

QUESTIONS FOR DISCUSSION OR SELF-REFLECTION

1. Why do you think it is important for an organization to be concerned about continuous improvement in its processes?

2. There is no consensus in the value of determining best practices. Do you think best practices obtained in other organizations is of value or not? Why?

3. If you were going to benchmark your company or your school with another, what process might you consider using? What steps would you follow, and what would be required on your part?

4. What are the ethical questions that might need to be considered in conducting a benchmarking project?

5. All of the processes that have been discussed in this chapter have, at one time or another, been treated as a fad rather than a core business process. What constitutes a fad? Why do you think businesses treat these processes as fads rather than embedding them in their cultures?

6. A sociotechnical systems approach requires that the organization pay attention to both the people and the technology side of an organization. How well do you think the processes discussed in this chapter meet this criterion?

9

Implementation: Global Level

OVERVIEW   This chapter explores the meaning of culture in a country context, describes the difficulties of changing organizational culture in the midst of varying country cultures, and suggests implications for OD practice in organizations consisting of varying country cultures and subcultures. In addition to considering specific OD-related issues, it also discusses common theories of culture applicable across disciplines, explores the emotional issue of globalization, and provides a self-assessment instrument for discussion purposes.

O f all of the issues confronting the OD field, perhaps one of the most difficult yet most important is the issue of doing OD work across national cultures and borders. We live in a world that is becoming increasingly small, given advances in technology—computers (including e-mail and the Internet), satellite and cable television, and cell phones, all of which enable us to be in touch instantly and always with any part of the world (almost). With few exceptions, all business organizations are impacted by the growing global economy: investment capital flows across the world; currency is exchanged as a commodity; purchases are made from around the globe, frequently from low-wage countries; workers are hired from across the globe (often not even requiring them to relocate); raw materials come from around the globe; the food we eat and the clothes we wear come from a myriad of countries; work is outsourced so that customer service problems in the U.K., for instance, are being addressed by workers in India; and so forth. There is no doubt that we live in a global economy.

For those people in OD, this business and personal reality is full of promise and challenge. As companies become involved increasingly in global contexts, OD professionals must understand: (1) their own culture thoroughly, (2) something of learning about other cultures, (3) what it means to be culturally sensitive, and (4) the difficulty of creating change in an organization's culture when the country culture in which that organization, or subsystem of an organization exists, is different from that of the OD professional or from the larger organization of which it is a subsystem. Each of these issues will be addressed in this chapter. As another type of implementation, Implementation at the Global Level is part of phase 5, as shown in Figure 9.1.

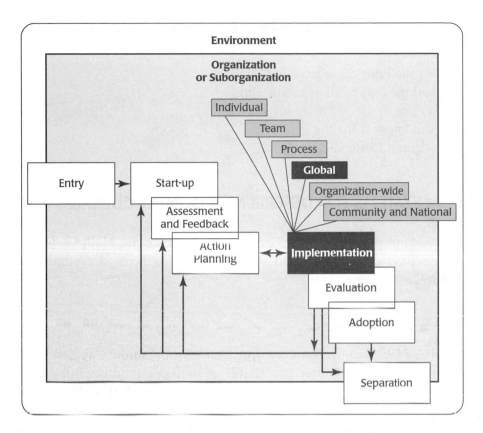

Figure 9.1 *Organization Development Process Model, Phase 5: Implementation at the Global Level*

A useful place to start the discussion is to reference the chart in Chapter 6 associated with the values clarification intervention. You probably had some difficulty in completing the chart. Seldom are we explicit about our own values, let alone the values of the dominant culture in which we live or the relevant subcultures in our own country. It gets even more difficult to think about the culture of other countries, especially when our experiences in those countries are limited. Yet, the starting point for considering global cultures is to understand our own values and our own culture well enough to be able to describe them to others. Once we can begin to do this, we are then in a better position to understand other cultures with which we might come in contact. As the poet T. S. Elliot noted:

> We shall not cease from exploration
> And the end of all our exploring
> Will be to arrive where we started
> And know it for the first time.
> —from "Little Gidding"

SYSTEMS FOR DESCRIBING COUNTRY CULTURES

This section will describe the contributions of Schein, Hall, Hofstede, Trompenaars, and Kluckhohn and Strodtbeck to our understanding of culture.

Schein's Contributions

Schein's (1985) concept of a cultural iceberg or onion was described and illustrated in Chapter 1 to enable us to understand organizational cultures better. This same schema, however, can be used to understand country cultures better. Just as an organization and its members have deeply buried assumptions, so do country cultures, making it very difficult to explain a culture, because assumptions are not something that are at the level of awareness. Thus, many books about cultures, especially travel guides, focus on the more easily explained—the languages, the customs (the do's and don'ts), the dress, the cuisine, the famous landmarks, sports, art, transportation means, the music, the history, currency, and so on. At the beliefs and values level, we often find countries explained in terms of their religions, superstitions, political ideologies, educational philosophies, and career aspirations. That is, these are areas that cannot be seen readily, but, with some probing, people are generally able to share what they believe or value in these arenas.

Assumptions, however, are those things that we *know* to be true, so well that we do not even question them. In many cultures, the following assumptions are simply accepted without question: Girls and boys should not attend school together. If women work, they should stop working when they marry; or, if they still continue to work, they should definitely stop working after childbirth. The primary role of child care belongs to the wife, while the husband has the primary responsibility for earning the family's income. An employee should have at least 4 weeks of vacation a year. (Try telling Italians that they will have only 1 week of vacation a year, and see what response you get! They are accustomed to six, regardless of how long they have been with a company.) Employees should retire at age 65. In many cultures, there is no awareness that these are even questions that might or should be asked. The assumptions control the answers without the question being asked. So, if one is to understand a culture deeply, it is at the assumption level that one must be knowledgeable.

Within the past 24 hours, I have personally experienced this phenomenon. First, I sent an e-mail to a group of five professional friends in Thailand. I entered their e-mail addresses randomly. One of the recipients was very upset that her name was last in the list. She was sure that I was sending a message that she was the least important person because her name was last. She insisted that, if I really didn't mean anything by the order of the names, they would have appeared in alphabetical order. Her assumption was that the order of the names was important and meaningful; my assumption was that order had no meaning. We have had subsequent conversation about this, and I think that we are both OK with understanding and clarifying our assumptions.

That same day, I was having a conversation in my office with a Japanese colleague. I have an allergic reaction to the many books in my office, so I had to blow my nose. In the U.S. culture, blowing one's nose is preferable to sniffling. In the Japanese culture and some other Asian cultures, blowing one's nose is considered rude. Realizing that from my Asian experiences, I turned my back and blew softly, but I was still reminded by my colleague that this was rude. It was—but only under the assumptions of her culture, not mine. So understanding one's assumptions becomes extremely important in doing cross-cultural work.

A comprehensive definition of *corporate culture* often cited is that of Schein (1985):

> Basic assumptions and beliefs that are shared by members of an organization, that operate unconsciously, and that define in a basic "taken-for-granted" fashion an organization's view of itself and its environment. These assumptions and beliefs are learned responses to a group's problems. They come to be taken for granted because they solve those problems repeatedly and reliably. (pp. 6–7)

While this definition is used to describe corporate or organizational culture, it applies equally to national culture or subgroups within national boundaries.

Culture, then, according to Marquardt, Berger, and Loan (2004), includes the following elements:

- A way of thinking, acting, and living
- [It] is *shared* by members of a group.
- Older members *pass* on to new members.
- Culture *shapes* the group's and each member's conscious and sub-conscious values, assumptions, perceptions, and behavior.
- It provides the group with systemic guidelines for how they should conduct their thinking, actions, rituals, and business. (p. 5)

Two technical and controversial terms often used in discussing culture are *emics*, the study of a culture by those who are part of that culture that leads to consensus by those who are inside the culture, and *etics*, the study of a culture by those outside the culture using scientific methods that must meet the test of scientific validity and reliability (Headland, Pike, & Harris, 1990). While this construct emerged from anthropological research, it has been widely used, and often reinterpreted, by other fields of study, including education and management.

Employees who are working internationally need to be aware of both the etics and the emics of the cultures in which they are working. However, in this world of easy transportation by air, it is not unusual for consultants, executives, and employees with special expertise to be in one country one week and in another the next. It may no longer be feasible or efficient for large numbers of global sojourners to learn a specific culture because they are not in a specific culture long enough to learn it well or to apply what they have learned about that culture.

Thus, many will find themselves working in cultures they will not understand well.

Hall's Contributions

Hall (1976) suggested that five primary variables distinguish high- and low-context cultures. A *high-context culture* is one that has implicit values, whereas a *low-context culture* has explicit values. Thus, a sojourner to Japan, a high-context culture, needs to understand that the culture does not state explicitly what is expected but assumes that people know what is appropriate or inappropriate, when decisions have been made, and when they are still under consideration. In contrast, a sojourner to the United States, a low-context culture, will get a little more help because expectations are stated explicitly (with job descriptions, policies manuals, performance goals, etc.). Hall referred to his model as the "silent language of culture," because so much of how culture affects individuals is unspoken.

The five categories in which Hall differentiated between high- and low-context cultures are

- time (mono- vs. polychronic),
- space,
- material possessions,
- friendships, and
- agreements.

A comparison of high- and low-context cultures appears in Table 9.1. The variables described in the comparisons between low- and high-context cultures include ones that have an impact on information exchange, or communications. Hall also made distinctions between cultures that have a *polychronic time culture* and those that have a *monochromic time culture* (see Table 9.2).

What is so critical to understand about Hall's contribution (and others who have explored differences in cultures) is that one type of culture is not better than the other; they are simply different. When involved in negotiations or interactions, it is easy for someone who is inexperienced in cross-cultural interactions (and even sometimes those who are experienced) to become frustrated and expect those from other

TABLE 9.1 Comparison of High- and Low-Context Cultures Based on Hall's Theories

HIGH-CONTEXT	LOW-CONTEXT
▪ Do not require a detailed exchange of information ▪ Rely on the knowledge they already have about the individual before the interaction ▪ Believe that status of the individual affects communication	▪ Prefer explicit, detailed exchange of information when two or more individuals are conducting business ▪ Commonly use facts, figures, and future projections in situations

TABLE 9.2 Comparison of Polychronic and Monochronic Time Cultures Based on Hall's Theories

POLYCHRONIC TIME CULTURES	MONOCHRONIC TIME CULTURES
▪ Are prone to multitasking and doing many things at once ▪ Are subject to interruptions ▪ Are committed to human relations ▪ Change plans often ▪ Base punctuality on the relationship with the person being visited	▪ Tend to be linear and do one thing at a time ▪ Treat time commitments consistently ▪ Adhere to long-term plans ▪ Follow rules of privacy ▪ Show respect for private property ▪ Emphasize promptness

cultures to behave the way we behave. Understanding how culture affects one's behaviors, however, can help remind us that we are simply operating under a different set of expectations.

· ·

During a trip in Calcutta, India, I was at the airport waiting to check in for a flight to Dhaka, Bangladesh. The process for checking in at this particular airport was pretty chaotic. Instead of a straight-line queue, there was a V-shaped wedge leading to the check-in counter. People were climbing over suitcases to get to the front of the queue. Two European men were in front of me in line, as we tried to form an organized queue, and it was apparent that they were becoming increasingly frustrated as they viewed what was happening. I had been through this process before, and I knew that we would all eventually get checked in, so I wasn't concerned. But, finally, it got to be too much for them, and one of them shouted out, "The problem with you people is that you don't have any system!" Of course they had a system; it just wasn't the kind of system to which this passenger was accustomed. He didn't understand his own assumptions for "how things should be" and was expecting others to behave as he was accustomed to behaving in Europe, being unwilling to adjust to the behaviors in Calcutta!

Hofstede's Contributions

Hofstede, under contract with IBM, explored a very large sample of employees in the 1960s for differences in country cultures based on a common company culture. He has generously allowed others to use his instrument, subsequently leading to a very large database that has expanded the number of countries and has allowed for updated profiles of countries, extending way beyond the original single-company sample.

More recently, Hofstede (2001) identified five variables on which he has claimed that country cultures, even those with considerable diversity, can be compared:

- **Individualism versus collectivism** entails, on the one hand, *individualism*—characterized by ties between individuals that are loose, with an emphasis on nuclear families—and, on the other hand, *collectivism*, in which people from birth onward are integrated into strong, cohesive in-groups, with an emphasis on extended families.

- **Power distance** is the extent to which less powerful members of the organization accept and expect uneven distribution of power. Small power distance suggests equality; large power distance suggests inequality.

- **Masculinity versus femininity** suggests whether a culture supports traditional masculine behaviors or traditional female behaviors, according to European norms. Masculine cultures have achievement as a motivator, social gender roles are clearly distinct, and people "live to work," whereas feminine cultures have relationship building as a motivator, social gender roles overlap, and people "work to live."

- **Uncertainty avoidance** is the extent to which members of a culture feel threatened by uncertain or unknown situations. Those with low uncertainty avoidance are willing to take risks, whereas those with high uncertainty avoidance are uncomfortable with uncertainty.

- **Confucian dynamism,** based on Confucian philosophy (dominant in eastern Asia, including China, Korea, and Japan), refers to short- and long-term perspectives; the emphasis is on what one does, not what one believes.

Several Web sites display scores on these five variables for a wide range of countries (see, e.g., www.cyborlink.com). They are easy to find with a search engine.

Recently I spent some time with a group of business executives from Guangzhou, People's Republic of China (PRC). We used the Hofstede framework to discuss differences and similarities between the two countries. Based on the Hofstede data, the two countries compare as follows on Hofstede's five criteria:

Factor	U.S.	PRC
Power distance	40	76
Uncertainty avoidance	46	36
Masculinity	62	50
Individualism	91	11
Confucian dynamism (long-term orientation)	29	96

Interesting dialogue ensued around these data. Participants argued that the "new Chinese" were not like this at all, that they were much more short-term thinkers and individually oriented, in contrast to what the numbers in this listing suggest. (The power distance statistics, however, were not questioned.) This point raises the criticism that has been leveled against Hofstede's data from the beginning: that it is dangerous to provide countrywide data because there are so many differences internally. Nevertheless, Hofstede has insisted that, in spite of internal differences, the statistics still suggest country-based differences.

Trompenaars's Contributions

Trompenaars (1994) also developed a set of variables that he claimed were useful in describing culture. These are similar to those suggested by Hofstede, with a somewhat finer distinction within some of the variables:

- Universalism versus pluralism (rules and procedures or relationships)
- Individualism versus communitarianism (me or the group)
- Specific versus diffuse (deep relationships or superficial)
- Neutrality versus affectivity (conceal or show emotions)
- Inner directed versus outer directed (ourselves or the environment around us)
- Achieved status versus ascribed status (what you do or who you are)
- Sequential time versus synchronic time (one after another or all at once)

Contributions of Kluckhohn and Strodtbeck

Kluckhohn and Strodtbeck (1961) suggested that culture orientation can be described with six variables:

- Relation to nature (subjugate, harmony, or mastery)
- Time orientation (past, present, or future)
- Basic human nature (evil, neutral, or good)
- Activity orientation (being, controlling, or doing)
- Relationship among people (individualistic, group, or hierarchy)
- Space orientation (private, mixed, or public)

STEREOTYPES AND GENERALIZATIONS

When we discuss theories about culture in class, my students frequently ask, "Aren't these theories just supporting stereotypes?" "How is this different from saying that U.S. Americans are loud and rude, or that Canadians have ice in their veins?" This reaction forces a discussion about stereotypes versus generalizations.

A *stereotype* is "a type of categorization that organizes previous experiences and guides future behavior regarding various groups" (Konopaske & Ivancevich, 2004, p. 148). Stereotypes can be both helpful and problematic. They are helpful because they give us a starting point to start thinking about some other culture. It would be impossible to interact if we had to begin from a zero point with everyone with whom we interact. They can also be problematic, however, in that, if no questions are raised about stereotypes, they can be applied inaccurately or inappropriately to people who do not fit the stereotype. So, though it may be true that most Canadians live in very cold climates (at least during the winter), many Canadians live in relatively temperate climates (e.g., those in Vancouver, British Columbia). And, while many U.S. Americans may be perceived as being rude because some tourists do not learn the norms of behavior in countries they visit, many more do.

Generalizations, however, are somewhat different from stereotypes. Rather than being based on experiences, as a stereotype is, they are based on data and apply to a majority of the members of a specific culture or subculture. Through variation, there is recognition that not everyone fits the conclusions. Furthermore, with additional research, the conclusions leading to the generalizations can be modified.

The distinction between stereotypes and generalizations based on research is extremely important for the OD professional. As Marquardt et al. (2004) advised:

> If coming from the United States, the [OD] professional usually represents the "typical American," along with the stereotypes associated with that culture. [U.S.] Americans are often described as impatient, individualistic, hardworking, self-centered, outgoing, open, and wealthy. . . . An [OD] practitioner needs to be conscious of stereotypical expectations. (p. 60)

I frequently receive comments in my international work that the person is surprised by my knowledge of the culture in which I am working, my willingness to try new foods, and my sensitivity to cultural and religious values. They often add, "That must be the Canadian part of who you are, because Americans aren't like that." Of course, there are Canadians who aren't like that (whatever "that" means in their eyes), and there are lots of Americans who *are* like that (again, whatever "that" means). Such overgeneralization is what happens when people do not adequately challenge their stereotypes.

GLOBALIZATION

Globalization is a word that generates considerable emotion, often negative. Yet, it is clear that globalization is inevitable (McLean, 2001), and, as Adler (2002) observed, "It is time for people to move beyond an awareness of the urgency of global competition and begin to develop skills for success in the global arena" (p. 3). According to Marquardt et al. (2004), "Globalization both symbolizes and creates a convergence of economic and social forces, values and tastes, challenges and opportunities" (p. 3).

Perspective (1998) has made the following observations about globalization:

> Globalization is dynamic and real, causing numerous and often radical changes in all but the most remote places. Depending on your point of view, circumstances, and prospects, the process can be seen as hugely positive—or grossly negative. But the issue of globalization and our collective response to it promises to define who prospers and who will not do well into the 21st century.
>
> Inasmuch as the pain caused by some aspects of globalization is undeniable, the real issue is whether the negative effects of its sweeping processes can be ameliorated—and the positive effects enhanced. Because, without doubt, the forward march of globalization itself is unstoppable.
>
> The negative effects of globalization can be softened only through new and higher levels of international cooperation and

consultation, filtered through a new system of moral values that puts human welfare and social justice ahead of the predominantly materialistic paradigm currently in vogue. The urgency for all peoples everywhere to cooperate together . . . can never be over-emphasized.

BECOMING A GLOBAL ORGANIZATION

Heenan and Perlmutter (1979) provided a useful model for identifying how individual organizations can be classified according to the extent that the organizations view their management potential as being global. Their *EPRG model* suggests four different approaches to how organizations might function:

Ethnocentrism – *Ethnocentrism* describes a preference for putting home-country people in key positions everywhere in the world and rewarding them more handsomely for work, along with a tendency to feel that this group is more intelligent, more capable, or more reliable than people from that nation.

Polycentrism – Cultures of various countries are quite dissimilar, foreigners are difficult to understand, and the organizations in that nation should be left alone as long as their work is profitable.

Regiocentrism – Advantages exist in recruiting, developing, appraising, and assigning managers on a regional basis.

Geocentrism – Integration occurs in diverse regions through a global systems approach to decision making.

The difference between an ethnocentric and geocentric organization is displayed graphically in Figure 9.2.

As an OD professional working in organizations that likely represent each of these models, it is helpful to understand which model best describes each organization. Then, as part of the assessment process and feedback phase, this information can be fed back to the client organization. It may be that the organization thinks they are more geocentric than they are. Helping them understand these four models can help them decide what they might do to redirect their focus.

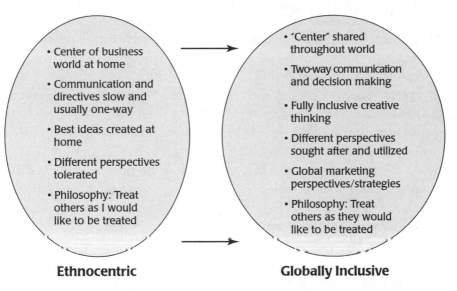

Ethnocentric   **Globally Inclusive**

Figure 9.2 *Corporate Worldview (from Tolbert, McLean, & Myers, 2002, p. 464; used with permission)*

OD INTERVENTIONS IN GLOBAL CONTEXTS

Most OD interventions focused on developing global organizations are not different from any of the other interventions suggested in this book, except that they may need modification based on individual cultural differences. The primary intervention that is used in a global context is training. Other interventions described here include global learning organizations, virtual team building, cross-cultural team building, cultural self-awareness, storytelling/sharing, job assignments, and blending. Each of these was described briefly in Chapter 5; those requiring more explanation as to the processes to be used are expanded on in this chapter.

Cross-cultural Training

As indicated in Chapter 5, a variety of approaches may be used to provide cross-cultural training. Unfortunately, much training that is offered is atheoretical and tends to focus on the do's and don'ts of traveling to other cultures. The U.S. State Department maintains a Web site on which information about most countries in the world is posted. This posting provides useful and relatively up-to-date information and, along with a commercial travel guide, can offer most of the *cognitive information* needed by a sojourner. From the list provided in Chapter 5 (p. 116), we may conclude that this is the least effective of all of the approaches to preparing people for an international or other cross-cultural assignment.

As we go further in the list, we see that the power of the training increases. A number of *experiential approaches* can be taken. One very popular simulation experience that participants consistently report as deeply moving and life changing is Bafa Bafa (Shirts, 1977), a group game where two teams take on the identity of two fantasy cultures, both of which have detailed and very different rules. Individuals then visit the other culture and attempt to assimilate into that culture by determining what its "rules" are and attempt to follow them. What is always amazing is that, during the debrief, after just an hour and a half, people have already identified with their culture and usually do not want to move to the other culture, even though their culture may have values that are not consistent with their own personal values. Participants also find out that they have quickly formed stereotypes about the other culture. When they discover how much of this has occurred in such a short time, they realize how deeply engrained their own stereotypes are and how difficult it is to move into another culture. This is the richness of experience that can never be duplicated through simply cognitive training.

Interaction with people from a target culture can be very useful in preparing to live in that culture, and it does not necessarily require moving to that country to have such an experience. Most universities have students enrolled who come from other countries. In our HRD program at the University of Minnesota, for example, we currently have students from 36 countries, and the university has students from more than 100 countries. Students will typically enjoy interacting with others about their country. Furthermore, people in metropolitan areas are likely to find pockets of various cultures. In the St. Paul–Minneapolis area, we have pockets of people, in addition to Native Americans, from Mexico, China, Vietnam, Laos, Cambodia, Korea, the Caribbean islands, Canada, many African countries, and so on. Each of these groups has more than 10,000 people in this one metropolitan area.

Every year, there is a Scottish Fair, a Celtic Fair, Cinco de Mayo, a Hmong festival, Kwanzaa events, and so on. Each of these will give the sojourner an opportunity to experience cultures of potential interest first hand without having to leave the country.

In an organizational setting, it would be relatively easy to bring together a panel of people from a range of cultures to share their experiences of coming to the country in which the organization is located. They could also share what you might expect in traveling to their country. Some companies ensure that potential assignees to another culture get an experience in that culture by sending them and their families to that country prior to their assignment for a week to one month. While this tactic might appear on the surface to be expensive, if it improves the likelihood of a successful assignment, it is well worth it.

Attribution or *culture assimilator* is a brief story containing a problem with a number of answers from which trainees are to select the right answer or best response. A culture assimilator is created by interviewing a number of people in the target culture and people who are experienced in traveling to that culture. The purpose of the first round of interviews is to identify stories that caused problems for those traveling to that country or that those in the country experienced as problematic from those who are traveling there. Once stories have been identified, a second round of interviews is conducted to identify responses used in the circumstances identified in the problem story. Finally, in the third stage, people experienced in the culture identify the best response. The author then provides a rationale for why that is the best answer and why the other options are not the best. Trainees select the option that they think is best, discussing their responses in small groups. The facilitator then shares the rationale provided by the author of the assimilator. See Appendix 9.1 at the end of this chapter for a sample focused on Venezuela (Tolbert & McLean, 1995).

An *integrated approach* simply means more than one of these approaches being offered to the same trainee(s). Although the benefits are clear, the costs in both time and financial resources go up.

Global Learning Organization

A process for creating a global learning organization within a corporate setting has been developed (Tolbert, McLean, & Myers, 2002). The process is depicted graphically in Figure 9.3.

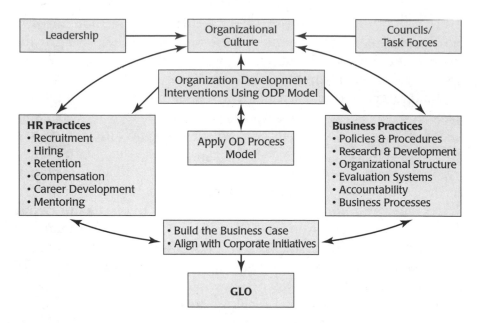

Figure 9.3 *Process for Creating a Global Learning Organization (Tolbert, McLean, and Myers, 2002; used with permission)*

According to Tolbert et al. (2002), the tenets within which the globally inclusive GLO change process is conducted are as follows:

- Create change buy-in and enrolment at all levels
- Provide effective leadership modeling and articulation of global vision
- Conduct culture audit, qualitative and quantitative, for designing OD interventions
- Create ownership of OD change interventions at all levels and functions
- Provide extensive team-building and empowerment opportunities
- Focus on personal and organizational work at the cognitive, affective, and behavioral levels
- Design training and education processes around learner readiness
- Build accountabilities for globalization into employee and executive performance management systems
- Link globalization efforts with all other corporate initiatives

- Provide measurement for progress around OD change efforts
- Provide challenge and support for all employees (p. 468)

Virtual Team Building

In some respects, virtual international or cross-cultural team building can be easier and more effective than face-to-face team building. Bringing together a group of people from a variety of cultures on a synchronous or asynchronous Web chat can be less threatening to people from some cultures than requiring them to speak in the presence of someone else, especially if power distance is a factor. Language can be an interesting variable in this process. Often people find it easier to read and write in a second language than they do conversing in that language. Conversely, people could feel more inhibited knowing that everyone on the chat will read what they are saying.

But Web chats are not the only way to build a virtual team. Video-conferences, teleconferences, and Webcams are other ways to create teams virtually, though each of these approaches is likely to be more challenging for team members for whom the language in use is not the native language.

Virtual team building can be enhanced in several ways, particularly on the Web. First, it can be very helpful to have people post a photograph of themselves and even of their families. A brief biography can also be helpful. Suggesting a set of etiquette guidelines for carrying on the Web chat in a respectful way, recognizing the cultures involved, can help to avoid some of the common problems that might occur through the reduced inhibitions that occur through web chats (see Appendix 9.2 for an example of such guidelines). Once the cultures from which the team members come are known, it is also possible to provide all participants with brief vignettes about each culture, supplemented by URLs (Web site addresses) that will provide additional information. Mediating the chat by a culturally mature individual (perhaps the OD professional) can also be helpful. When a breach of cultural sensitivity occurs, the OD professional can step in and explain what the breach was and how it might be avoided in the future. A potential problem, however, is that people from some cultures will be very upset with what they perceive as public criticism. In that case, the mediator may wish to send a private e-mail to the person who made a cultural faux pas.

Cross-cultural Team Building

In contrast with virtual cross-cultural team building, what is being referenced here is a face-to-face team building. As indicated in Chapter 7, the most effective team building is what emerges from the natural business of the team. When people from different cultures come together naturally in a work team environment, the facilitator will likely find it useful to have people share the stories of their backgrounds, including their cultural backgrounds. The OD facilitator could be prepared ahead of time to introduce to the team the implications of having this particular mix of cultures working together, being careful to stipulate that individuals might well be different from the generalizations that exist about each culture. Furthermore, as with the virtual team building, the OD professional should be prepared to use his or her process consultation skills to reflect back to the team any instances in which cultural norms have been violated. This will require that the OD professional be well grounded in his or her own culture and knowledgeable about a wide range of cultures, and it may require more than one OD professional, representing more than one culture.

Cultural Self-Awareness

The importance of cultural self-awareness cannot be overstated. In Chapter 6 (Appendix 6.2), you completed an exercise that asked you to think about your own culture, as well as other cultures. In this chapter, in Appendix 9.3, is another exercise to help you understand your own values. A third exercise is included in this chapter, too—a work in progress that might help you see yourself in different cultural contexts (see Appendix 9.4). Anything that can be used to help individuals understand their own culture and their own cultural awareness will assist in preparing them for global assignments or participation with team members from other cultures. (More details about Appendices 9.3 and 9.4 are in the Questions for Discussion section at the end of this chapter.

Storytelling/Sharing

The narrative or storytelling can be a rich source of information about cultures that will help others learn about a specific culture. Autobiographies (Karpiak, 2005) can be a valuable source of reflection for the individual (about both life events and the meaning of life in a cultural context) and for others with whom the stories are shared. Having people who are preparing to participate in an assignment in a different culture or having team members from different cultures write chapters of their lives can be a rich learning experience.

There are other ways in which stories can be valuable sources of cultural information. Simply looking at the proverbs that are popular in a country, for example, may say much about that culture's values. Consider the following examples and what they might imply about the various cultures:

U.S. Proverbs
Waste not, want not.

He who holds the gold makes the rules.

If at first you don't succeed, try, try again.

The early bird gets the worm.

Chinese Proverbs
A man who waits for a roast duck to fly into his mouth must wait a very, very long time.

A man who says it cannot be done should not interrupt a man doing it.

Give a man a fish, and he will live a day; give him a net, and he will live a lifetime.

Other Proverbs
No one is either rich or poor who has not helped himself to be so. (German)

Words do not make flour. (Italian)

Wealth that comes in at the door unjustly, goes out at the windows. (Egyptian)

Discussing the cultural implications of such proverbs, and adding to these, can be a helpful introduction into a culture.

Likewise, looking at fairy tales or children's stories can communicate what the older generation is trying to convey to children about that culture. Consider "Goldilocks and the Three Bears"; the message of this story is moderation in all things. Metaphors and similes, likewise, provide rich insight into a culture. Of course, locating these materials can be time-consuming and probably not cost-effective for an individual sojourner. But in a context where many individuals are likely to be involved, the time spent can be very worthwhile.

Although not for public consumption, a diary or journal, written while going through training or while on an assignment in a different culture, can provide another useful source of information for reflection—about both your own culture and the culture you are experiencing. It can also be helpful in analyzing your responses to specific cultural contexts, so you can learn from the experiences and modify your responses to those cultural contexts for the future.

Job Assignments

One of the most effective ways to help someone in an assignment in a different culture is to provide adequate support before the journey, during the journey, and on the return from the journey. We've already talked about ways to prepare people for a journey. While on the journey, you can support them through a Web site, through active e-mail communication, and through a group of support people in that culture. Support after return can occur through debriefing, giving the person time to readjust to the culture, ensuring that newfound knowledge and expertise are used, connecting the person with others who have had a similar experience, providing a job comparable to the one before the assignment, and so on. The point here is that people working in a different culture need a guided experience to maximize what they gain from the direct involvement in another culture.

Blending

Helping organizations to blend the best of what exists in their organization wherever it is found around the world can be a challenging and rewarding experience. This process requires understanding cultural contexts so that immutable cultural norms are not violated, but it also means taking risks in violating cultural norms that you perceive are not as critical as others. How this might be done is illustrated in the following case of Sumitomo 3M in Japan (McLean, Kaneko, & van Dijk, 2003).

This case study shares the journey of Takekazu Kaneko, executive vice president of Sumitomo 3M Limited (Japan) during his 3-year sojourn at 3M Corporate Headquarters in St. Paul, Minnesota, resulting in the development of 21 action plans to change HR policies and systems to be implemented on his return to Japan as executive vice president. The case study presents the process whereby the 21 action plans were developed, the process of implementing them on Kaneko's return to Japan, and the resulting outcomes.

Action Plans for Cultural Change

Takekazu Kaneko, as head of the finance department, became something of a "hero" within 3M when he successfully guided the 3M Company in Japan through the very difficult currency crisis of 1997, making a profit for the company while other companies were losing significant amounts of money. Following this experience, he was assigned to headquarters in St. Paul, in part for acculturation purposes, in part to prepare him for a more senior management role in Japan, and in part to serve in the top finance position for 3M's Asia–Pacific Region. In this role, he had the opportunity to travel extensively, "together with top 3M executives, giving him plenty of opportunities to get to know each other well and to exchange views on a variety of subjects" (Gundling, 2003, p. 312). Gundling (2003), a consultant who was actively involved in supporting Kaneko's journey, has briefly described some of the process leading to the development of the action plans.

Part of Kaneko's assignment was to prepare for his return to Japan at the end of his assignment to assume the role as VP of HR in the company. He had extensive conversations with HR professionals at headquarters and HR professionals from Europe. He also had extensive conversations (estimated at 120) with stakeholders in Japan. A number of benchmarking meetings also were held with HR professionals in other companies in Japan, both locally and foreign owned.

Another major factor in the development of a set of action plans was Kaneko's involvement in a 1-year weekly seminar for high-potential HR managers at 3M's headquarters. These seminars were conducted by John Fossum, representing human resources and industrial relations, also a professor at the University of Minnesota, and me, representing HRD. Our assignment was to facilitate a weekly seminar that would challenge 3M's culture based on current research. I met twice with Kaneko and Gundling to review the action plans that Kaneko was preparing for implementation on his return to Japan.

The purpose of the action plans was to create "a new corporate culture" that would accelerate "employee innovation and business growth with a personal sense of freedom, excitement and accountability" (Kaneko, 2000, p. 1). The 21 systems to be impacted, with the actions to be implemented, were developed as follows (later to be referred to as HR Plan 21):

1. Compensation: Overhaul system for managers; implement new system for general employees
2. Job Grade: Define and open for management employees; implement for general employees
3. Dual Ladder: Redesign to attract technical people
4. Promotion: Reduce minimum age requirements; positive promotion of excellent young employees
5. High Potential: Identify high potential employees; provide leadership training.
6. Job Posting: Build system for below manager level
7. Training Programs for Senior Employees: Develop new system
8. Information Sharing and Employee Participation: Create more communication channels; promote information disclosure
9. Corporate Structure: Change number of Board Members and reduce one management layer
10. Relations with Labor Union: Increase communication and collaboration
11. Position Retirement: Restructure system
12. Education and Training: Develop and modify existing programs; introduce six sigma and coaching
13. Utilization of Women: Promote EVE 21 activities; promote sales representatives [for] minor career women; start trial mentoring system

14. Succession Planning: Improve existing process
15. Job Rotation: Focus on Hipo's [high potentials]
16. HR Department Reengineering: Shift paradigm in HR department
17. Recruiting: Improve screening process
18. FSE Assignments and Overseas Travel: Focus on younger employees; change travel policy
19. Pension Fund: Outsource ALM and change investment banks; overhaul pension system
20. Office Environment: Update facilities with women employees' input
21. Dress Code: [Implement] business casual (Kaneko, 2000, pp. 2–3)

I expressed considerable skepticism about the probability of these action plans succeeding, in spite of the extensive collaboration that had occurred. I especially raised concern about how culturally appropriate the action plans were to impact the seniority system currently in place and the lack of opportunities for women in the Japanese company. Although Kaneko agreed that these would be difficult, he also indicated that they were important action plans, both from his own value set and from the perspective of headquarters and employees and management in Japan. In 2000, Kaneko returned to Japan as executive vice president of human resources (and several other functional areas).

Implementation of Action Plans
At the time of Kaneko's return to Japan, the company was still typically Japanese—"lifetime employment, promotion by seniority, and a company union" (Gundling, 2003, p. 312). The first thing that was needed to implement the action plans was to gain additional support from other members of senior management. Surprisingly, this process went amazingly smoothly. Two other major stakeholders were not so easily convinced: the union (and senior employees) and supervisors. Several meetings were held with both groups to clarify the implications of each action plan and discuss the advantages of each to both groups. The slippage in the Japanese economy added additional stress, requiring more early retirements and greater performance management.

Some formal steps were undertaken. Kaneko "created an HR reform steering committee composed of key company opinion makers, and another advisory group of employees representing different functions, ages, and genders" (Gundling, 2003, p. 314). Kaneko also appointed a woman manager, brought personnel with strong business experience into HR, and made some basic policy changes, such as changing the dress code and displaying employee art. Other action plans were pilot tested before widespread implementation.

Success in Implementing the Action Plans
Three years later, in 2003, I met with Kaneko at Sumitomo 3M headquarters in Tokyo to discuss the outcome of the action plans. At that time, all 21 of the systems had been implemented to various extents. As I had predicted in 2000, the two areas that proved to be most difficult were the improved use of women and items related to job seniority, both of which are deeply entrenched in the Japanese culture.

Nevertheless, as Gundling (2003) observed:

> More changes have taken place in human resources practices at Sumitomo 3M than anyone would have previously thought possible—all aligned with the corporate goals of accelerating the pace of growth while increasing operating efficiency in total, nineteen of twenty-one changes proposed in Kaneko-san's initial plan have been implemented or are under way. . . . The effects of the change effort have predictably affected the company's atmosphere and, in spite of the tough economic climate, Sumitomo 3M has become the most profitable location for the company worldwide. (pp. 314–315)

After the HR Plan 21 was completed, it was evaluated by an ad hoc task force team led by a business executive director. The conclusion was that the work environment had improved by implementing the new corporate culture, and, while impossible to prove a direct cause-effect relationship, significant improvements occurred following the implementation of the HR Plan 21 (see Table 9.3).

TABLE 9.3 Apparent Financial Benefits from HR Plan 21

MEASURE	1998–2001 PREIMPLEMENTATION ANNUALIZED GROWTH (%)	2002–2003 POSTIMPLEMENTATION ANNUALIZED GROWTH (%)
Sales	4.6	8.1
Profitability	7.1	22.0
New product sales	8.5	11.1
Productivity	5.0	11.7

In spite of these excellent performance figures, there was a perceived need to continue to shift to a more contemporary corporate culture to provide more freedom and excitement for employees. Kaneko (2003) himself concluded, "We completed our goal—the introduction of the programs—at the end of March 2003, as planned" (p. 1). While acknowledging the changes in culture, Kaneko (2003) also acknowledged the need for continuous improvement:

> Have you stopped thinking about age or gender in the work place? Is feedback about your personnel rating or coaching honest and open? Can you operate beyond organizational barriers? Can you gain the new experiences you have planned for your career-building without difficulty? Is information communicated appropriately and timely to every corner of the organization? In reflecting on these questions, many of you may answer, "Not enough or not yet." (p. 1)

He went on to underscore the importance of a new 2-year corporate culture change effort, designed to "create a company that can grow under any economic situation, by fostering independent and energetic employees with a spirit for challenge" (p. 2). To bring about this ongoing cultural change, the task force team developed critical business culture components using six sigma methodology.

Conclusions about Blending

Based on this case, the following characteristics may be necessary to make corporate change, generally as well as specifically across cultures:

1. Support from top management at headquarters is critical.

2. Widespread involvement of employees and management in the Japanese company made the transformation more likely.

3. Provision of extensive training and development for the change agent assisted in preparation for the change process.

4. Selection of a change agent with an extensive record of previous successes dramatically increased the chances for success.

5. Benchmarking of *processes* used by other Japanese companies highlighted areas where culture change was most likely to succeed with the Japanese culture.

6. Sufficient (and extensive) time was provided to develop a detailed and well-thought-through set of action plans.

7. Sensitive culture change is possible even when it is counter to national culture.

8. Culture change is most likely when the benefits of the changes are obvious to those affected by the changes.

9. Use of the PDCA (Plan-Do-Check-Act) Cycle, with a pilot implementation before widespread implementation, helps to identify changes in the process that will improve the outcome. (McLean, Kaneko, & van Dijk, 2003, 1-1-1-7)

DESIRABLE CHARACTERISTICS FOR PEOPLE ENGAGED IN GLOBAL OD WORK

Not every OD professional will be competent to work across cultures. Researchers have made many attempts to identify the desirable characteristics for those involved in cross-cultural, international work. For example, from their review of the literature, Marquardt et al. (2004) identified the following mix of characteristics and competencies needed by successful global HRD consultants:

- Cultural self-awareness
- Knowledge and appreciation of other cultures
- Global perspective and mind-set
- Respect for the values and practices of other cultures
- Cultural flexibility, adjustment, and resiliency
- Acculturize training programs and events
- Communication skills
- Cultural empathy
- Patience and sense of humor
- Commitment to continuous learning (p. 77)

McLean, Tolbert, and Larkin (2005) conducted a thorough review of the literature in support of developing the instrument in Appendix 9.4. The instrument is provided here for discussion only, as it is still a work in progress. We concluded that the professional working across cultures is likely to be most successful if he or she has the following characteristics:

- Flexibility
  Is reflective
  Is willing to think "outside the box"
  Is willing to change behaviors

- Adaptability
  Can actually change behaviors

- Cultural awareness/values
  Values other cultures
  Values one's own culture
  Knows one's own culture
  Values diversity
  Knows other cultures

- Ambiguity
  Is comfortable with the unknown
  Doesn't need to be right
  Finds it acceptable not to have one answer
  Realizes multiple answers exist

- Relationships
  Demonstrates resiliency

Genuinely likes people

Has a sense of humor

Has sound communication skills (speaking, listening)

- Motives (why an individual wants to work cross-culturally)

Cares about career development (impacts experience positively)

Is interested in personal growth (impacts experience positively)

Has a sense of adventure (impacts experience positively)

Wants to help others—mutual (impacts experience positively)

Wants to escape current circumstances (impacts experience negatively)

Wants bragging rights (impacts experience negatively)

Feigns "helping" others—nonreciprocal (impacts experience negatively)

These are also the factors measured with the instrument in Appendix 9.4.

In Marquardt et al.'s (2004) view,

> to be effective across cultures, [OD] professionals must be aware of the impact of language, verbal and nonverbal; recognize the cultural aspects that impact the delivery of the program and adjust their delivery accordingly; plan logistics, such as scheduling sessions and meals, around the norms of the local culture; and use the most appropriate methods for evaluating results and providing feedback. (p. 69)

CHALLENGES FACING GLOBAL OD PROFESSIONALS

As interesting as doing OD is in a global context, there are many challenges. A partial list follows:

- **Corruption** in some countries is taken for granted, and to work in those countries, you may have to accept a certain level of corruption. You will need to struggle with where your own values are and how they influence the work that you do. (See more about corruption in Chapter 15.)

- **Language** is a major conveyor of culture. When you work in a culture whose language you do not know, requiring that your

host use your language or that you use an interpreter, you lose
a lot of information about the culture and the business context.
Using an interpreter also cuts down on the amount of communication that takes place—everything takes at least twice as long
to say. I have also had difficulty in working with interpreters
who wanted to do much more than just translate; they also
wanted to add their own observations and comments, and I
was never sure exactly what was being said or added.

- **Travel** requires you to be away from your family and friends,
  sometimes for long periods. Living in a hotel, eating all meals
  out, and flying from country to country may sound appealing
  in the beginning, but it can quickly lead to loneliness and
  stress. If you are an introvert, such stress can quickly become
  overbearing.

- **Lack of resources** may be a problem. Often the organizations
  with which you might most like to work may simply not have
  the resources to pay you more than your travel expenses. This
  is certainly truer in some countries than in others. My answer
  to this is to take such jobs if I believe I can make a major contribution to humanity and if I believe that I can learn something
  while offering my services. I have also been left wondering
  when my travel expenses haven't been reimbursed after 3
  months whether I would ever see the money. Fortunately, to
  date, I always have. However, many professionals might not be
  able to wait so long for such reimbursement and may not be
  able to take an international consultation if the pay does not
  match their needs.

- **Differences in work ethics** can also surface as an issue. I have a
  strong work ethic. When I am traveling to another country, I
  want to maximize my time there, so I am willing to work hard
  and long hours to accomplish as much as possible. In some
  countries, however, this is seen as crazy behavior. If we don't
  stop for an early afternoon break and a 4-hour dinner, then we
  haven't affirmed our relationship. So I must battle with my own
  work ethic to support the desires of those from the host culture.

- As a North American, I also have a *concept of time* that supports the notion of "use it or lose it." This point adds to my work

ethic issue, and I have to work hard at keeping time in its proper perspective for that country. It is actually a good feeling to be working in a culture where time is not something that "gets used up," and I can relax a little and not feel as pressured by time.

- **Conflict** is another area in which the OD consultant needs to be very aware. As a process consultant, part of our task is to give feedback. Yet, receiving feedback, especially publicly, can be a major source of loss of face in some cultures. Likewise, public disagreement can also be seen as unacceptable. During a team-teaching experience in the United States where a colleague and I publicly disagreed about a theory, the Asian students in the audience were noticeably afraid. We asked them what was going on for them, and they indicated that they were afraid that verbal disagreement would lead to physical violence. We used this as an excellent learning moment to explain the academic value of disagreement and that the two of us were good friends who simply chose to disagree.

- The *role of women* can be restricted in many cultures in which one may choose to work, though Adler (2002) suggested that the opportunities for women in international assignments is almost the same as for men, even in cultures where roles for women in that culture are not the same as for men. Saudi Arabia is a country in which I do a considerable amount of work, and it is difficult even for a non-Saudi woman to work in that context, except in traditional female roles as nurses, teachers, and administrative assistants. How one chooses to deal with this issue as a male will reflect his values. Will working there perhaps open opportunities to change the culture? Is it appropriate to attempt to change the culture, even in small ways, when one feels strongly about a value?

- **Bureaucracy** is another problem that OD professionals might experience in some countries, especially if they come from a culture in which bureaucratic systems are not prevalent or are a little more flexible than the country in which they find themselves.

In spite of these challenges, I have found my work in cultures other than my own to be extremely rewarding. That is not to say that you do not have to be constantly aware of your own culture and the culture in which you are working. And, certainly, there are times when the stress does get overwhelming. In spite of that, however, the rewards, for me, far exceed the challenges. I believe that I grow with every new assignment. I hope you find opportunities you might have for international work to be equally rewarding.

CHAPTER SUMMARY

Preparing an organization to become global has become almost essential for any organization attempting to be competitive in today's global economy. Although globalization does have its drawbacks, it is inevitable that it will continue. Our role as OD professionals, then, is to help our organizations become global.

Many theorists have suggested models to help us understand not only our own culture but also the cultures of others. While never providing a perfect description of any one individual from a culture, the generalizations of these theories and their supporting research can be extremely helpful to the OD professional. A number of specific interventions that might be used by the OD professional include cross-cultural training, global learning organizations, virtual team building, cross-cultural team building, cultural self-awareness, storytelling/sharing, job assignments, and blending.

Finally, this chapter described characteristics of successful professionals working in another culture, along with the challenges facing the OD professional working in a global context.

QUESTIONS FOR DISCUSSION OR SELF-REFLECTION

1. Make a list of everything you can see in the room in which you are reading this chapter. List where you think each product was manufactured. Most products have a label on them indicating where they were manufactured. Think about what you have eaten today (or yesterday). Where was the food grown? What are the implications of this exercise?

2. Describe to someone else what your core values are and where they came from.

3. Describe to someone else the dominant culture of the country in which you live, as well as at least one subculture within that country.

4. How does being able to describe your own values and culture enable you to understand other cultures better?

5. Check one of the Web sites for Hofstede's ideas, and determine the values for your country and one other country of interest to you. Do you agree with what these results show?

6. Appendix 9.3 of this chapter shares a self-assessment tool to help you explore your own stance on several of the variables reviewed. These items are set up as dichotomous variables on several factors related to the purpose of life, space, time, and values. When I use this tool in class, I use a human bar chart approach: Students select items of particular interest, and then they line up according to their response (from 1 to 5). As they stand in their human bar chart, they talk about why they selected the number they did. This quickly leads to the conclusion that there are not "right" and "wrong" answers—only different ones. Otherwise, you might want to complete the exercise and then discuss your responses with a partner.

7. List several stereotypes for a variety of countries. How accurate do you think these stereotypes are? If you believe the stereotype, how would it affect how you would interact with someone from that country?

8. Complete the culture assimilator provided in Appendix 9.1, and then discuss your responses with a partner.

9. Identify four or five of your favorite nursery rhymes, fairy tales, or children's stories. What do they say about your culture and what is considered important in that culture?

10. Identify four or five proverbs that you heard while growing up. What do they say about your culture and what is considered important in that culture?

11. Complete the instrument in Appendix 9.4. Determine your strengths and your weaknesses relative to being a successful OD professional working in a global context. Discuss the results.

APPENDIX 9.1
VENEZUELAN CULTURE ASSIMILATOR
(from Tolbert & McLean, 1995, pp. 14–15; used with permission)

Edward, a U.S. business professional, was having a business lunch with Carlos, the owner of a printing company. Edward was having his company's letterhead printed by Carlos. As they were leaving, Edward wanted to share some new ideas for layouts with Carlos. Carlos said he would be happy to see them. Edward asked if he could bring them by his office the next day, and they could go over them in about an hour or so. Carlos said he would be happy to do it and told him to drop by at about 2 p.m.

The next day Edward went to Carlos' office at 2 P.M., and Carlos was not there. The secretary said that he left at about 1:30, and he would not be returning for the day. Edward said that there must be some mistake as they had made these arrangements yesterday at lunch. The secretary said that she did not have an appointment scheduled, and she was sorry. Edward was very angry about the inconvenience. He was debating about whether or not to cancel his agreement with Carlos and take his business somewhere where he could be better served.

How would you explain the fact that Carlos was not there?

a. Carlos was not interested, and he did not know how to let Edward know. Carlos made the appointment casually hoping that Edward would forget about it.

b. The appointment was agreed upon over a business lunch, and evidently Carlos was not sufficiently organized to remember himself or to call his secretary to tell her to write it down. Thus it was forgotten.

c. Secretaries handle the agenda, and if they are not told about appointments, then they do not exist. Typically, in Venezuela, business professionals do not keep their own schedules.

d. Carlos did not really feel that he had committed himself; for Carlos it was only a tentative possibility.

Rationales for Venezuela Cultural Assimilator

1. You selected a. While it may be true that Carlos did not know how to say no to Edward, there is nothing in the scenario that indicates that Carlos hoped that Edward would simply forget. It is just as likely that there is a simple break-down in communication between Edward and Carlos or Carlos and his secretary. Please choose again.

2. You selected b. You may be responding to the stereotype that Venezuelans are not sufficiently organized. In any culture, casual arrangements can be overlooked; however, in Venezuela, the presumption is that all appointments are made with secretaries. Carlos assumed that Edward was not planning to follow up on their planned meeting since Edward did not call the secretary and confirm the appointment. Please choose again.

3. You selected c. This is the best response. You will find that secretaries are responsible for booking appointments and managing schedules for some business professionals. Check and confirm with the secretaries of those with whom you want to meet, especially when the appointment was made in a social environment like lunch.

4. You selected d. Regardless of how tentative or how certain the appointment, Carlos would have assumed that Edward was not serious about keeping the appointment when he discovered that Edward had not confirmed the appointment with his secretary. There is another response that addresses this Venezuelan business tactic more clearly. Please choose again.

APPENDIX 9.2
GUIDELINES FOR WEB CHATS/E-MAILS

- Be realistic in your expectations about getting a response. Expect at least 48 hours for a reply, longer if over the weekend or if the person is out of town.

- Remember that any message sent by Internet is totally void of nonverbal feedback. Messages that would be perfectly appropriate when delivered verbally may be considered rude and inappropriate on the Internet. Some efforts at providing nonverbal feedback can be used (e.g., :-) smiley face), but they aren't very effective. Sarcasm and irony, in particular, often translate poorly on the Internet.

- Don't feel rejected by single responses (e.g., yes). One of the advantages of the Internet is that short, efficient messages can be sent appropriately. You also owe it to recipients to keep your communications short. Ask your question. Make your comment. Seldom will an e-mail message exceed a paragraph.

- Don't type in solid caps. It is difficult to read and is perceived as "screaming." The one exception to this is if you want to respond to multiple components of a message. In that case, you may want to reply to the message and embed your responses in solid caps in the body of the original message.

- Exercise all rules of good etiquette that you would follow in formal communications. Internet messages are public documents and may have legal ramifications. Don't say anything that you would not say publicly.

- Don't get lazy with your writing. Just as with formal writing, you convey much about yourself with how you write.

APPENDIX 9.3
VALUES SELF-ASSESSMENT
(adapted from Harris & Moran, 1979, pp. 46–47,
used with permission from Elsevier)

Pairs of contrasting attitudes are presented below. Use the number 1 to indicate full agreement with the item on the left, a 5 for full agreement with the item on the right, a 3 for a neutral position, and a 2 or a 4 for positions that lean toward the left or right, without full agreement.

_____ 1. The individual can influence the future (where there is a will, there is a way).

Life follows a preordained course, and human action is determined by the will of God.

_____ 2. The individual can change and improve the environment.

People are intended to adjust to the physical environment rather than to alter it.

_____ 3. An individual should be realistic in his or her aspirations.

Ideals are to be pursued regardless of what is "reasonable."

_____ 4. We must work hard to accomplish our objectives (Puritan ethic).

Hard work is not the only prerequisite for success. Wisdom, luck, and time are also required.

_____ 5. Commitments should be honored (people will do what they say they will do).

A commitment may be superseded by a conflicting request, or an agreement may only signify intention and have little or no relationship to the capacity of performance.

_____ 6. One should effectively use one's time (time is money that can be saved or wasted).

Schedules are important but only in relation to other priorities.

_____ 7. A primary obligation of an employee is to the organization.

The individual employee has a primary obligation to family and friends.

_____ 8. The employer or employee should be able to terminate his or her relationship.

Employment should be for a lifetime.

_____ 9. A person can only work for one company at a time (we cannot serve two masters).

Personal contributions to individuals who represent an enterprise are acceptable.

_____ 10. The best-qualified persons should be given the positions available.

Family considerations, friendships, and other considerations should determine employment practices.

_____ 11. A person should be removed if not performing well.

The removal of a person from a position involves a great loss of prestige and should rarely be done.

_____ 12. All levels of management should be open to qualified individuals (office assistants can rise to become company presidents).

Education or family ties should be the primary vehicles for mobility.

_____ 13. Intuitive aspects of decision making should be reduced; efforts should be devoted to gathering relevant information.

Decisions are expressions of wisdom by the person in authority; any questioning would imply a lack of confidence in that person's judgment.

_____ 14. Company information should be available to anyone who needs it within the organization.

Withholding information to gain or maintain power is OK.

_____ 15. Each person is expected to have an opinion and to express it freely even if those views do not agree with colleagues' views.

Deference is to be given to persons in power or authority and to offer judgment that is not in support of the ideas of one's superiors is unthinkable.

_____ 16. A decision maker is expected to consult persons who can contribute useful information to the area being considered.

Decisions may be made by those in authority, and others need not be consulted.

_____ 17. Employees will work hard to improve their position in the company.

Personal ambition should be frowned upon.

_____ 18. Competition stimulates high performance.

Competition leads to unbalance, which leads to disharmony.

_____ 19. A person should do whatever is necessary to get the job done (one must be willing to get one's hands dirty).

Various kinds of work have low or high status, and some work may be below one's "dignity" or place in the organization.

_____ 20. Change is often an improvement and a dynamic reality.

Tradition should be revered and the power of the ruling group is founded on the continuation of a stable structure.

_____ 21. What works is important.

Symbols and the process are more important than the end point.

_____ 22. Persons and systems should be evaluated honestly, whether negative or positive.

Persons should be evaluated but in such a way that individuals not highly evaluated will not be embarrassed or caused to "lose face."

APPENDIX 9.4
DISCOVERING GLOBAL EFFECTIVENESS PROFILE
(from McLean, Tolbert, & Larkin, 2005;
used with permission; copyright © 2005)

For each statement that follows, six numbers are provided. If you strongly agree with the statement, circle 6. If you strongly disagree with the statement, circle 1. If you are less certain about your choice, circle a number closer to the middle. In every case, you will have to indicate a preference by agreeing or disagreeing.

If you do not have any experience similar to that described in any item, try to imagine yourself in that situation, and make a choice about what you think you would do or prefer.

Remember that your responses are confidential. Unless you choose to share your responses with others, you are the only one other than the researchers who will see your profile. If you try to respond in a way that you think is favorable, rather than how you truly feel, the result of this experience will not be as meaningful for your own learning as it would be otherwise.

Example When choosing a restaurant, I prefer to go to   1 2 3 4 5 6
a restaurant that serves food that is common
in my country.

If you clearly prefer to go to a restaurant that serves food that is common in your country, circle 6. If you prefer to go to a restaurant that serves food that is common in your home country, but you don't have a strong preference, you would circle 4 or 5. Likewise, if you clearly prefer to go to a restaurant that serves food that is *not* common in your country, circle 1. Circling a 2 or a 3 indicates disagreement with the statement, but not as strongly.

So, the scale you will be using is:

1	2	3	4	5	6
STRONGLY DISAGREE			**STRONGLY AGREE**		

1. I prefer to return to a favorite travel location rather than travel to a new location. 1 2 3 4 5 6

2. While in another country, I mistakenly use a hand gesture that is considered obscene in that country. When someone points out my error, I apologize. 1 2 3 4 5 6

3. I am fluent in a second language. I welcome the opportunity to use these skills within my company. 1 2 3 4 5 6

4. My primary reason for wanting an international business experience is that it will help me grow personally. 1 2 3 4 5 6

5. When ordering at a restaurant, I prefer to choose a food item I have not tried before. 1 2 3 4 5 6

6. I am invited to attend a play or concert that will be conducted in a language I do not understand. I accept the invitation. 1 2 3 4 5 6

7. I am asked to be a consultant on a global project. My suggestions are continually ignored by the multi-country team. I withdraw, making suggestions only when I am asked. 1 2 3 4 5 6

8. My primary reason for wanting an international business experience is that it will help me forward my career. 1 2 3 4 5 6

9. The company for which I work is engaged in a global continuous improvement initiative. In this effort, I believe that it is important to reflect from time to time on how past developments and progress impact our current work. 1 2 3 4 5 6

10. I become ill while in a host country. I trust the doctors to do a good job even though they do not speak my language. 1 2 3 4 5 6

11. Following a large international company event, I choose to join an informal international group for continued socializing. 1 2 3 4 5 6

12. My primary reason for wanting an international   1 2 3 4 5 6
    business experience is that it will provide me with
    a sense of adventure.

13. While preparing for a 2-year assignment in another   1 2 3 4 5 6
    country, my spouse and I discuss schooling arrange-
    ments for our children. I prefer a school that is
    similar to one in which they are currently enrolled.

14. While traveling in another country, I use that   1 2 3 4 5 6
    culture's normal way of greeting people.

15. While on an international assignment, our   1 2 3 4 5 6
    company asks for volunteers for community
    programs. I choose not to volunteer.

16. My primary reason for wanting an international   1 2 3 4 5 6
    business experience is that it will help me improve
    my image with my co-workers.

17. I consider whether an e-mail message being sent   1 2 3 4 5 6
    to another country should be composed differently
    from those I send in my own country.

18. When meeting people from different cultures,   1 2 3 4 5 6
    I refrain from asking questions about their culture
    as I do not want to appear ignorant or make
    them uncomfortable.

19. When visiting another country, I often do not   1 2 3 4 5 6
    understand comments that cause others to laugh,
    even though everyone is speaking in my language.
    I attempt to discover why the comments are
    considered funny.

20. My primary reason for wanting an international   1 2 3 4 5 6
    business experience is that it will help me help others.

21. When I arrive at my international destination, my   1 2 3 4 5 6
    host is not there to meet me. I have never been in this
    country, do not speak the native language, and can not
    reach my host. Even after a few hours have passed, I
    continue to wait, confident that my host will arrive.

22. I am assigned to a country in which I have difficulty   1 2 3 4 5 6
    understanding many of the cultural differences. I do
    not get along with my assigned liaison. I analyze the
    cultural reasons why we do not work well together.

23. When facilitating an international brainstorming 1 2 3 4 5 6
    session to generate ideas, I wait until all ideas have
    been presented before making judgments about the
    usefulness of the ideas.

24. My primary reason for wanting an international 1 2 3 4 5 6
    business experience is that it will help me escape un-
    desirable current circumstances and make a new start.

25. At a business meal in another country, I am not 1 2 3 4 5 6
    familiar with the eating utensils provided. I choose
    to use my preferred utensils.

26. While in another country preparing to make a 1 2 3 4 5 6
    presentation, a co-worker offers to share experi-
    ences from that country. I decline as I do not want
    to be biased by anyone's perspective.

27. When a colleague from another country and I have 1 2 3 4 5 6
    a different solution to a business problem, I listen
    fully to their recommendations before stating
    my opinion.

28. My primary reason for wanting an international 1 2 3 4 5 6
    business experience is that it will allow me to
    experience a style of living that is superior to my
    current lifestyle with servants, better house, lower
    cost of living, and so forth.

29. I am invited to join my international host and 1 2 3 4 5 6
    colleagues for dinner. Throughout the dinner, they
    speak in their language, which I do not understand.
    I am frustrated.

30. At an international dinner party, my colleagues 1 2 3 4 5 6
    ask me what I value most in my culture. This is
    easily answered as I have thought through my
    cultural values.

31. When in another country, my attempts at humor 1 2 3 4 5 6
    are often met with silence. I keep trying, knowing
    from experience that my humor is appreciated; it
    will be appreciated in this country once the people
    get to know me.

32. My primary reason for wanting an international 1 2 3 4 5 6
business experience is to learn how businesses
operate in other cultures.

33. On an international business trip, I brought along 1 2 3 4 5 6
work that I planned to complete in the evenings.
My hosts made other plans for my evenings.
Although I do not want to participate, I do so at
the expense of my planned work.

34. When asked by someone from another country 1 2 3 4 5 6
about the religious values of my country, I avoid
the question, as it is too personal and inappropriate.

35. I am an advisor for an international Research and 1 2 3 4 5 6
Development team. During a team meeting, an idea
is selected that I know is difficult, if not impossible,
to produce. I say nothing because the team has
already selected the idea.

36. My primary reason for wanting an international 1 2 3 4 5 6
business experience is to learn best practices and
principles regarding diversity to apply in my
home country.

37. I am on the food committee for a reception for 1 2 3 4 5 6
company representatives from three countries.
As the majority of attendees are from my home
country, we choose food primarily from my
home country.

38. I am on a work assignment outside of my home 1 2 3 4 5 6
country. I prefer not to drink the beverage(s)
traditionally served with the meal. I ask my
liaison ahead of time to help arrange for my
preferred beverage.

39. In business cultures, I often use humor. When in 1 2 3 4 5 6
the same situation with someone from another
country, I use logic because I fear that my humor
and what is humor in their country could create a
barrier between us.

40. My primary reason for wanting an international business experience is to learn about and experience different types of organizational structures. 1 2 3 4 5 6

41. At an international business banquet in my honor, the main course is food that I have never tried. It looks strange to me, but I try it anyway. 1 2 3 4 5 6

42. In an effort to value others, I attempt to treat everyone the same. 1 2 3 4 5 6

43. At an international reception, I hear someone telling a joke that is disrespectful of colleagues from another country. I do not laugh with the group. 1 2 3 4 5 6

44. My primary reason for wanting an international business experience is to help improve business structures and styles in other countries. 1 2 3 4 5 6

45. When working on a global business project, I am comfortable not knowing exactly what the end result will be. 1 2 3 4 5 6

46. While on a business trip to another country, I find that my views on many issues are different from my hosts'. I ask questions to determine how and why their views are so different from mine. 1 2 3 4 5 6

47. While traveling in another country for the first time, I am asked what to do in a particular business situation. I offer several suggestions, but the person who made the request wants only one solution. I choose what I think is the best suggestion and present it. 1 2 3 4 5 6

48. My primary reason for wanting an international business experience is to gain prestige. 1 2 3 4 5 6

49. An international team member suggests improvements to our global project after our team has worked months to obtain final approval. We decide to move forward as our colleague has had sufficient time for input earlier. 1 2 3 4 5 6

50. When traveling in another country, I try to find out how my behaviors will need to change if I am to be effective. 1 2 3 4 5 6

51. When speaking in my language with someone whose native language is different from mine, I speak at my normal pace and enunciation, while attempting to determine if I am understood. If I am not, I then speak more slowly and distinctly than I would normally. 1 2 3 4 5 6

52. My primary reason for wanting an international business experience is to receive higher pay because of hardship posting. 1 2 3 4 5 6

53. When visiting my company's facilities in another country and finding that a process used at home is not working well there, I attempt to discover how the process needs to be modified to work better in that country. 1 2 3 4 5 6

54. I usually continue my normal tipping practices when I travel outside of my country. 1 2 3 4 5 6

55. While working as a troubleshooter in another country, a colleague and I, from different countries, are having trouble agreeing on a solution to a problem. To avoid conflict, I go along with my colleague's solution. 1 2 3 4 5 6

56. My primary reason for wanting an international business experience is to learn or practice another language. 1 2 3 4 5 6

57. I prefer not to be around smoking. The international meeting I am attending is filled with people smoking. I ask the organizers to prohibit smoking during sessions. 1 2 3 4 5 6

58. When traveling to a country that is new to me, I wait until I arrive in the country to learn about it to avoid becoming biased by others' experiences. 1 2 3 4 5 6

59. If I have difficulty understanding someone whose   1 2 3 4 5 6
    native language is not mine, I keep our conver-
    sation short.

60. My primary reason for wanting an international   1 2 3 4 5 6
    business experience is to get bargains by purchasing
    goods at low prices.

61. In the middle of my presentation to an international 1 2 3 4 5 6
    audience, the audio part of a video fails. I keep the
    video running and paraphrase the audio, as I know
    the video.

62. While at a reception where one-quarter of those in   1 2 3 4 5 6
    attendance are from another country, I choose to
    spend most of the time with people from a country
    other than my own.=

63. I try to understand other people's thoughts and   1 2 3 4 5 6
    feelings when communicating with them.

64. My primary reason for wanting an international   1 2 3 4 5 6
    business experience is to travel at company expense.

65. In another country, my host is not able to provide 1 2 3 4 5 6
    me with a computer during my four-week visit.
    I explain that I cannot complete my work under
    these circumstances, and they will need to provide
    me with a computer.

66. I know the appropriate customs used in another   1 2 3 4 5 6
    country when being introduced to someone of the
    opposite sex. Nevertheless, I wait for the other
    person to set the example.

67. I am comfortable meeting and relating to people   1 2 3 4 5 6
    who are from other cultures and quite different
    from me.

68. My primary reason for wanting an international   1 2 3 4 5 6
    business experience is to provide educational
    experiences for my family.

Discovering Global Effectiveness Profile Feedback

Enter the number you have circled for each question in the appropriate cell in the table below. If a question number has an *R* after it, enter 1 for a 6, 2 for a 5, 3 for a 4, 4 for a 3, 5 for a 2, and 6 for a 1. When all cells have been filled in, total each column.

FLEXIBILITY, ADAPTABILITY, & AMBIGUITY	CULTURAL AWARENESS	RELATIONSHIPS	MOTIVES
1R.	2.	3.	4.
5.	6.	7R.	8R.
9.	10.	11.	12.
13R.	14.	15R.	16R.
17.	18R.	19.	20R.
21.	22.	23.	24R.
25R.	26R.	27.	28R.
29R.	30.	31R.	32.
33.	34R.	35R.	36.
37.	38.	39.	40.
41.	42R.	43.	44R.
45.	46.	47R.	48R.
49R.	50.	51.	52R.
53.	54R.	55R.	56.
57R.	58R.	59R.	60R.
61.	62.	63.	64R.
65R.	66.	67.	68R.

Interpretation.   Look at the totals for each column. The column with the highest total is your greatest strength, and the one with the lowest total is the area of greatest need for development. The lowest possible score is 17, and the highest possible score is 102. Normative data have not yet been established, but preliminary data suggest that a score of 80 or higher is a strength, while a score of 60 or lower is a weakness. Although reliability has been established, validity is still to be established.

10

Implementation: Organizational Level

CHAPTER OUTLINE

Organization Design
Company-wide Survey
Learning Organization
Organizational Learning
Culture Change
Accountability and Reward Systems
Succession Planning
Valuing Differences/Diversity
Mission, Vision, and Values/Philosophy Development
Strategic Planning
Large-Scale Interactive Events (LSIEs)
Open Systems Mapping
Future Search
Open Space Technology Meetings
Chapter Summary
Questions for Discussion or Self-Reflection

OVERVIEW   At the organizational level, the most important interventions improve strategic thinking and strategic alignment. Important OD contributions to this process included in this chapter are organization design; company-wide survey; learning organization; organizational learning; culture change; accountability and reward systems; succession planning; valuing differences/diversity; mission, vision, values, and philosophy development; strategic planning; large-scale interactive events; open systems mapping; future search; and open space technology meetings.

We turn now to those interventions that are intended to impact the whole organization. As recognized in Chapter 5, however, within systems theory, all of the levels covered in the preceding chapters also impact the whole organization in some way. Although I have categorized the interventions to fit into different levels of targets of impact, the distinction in levels (and thus in these chapters) is somewhat artificial. Implementation targeted specifically at the organizational level is one more aspect of the implementation phase, as identified in Figure 10.1.

As is true with all chapters included in the implementation phase, an almost limitless number of interventions could be used to accomplish organizational effectiveness across the whole organization. This chapter will focus on only a sample of such interventions.

ORGANIZATION DESIGN

As most organizations are already in existence when OD professionals get involved (though that doesn't have to be the case), organizational structure or design for the OD professional usually involves organizational *re*structuring, mergers and acquisitions, outsourcing, and downsizing.

Cummings and Worley (2005) suggested that five factors need to be considered in an organizational restructuring: the environment, organization size, technology, organization strategy, and worldwide operations. Each of these factors influences how an organization will structure itself.

Organizational Structuring or Restructuring

Managers who are unfamiliar with OD often think primarily about the structure of their organization when they think about OD. Reorganiza-

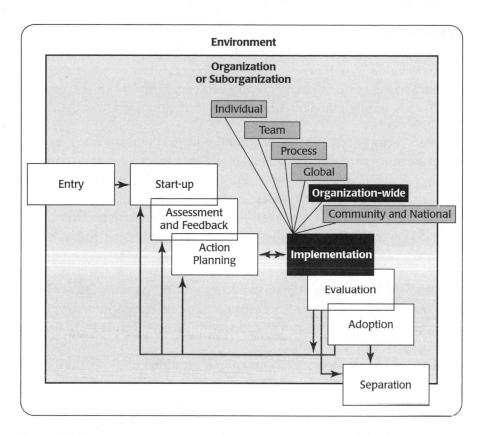

Figure 10.1 *Organization Development Process Model, Phase 5: Implementation at the Organizational Level*

tion of the organization's structure is frequently seen as a way to improve organizational performance, though there is little research to suggest that any one approach to structure produces better performance than another. Several simple models of organizational structure will be described briefly here. In most organizations, structures are much more complex.

Functional Structure. *Functional structure* is probably the easiest to create and understand. Basically, each functional area, such as operations, production, R&D, human resources, finance, legal, marketing, and so on, is managed by a manager who is usually a specialist in the area managed.

Divisional Structure.   In contrast to the functional structure, the *divisional structure* is organized by product line. Each product line division is self-contained; each product line is then organized by function. Each product has a senior manager, and each function within the product line has a separate manager who reports to the division manager.

Matrix Structure.   A *matrix structure* tends to be more complex than either of the structures described so far. Its objective is to attempt to maximize the strengths of both functional and divisional structures, while minimizing the weaknesses. Each person basically reports to two managers: a functional manager and a product manager. This can be extended even further by adding a geographic manager (e.g., "Asian Region").

Process Structure.   Organization occurs around common processes— for example, providing quality customer service, researching new products and services, distributing products to the marketplace, managing the organization, and so on.

These basic *process structures* can be modified in almost unlimited ways. What is critical to the OD professional is to understand what the objective is in a restructuring. Change for the sake of change is going to use resources ineffectively and could cause considerable unrest and possibly harm in the organization.

Another structural question that is almost perennial is whether an organization should structure its functions as centralized or as decentralized. Burke (2002) suggested that this is no longer the right question; the question is not either/or but, rather, how to do both simultaneously when appropriate. Finance, for example, might well be centralized, while human resources are decentralized.

Mergers and Acquisitions

Just as there are many ways to structure an organization, so also are there many ways for structure to emerge from a merger or acquisition. Schmidt (2002) suggested four major ways to structure a company after a merger or acquisition:

- *Limited integration* – Basically, with limited integration, the two companies continue to operate as they did before the merger or acquisition, with a holding company functioning as the overarching organization.

- *Dominant company* – Under the dominant company approach, the dominant, or acquiring, company absorbs the acquired company.

- *Mutual best of both* – As its name implies, in mutual best of both, a new company emerges as an integrated entity, drawing on the best from each of the two companies involved in the merger or acquisition.

- *Transformation to new company* – Though similar to the approach immediately preceding, transformation to new company adds the incorporation of totally new company practices and external best practices in creating the integrated new company.

As with the restructuring of organizations, there is no best way to respond to the needs created by a merger and acquisition, at least in terms of how the new company is to be integrated. Mergers and acquisitions do typically lead to downsizing of both organizations.

Using grounded theory methodology, Johansen (1991) developed a model of individual response to significant organizational change, specifically a merger or acquisition leading to downsizing. Although the model (see Figure 10.2) is presented in a logical sequence as a series of steps, this presentation is done only for reasons of understanding and clarity. Change, and people's response to change, is not linear and not necessarily logical. To understand any change event, it must be considered in context.

People constantly scan their environment for potentially significant change events. They talk with each other about these events, and through this process they come to an understanding of the relative importance of their findings. Once an event is identified as potentially significant, they conduct an analysis of what the change might mean to them. This analysis causes stress, and people take action to change the course of the event and/or lower their feelings of stress. Assuming that adequate time is available, they will take action and then reassess their position in relation to the change, perhaps leading to additional coping actions. At some point the event actually happens. It is easier to mark the start and finish of some events than of others. Once the event has happened, people assess the effects of the change. The results of this

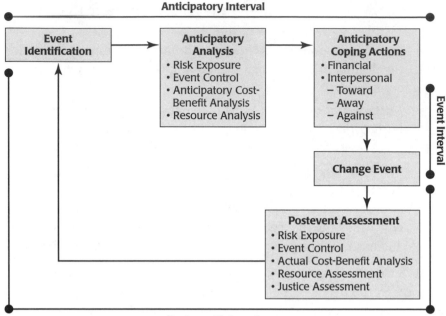

Figure 10.2 *Individual Responses to Significant Organizational Change (used by permission of the author, Barry Craig Johansen)*

assessment may lead to stress, as well as to actions that deal with the effects of the event and *its* associated stress. This process continues until the stresses generated by other events are perceived to be of greater urgency than dealing with the past event. At this point the past event is put on the back burner or is forgotten as the person deals with the new conditions. Perhaps the event is revisited in the future, perhaps not, depending on how the environment and events evolve. The OD professional and company management need to understand how this cycle functions for employees.

Outsourcing and Downsizing

An organization might downsize for many reasons: improved technology, a merger or acquisition that has resulted in duplicated personnel, a downturn in the economy and/or demand for the organization's products or services, improved processes, flattening of the organization with fewer middle managers, replacement of regular employees with contract employees, and outsourcing—the movement of some aspect of an organization to some other company, increasingly in an international context.

Outsourcing is almost always a result of an effort to move production or a service to an organization or company where comparable quality can be provided at a lower cost. We saw this happening in large numbers in the 1990s and continuing today, with many organizations' information technology (IT) and customer service areas being transferred to India. Manufacturing, which once moved to Korea, Japan, and Taiwan, is now moving to China, Indonesia, and the Philippines—all to take advantage of lower personnel costs.

Organizations will often try to downsize with minimal impact on their employees, through attrition, early or planned retirements, regular turnover, redeployment to other functions or other locations, extended vacations without pay, and, finally, layoffs. How downsizing is done will often affect the organization's reputation and future potential for attracting and retaining employees.

· ·

The market for a computer peripheral company with which I was working on TQM suddenly collapsed because of increased competition. The company tried to continue with its regular workforce, but it became apparent after a month that the payroll needed to be cut dramatically. The CEO met with employee groups to discuss what options might be taken. Layoffs were discussed, but the employees unanimously rejected such an approach. Instead, they recommended that every employee move from 5 days to 4 days of employment. Some employees volunteered for a temporary leave of absence without pay. Others agreed to take an extended vacation without pay. This continued for about a year, after which time TQM efforts had established the company at the top of the industry, again, and its need for employees actually doubled over the precrisis level. Employees were so impressed with the way that the company had handled the downsizing that these already-loyal employees became even more devoted to the company.

. . . .

> Another manufacturing organization with which I was working on TQM was a unionized environment. The union was not happy about working on TQM because its members anticipated, accurately, that the TQM activities would result in improved processes for which fewer employees would be needed. After reviewing its personnel records carefully, the company determined that a number of employees, about the number that the company thought would become surplus, were nearly ready to retire. The company signed an agreement with the union that it would not lay off workers as a result of the TQM activities, but it would, instead, use anticipated attrition to take care of the surplus personnel situation. About 10 positions became surplus as a result of the TQM activities, and the company honored its agreement, allowing the anticipated regular retirements to take care of the surplus.

. . . .

There is little empirical evidence to suggest that downsizing in the United States has been successful. If not handled well, the remaining employees often feel betrayed, afraid that they will be next. They become overworked because they have to do the work of others, as well as their own, and experience increased stress and illness, disruption in family life, and other unpleasant outcomes. All of these responses have the potential of leading to decreased productivity. Rather than downsizing in order to achieve increased productivity and quality, organizations can look at other options, including increasing market share and revenues, thus reducing the per-unit cost of production.

COMPANY-WIDE SURVEY

Chapter 4 provides detailed information on how to accomplish a company-wide survey. The event of conducting the survey is, in itself, an intervention. If done correctly, the survey will incorporate employee input and participation, not only in designing the survey but also in analyzing the data and providing feedback to employees. It is vital to realize that conducting the survey creates expectations on the part of employees that something will be done with the data. If the organization ignores the information that it gains from the survey, employee morale is likely to decrease. In fact, the same negative outcome is likely to occur if something is done in response to the survey, but it does not meet employees' expectations. The whole survey-feedback-planning-implementation process is a common and important intervention for the OD professional.

LEARNING ORGANIZATION

As popularized by Senge (1990), a *learning organization* is "an organization that has woven a continuous and enhanced capacity to learn, adapt and change into its culture. Its values, policies, practices, systems and structures support and accelerate learning for all employees" (Nevis et al., 1995, p. 73). Some of the characteristics of a learning organization include the following actions:

- Embraces change
- Encourages managers to be coaches, mentors, and facilitators of learning
- Has a culture of feedback and disclosure
- Has a holistic, systematic view of the organization and its systems, processes, and relationships
- Has shared organization-wide vision, purpose, and values
- Has systems for sharing learning and using it in the business
- Provides frequent opportunities to learn from experience
- Spreads trust throughout the organization
- Strives for continuous improvement
- Views the unexpected as an opportunity to learn. (Marquardt & Reynolds, 1994, p. 23)

Another characteristic not included in this list is the ability to learn from both successes and failures, and to see failures not as something for which someone is to be punished but something from which to learn. The challenge for the OD professional, though, along with the organization, is how to create an organization that is a learning organization. It is easy to state the desired outcome characteristics, as included in the list, but it is much more difficult to create an alignment between the behaviors of an organization and these desired outcomes. Responsibility will reside with management to make a transition into becoming facilitators of learning, rather than the more traditional roles performed by managers.

Watkins and Marsick (1996) provided seven imperatives for managers who desire to create a learning organization:

- Create continuous learning opportunities.
- Promote inquiry and dialogue.
- Encourage collaboration and team learning.
- Establish systems to capture and share learning.
- Empower people toward a collective vision.
- Connect the organization to its environment.
- Use leaders who model and support learning at the individual, team, and organizational levels.

Perhaps the most effective way for the OD professional to assist an organization that wants to become a learning organization is to coach managers to become learning facilitators in the broadest sense.

Another concern with the concept of the learning organization is that we do not have definitive research suggesting that the existence of a learning organization leads to improved organizational performance (Ellinger, Ellinger, Yang, & Howton, 2002).

ORGANIZATIONAL LEARNING

Organizational learning is often used synonymously with *learning organization*. While the distinction may not be significant, organizational learning is the process an organization uses to become a learning organization. The seven imperatives quoted earlier from Watkins and Marsick (1996) are the things that management must do to embed organizational learning into the organization so it will become a learning organization.

CULTURE CHANGE

Culture change is really what OD is about. However, keeping in mind Schein's cultural iceberg (from Chapter 1), it is obvious that making superficial change ("above the water") is much easier than creating a truly different and improved culture that goes "under the water" to influence the core assumptions of the organization and its leadership. Consider the case of Sumitomo 3M presented in Chapter 9. It was easy to change the dress code (clearly above the water). But it was most difficult to change the promotion process to result in more senior female executives or more executives under age 30 getting promoted. Not only were deep assumptions of the organization being challenged, but national culture also played its part in making such changes difficult.

According to Burke (2002):

> Examples of significant and successful organization change . . .
> are exceptional. Most organization change is not significant or
> successful. Organizational improvements do occur, even fre-
> quently, and do work, but large scale, fundamental organization
> change that works is rare. (p. 1)

He went on to suggest his reasons for why he thinks this is so: Deep change of organization culture is difficult; change is most needed when organizations are at their peak, yet it is difficult to convince organizational leaders of this need; and, finally, our knowledge and skill at making such change is limited.

Strangely, it seems to be easy to influence a culture in a negative direction. Consider, for example, how quickly a culture can change when an incompetent, insensitive leader or manager is put in place. Thus, the task of almost all of OD is to help an organization improve its culture. Everything discussed in this book is directed at positively influencing organizational culture.

From a systems perspective, all components of an organization work together to create its culture. Thus, when attempting to bring about change in the culture, it is important to view the organization and its culture holistically. One aspect of a culture may come to the fore at a given point in time, but the whole organization will always be intimately connected, even while other aspects appear to be in the background.

Another factor contributing to the difficulty of culture change is that most organizations do not have a singular culture. Rather, cultures are usually made up of many subcultures. Thus, the effort to bring about culture change requires that the focus of the OD effort be on the subcultures while also focusing on the overall organizational culture.

Furthermore, as discussed around systems theory, changes in the culture of a subgroup will create changes in the organizational culture, yet it is impossible to predict what those changes will be.

Changing culture by focusing on changing culture is doomed to failure. Considering Schein's cultural iceberg, the deeply held values, attitudes, beliefs, and assumptions are too deep to address directly. Thus, to change culture, we address behaviors, especially those that are the most easily influenced. So, to change culture, focus on the behaviors that, if changed, are most likely to influence the deeper attitudes. Culture change is extremely complex.

ACCOUNTABILITY AND REWARD SYSTEMS

Both accountability and reward systems are part of a bigger system—performance management. Most of the issues related to performance management fall into the responsibility area designated for human resources. However, because the components of performance management have such a major impact on the culture of an organization, it is essential that I make a few comments here about the OD issues associated with performance management.

The OD professional can ask many questions to help HR create a performance management system that supports the goals of the organization and helps create the kind of culture that is desired:

- How do we determine an individual's contribution to the organization when everyone works within a system that can either support or inhibit outcomes?
- Should we be concerned about reward systems at the individual, team, business unit, or organization level?
- What is the relationship between intrinsic (from within) and extrinsic (from the outside) motivation?
- How should employees learn how well they are performing?
- What role should employees have in creating their performance managements system?
- How should the performance management system be communicated to employees? Should there be secrets regarding salary, bonuses, and the like?

What role can OD play in helping HR answer these questions? First, OD needs to continue to remind HR of the importance of systems thinking. While it is not clear what portion of one's performance comes from individual effort and skill and what portion comes from the system itself, it is clear that the system has a major role in the process. Care, therefore, must be taken in not assuming that the individual is the sole determinant of that individual's performance.

OD can also help HR in recognizing that no performance appraisal system has yet been created that accomplishes what the organization is hoping to accomplish. Preparing managers and supervisors to be coaches who give feedback on a regular, ongoing, immediate basis is far superior to a once-a-year feedback system based on typical perform-ance appraisals. Furthermore, as indicated in Chapter 6, *multirater appraisals* are not very useful because of the different perspectives of performance and the lack of agreement between groups. With an ongo-ing feedback system, employees who have been placed in the wrong position, not received sufficient training, or inappropriately hired will be quickly identified.

There is also often an assumption that employees are motivated only through extrinsic rewards. As a result, many organizations over-emphasize salary, bonuses, and benefits. However, when employees feel that they have been fairly treated with extrinsic rewards, most employ-ees are intrinsically motivated. They want opportunities to excel in their job, to feel as if they have achieved something important, to be recognized for their contributions simply with a comment from others, and so on.

Secrecy is often characteristic of salary and bonus systems, espe-cially among managers. The assumption is that any perception of unfair treatment will lead to low morale and perhaps even conflict among individuals. Another perspective, however, is that secrecy implies that something unfair is going on, and, even when employees might be treated fairly, the perception of unfair treatment negatively affects morale. The best approach is to encourage openness and to ensure that a fair system is in place so employees will clearly understand any differ-ences that might exist.

Goal setting is another category of performance management. *Management by objectives (MBOs)* has been around for a long time, but it has disappeared from many organizations because of all of the problems associated with this approach. Since MBO objectives are set within a particular systems context, they are not based on the capabilities of the system as a whole. Also, they tend to be applied unevenly across the organization. Reaching the objectives set for one year can unreasonably increase the objectives for the next year. Objectives can actually limit performance: employees slow down once the objectives have been met, unimportant objectives are set, and on and on the list of problems can go. Appropriate goal setting has been addressed in much more detail in Chapter 8.

A friend is employed as a salesperson for a company that sells used large computer systems. He is extremely effective, selling a volume far greater than anyone else in the company. Early in his career, he found that when he reached his objectives, the company dramatically increased his objectives for the following year, without any additional compensation. He is well compensated, so he has decided that he will continue *just* to meet the objectives set for him by his company. Once he has accomplished this point, which maximizes his income, he stops selling. He takes vacations. He travels. If he does make a sale that would cause him to exceed his objectives for the current pay period, he holds the invoice until the next pay period. Who benefits from this? Certainly not the company. It loses a huge amount of revenue by following such a system. The company would benefit greatly by having him continue to sell throughout the year. The salesperson would benefit with a higher income if he could continue to sell throughout the year without being penalized by negative consequences. Here is an MBO system that appears to cause problems for everyone!

The practice of including employees in decisions that are related to reward systems is one approach that can help ensure that the systems are perceived as fair.

I was working for a family-owned, hobby distribution company that had made the decision to improve its culture to support the basic premises of total quality management. We had conducted employee surveys and interviews that indicated that there was widespread concern on the part of employees that salaries and benefits were not comparable to those in the community and the industry. Survey results also indicated that employees believed that inequities were present within the organization, especially in the way in which year-end bonuses were given.

The quality steering team, consisting of employees, supervisors, and managers, agreed that it would be useful to explore the reward systems as a component of TQM. Before looking extensively at the existing rewards system, the steering team discussed where they wanted to be in relation to both the industry and the community. They decided that they wanted to pay slightly over the average in both the industry and the community to help with recruitment and retention, yet hold expenses at a reasonable level to support the continuing operation of the company. It was decided to target pay at the 60th percentile. With that decision made, the next step was to determine the existing rewards system and to determine where pay fit relative to the industry and community. While the HR manager had regularly accessed community and industry surveys in determining pay, it was always done within the context of HR and was not shared widely within the company.

So, the next step in the process was for the steering team to participate in deciding what databases to use in determining the distribution of pay both in the community and in the industry. They determined that they were just under the 60th percentile, so modest pay increases were recommended to bring the pay to just over the 60th percentile. Benefits were also included in the databases, and the steering team determined that these were actually above the target. So, although no significant changes were made in the rewards system, employee morale was significantly improved with the knowledge that they were at or above the target the steering committee had set and because there were no longer any secrets. The steering committee also decided that a matrix that combined a skills-based approach with seniority would be fair to everyone.

The last issue that the steering committee discussed had to do with the bonus system. This was a system that had been created by the top three officers in the company and had never been shared or explored publicly before. The steering team reviewed the system in place, decided that it was not fair to the individuals involved, and developed a new system for bonuses based on company performance. Although there was some concern about whether senior management would accept the proposal, the steering committee was pleasantly surprised when it was accepted without change. The new system was explicit and removed the possibility of individual favoritism. It also spread the bonus system over the whole employee system, based on base salary, rather than limiting it only to senior managers. The experiment of opening the system more broadly across the employee base was deemed to be a great success.

SUCCESSION PLANNING

Preparing individuals for future positions, especially in this world of rapid turnover and an aging population, is widely recognized as critical for the success of an organization. However, many organizations find it easier to support *succession planning* in its rhetoric than in its practice.

Tippins (2002) noted that succession planning is typically approached through four steps:

1. Identification of key positions for which succession planning is important
2. Determination of relevant knowledge, skills, and abilities required for the key position
3. Assessment of the talent pool on relevant knowledge, skills, and abilities
4. Development of employees who are deficient in some area (p. 252)

In many organizations, high-potential employees are identified, either through an assessment center, consisting of psychological tests and minisimulations, or through an ongoing appraisal system. These *"hipos"* (high-potentials) are often then given special job opportunities for development and extraordinary additional opportunities to participate in development activities. While this approach is likely to prepare some few individuals for succession, as needed, there is no guarantee that they will stay with the organization. Moreover, the potential downside of this arrangement is in discouraging and disappointing employees who are not selected, creating overall decline in morale. However, a company faced with the potential of high retirements or high turnover may not have an alternative.

Another challenge for OD professionals is in deciding who should have access to the information. In some organizations, those in the hipo pool do not know that they have been so labeled. In other organizations, this designation is common knowledge. In spite of the potential consequences, I lean in the direction of open knowledge regarding succession planning. Secrecy, unless absolutely essential, creates an organizational culture that breeds rumors, discontent, and dysfunctional communications. Each situation, of course, will be different.

VALUING DIFFERENCES/DIVERSITY

Most organizations have recognized the need for some emphasis on diversity, though this often focuses on specific protected classes, such as gender, age, ethnicity, race, religion, nationality, and sexual orientation. Many other sources of diversity in organizations are not protected, including geographic origin (urban/rural, West Coast/Midwest, North/South), and even ideas, politics, and ideologies. Diversity of thought, at least, is essential in fostering new ideas and new approaches, enhancing customer bases, and generally leading to innovation and creativity.

Several organizations approach diversity from a training perspective. Little evidence, however, indicates that diversity training actually changes how diversity is valued in an organization. People intuitively and/or rationally assess the culture of the organization to determine whether diversity is seen in positive ways or whether it is simply tolerated or not even recognized. Protected classes are often given at least lip service to protect the company against legal action. But creating a climate for truly valuing diversity in order to maximize its benefits is not easy and is the responsibility of the organization. Experiential exposure, self-reflection, small-group interactions, and to some extent training can all be beneficial in creating a positive environment.

Diversity is an important issue for organizations for three (and probably more) reasons. All have to do with performance. First, if an organization does not value diversity, then it may overlook the most competent people for positions within the organization. Second, given the demographics in most countries, especially in the United States, the population of consumers and industrial buyers is increasingly represented by people from protected categories. Having people from groups similar to these diverse consumers and buyers in important organizational positions may provide a competitive advantage, though the research suggests that, in spite of its apparent logic, this may not be so (Gray, 2005). Finally, if employees from protected categories feel that they are not valued, this perception will likely affect their morale, leading to diminished productivity.

Helping organizations move forward on the topic of diversity can be a very difficult task, and there are no easy answers as to how this progress can happen. Certainly, one of the most effective ways is for the organization to model the outcomes desired by having role models in positions of authority in the organization. These should not be token placements but people who are clearly competent in the work that they do.

One of the most common approaches to creating an organizational culture that values diversity is to offer training. But what that training should be and how effective training in this difficult area can be with adults are both difficult questions. Perhaps the best that can be expected from training in this area is sending a clear message that disrespectful and discriminatory behavior will not be accepted. Perhaps it will take a long time, if ever, to move an organization to valuing diversity solely through training.

Another approach that some organizations have tried is to have groups organized around different protected classes of employees to address business issues that the group believes affects that group. The idea is that employees can then communicate with management about barriers to full acceptance of diversity. This approach might work when management sees diversity as a high priority for its success as an organization. But, when management is not committed to valuing diversity, the formation of such groups will create unfilled expectations, leading to even more frustration, and it may also be a way to trivialize and set aside the concerns of such groups.

MISSION, VISION, AND VALUES/ PHILOSOPHY DEVELOPMENT

OD professionals are often called on, as part of a strategic planning or strategic review intervention, to facilitate the development of the organization's mission, its vision for the future, and the values/philosophy it will use to accomplish that vision. Unfortunately, there is no common acceptance of the meaning of *mission* and *vision*, and these terms may actually be used in opposite ways. *Mission*, for me, refers to the organization's purpose or reason for being. *Vision* is a statement of how the organization would like to look at some time in the future and includes the values or philosophy for which it would like to be known.

Mission statements are usually short, catchy statements that are easily remembered and communicate what the organization's purpose is. A good mission statement will be explicit enough to be helpful in managing the organization and will set it apart from its competitors. It should also be broad enough to accommodate changes in technology and in future markets. What follows is an example of a mission statement that meets the criteria described here. It will be used, later, to illustrate the development of a vision statement.

In the 1990s, Delta Air Lines created the following mission statement (used with permission):

We want Delta to be the WORLDWIDE AIRLINE OF CHOICE.

The purpose of a *vision statement* is to capture the organization's vision for its future. The statement can be constructed by a senior management team, a cross section of employees, a board of directors, or others charged with creating a viable vision for the organization. The vision statement is a longer statement than a mission statement; it should specify what the organization does, who it does it for, what values will be used to meet the vision, and so on.

The following questions are ones I often use with organizations to help them think about their future and where they are heading. This is not to say that the answers to all of these questions are simply integrated into a vision statement. Rather, these questions cause participants to think about the future. The team will then decide, based on its responses, what it wants to use in constructing the vision statement in order to set a direction for the organization and its employees.

Questions for Creating a Vision Statement for XYZ Corporation

1. What needs should the services or products of XYZ meet?

2. What services or products should XYZ deliver?

3. To whom should XYZ deliver its services or products?

4. Where should XYZ deliver its services or products?

5. What technologies should XYZ use?

6. Where should XYZ deliver its services or products?

7. What are the expectations of XYZ's stakeholders?

8. Who will XYZ's future competitors, suppliers, and partners be?

9. What is the public image that XYZ should pursue?

10. What is the image that you want employees to have of XYZ?

11. What is the image that you want suppliers to have of XYZ?

12. What is the image that you want customers to have of XYZ?

13. What are the values/standards that should underlie the work of XYZ?

Delta Air Lines created the following vision statement to accompany its mission statement (used with permission):

WORLDWIDE, because we are and intend to remain an innovative, aggressive, ethical, and successful competitor that offers access to the world at the highest standards of customer service. We will continue to look for opportunities to extend our reach through new routes and creative global alliances.

AIRLINE, because we intend to stay in the business we know best—air transportation and related services. We won't stray from our roots. We believe in the long-term prospects for profitable growth in the airline industry, and we will continue to focus time, attention, and investment on enhancing our place in that business environment.

OF CHOICE, because we value the loyalty of our customers, employees, and investors. For passengers and shippers, we will continue to provide the best service and value. For our personnel, we will continue to offer an ever more challenging, rewarding, and result-oriented workplace that recognizes and appreciates their contributions. For our shareholders, we will earn a consistent, superior financial return.

STRATEGIC PLANNING

There are many approaches to *strategic planning*, including SWOT (strengths, weaknesses, opportunities, threats) analysis, PEST (political, economic, social, technological) analysis, and *scenario planning*. Each will be described briefly, recognizing that strategic planning is a huge topic around which many books have been written.

Most, but not all approaches to strategic planning include the following steps:

1. Create a mission statement to last about 10 years.
2. Create a vision statement to last 15 to 20 years.
3. Create a philosophy/values statement or incorporate it into the vision statement.
4. Conduct a scan (discussed in the next section) to analyze the environment and competitors.
5. Create strategies/goal categories to be implemented in 3 years and 5 years.
6. Within each strategy category, create tactics to move the organization for the next year toward accomplishing that strategy/goal.
7. For 3- and 5-year strategies, do decision trees (described later in this chapter) to determine what needs to be done each year to insure that steps are taken in the appropriate year to have the goal accomplished on time.

All approaches to strategic planning require that the organization be skillful in doing scans (step 4), both externally and internally. This concept will be discussed before each approach is described.

Scans

A strategic plan is always set within the context of the environment in which the organization functions and the internal capabilities of the organization. Both external scanning (also called *environmental scanning*) and internal scanning are essential for understanding these factors of the organization. An *external scan* requires that the organization gather considerable information about the industry, competitors, the marketplace, government regulations, demographics, technology, economic development, global trends—anything that might influence the future of the organization. Such information might be found in industry reports, government reports, industry-specific journals, industry conferences, and so on. *Internal scans* will typically include both historical and present data. Such information is generally gathered through interviews with key stakeholders, annual reports, planning documents, analysts' reports, customer surveys, employee surveys, marketing reports, board meeting minutes, human resource databases, and anything else that would provide information about the organization. Don't make the assumption that any one individual or any one team has all of this information. The useful and necessary data are spread throughout the organization.

SWOT and PEST

Both of these approaches are based on the extensive research that was conducted in doing the scan. Typically, whatever team is brought together to do the strategic planning, brainstorming (see Chapter 7) is used to identify the important factors that fit under each of the categories: strengths, weaknesses, opportunities, and threats for the SWOT analysis; and political, economic, social, and technological factors likely to affect the organization for the PEST analysis.

   With this background, the team then needs to establish the strategies that it will use to maximize its opportunities (assuming SWOT is being used) and to minimize its threats. A *strategy* is a broad category used to achieve an organizational goal. For each agreed-on strategy, the team creates one or more *tactics*, specific steps used to accomplish that strategy.

   Finally, to ensure that the tactics can be applied within the time frame that has been established, decision trees are sometimes used. A *decision tree* (see Scholtes, 1988) starts with the expected time frame for the tactic to be completed. Then, incrementally, decisions that must be accomplished before the final step are listed, with the costs associated with each step and the length of time that it will take to complete the task.

· ·

In a strategic planning process with a retail organization, discussion took place regarding the construction of a pilot "super-store," to be in place in 5 years. As the decision tree process was applied, the planning team discovered that they couldn't complete the project in just 5 years, and the cost for accomplishing the project quickly far exceeded economic benefit. The team decided to continue with the idea, but to move it out beyond 5 years and to put steps in place over the next 3 years that would allow them to accomplish the task within 8 years, instead of 5.

· ·

Scenario Planning

Another approach to strategic planning, scenario planning, is still remembered as having saved Shell Oil Co. in 1974 from the oil embargo that caused huge losses in all other oil companies, and the process is receiving renewed emphasis (Chermack, 2004). This is not a predictive approach. Under scenario planning, all possible (and even improbable) changes in the environment are considered and developed into a story. Strategic responses are then developed for each story without knowing how the environment will actually change. Then, regardless of what happens in the future, hopefully, plans have been put in place to be implemented immediately, as needed and as appropriate.

· ·

The executive committee of a large multinational corporation heard of scenario planning and liked the idea of implementing it. The company appointed a committee (with no members from the executive committee on it) to create a set of scenarios for 10 years in the future. The team worked for 6 months on a weekly basis, conducted extensive research, talked with suppliers and even competitors, and then created 12 extensive scenarios.

The team then met with the executive committee to present the scenarios. A half day was set aside, and the team made an elaborate presentation of the scenarios. After the presentation, members of the executive committee asked a number of questions and then dismissed the team members. They continued to meet for the rest of the day.

Following the meeting, the executive committee reported to the team that they had selected scenario 6, as that was the most desirable outcome. They would put their time, energies, and resources into responding to that scenario. Clearly, they did not understand the purpose of scenario planning and basically wasted the 6 months of work accomplished by the team. The chair of the team met with the executive committee in an effort to educate it about how the scenarios should have been used, but the committee was not responsive. If any of the other scenarios should happen, this organization will not be prepared, in spite of the good work done by the scenario planning team.

LARGE-SCALE INTERACTIVE EVENTS (LSIEs)

An LSIE is attended by as many as 1,500 people (Sullivan, 1997), all meeting in one place for a 2- to 3-day period. In such an event, participation is extended to all possible stakeholders, such as employees, shareholders, customers, and suppliers. The primary intent of an LSIE is to enable whole systems changes to occur rapidly throughout the organization, rather than having the change trickle gradually throughout the organization.

The characteristics of an LSIE can be summarized as follows (McLean & Kamau, 1998):

- They are based on the principles of small groups (Dannemiller & Jacobs, 1992), though they are typically larger than 100 and can be as large as several thousand, and they typically meet for a period of only 2 to 3 days.
- Because they target the whole system, they are typically made up of representatives from all levels, all geographic locations, and all functional areas of the organization, creating what is called a *max-mix* in LSIE jargon (Sorenson, 1996).
- The intent in an LSIE is for a democratic environment (Sorenson, Gironda, Head, & Larsen, 1996) in which each

participant has an equal chance to contribute, though it is unlikely that such a culture can be created in just a few days if it is not already part of the organization's culture.

- Because each person is involved in the process, the expectation is for an increased commitment to change.

- Change is implemented more rapidly because there is no longer a need for gradual sharing of the needed changes throughout the organization.

- LSIEs are also seen as useful in breaking down existing *silos*; relationships develop during the LSIE that go beyond department boundaries.

- LSIEs are interactive in nature and include consensus, collaboration, and shared ownership of decisions.

DeVogel, Sullivan, McLean, and Rothwell (1995) raised the possibility that LSIEs might lead to the "illusion of participation," in which large numbers of people interact to make decisions, but where the traditional decision makers actually make the decisions.

. . . .

I had the opportunity, with one of my doctoral students, to participate solely as an external evaluator of an LSIE that was conducted by another set of hired OD consultants within a large, state government agency (McLean & Kamau, 1998). The executive team and the managers in the agency met and made the decision to hold an LSIE for the entire organization. They also decided that the event would be planned by a representative group of persons from the entire organization, the design team. The design team was made up of nine volunteers largely unknown to each other, along with two OD consultants. Neither of us (my doctoral student and I) had any responsibility for or any role in the activities, except as evaluators.

We observed a 3-day planning meeting of the design team. We also observed the staging day—a day before the actual LSIE. Staging the event was done by the two OD consultants hired for that purpose, the design team, and the support team. The support team consisted of two office staff from the consultants' organization, support staff from the client organization, and volunteers who were learning how to conduct LSIEs. Finally, we observed the entire 3-day LSIE. The event included 468 people from a government agency with 534 employees and the hired OD consultants and their staff members. Attendance at the event was "required," not voluntary.

We conducted 1-hour interviews with 22 people within a month after the LSIE and with 21 of these 22 nine months after the LSIE (one person had left the organization). We learned that the LSIE entailed free interaction and high expectations of what could be achieved, but there was a slow pace of implementation of the resulting recommendations. We also discovered that minimal individual and organizational change occurred immediately after the event. Persons had volunteered to participate in the follow-up activities, but little action was taken during the first month after the LSIE. My student and I discovered that there also existed consultant–client incongruencies over the duties and responsibilities of the hired consultants regarding follow-up activities.

Later, we reported that, after 9 months, participants still remembered the event (Kamau & McLean, 1999). The LSIE had resulted in an acceleration of some changes. Most of the changes that occurred in this organization, it was believed, would have occurred with or without the LSIE. The changes that did take place as a direct result of the LSIE were considered "cosmetic" by some participants. The information gathered during the event led to a better understanding of internal and external customers. However, the time spent (3 days) on the LSIE was considered to be too long—the participants would have preferred a shorter period. They thought that LSIEs should focus more on gathering and delivering information than formulating strategic plans.

A power base that will endure over time in an organization should be identified and targeted for implementing the organizational change. In this case, the management team should have been involved more in the planning and the execution of the LSIE, because the management team was considered more permanent than the "genuine, but transient" executive team.

The value of holding an LSIE lies in the information that is collected. The participants are able to give information more freely in an LSIE because of the broad involvement of employees and the increased trust level with what they perceive as objective third-party facilitators. It is important to analyze and use that information properly. It is also possible to use LSIEs to deliver information (e.g., policy matters) to a wider audience in a participative manner.

OD consultants, whether internal or external, planning on using LSIEs need to recognize that they will need to spend more time on the implementation phase following the LSIE rather than assuming that change will be achieved during the event. Information collected during an LSIE can be overwhelming to the client organization, and help is needed to analyze the information and arrange it in a meaningful and useful form. When internal OD does not exist, an external OD consultant should plan on spending more time to help with follow-up activities. Planning for follow-up activities is as important as the planning for the LSIE itself. OD consultants should anticipate the problems organizations may encounter and coach the leaders accordingly.

OPEN SYSTEMS MAPPING

Open systems mapping starts with the assumption that an organization, in the language of systems theory, is an open system. The organization interacts to different degrees with the environment. Open systems mapping is a process, often used in large groups, to determine how this interaction takes place. It is often used, then, to help the organization determine its mission, based on what it currently is and what it would like to be. Once this gap is identified, the organization can then decide what it needs to do to get there.

Mapping the system as it is and then mapping where people want the organization to be in the future may be a way to make these visions more concrete. Heap's (n.d.) approach uses a verbal, columnar approach in which (1) the system is described, (2) the factors that influence or are influenced by the system are listed, (3) the nature of the relationship is described, and (4) the emotions people feel about the relationship indicated. For example, (1) a manager (2) interacts with subordinates (3) in a friendly and supportive way (4) that makes people feel happy.

. . . .

Heap (n.d.) also suggested that pictures could be used to describe the relationships and emotions. I have participated in two open systems mapping sessions. Both sessions were facilitated in a similar way. Sheets of butcher paper were laid out on the floor, a large circle was drawn in the center of the butcher paper to represent the organization, and we then began drawing images to express relationships that existed with the organization and our feelings about those relationships. Having discovered that I am more of a verbal than a visual communicator, I found the process to be quite challenging. That reaction seemed to reflect the basic feelings of others in the group, but, as the group consisted of mostly males, a gender influence may have been in effect.

FUTURE SEARCH

Many see future search as a specific application of an LSIE. Weisbord and Janoff (2000) developed the concept of future search. As described in Chapter 5, future search brings together a cross section of members of a system who meet in a large-group planning session to explore the past, present, and future related to a specific, focused task.

Weisbord and Janoff (2000) recommended that 30 to 64 stakeholders, with one-third coming from outside the system or organization, would be involved. The process begins with the participants telling stories about their shared past, knowing that there will be inconsistencies and contradictory recollections of that past. Even those from outside the organization will have shared information because of country history, interaction with similar organizations, common values, and so on. Participants then explore the present and the global trends affecting that present. This information is often recorded on a large sheet of paper, with subsequent prioritizing of the trends also noted. To imagine the organization's future, typically 5, 10, and/or 20 years in the future, diverse subgroups, formed by their interests in a specific theme, get together to create concrete verbal images of that future. Each subgroup also describes the barriers they would have had to overcome to get to the future they envision. All participants in the future search then create a list of common futures (what they agree on), possible projects to get there, and unresolved differences. Participants then decide on what specific project each participant wants to work on and then they cluster with others interested in working on the same project to determine next steps.

The benefit of this approach is that the facilitator has no specific outcome in mind, nor is there any preconceived sense of problems, solutions, projects, and so on. Everything that emerges from the exercise resides with the participants, with the facilitators only overseeing the process.

. . . .

I was a participant in a future search cosponsored by the Academy of Human Resource Development and American Society of Training and Development, with the objective of looking at the future of the profession of human resource development. For those interested, the complete process is described by Dewey and Carter (2003). Twelve common group themes emerged for the future of human resource development (pp. 252–254):

- Creating synergy between research and practice
- Leveraging available technology without losing the human touch and social component of learning
- Striking a healthy balance between work life and personal life
- Striving to create humane workplaces
- Acknowledging intellectual capital as the life blood of the organization (the true "bottom line")
- Developing a sense of social responsibility
- Embracing globalization
- Embracing multiculturalism
- Partnering in the fundamentally changing role for education
- Managing knowledge and learning effectively
- Developing partnerships and collaboration internal and external to the organization
- Fostering lifelong learning

These visions are ones that OD professionals could probably accept for its future as a profession. My own reaction to the outcome we produced, however, was that this was a laudatory list of *present*, quality HRD. Nothing in this list really suggests any future vision, except for the fact that there is a gap between our desired present and our actual present.

. . . .

OPEN SPACE TECHNOLOGY MEETINGS

These meetings are based on the dialogue process (see Chapter 7), but they are also a subset of LSIEs. According to Corrigan (2002), "The goal of an Open Space Technology meeting is to create time and space for people to engage deeply and creatively around issues of concern to them." It can be used to address a wide range of issues, including "strategic direction setting, envisioning the future, conflict resolution, morale building, consultation with stakeholders, community planning, collaboration and deep learning about issues and perspectives" (Corrigan, 2002).

After identifying issues to be addressed, each issue is posted on the wall with an agenda and time specified to meet to address the issue. Participants decide which issues they choose to attend, and dialogue technology is used. Ideas are then captured on flipcharts and are posted on a results wall. People have the freedom to address any issue they want, as well as the freedom to express any opinion they wish about that issue.

According to Corrigan (2002), the following principles and law operate:

- Whoever comes are the right people.
- Whatever happens is the only thing that could have happened.
- When it starts is the right time.
- When it's over, it's over.

The Law of Two Feet applies:

If you find yourself in a situation where you are not contributing or learning, move somewhere where you can.

CHAPTER SUMMARY

This chapter focused on some examples of OD interventions designed with a primary focus on the whole organization, recognizing that all OD interventions affect the whole organization in some way. Culture change, while one of the most difficult of outcomes to realize, is really what most of OD is about. Thus, by addressing the behaviors and norms above the water of Schein's cultural iceberg, OD professionals can hope to influence the organizational culture.

Similar comments can be made about several of the targets of the interventions included in this chapter. Valuing diversity, for example, is influenced by deeply held assumptions; by addressing behaviors, we hope to influence culture. Thinking in strategic ways is driven by one's beliefs and values, yet some form of strategic plan is needed to provide direction to the organization. Values are incorporated into mission and vision statements. The design of accountability and reward systems almost always contradicts research, yet how organizations put these areas in place often reflects the values of the organizational leadership. Similar observations can be made for most of the interventions contained in this chapter. As suggested, creating culture change is a complex process!

QUESTIONS FOR DISCUSSION OR SELF-REFLECTION

1. Consider each of the structures suggested in this chapter. List the advantages and disadvantages for each structural model.

2. How can the OD professional help diminish the pain caused by downsizing, outsourcing, or the loss of jobs to a merger or acquisition?

3. What do you believe provides the strongest motivation for you to perform at your best as a student? As an employee? What is the relationship between intrinsic and extrinsic motivation factors for you?

4. Write a personal mission statement and a personal vision statement. Discuss their value.

5. Create a number of scenarios for your own future. Discuss one or two of these, suggesting how scenario planning might serve you better than a more static strategic plan.

6. Your class or a group of employees may wish to participate in an open systems technology meeting.

11

Implementation: Community and National Levels

CHAPTER OUTLINE

Organization Development at the National Level: What in the World Is It?

Why Is OD at the National Level Growing in Importance?

Processes Used in Doing OD at the National Level

Barriers to Establishing National Development Policies Based on OD Principles

Attributes of Excellent National Development Policy Based on OD Principles

Outcomes of Excellent National Development Planning

Conclusion

Chapter Summary

Questions for Discussion or Self-Reflection

OVERVIEW A relatively recent phenomenon, especially in the global context, has been the application of OD principles, values, and techniques in community contexts and at national levels. In a world increasingly threatened with violence, the skill set of experienced OD professionals has the possibility of offering that expertise to communities, nations, regions, and worldwide nongovernmental organizations (NGOs) to help build stronger communities and to counter widespread violence.

As specified in Chapter 1, an *organization* is any group of two or more coming together with a common purpose. Historically, the focus of OD work has been on for-profit and not-for-profit organizations, including subsystems of those organizations. Increasingly, however, there has been an awareness of the importance of the skills of OD in developing communities, nations, regions, and worldwide NGOs. This emerging focus is consistent with the Implementation phase of the ODP model (see Figure 11.1).

The OD Institute has been very influential in sending teams of OD professionals to areas of the world where conflict between groups has been prevalent. Teams have been sent to Northern Ireland, South Africa, the Balkans, and other locations. The intent in each situation has been to contribute the conflict management skills resident within the field of OD to help groups that have been in conflict confront the source of their conflicts and find ways to coexist in healthy ways. It is not possible to point to proven cause-effect breakthroughs with such excursions, but they do show promise. However, as OD teams tend to be outsiders who are in communities for a limited amount of time, developing OD professionals within the communities is another promising approach for making significant contributions to peace efforts.

During a U.S. State Department project in Kyrgyzstan, from September 2001 through December 2004, a colleague and I, with others, conducted an extensive needs assessment of K–12 administrators and developed two master's degree programs in educational leadership (McLean & Karimov, 2005). As a by-product, our work influenced educational policy on everything

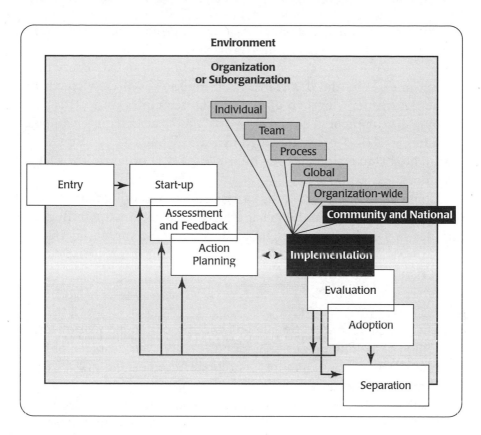

Figure 11.1 *Organization Development Process Model, Phase 5: Implementation at the Community and National Levels*

from reinstituting public kindergartens to establishing boards of directors for universities and continuing education for K–12 administrators. The codirector in Kyrgyzstan claims that the work laid a foundation for democracy that led to the recent peaceful overthrow of the corrupt government. OD skills in the project included cross-cultural training, collaboration, network building, team building, conflict management, and education.

Efforts are also under way to develop OD expertise in communities that are potentially sources of conflict through the offering of academic programs in these areas. For example, the University of Minnesota has been offering its human resource development professional certificate, including a course in OD, in Saudi Arabia since 1999, and it began offering courses for a master's degree in 2005. Ohio State University offers courses in Kuwait, and the United Arab Emirates is already committed at the government level to applying OD principles and skills in its ongoing development. The University of Illinois at Urbana-Champaign conducts its HRD program in Kenya and Thailand, while George Washington University has been offering its HRD program for years in Singapore.

Community development has long been seen as critical in Thailand (na Chiangmi, 1998), and explicit efforts have been made in Buddhist temples in Thailand to use OD to develop the temple and those it serves, with a national annual award given to the temple that does so best (Yamnill & McLean, 2005).

. . . .

Lim (2005) described an innovative approach in the tension-torn region of the Philippines—Mindanao—under the auspices of the Notre Dame Foundation for Charitable Activities, Inc. (NDFCA), Women in Enterprise Development. In spite of a peace agreement between the government of the Philippines and the Muslim National Liberation Front (MNLF), conflict continues in this region. In addition, the Communist New Peoples' Army (NPA) has experienced resurgence, and the indigenous peoples of the region, the Lumads, have serious unmet needs. Through the establishment of community learning centers, with support from UNESCO and the United Nations' Multi-Donor Program, NDFCA, a Christian-based organization, offers its services to all without distinction—Muslims, Christians, and indigenous people. The primary focus has been on capacity building that has included some of the following services: out-of-school children and youth literacy education, adult literacy education, continuing education, training, advocacy, peace education, gender fairness, enterprise development, and political activity. As Lim (2005) explained:

> Educating toward a culture of peace for our learners is a major concern. Lessons integrate: the concept of peaceful and indigenous resolution of conflict; of respect for the fundamental

rights and freedom; of promoting cultural understanding, tolerance and solidarity; cultivating inner peace and to live with others in peace and compassion. (p. 2445)

In so many ways, this story in the Philippines represents the power of the kinds of skills that OD professionals can contribute to nations. Lim has a background in development and served, prior to her current executive director position, as dean of a business school in the region.

. . . .

These are not unique stories. Individual OD professionals, consistent with the OD Code of Ethics developed by The OD Institute (see Chapter 15), have chosen to make their voluntary contributions (known as *pro bono*, literally "for good," or free service) to organizations that serve the community.

ORGANIZATION DEVELOPMENT AT THE NATIONAL LEVEL: WHAT IN THE WORLD IS IT?

The application of OD skills that have been used successfully in organizations and their subsystems is moving to communities, nations, regions, and even more broadly. This trend is consistent with what I see as parallel to the same movement that is taking place in HRD, the umbrella for organization development for some (e.g., McLagan & Suhadolnik, 1989), as suggested in Chapter 1. In that context, consider this definition of HRD:

Human resource development is any process or activity that, either initially or over the long term, has the potential to develop . . . work-based knowledge, expertise, productivity and satisfaction, whether for personal or group/team gain, or for the benefit of an organization, community, nation, or, ultimately, the whole of humanity. (McLean & McLean, 2001, p. 10)

I have suggested in Chapter 1 that we can easily replace the opening term, *human resource development*, with *organization development* and, with some other minor changes, create the following global definition for organization development:

Organization development is any process or activity, based on the behavioral sciences, that, either initially or over the long term, has the potential to develop in an organizational setting enhanced knowledge, expertise, productivity, satisfaction, income, interpersonal relationships, and other desired outcomes, whether for personal or group/team gain, or for the benefit of an organization, community, nation, region, or, ultimately, the whole of humanity.

Many countries have already applied this definition, though under the label of national human resource development. In discussing this movement, much of the rest of this chapter draws heavily on an earlier monograph (McLean, Osman-Gani, & Cho, 2004), specifically on select articles (i.e., McLean, 2004; Cho & McLean, 2004).

Organization development, when viewed from a national perspective, goes beyond workplace organizations to include employment, preparation for employment, education, health, culture, safety, community, tourism, and a host of other considerations that may not typically have been perceived historically as the focus of OD. Yet, within the growing concept of national and regional open systems thinking, there is a need for a unified, synthesized approach to the planning and influencing of these issues within each country or region. Given the size of the issues involved, it is clear that OD cannot hope to undertake the scope of this approach alone. As I have emphasized throughout this book, it is essential that OD professionals collaborate in these community, national, and regional development undertakings. Professionals in economics, social work, urban and rural planning, education, politics, business, health care, and every other area that touches on these issues will need to work together to help people and communities move forward. Two such examples of how OD might make a contribution in such a way follow.

First, consider the view that there is no one on Earth who is not potentially subject to AIDS/HIV infection. Combating this issue will take the work of medical researchers, medical personnel, educators, social workers, and many others, including, as I am suggesting, OD professionals who understand the process of change and what it will take to address cultural issues that continue to put individuals at risk. For example, OD professionals, working primarily through consortia of business organizations, have been addressing the question of what businesses in Thailand must do to help alleviate the impact of AIDS/ HIV on workers and business organizations (Virakul & McLean, 2000).

A second example is the overwhelming tragedy of the tsunami in December 2004. Never in modern history has there been such an extensive natural tragedy in terms of loss of personal lives and property damage affecting so many countries. The long-term recovery process will require years. The immediate-term recovery process required tens of thousands of volunteers and professionals from many countries working together. It demanded incredible coordination and cross-cultural understanding. I do not know how many OD professionals took part in the recovery process, but, given the skill set of OD professionals, they likely played a significant role. I am personally aware of OD professionals being involved in the rebuilding of villages in Sri Lanka. Unfortunately, many such opportunities exist in the world, for which OD professionals could well take some responsibility in facilitating solutions.

So long as cultures and country circumstances remain different, there will never be an overarching definition for OD in a global context—nor should there be! Given the importance of ambiguity and the influence of culture that are core elements in OD, each community, country, and region will create its own modifications to the suggested definition. Failure to provide a unified definition will leave some people uncomfortable, but that is the way it is in a world of diverse cultures.

In part, the emphasis in the proposed global definition of OD on nation has emerged from the shift that has occurred in many countries (e.g., Kenya, Korea) from governmental 5-year development plans to a national focus couched in the language of HRD/OD. In Singapore, this movement is referred to as *human capital development*; the government there has always given top priority in strategic planning to national development (Osman-Gani & Tan, 1998, 2000). Recently, the Korean Ministry of Education was renamed the Ministry of Education and Human Resource Development (Cho & McLean, 2002; Moon & McLean, 2003), with efforts to use OD principles to pull together in a collaborative way the work of more than 20 ministries coordinated under the Minister of Education and Human Resource Development.

Another example of the growing importance of OD at the regional level is reflected in the work of the HRD Working Group of Asia-Pacific Economic Cooperation (APEC), a group that "is widely considered to be one of the most dynamic of the eleven working groups in APEC, with HRD as one of the APEC economic leaders' six priorities" (Zanko & Ngui, 2003, p. 13). Its areas of concern suggest significant components of the proposed global definition of OD: "education and training issues that are cast very widely to include basic education, industrial training, productivity and equity in labour forces and workplaces, creation of comparable labour market data, lifelong learning and management development" (Zanko & Ngui, 2003, p. 13).

WHY IS OD AT THE NATIONAL LEVEL GROWING IN IMPORTANCE?

OD at the national level is of rising significance for several reasons:

- For many countries, their people are their primary resource. Without natural resources, many countries must look to their human resources. Japan and Korea are prime examples of countries that have succeeded because of their emphasis on developing their people when they do not have access to natural resources.

- Development work is critical for national and local stability. Countries that do not have sustainable development and that have high unemployment rates leading to high levels of poverty are countries that reflect a lack of stability. Developing people is one approach to alleviating these conditions.

- If we are ever to break the cycles of welfare, poverty, violence, unemployment, illiteracy, and socially undesirable employment, we must provide integrated and coordinated development mechanisms, such as those available through OD.

- Working in collaboration with other professionals, OD has the potential to improve individuals' quality of work life.

- There is an increased need to deal with the ambiguity of global *coopetition* (the simultaneous need for cooperation and competition). Many small countries, in particular, are finding that it is essential to cooperate with their neighbors even when they are competitors (e.g., the many small islands of the Caribbean that are competing for tourists). OD professionals have (or should have) a high degree of comfort with such ambiguity.

- The demographics of many developed countries, among other explanations, suggest a potential labor scarcity (fewer younger workers with an aging workforce that does not have the currently requisite skill sets), whereas other countries (e.g., Saudi Arabia) have a surplus of young workers, requiring some coordinated response from industry and government agencies and across national governments.

- The impact of AIDS/HIV on populations worldwide, but especially in developing countries, is potentially damaging to the present and future populations, workforces, and economies of many countries. A response is required to diminish the incidence and impact of AIDS/HIV. A national focus on OD is one approach that might do this.

- Dynamic changes in technology keep pressure on for enhancing the skills of all people.

An economist back in 1986 stated that "developed, educated, motivated people are an unlimited resource . . . [while] undeveloped, uneducated, unmotivated people are a monumental drag on an economy in the internationalized information era" (Marshall, 1986, p. 1). Of course, one could also see such a population as an unparalleled opportunity for development and advancement of a nation, if the nation responds appropriately.

Briggs (1987), also an economist, concluded, "While economists in general and policymakers in particular have focused upon physical capital as the explanation for long-term economic growth, it has actually been human resource development that has been the major contributor" (p. 1213). These observations underscore the importance of using OD skills for continuing development at the national level.

PROCESSES USED IN DOING OD AT THE NATIONAL LEVEL

A previously cited monograph (McLean et al., 2004) summarizes how 13 countries and regions have used OD concepts to formulate national development policies. In this process, most countries became involved with debating and discussing the various issues to diagnose what was wrong with the country's education system, as well as economic, social, cultural, and human resource development systems; and what could and should be done in response to such an analysis. Expert committees were appointed; a number of seminars and conferences were held in various parts of the country; many issues were raised and suggestions made, debated, and discussed. Through lengthy and controversial processes, national systems were designed and developed. The emerging policies were often influenced by the power dynamics of the different ministries, and the complexity and multidimensionality of each country.

Five emerging models for development were identified in this research: centralized, transitional, government initiated, decentralized/ free market, and small nation. There is no "pure" model; each country, even though it is categorized as fitting into one or the other of the models, may also incorporate components from other models. Much of what follows in discussing these models has been gleaned from an earlier work (Cho & McLean, 2004).

Centralized Model

Under this model, the state is responsible for providing education and training with a top-down approach from the central government to local governments and to private enterprises and their agencies, as seen in the Chinese model (Yang, Zhang, & Zhang, 2004). The central government plays a critical role in planning, implementing, and assessing development policies and strategies. Entrepreneurship, intrapreneurship, and personal initiative are often discouraged by a top-down management style, as with the Polish model (Szalkowski & Jankowicz, 2004). There are no serious or reputable agencies beyond the government that are responsible for development policymaking. Furthermore, there is a strong interest in the social dimension of development. Rooted in a strong collectivist context, this model tends to have strong social and moral implications.

Finally, development policies within this model are still usually linked to 5-year national plans of development, as in the case of Mexico (Rangel, 2004) or Kenya (Lutta-Mukhebi, 2004), both of which are in the industrialization economic development stage. The government plays a major role in economic development, while the corporate sector plays a minor role in that its market share is small, and it depends on technology from advanced countries.

Transitional Model

This model applies to countries under transition from the centralized model to a government-initiated or decentralized model. Development policy is featured in the tripartite approach drawing on employers, unions, and the government. The tripartite relationship ensures that there is agreement over the strategies and the necessary steps for implementing development policies. Therefore, a major role emphasized for national development policy is on coordination.

Second, national development policies under this model take a multidepartmental approach. Development policies are typically promulgated by different ministries, such as the Ministry of Industry and Resources, Ministry of Culture and Tourism, Ministry of Information and Communication, Ministry of Education, and Ministry of Labor. These offices are potentially in conflict and sometimes repetitive. The government may then be called on to plan and initiate coordinated development policies. In Korea, for example, this coordination occurs through the office of the Vice-Prime Minister of Education and HRD (McLean, Bartlett, & Cho, 2003).

The concept of national development policy in India (Rao, 2004), through the Ministry of HRD, has been limited to education and culture, and the broader national development policy system has not been integrated due to the country's complexity and multidimensionality. In this context, India can be considered to be a very weak version of this model. The Singaporean model (Osman-Gani, 2004) lies between the transitional model and the government-initiated model in that Singapore's human capital development plan is featured by a committed government, a network of agencies, and a commitment to tripartism. In addition, Singapore has the People Developer system, similar to the Investor in People system in the U.K.

Government-Initiated Model toward Standardization

The U.K. example of national development policy is seen as exerting some influence over its former territories and beyond. It illustrates an approach that uses a variety of development initiatives taken by the government. The majority of approaches have been consultative and based on a stakeholder view of human resources and the economy. Worker competences are controlled by the National Occupational Standards and Modern Apprenticeship Frameworks that are managed by Sector Skills Councils. The Learning and Skill Council, which is composed of representatives from employers, learning providers, and community groups working to provide human resource development services to satisfy local needs, plans and funds all post-16 education other than the university sector. Investor in People (IIP) awards have attracted interest from corporate sectors and have placed the function of developing people on the agenda of large corporations, though it does not easily meet the needs of small to medium-sized enterprises. The general move in the development of people in the U.K. is toward standardization, which risks a unitary approach (Lee, 2004).

South Africa (Lynham & Cunningham, 2004), Australia, and other former British territories have followed the U.K. model to a large extent, though some components, such as Investor in People, are not designed and implemented in the current systems. Standardization is accomplished in many of these countries through National Vocational Qualifications (NVQs), in which competencies are specified for different levels of education and expertise.

Decentralized/Free Market Model

Under this model, the major forces pushing development efforts come from the competitive market. The development of people has been normally regarded as activities at the enterprise level. The private sector is mostly responsible for education and training, although the state supports the private sector in an indirect way.

Second, this model is based on a firm individualistic value in which individuals are responsible for their own learning and growth. The Canadian model (Cooper, 2004) fits this category as, presumably, does the model present in the United States.

Small Nation Models

Because more than 190 countries currently belong to the United Nations, it is important to consider this model as, by far, the majority of nations in the world fit into the small nation category. Small countries may need to take different approaches toward development, often in cooperation with other small nations in their region. So, we find nations in the Pacific Islands cooperating (Bartlett & Rodgers, 2004), just as St. Lucia cooperates with other small countries in the Caribbean (Scotland, 2004). The model is a difficult one for countries to participate in because, on the one hand, the countries are in competition with each other, especially in the tourism industry, while, on the other hand, they need to cooperate to gain the benefit of pooling resources. This is a perfect example of the concept of coopetition in which small nations, such as those in the Caribbean, must both cooperate in marketing to gain more tourists to the area and still compete so tourists will choose one specific island.

In the Pacific Islands, a number of regional intergovernmental organizations have played a key role in promoting development for the region. These include the Secretariat of the Pacific Community (SPC), the Pacific Islands Forum Secretariat (PIFS), South Pacific Board of Educational Assessment, and the University of the South Pacific.

Another characteristic of the small nation model is the participative processes that are possible. Because the nations are small, it is not difficult to get people together and to hear from every sector of the nation.

BARRIERS TO ESTABLISHING NATIONAL DEVELOPMENT POLICIES BASED ON OD PRINCIPLES

While most of the country cases reported in the monograph focused on the successes in moving toward a national development policy, each country had some difficulties in moving toward establishing a national development approach. Though not comprehensive, the following list suggests some reasons why countries might have difficulty in establishing a national development policy:

- The labor market is imperfect and unpredictable. We cannot know what skills and competencies will be needed in the future. And by the time the future arrives, the labor market is unbalanced. So students who have prepared for careers that were "hot" 5 years ago find that the supply of available workers in that field exceeds the demand, while a new labor demand has emerged for which too few students have prepared themselves.
- Everyone tries to do the same thing. For example, the IT and customer service labor markets, which are moving off-shore

from the United States and Europe in large numbers, are likely, ultimately, to lead to a glut in the labor market. When technology changes, or when wages in one country become too high for the desired level of productivity, what will countries like India, the Philippines, Malaysia, and other Asian or African nations do? Will they be prepared for the next major wave of off-shoring?

- Mobility of labor can upset the best of plans. Often this development is put in the context of a "brain drain." This phenomenon is often experienced by countries in which the standard of living is low but that have been successful in producing personnel who are well qualified in areas of high global labor market demand.

- The desire to have freedom of choice may impede governmental action. For example, government desires to limit the number of higher education institutions is impeded by the desire of people to earn degrees regardless of whether there is demand for graduates of a particular major. Kyrgyzstan is a perfect example of where this problem exists (Albaeva & McLean, 2004). Current higher education reforms in Kyrgyzstan have reduced higher education institutions from 114 to 8 that will receive financial support from the government. The result is a monopolistic environment in which each major is offered in only one institution that is government subsidized. Furthermore, in a country with extremely high unemployment (approaching 40%), one of the most popular majors is American studies, for which there is virtually no demand in the workplace.

- National development planning, to some people, sounds too much like communism, socialism, and centralized planning. As we saw in the five models, the centralized model does exist— but the other four models described here do *not* rely on a centralized planning perspective.

- Is national development planning simply camouflaging the old 5-year plans? Again, it is clear that, for some countries, such is the case (e.g., Kenya, People's Republic of China). However, several other countries have not done this, and, even among those countries that do use 5-year plans, many have a head start in coming to grips with the concept of national development policy.

- Serious social problems impede the national development in some countries. For example, the HIV/AIDS situation in India, Kenya, Thailand, and South Africa has a huge impact on the country's economy, such as health costs, loss of a productive workforce (including teachers), orphans, and absenteeism. Such countries must come to grips with this issue if it is to have a viable national development policy.

ATTRIBUTES OF EXCELLENT NATIONAL DEVELOPMENT POLICY BASED ON OD PRINCIPLES

In spite of these barriers, many countries are moving toward the successful use of OD principles for setting national policy. Specifically, OD principles of planning, collaboration, team building, conflict management, ambiguity, flexibility, long-term focus, needs analysis, and evaluation all fit. In fact, the application of the ODP model appears to be as appropriate for use in nations as in organizations.

Some of the attributes that might be mined from the cases explored in this chapter include the following:

- There is no one "right" way to create national development policy. How national development policy is created will vary from country to country based on country characteristics (McLean & McLean, 2001).
- Approaches to developing national development policy provide a shifting and differential balance between central, regional, and local planning.
- National approaches to development policy planning must be flexible, allowing for quick responses to changes in the worldwide, regional, national, and local economies and labor markets. Those models that presume to predict the future or to establish standards after lengthy and extensive study are likely to be too rigid to respond quickly enough to the needs of the marketplace. Ambiguity arises in the apparent conflict between OD's long-term perspective and the need for quick response.
- When individuals lose jobs through no fault of their own, government policy must provide for training and retraining, education and reeducation, relocation, and compensation. A

social and economic fallback system must be in place for all members of the society.

- Excellent national policies for development will be nondiscriminatory, being designed for everyone, from birth to death.

- Quality national policies for development will dynamically encourage rather than mandate (e.g., eliminating overlap in higher education institutions, attracting students to needed fields of study and away from those with excess, providing incentives to pay higher salaries in areas where labor is needed, etc.).

- There will be a clear statement of mission for government agencies, to eliminate any duplication of government services. This is key to excellent development policy creation, and it is probably one of the most difficult to implement. How to move past jealousies, power struggles, turf battles, and other destructive conflictual activities remains a key, but extremely difficult, necessity.

- The creation of national development policies will use OD principles to emphasize coopetition with other countries in the region, and perhaps even with any country willing to partner. In today's market-based economies, it may be difficult for most countries to deal with the ambiguity of coopetition, especially in countries where dichotomous, we-they thinking predominates.

- The role of the political system will be well defined. Within the centralized model, of course, the political system will take the lead; in the transition model, the government will be a part of the tripartite system providing the leadership. In decentralized systems, on the other hand, any influence from the political system will be viewed as interference.

- Leadership for excellent national development policy creation will be interdisciplinary.

- Leadership will consist of the *very best minds available* (not limited to family members, cronies, political friends or politicians, civil servants, and not necessarily even just citizens of the country *unless* they are truly the best minds available). Decisions about membership and leadership will depend on the national development model in place.

- Excellent national development policies must be flexible while remaining visionary. This probably means that there will be no 5-year plans—they are too far out and inhibit flexibility. At the same time, consideration must be given to possible scenarios for at least 20 years ahead—with the hope that the best minds will be able to surface scenarios that might be close to what will actually happen.

- It will not be constrained by the culture of the country, while still considering country culture. This is another tricky and ambiguous situation that must be handled wisely.

- National development policy will be heavily biased toward research and theory, while remaining thoroughly practical.

- Evaluations will include both qualitative and quantitative measures. Existing country cases appear to be silent on the issue of evaluation. We do not know what criteria countries will use to determine success, nor are we informed about how those evaluations will take place. So, although most countries put considerable emphasis on the upfront analysis of needs, none identified in the literature is concerned about evaluation. When such plans are put in place, they need to be both data driven as well as anecdotal.

- Objectives will be established based on the capabilities of the new, envisioned system, not just on wishes, desires, and needs.

- Budgets to support national development will increase dramatically annually, gradually replacing social welfare and defense budgets. In spite of the positive development plan laid out in the last two plans in Kenya, its current budget is insufficient to cover the most basic needs of the nation, such as teacher salaries, minimal educational facilities, and so on.

- Tax incentives may encourage the use of quality OD processes in the development of people and organizational cultures, though the entire issue of funding is a difficult one.

- Work–life balance will be encouraged with family-friendly policies. There must be a recognition that, with a holistic perspective of national development, economic development alone is not enough. This is one of the major problems in a country such as South Korea, where long working hours mean

> absence from the home and discrimination against women moving into the workplace.

- Social factors must be addressed. When workers and potential workers are confronted with poverty, illness (e.g., HIV/AIDS), family abuse, discrimination of various sorts, political oppression, and so on, it will be impossible for the population to thrive and for national development policies to succeed.

Unfortunately, we have few cases to point to of real success in developing national development policies. Singapore probably comes the closest to economic success, but others might question whether applying a similar approach in other countries would lead to equivalent success.

OUTCOMES OF EXCELLENT NATIONAL DEVELOPMENT PLANNING

The following list of desirable outcomes may be perceived by some as idealistic. Nevertheless, progress in moving toward each is occurring in those countries that are beginning to use OD principles for national development.

- Functional illiteracy will be eliminated—among youth and adults.
- Employment in socially undesirable occupations (prostitution, drug dealing, and illegal activities) will steadily decline because of the availability of attractive, alternative employment and a personally and socially supportive environment.
- There will no longer be a need for child labor; all children will receive adequate education while having their physical needs met, along with those of their families (Budhwani, Wee, & McLean, 2004).
- The "right" mix of people will emerge from excellent national development policy planning. Creative approaches will be needed to attract people to occupations and preparation programs that are not deemed to be socially acceptable (e.g., plumbers, construction workers, hotel workers, etc.).
- The quality of primary and secondary education will improve and be more comprehensive in its curriculum; teachers will be

adequately paid, and appropriate facilities and supplies will be provided.

- The quality of higher education institutions will improve as their quantity decreases; again, faculty will be adequately paid, and appropriate facilities and supplies will be provided. In addition, academic freedom will be affirmed and carried out with the blessing of the political system.

- Less money will be spent in traditional forms of national development, such as remedial basic education, proprietary schools, and long-term degree programs for which there is little demand, while increasing funds will be available in nontraditional forms of development, such as online e-learning, structured on-the-job training, apprenticeships, and so on.

- Increased legal and encouraged flow of labor across national boundaries will occur to seek labor market equilibrium. This movement will likely continue to be fought by developed countries that have a disproportionate share of the world's economic wealth.

- A balanced approach to population growth will be taken. This may need to come from more open borders for immigration. Looking not too far into the future, many countries are aging; some, such as Italy, are facing a dramatic decrease in its population. At the same time, other countries continue to grow beyond their ability to support their populations. OD applied at the cross-national and global organization levels may well help build needed equilibrium in world populations.

- Progress will be made toward full employment without underemployment.

- Education, training, provision of medical support, culture change, provision of condoms, and social worker support will bring about improvements in the health situations of countries using OD principles for national development, especially relative to HIV/AIDS—in spite of religious and cultural restrictions.

- Perhaps, as suggested by Freire (1972), people will be able to function fully as members of society rather than being acted on.

- "If human resources are truly 'the wealth of nations,' their development carries with it the parallel responsibility to recognize that their contribution to the economy must enhance the quality of life on this planet and not lead to its enslavement, impoverishment, or extinction" (Briggs, 1987, p. 1236).

CONCLUSION

Cynics believe that conversation about national development based on the principles of OD is idealistic, but, at our core as OD professionals, aren't we idealists? We dream of developing individuals to have improved lives. We dream of developing organizations that are productive, safe, supportive, nurturing, successful, competitive, financially secure, ethical, and profitable. Are these goals too idealistic?

Why should we dream for less for our nations, our regions, and our common humanity than what we dream for individuals and organizations? Our OD efforts in national development will not be perfect, but they can and should move us along on our pathway to improved humanity. This will not be an easy journey, but it is a journey that we must take—as a profession and as members of that profession.

CHAPTER SUMMARY

Interest has risen in recent years in applying OD principles at community and national levels for the creation of development policies. The interest is in coordinating the efforts of multiple ministries to eliminate duplication and to fill in any gaps that might exist. Such national development plans include education, training, economic policy, enterprise development, health, safety, technology, and other aspects that influence and affect the quality of life for the country's citizens and residents. Drawing on recent research that investigated the national development policy planning of 13 countries, this chapter explored the barriers to effective development planning, the characteristics of outstanding national development planning, and the outcomes to be expected from excellent national development planning that uses OD principles.

QUESTIONS FOR DISCUSSION
OR SELF-REFLECTION

1. Why do you think that interest in using OD principles at the community and national levels has recently increased?

2. Considering the five models for using OD for national development policy planning, what do you see as the advantages and disadvantages of each?

3. Why do you think that the United States fits into the free market model? Do you think the United States would be better served with some other model?

4. How does country culture influence the model that prevails in a country?

5. What steps might be taken to reduce the barriers to the effective application of OD principles at the national level?

6. Consider the situation described in this chapter about the peace efforts in the Philippines. What OD principles do you see being applied there?

7. Consider the HIV/AIDS pandemic. What OD principles might be applied to diminishing the impact of this illness?

12

Evaluation of Processes and Results

CHAPTER OUTLINE

OVERVIEW   Unfortunately, evaluation is often ignored by OD professionals and their clients. In this chapter, the importance of evaluation is stressed, along with some suggestions of how evaluation can be done so as to counter the objections often put forward. Many approaches to evaluation are reviewed, with advantages and disadvantages of each. Again, because it is always impossible to *prove* direct cause and effect with OD, triangulation (use of multiple approaches) is emphasized. Formative (during the process), summative (at the end of the process), and longitudinal (over time) evaluation are discussed. (This chapter draws heavily from McLean, 2005.)

Evaluation is an important phase often overlooked by practitioners. The difficulty in conducting a viable evaluation is often cited as the reason why evaluations are not conducted. This chapter explores the reasons for conducting evaluation, the pros and cons of the most popular approaches to evaluation, and suggestions for a workable, though not perfect, means of carrying out acceptable evaluations.

According to the ODP model, the Evaluation phase (see Figure 12.1) follows the Implementation phases with significant overlap. It is critical that the decision about how to evaluate be made during the Start-up and Action Planning phases. The overlap that occurs between the Intervention and Evaluation phases is critical because evaluation, ideally, is formative as well as summative. That is, evaluation should be occurring on an ongoing basis throughout the change efforts (*formative evaluation*), as well as at the end of the process (*summative evaluation*). In many organizations, such evaluation also occurs on a repeated basis, long after any specific intervention (*longitudinal evaluation*).

The purpose of evaluation is to allow the OD professional and the client organization to make immediate adjustments while in the process, and to determine whether the change effort should be institutionalized throughout the organization (adoption) or whether the cycle needs to begin again to find a more effective intervention. Evaluation is also used to determine the effectiveness of the OD professional, though such an approach is often misplaced. The OD professional is able to do only what the client organization allows him or her to do. Thus, failure to experience the benefits from the intervention could well reflect the

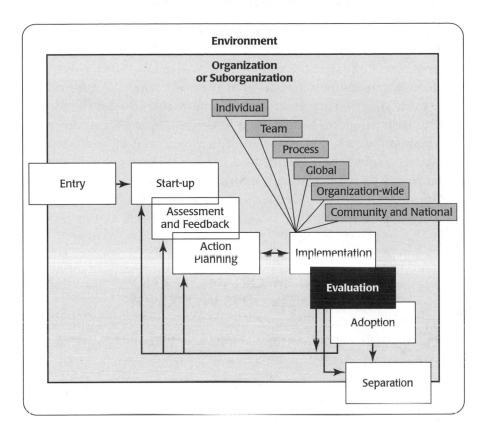

Figure 12.1 *Organization Development Process Model, Phase 6: Evaluation*

choice of the wrong intervention; a changing environment from the time of the assessment; an uncooperative, time- or resource-deficient, or unskilled client organization; or the incompetence or mistake of the OD professional. Separating out the cause of failure is a useful process to enhance learning of all of the parties, but it is extremely difficult to do.

Evaluation in OD is consistently seen as an important phase in the professional application of OD. In spite of its importance, evaluation has proven to be difficult to perform in a way that the results are widely accepted. The difficulty of performing evaluations may lead to the subsequent failure to include evaluation.

DEFINITION

According to Fitzpatrick, Sanders, and Worthen (2004), there is no "uniformly agreed-upon definition of precisely what the term *evaluation* means" (p. 5). They went on to define *evaluation* "as the identification, clarification, and application of defensible criteria to determine an evaluation object's value (worth or merit) in relation to those criteria" (p. 5). From the OD field, Beckhard and Harris (1977) defined *evaluation* as "a set of planned, information-gathering, and analytical activities undertaken to provide those responsible for the management of change with a satisfactory assessment of the effects and/or progress of the change effort" (p. 86).

WHY IS IT IMPORTANT TO KNOW HOW WELL OD IS WORKING?

Why should we evaluate our interventions or determine whether what we have done has made any difference?

- **To determine future investments in OD** – Why would an organization put more money into OD if it is not convinced that OD is making a difference?
- **To improve OD processes** – There is always room for improvement—nothing is ever done perfectly.
- **To identify alignment of OD with business strategies** – The organization is much more likely to support a function if the perception is that the function is trying to accomplish the same things as the organization.
- **To build intellectual capital within the organization** – Without a means to determine whether what was done was effective, it is difficult for the organization to learn more about its function and what it should be doing.
- **To stop doing what is not effective** – This cannot be done without having some way to determine what has been effective and what has not been effective.
- **To be accountable to stakeholders, and ensure employee and management accountability** – In today's era where corporations

are viewed as being irresponsible, *accountability* is a key word in the business environment, and it will continue to be well into the future.

- **To reflect on and improve the overall climate and health of the organization** – Creating a healthy work environment is a major role for OD, and whether this has been done cannot be known without evaluation.

- **To avoid fads and "flavors of the month"** – For some reason, OD seems particularly vulnerable to fads. Evaluation can be a means for OD to determine whether a new intervention is truly a quality improvement or whether it is simply the next best way for the most recent author of a bestseller to improve his or her income! Unfortunately, clients may have difficulty with ambiguity and go looking for the simple "magic bean" that will give them the answers to all of their complex problems. Such a "bean" does not exist, and ongoing evaluation will remind clients that one tool or one approach is not going to answer all of their problems.

- **To support the organization's global competitiveness so the organization stays in business** – This is another way by which evaluation can support the organization's strategy.

- **To lead the organization in keeping employees motivated and productive** – Again, evaluation will help OD know whether it is being successful in accomplishing this task.

- **To improve OD's ability to help the organization work its way through today's complex and often chaotic business environment** – Ongoing and frequent feedback will help OD know whether it is effectively assisting the organization in today's complex environment.

- **To improve OD's image within the organization by showing how much it contributes to the organization's success**

WHY IS EVALUATION OFTEN BYPASSED?

The argument for conducting evaluation in OD is strong, yet there are also reasons why evaluation is *not* conducted:

- It is very difficult to do, especially if there is insistence that cause-effect relationships be established between interventions and outcomes.

- The client organization may be so pleased with the obviously positive outcomes of the interventions that it does not believe an evaluation is necessary.

- Conducting an effective evaluation can be time-consuming and costly, and the client organization may believe that it has other priorities for its time and financial resources.

- The OD professional may be concerned about his or her reputation if the results of the evaluation are not positive; thus, the OD professional does not push the client to conduct the evaluation.

- If the evaluation results are not positive, the sponsor within the client organization may be concerned that his or her credibility will be on the line for having made the decision to pursue this OD process.

- Neither the OD professional nor members within the client organization may have the expertise to conduct the evaluation.

- There may be concern that the OD professional will not be objective in conducting the evaluation of his or her project, and the client organization is not willing to bring in someone else to do the evaluation.

- Both the OD professional and the members of the client organization are so confident of their expertise in implementing interventions that they do not even question whether the interventions have been successful.

- Separation takes place before the evaluation phase is reached.

Underlying all of these barriers is the very complexity of change itself. Golembiewski, Billingsley, and Yeager (1976) suggested that there are three levels of perception of change to be addressed by OD. *Alpha* (some refer to this as *first-order*) *change* is change that is consistent with present processes, values, and understandings in the organization. For example, customer service training may improve customer service in an organization that values customer service. Since this change occurs on a stable measure, it is the easiest to evaluate because it gets better, gets worse, or stays the same. *Beta* (or *second-order*) *change* is a change in understanding what matters with a stable measure. Reward systems, for instance, may actually decrease employee satisfaction, even with an increase in compensation, because more teamwork may have helped employees see the importance of team rewards rather than individual rewards. *Gamma* (or *third-order*) *change* occurs when a fundamental change occurs in the importance of the measure itself that is applied. For example, in the prior example, teamwork may have created a change in the perception of what is important to employees; rewards may no longer be significant, being replaced by the importance of relationships. Alpha change is the easiest of the three to measure, though it is clearly still not simple; gamma change is by far the most difficult to evaluate

APPROACHES TO SUMMATIVE EVALUATION

Turning now to specific approaches to evaluation, keep in mind that there is no single best approach. As much as many people are uneasy with ambiguity and would like *the* answer on how to do evaluation, there will never be such a solution to this very complex question. No matter what approach is ultimately chosen for evaluation, problems will arise. Looking for a problem-free solution to this question is like searching for the pot of gold under the rainbow or for Jack's magic beans—each is a fantasy!

Repeating the Same Measure as That Used in the Assessment Phase

This approach assumes that something triggered the awareness of the need for the intervention in the first place. Perhaps it occurred through some form of employee feedback system (either interviews or surveys) that some organizations use on an annual or biennial basis. Perhaps it was feedback from customers through focus groups or some form of written or Web-based survey. Perhaps a problem with quality or production identified through *statistical process control (SPC)* charts indicated the need for an intervention. Regardless of the process used, repeating that process may indicate whether or not the intervention was effective in changing whatever problem was originally identified.

Strengths in the Repeated Measurement Process.   In some respects, this approach may have the greatest validity, because it replicates the very process that indicated a problem or a need for the intervention in the first place. It carries with it high impact because the system was willing to accept the original input that there was a problem; showing that there is no longer a problem or that there is less of one, therefore, will have a high degree of credibility within the system. Furthermore, whatever measures were used originally are already in place, reducing the costs of having to create new measurement instruments. Finally, the stakeholders who had created an awareness of the need for the intervention initially will feel validated and listened to when they are again consulted regarding the impact of the intervention.

Weaknesses in the Repeated Measurement Process.   If the original process included interviews or surveys, it may be time-consuming and expensive to repeat the measures. In addition, as employees and customers tire of completing surveys, there may be a low response rate, or the process may not be taken seriously. The respondents or participants in the Evaluation phase may also very well be different from those who took part in the Assessment phase.

There may also be a temptation to change questions, add questions, or delete questions from those contained in the original Assessment phase, because of emerging interests. While such actions may be helpful in answering some new questions, they do jeopardize the value of the information for evaluative purposes. Also, if the original process was not valid or reliable, repeating it will still not yield valid or reliable outcomes. Finally, if technical processes have been involved (e.g., SPC), management (and even the OD professional) may not know how to interpret the results.

Return-on-Investment Models (Human Resource Accounting)

Return-on-investment (ROI) models, and a similar approach called *human resource accounting,* attempt to convert all inputs and outputs into financial terms. They then determine how much the OD intervention or function has contributed to the organization, resulting in a percentage that indicates what the return on OD investments has been. This figure provides opportunities to compare human capital investment to investment in other types of capital.

ROI begins by accepting that the important contributions of OD are to the organization's bottom line. Because there is no way to make a perfect connection or link between OD inputs and outputs, estimates are provided by managers and supervisors or other subject matter experts, based on their best guesses, or the organization may require the use of control and experimental groups (discussed later).

The rationale for this approach is that businesses function on finances and often make decisions based on the bottom line. Thus, the argument is that OD must justify itself in the organization by showing that OD makes a greater contribution to the financials of the organization than an alternative investment would make. One might ask, however, how well ROI can be applied given the difficulty of being able to determine cause-effect relationships. Organizations try to use anticipatory (i.e., based on knowledgeable guesses) ROI to answer such questions as, Should we build a new warehousing facility? Typically, however, such guesses tend to be very unreliable. ROI is difficult to apply regardless of the organizational support function involved (e.g., advertising, marketing, finance, accounting, facilities, purchasing, administration, etc.). It is as challenging for these functions to make the ROI case in an organization as it is for OD.

The formula for determining ROI is

$$ROI\ (\%) = \frac{Benefits - Costs}{Costs} \times 100$$

Strengths of ROI Models.   The allure of ROI models resides in the fact that they provide organizations with quantitative information in monetary terms. As this approach uses the currency of business, it is in alignment with the business objective and, therefore, often with its strategies.

This is the approach most familiar to managers, improving communications about benefits between OD professionals and management. As a result of this improved communications, there is greater potential for improved decision making, by management and by OD professionals. In fact, the process involves management directly in the computation of the ROI numbers, thus engaging them actively and explicitly with the OD process. It also becomes difficult for management to argue with its own numbers. Finally, the focus is on OD as an investment, not as an expense, thus influencing how dollars spent on OD are viewed.

Weaknesses of ROI Models. In spite of many people's efforts to use ROI in evaluating OD, and even in spite of the demand by some organizations that use an ROI approach, ROI is, unfortunately, impossible to measure because of intervening variables. Thus, no direct cause-effect evidence can be developed. ROI is not the perfect solution for many other reasons:

- Estimators do not agree (i.e., there is low interrater reliability) as to what the numbers to be used are.
- Because there is no way to determine accurately what the numbers are, they are based only on guesses.
- The use of control groups can reduce the impact of good programs on the organization because they are not being implemented organization-wide from the beginning, but the benefits are restricted only to those people in the experimental groups. If the programs are beneficial, the whole organization wants to benefit right from the beginning (see the later discussion on control groups for more on this point). Of course, they can also limit the impact of poor programs.
- ROI can be expensive to implement because of the time needed from the active involvement of management and other personnel in the process. One could well argue, however, that their involvement is desirable in *any* OD activity.
- ROI is based on the false assumption that other aspects of business can prove ROI.
- In a rapidly changing world, ROI takes too long, an argument also posed against the use of OD itself.
- Not all intangible benefits are financial (e.g., employee satisfaction, ethical business decisions, etc.). Some have tried to assign financial value to intangible benefits, with varying degrees of success. For example, research in an organization could identify the likelihood of an employee staying in the organization rather than leaving based on measures of satisfaction. Financial numbers can be assigned to employee turnover. Again, getting accurate measures is difficult and time-consuming.
- Strategic positioning may result in low or negative ROI. Zero percent or even negative ROI may be better than the alternatives that could lead to a greater loss.

- Costs often omit important factors, such as depreciation, overhead, and lost productivity. Of course, the response to this concern is to ensure that all applicable factors are included.
- ROI could be politically sensitive (as any evaluation approach might), by overstating benefits that actually occur from other functions and overassigning costs to other functions.
- In spite of widespread rhetoric in support of ROI, it is difficult to identify successful applications. If desired and if practical, many organizations would be using it.
- With ROI, as with other approaches, it is easy to manipulate results.

As Pipal (2001), director of T&D for Worldcom, concluded, "ROI in industry today is dead. Change occurs so rapidly that there isn't time to use traditional ROI. Financial benefits have to be so great that no one asks about ROI." The history of Worldcom's acquisition by MCI underscores how rapidly change can occur.

Kirkpatrick's Four Levels for Evaluating Training

Probably the most widely used evaluation approach in training and development, seen by some as an OD intervention, has been *Kirkpatrick's four levels of evaluation*. First popularized in the late 1950s and early 1960s, Kirkpatrick (1998) has updated the model, and it continues to be widely used.

According to Kirkpatrick, four levels need to be evaluated:

- reactions (usually measured by a short survey, though focus groups are sometimes used);
- learning (usually measured with a written test or a demonstration of performance);
- behavior (based on observations of a supervisor, a third party, or self-report);
- and organizational impact (bottom-line measures).

Some have suggested that we should add community or national impact (using macroeconomic measures). Others, however, have been critical of this model; perhaps the most visible critic has been Holton (1996).

Strengths of the Four-Level Model.   Kirkpatrick's model has proven to be capable of withstanding decades of use and review for many reasons. Perhaps the two most common are that the model is simple and easy to understand. Furthermore, because of their long-term and extensive use, the four levels are well understood, providing the profession with a common vocabulary. There is also the implication of a systems perspective because the system is multivariate and explores a variety of outcomes that one might expect from an OD professional.

Weaknesses of the Four-Level Model.   In spite of its widespread use, however, many weaknesses are associated with the use of Kirkpatrick's four levels:

- There is a lack of research validation; research has shown a weak link between reaction and learning on performance.
- The use of the word *level* is inappropriate; one level does not lead to the next, as implied by the term.
- This approach does not help in identifying how to do level 4 evaluation, by far the most important and most difficult of the four levels.
- It provides excuses for not doing a systematic evaluation of all four levels.
- It is simplistic, a taxonomy rather than a model (Holton, 1996).
- It is designed primarily for evaluating training and may not fit other OD functions very well.

The four levels are much more likely to be used in evaluating training and development efforts than other OD concerns. In spite of the problems associated with the use of this approach, it is unlikely that it is going to disappear, given its simplicity and widespread use.

Balanced Scorecard

According to Kaplan and Norton (1996), strategy formulation and evaluation should be undertaken from four perspectives, with appropriate questions that need to be answered for each of these categories:

Financial perspective – What must we achieve to satisfy our owners?

Customer perspective – What must we achieve to satisfy our customers?

Internal business perspective – What processes must we excel at?

Innovation and learning perspective – What must we do to ensure that we learn and grow?

More extensive questions to be asked in building a *balanced scorecard (BSC),* according to Becker, Huselid, and Ulrich (2001), include these:

- Which strategic goals/objectives/outcomes are critical rather than merely nice to have?
- What are the performance drivers to each goal?
- How would we measure progress toward these goals?
- What are the barriers to the achievement of each goal?
- How would employees need to behave to ensure that the company accomplishes these goals?
- Is OD providing the company with the employee competencies and behaviors necessary to achieve these objectives?
- If not, what needs to change?

Balanced scorecards are very popular today, not only for OD, but also for other business functions. In spite of their popularity, however, they, too, are not the perfect solution to our evaluation problems.

Strengths of BSC in OD Evaluation.   Perhaps the reason why this approach has been so popular is because it appears to be strategic and focuses on the bottom line. In addition, it centers on the organization's strategy implementation, which requires constant change and flexibility. Moreover, the performance measures used do not usually get old. Other reasons for its widespread use include that it is currently popular, with vocabulary that is becoming increasingly familiar; it distinguishes between deliverables and doables (Becker et al., 2001); and its focus is on human capital (85% of a company's value).

Weaknesses of BSC in OD Evaluation.   The balanced scorecard approach shares many of the problems of ROI evaluation. Notable among these are the following:

- Determining quantitative measures for the most important outcomes is difficult; the system forces attention on the most easily measured outcomes.
- There is no established cause-effect link between innovation and learning and other perspectives.
- BSC is an overly simplistic strategic model (focusing its questions in just four areas).
- Start-up costs, for training and for developing systems, are high.
- BSC goals can become obsolete quickly (contrary to one of its stated strengths), unless consistent effort is made to keep them up-to-date.

I am unaware of any successful application of the BSC approach to the evaluation of OD. If such reports surface, this approach probably would be much more widely used.

Control Group Experiment

Using control and experimental groups to determine whether differences exist between those who have experienced a given intervention and those who have not is probably the most powerful approach that can be used, when it is feasible. However, it is seldom implemented in a business setting for a variety of reasons:

- Small numbers are often set aside for either the experimental or control group or for both; when this happens, it is difficult to obtain statistical significance.
- Similarly, if small numbers of participants are used, employee anonymity may be violated.
- For business (and perhaps even legal) purposes, all employees may need the intervention at the same time.
- Because of schedules, work team or union agreements, or other points, it may be difficult to assign employees randomly.
- The purpose of doing business is to do business, not to conduct research. Furthermore, there may not be the expertise needed to conduct such experiments.
- It may be difficult to have those experiencing the intervention working together with those who have not experienced the intervention.

- Such an approach may be very time-consuming before an answer to the evaluation can be determined. This longer period of time also could make the process very costly.

- If the intervention is truly effective, it may cost the organization to have only half of the employees receiving it. There will be a time lag while half of the employees is receiving the intervention if it is deemed to have been effective. Of course, if the intervention is ineffective, such an approach may protect the half that was not involved.

This approach is seldom used in organizations, whether for the purposes of evaluation or research. As a result, we often do not have the evidence we would like to identify interventions that are most effective for organizations.

Systems Perspective Evaluation

A *systems perspective evaluation* recognizes that no one of the preceding approaches to evaluation can be effective. Rather, there is an affirmation of the concept of triangulation; the use of multiple measures provides a variety of ways to look at the effectiveness of the intervention.

In a systems perspective, OD works as a partner with management personnel to identify the information they want from evaluation and to determine what deficiencies they are willing to accept. Then, OD uses multiple forms of evaluation to provide a broader perspective of OD outcomes. In this approach, OD establishes with stakeholders criteria and outcome levels desired prior to the intervention. Then, both qualitative and quantitative feedback is included in reports, with the measures being identified to determine OD performance. Using all of these factors, the ultimate goal is to perform the job *so well* that no one questions the value-added of OD.

LONGITUDINAL EVALUATION

Longitudinal evaluation is extremely important in understanding an organization's ability to sustain the change efforts created through OD interventions and to guard against the tendency of organizations to regress back to the preintervention state. Longitudinal evaluation does not require any different an approach to evaluation than those methods reviewed in the summative evaluation section of this chapter. But it does require the ongoing commitment of the client organization and the OD professional to continue to gather information to determine whether the effects of the change are remaining in place. Longitudinal evaluation also makes it easier to identify changes in part of the organization that were not directly the target of the intervention, consistent with our understanding of systems theory.

One way that such an approach might be more easily justified to the organization is to present longitudinal evaluation as a regular basis of doing assessment for future action planning and interventions, while at the same time providing the necessary longitudinal evaluation. Seldom do organizations take full advantage of longitudinal evaluation because of the costs and a lack of full understanding of the benefits that an organization can realize from the process.

Some cautions are necessary for those organizations considering longitudinal evaluation. First, employees or others involved in this evaluation may become tired of the process if it is repeated too often with too little time between stages, especially if it requires an active response on their part, as with an interview or a survey. Ongoing collection of data, as through customer satisfaction programs or statistical process control (SPC) might help an organization avoid this problem.

Another problem is that caused by beta or gamma change, as described earlier. With changes in how a particular variable is viewed or with a shift in what variables are important in the organization, longitudinal evaluation may not be able to pick up important, but previously unmeasured, factors.

Finally, from a systems perspective, a problem may arise with longitudinal evaluation in that changes in the system (e.g., the economic environment) affecting the evaluation results might have nothing to do with the intervention under review or the variable being measured.

APPROACHES TO FORMATIVE EVALUATION

Formative evaluation, that which takes place during the intervention, is especially helpful in building in flexibility, enabling rapid shifts in interventions that are being implemented. With formative evaluation in place, it will not always be necessary to return to the beginning of the organization development process cycle. Moreover, many of the sources of formative evaluation are, in fact, parts of the OD interventions themselves.

By its nature, process consultation is a form of evaluation and feedback that is ongoing. The OD professional reflects back to those involved in the OD intervention his or her observations on what is being seen and how that is affecting the process. Some of the interventions described in earlier chapters not only create change, but also provide feedback on how well the process is going.

I referred earlier to statistical process control, a process of using various statistical tools to provide information about the performance of the processes that are in place in the organization. Run charts and control charts, important tools in SPC, show clearly in graph form when improvements are continuing as desired and when progress has stalled or even started to move in an undesirable direction. Close monitoring of the charts will provide immediate feedback. One problem is that organizations may not allow enough time for sufficient data to accumulate to represent what the system is really performing. It can help to identify whether the variation in a system is a result of normal variation or if there is a special cause (e.g., a bad batch of raw material). Too quick a response can result in *tampering* with the system—responding to symptoms rather than using the results to identify root causes—resulting in even more problems within the system.

A number of approaches can be used to provide formative evaluation in a team setting. In Chapter 7 on teams, a formative tool, the *sociogram*, which provides a visual representation of the interactions that take place during a team meeting, was described.

It is also useful for OD professionals to seek feedback on the quality of their work so that they can make necessary adjustments along the way. Sometimes something as simple as having a conversation and asking the client how things are going is sufficient. If many people are involved in the client organization, a form can be created to invite feedback from client members with whom the OD professional is interacting.

It is never really a question of whether one should do formative or summative evaluation. Both are important and serve different purposes. A competent OD professional working with an organization committed to continuous improvement will use all three approaches—formative, summative, and longitudinal.

OD'S STRATEGIC IMPERATIVES RELATED TO EVALUATION

Given that each individual approach to evaluation has at least as many weaknesses as strengths, we can identify some lessons to be learned that will help OD perform its functions most effectively:

- Tie every OD activity to the organization's strategy (which implies knowing the organization's strategy).
- Know what the client expects from OD—if the expectation is valid, deliver it; if invalid, help the client understand why and what is valid.
- Work strategically with partners in the company.
- Measure what is important to the client.
- Share the outcomes of effective OD widely within the organization.
- Foster learning within the OD group and steering team ("What can we learn from this?").
- Use triangulation—multiple measures that show the same outcomes will provide stronger evidence of the contributions OD has made.

CHAPTER SUMMARY

It is important to gather information that will provide feedback on how well what we have done during the Action Planning and Intervention phases is working. Three time frames are commonly used in evaluation: formative, done during the change process itself; summative, conducted at the conclusion of the change process; and longitudinal, conducted periodically over time after a specific change process. Many approaches can be used in these evaluation processes; we reviewed several in this chapter, along with each one's strengths and weaknesses. In spite of the pressure to find the "best" approach to evaluation, no single approach can overcome every objection. The most effective response to this concern is to tie OD efforts to the strategies of the organization and to use triangulation, multiple approaches to evaluation, to overcome some of the problems resident in each approach.

Evaluation is essential and should not be ignored. It allows for prompt responses to indicators that the process is not going well and needs to be adjusted. It is also essential for both the OD professional and the client organization to learn from the work that they are doing together.

QUESTIONS FOR DISCUSSION
OR SELF-REFLECTION

1. Why do you think I have concluded that evaluation is essential? Do you agree or disagree?
2. If you could select only one of the many approaches reviewed in this chapter, which would you choose and why?
3. Which of the many approaches reviewed in this chapter do you believe is the weakest? Why?
4. How do you see formative, summative, and longitudinal evaluation interacting?
5. What approaches other than those suggested in this chapter do you think might be used for formative evaluation?
6. Given that no one approach to evaluation meets all of what we would like it to do, how do you think triangulation can contribute to the Evaluation phase?
7. How do you think the results of an evaluation process should be used?

13

Adoption of Changes and Follow-up

CHAPTER OUTLINE

Three-Step Change Model
Continuing Attention to Change
Adoption Requires Joint Planning
Factors Influencing the Adoption Process
Resistance to Change
Chapter Summary
Questions for Discussion or Self-Reflection

OVERVIEW Adoption of change is a controversial phase in today's dynamic and rapidly changing world. Some argue that change is so rapid that an organization cannot afford to adopt or institutionalize a change but must be in the process of constant change. Opponents of this theory argue that the culture has not changed until there is evidence that the change has been adopted or institutionalized. Reconciling these two perspectives will be the goal of this chapter.

Through the Implementation and Evaluation phases, we have discovered that the change that was proposed in the Action Plan was successful in the pilot or initial application of the change. From this success, the organization has now decided to adopt the change throughout the organization.

As we see from the ODP model in Figure 13.1, once the Adoption phase has occurred, we return to the beginning of the cycle or move to the Separation phase. With a commitment to continuous improvement, the cycle begins again, exploring the newly created culture and its processes to determine how they, too, can be improved, with the possibility that an even better adaptation to the organizational culture can be found. In this process, the newly implemented and adopted cultural component may need to be replaced, with a new adoption following another pilot implementation. Let's consider the Adoption phase—and the change it entails—in more detail.

THREE-STEP CHANGE MODEL

Lewin (1947) suggested that there were three steps to bringing about change in an organization: Unfreeze, Move, Refreeze. The idea behind this *three-step change model* is that the desired changes are first identified through an assessment process. Those aspects of the organization that are keeping it from developing as desired are identified. Then, the task of the OD professional is to help the organization free itself from those aspects, through education, awareness, and experience. Once the culture is "unfrozen," the next step is to move it in the desired direction through the various interventions that have been reviewed earlier in this book. When the organization has moved in the desired direction and has reached the desired state, it should then be "refrozen" or set into

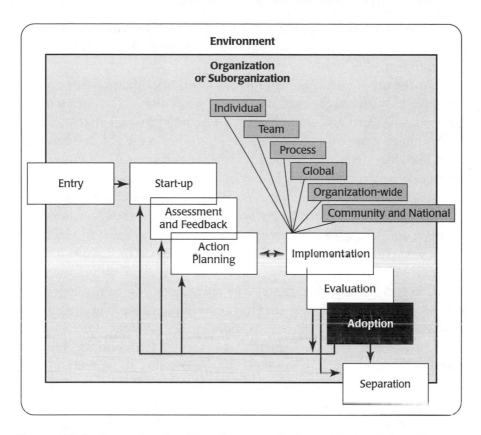

Figure 13.1 *Organization Development Process Model, Phase 7:*
Adoption

the culture or practices of the organization. This refreezing is the Adoption phase. Adoption thus serves two functions: it makes it less likely for the original target to revert to the prechange stage, and it enables the desired change to be distributed broadly throughout the organization.

As indicated in the overview, however, some OD professionals do not believe that this model is effective today. They argue that the world is much too dynamic for the static nature of the "refreezing" step. Rather, they argue that the model should be "Unfreeze, Move, Move, Move." There is some validity to this concern and to the model they propose. Many organizations (and even nations) are faced with the necessity of having to respond quickly and frequently to a changing environment, to changing regulations, to a changing marketplace, to changing competitive pressures. Each of these factors makes the refreezing step an unwise or even dangerous one because it puts the organization into a place where it cannot respond quickly enough to the dynamism of its environment.

On the other hand, not all factors of an organization are equally subject to dynamic changes or in need of dynamic responses to the environment. And one could argue that people are not capable of constant change without having some solid ground on which to base their lives and their decisions. So perhaps the solution to this apparent contradiction is, like much of OD, not an either-or decision but modifications as the circumstances warrant. Thus, in certain circumstances for one organization, a more static model might be perfectly appropriate, while in another, with a different set of circumstances, the model needs to be very dynamic. And in a third organization, a midpoint between these two positions might be possible. Likewise, even within one organization there might be rationale for using both positions, depending on the nature of the change that has been implemented successfully, so that some changes can be seen as more static, whereas other changes need to be viewed, implemented, and reviewed with considerable dynamism. In any case, probably no change is going to be truly permanent, and, to some extent, change is a given in every organization to one degree or another. Organization members who believe that permanence does and should exist may have to adjust their thinking. Those who resist altering their view may find themselves permanently separated from the organization while the organization proceeds with adopting the change.

Another view related to change is that there are different types of change. E- and O-change models were reviewed in Chapter 1. Similar to these models, Weick and Quinn (1999) suggested that OD needs to focus on both *continuous change*, which is ongoing, evolving, and emergent, such as found in continuous improvement approaches, and *episodic change*, which is intentional, infrequent, discontinuous, and dramatic.

Given the ambiguity associated with change, it is possible that the OD professional needs to balance both change and stability, both continuous and episodic change. For example, an organization may have as a core underlying value the importance of excellent customer service. But the environment and the organization's customers may call for different ways to reflect this core value, either as times change or to meet individual customer preferences, requiring significant change in the organization. For example, an airline with a core value of superb customer service may find itself opening local ticket offices and then closing them at a later date as improved Web sites take away the necessity for in-person customer service. Thus, the OD professional in this situation would need to remind the client organization of the continuing importance of excellent customer service, while at the same time facilitating the organization's discovery of the best ways to provide better customer service on a continuing basis.

CONTINUING ATTENTION TO CHANGE

Regardless of which perspective one takes of Lewin's (1947) change model, one should not assume, just because a change has been put in place (adopted), that it will remain in place exactly as it was when it was first adopted. Nor should it be assumed that what has been adopted will always continue to be the best process or action for the organization. In fact, systems may regress to what they were. So, if sufficient ongoing attention is not paid to the change to ensure that it remains in place until it becomes embedded in the organization, the organization, and those in leadership roles within the organization, may revert to the way things were.

Management oversight, typically through an executive steering committee, will be important in ensuring that major changes are adopted systemwide. Of course, this assumes that management understands the importance of the change and has made a commitment to the change. It also assumes that management has the required discipline to support desired change, especially through the implementation of appropriate reward and recognition systems to encourage change-enabling behavior and discourage change-debilitating behavior. As discussed in detail in Chapter 12 on evaluation, having measurement systems in place to track progress of the change will help in the Adoption phase.

Focus on continued communication throughout the organization is another factor to encourage continued attention to the desired change. There is also a need to protect against the "not invented/born here" syndrome. Management in other units/departments/functions may not feel that the pilot adequately represented how their part of the organization will benefit from the change so they do not buy in. Finally, getting rid of the old system will protect against reversion to that system.

All of these issues have implications for the Action Planning phase (planning who will be involved in the pilot, selecting who will be on the steering committee, deciding how progress will be measured and tracked, etc.). This process is iterative; the action plan may need to be adjusted as management, the steering team, and the OD professional learn through the implementation.

One of the advantages of an internal OD professional is the greater ease in monitoring the adoption. An external OD professional has no way to monitor the adoption unless he or she is continuously contracted by the organization. Even then, the external professional may be called on to work in a part of the organization not connected to where the original adopted change was made. In this situation the external professional will not have the opportunity or the permission of the organization to observe or monitor the adopted change.

One advantage an external OD professional might have in the Adoption phase is that, in going away from the organization for a while, perhaps 6 months to a year, and then coming back to do a follow-up assessment, he or she will be able to see more clearly whether the change has truly been adopted. The internal OD professional will be experiencing the change day to day and may not see it taking place. The external OD professional will have the picture upon leaving the organization and then upon returning several months later.

ADOPTION REQUIRES JOINT PLANNING

As with many aspects of OD, the Adoption phase requires joint planning between the process owner(s) and the OD professional. This type of mutual interaction and support ideally has been present throughout the OD process, according to the OD value of interdependency. However, it is especially necessary during the Action Planning, Implementation, Evaluation, and Adoption phases, as these are the stages that clearly require deep understanding of the organization's culture and the process expertise of the OD professional. If data from the Evaluation phase identify that the implementation has not been successful, then the Adoption phase should be skipped and the ODP cycle begun again.

FACTORS INFLUENCING THE ADOPTION PROCESS

The degree to which an organization is able to adopt, or institutionalize, the outcomes of the OD intervention depends on a variety of critical factors, each stemming from key factors inside and outside the organization. First, the combined efforts of the OD professional and the client organization to carry out the intervention in the first place play a large role in the success of the institutionalization process. Second, the degree of involvement of the organization itself is key to successful OD intervention adoption. As has been discussed earlier and will be considered in detail in the next chapter, at some point, the OD professional, whether internal or external, must begin to separate from the change effort. This separation can only be done successfully if the organization has been fully engaged in the intervention process. The third critical factor in determining the success of OD adoption is the degree to which the organization, its subsystems, and individuals employ the newly proposed and enacted changes.

Five Key Features of OD Interventions

Cummings and Worley (2005) stated that five key features of OD interventions can affect their subsequent institutionalization: goal specificity, programmability, level of change target, internal support, and sponsor.

Goal Specificity.   Goal specificity requires that the OD professional and critical organization members set specific goals to reach the desired outcomes. Though there are broader, underlying goals that guide the organization (e.g., organizational mission and vision), goals must be broken down into individual steps in order to move the process forward in manageable, efficient, and effective ways. Breaking down goals into manageable steps ensures that organizational members will not get overwhelmed and helps them maintain a clear perspective of where they are and what needs to be done to reach the desired state.

Programmability.   *Programmability*, according to Cummings and Worley (2005), "is the degree to which the changes can be programmed. This means that the different characteristics of the intervention are clearly specified in advance, thus facilitating socialization, commitment, and reward allocation" (p. 193). Of course, this factor might be applied more easily and appropriately to structures and processes than to people. In other words, the intervention must be clear to all involved, establishing further the need for goal specificity. Once the organization and its members understand the intervention fully, management with the help of the OD professional, if required, can move toward establishing and strengthening organization-wide commitment.

Many organizations are struggling to put in place performance management systems that are perceived by employees to be fair and helpful, while supervisors and managers want something that is simple, not time-consuming, and nonconfrontational. These are not criteria that are easily met.

A large organization with which I have been associated has just spent millions of dollars on revising its performance management system, but it is now having a very difficult time in getting it accepted. Specificity was lacking, resulting in a system that combines performance feedback, developmental needs, and compensation and promotion decisions. This is asking for too much from a single system, and employees, who were expecting a system that would be developmental without being tied to compensation decisions, were unhappy. Supervisors and managers, who were not completing performance appraisals under the old system because they were too time-consuming, are now finding the new system even more time-consuming. Without specificity of goals, the institutionalization appears to be failing. Even with the best of IT experts working with the system, it appears that the intervention will not succeed. It also will not succeed if supervisors and managers will not do the work to get the data to input into the system. In fact, it now appears that the organization, after this huge expenditure, will need to start over because the implementation was simply not done correctly the first time around.

Level of Change Target.   The *level of change target*, the third factor of intervention that can affect the institutionalization processes, refers to clearly specifying the target for change within the organization. Is the target of the change the entire organization, one or two departments, or a specific work team or committee?

Once the target has been identified, the OD professional is responsible for ensuring that the scope of the change is neither too small nor too broad, causing the change to lose its momentum. If too small, the OD professional must outline specific steps to make sure that the change effort does not unintentionally lead to the creation of an undesired minisubculture within the organization. (Sometimes subcultures may be desirable, but they should be planned.) Rather, the OD professional must always be aware of the interconnectedness of each part of the organization to the larger whole—striving, ultimately, toward the organization-wide mission.

Internal Support and Sponsor.   Internal support and *sponsorship* are the last two factors that impact the success of the institutionalization process. *Internal support* refers to the internal team, preferably guided by top management, an internal professional, or an assigned team leader from within the organization, to ensure that the OD intervention is successfully followed through to begin the long-term process of adoption. Without continuing support from key members within the organization, the likelihood of permanent and widespread change is minimal, and it is much more likely that the organization will fall back into its old patterns.

The role of the sponsor is to "initiate, allocate and legitimize resources for the intervention. Sponsors must come from levels in the organization high enough to control appropriate resources, and they must have the visibility and power to nurture the intervention and see that it remains viable" (Cummings & Worley, 2005, p. 194).

Key Factors to Ensure That Change Remains

Once the organization takes ownership in adopting the intervention, certain key factors must be present to ensure that the change remains in place: (1) socialization, (2) commitment, (3) reward allocation, (4) diffusion, and (5) sensing and collaboration.

Socialization.   *Socialization* refers to the "transmission of information about beliefs, preferences, norms and values with respect to the intervention" (Cummings & Worley, 2005, p. 194). In other words, the internal professional team or key members of the organization have the responsibility to communicate to members of the organization the progress and status of the changes occurring within the organization. As posited by Cummings and Worley, "transmission of information about the intervention helps to bring new members onboard and allows participants to reaffirm the beliefs, norms, and values underlying the intervention" (p. 194). In addition, establishing commitment ensures that people within the organization become committed to those beliefs, norms, and values that support the intervention and the continuing institutionalizing process.

Commitment.   Murrel (2000) expanded the concept of organizational commitment, asserting that the extent of the organizational change effort, and, ultimately, the success of the adoption stage, is determined by the extent to which individuals are committed to change. However, for people to reach the desired level of organizational commitment, the OD intervention must be implemented at the right depth. That is, the intervention must not be too superficial or too overwhelming for employees to handle. Murrel listed three phases of depth:

- *Depth is too shallow* – Superficial issues fail to engage people. The whole approach is treated as one more program of change with very little ownership. It lacks authenticity as concerns true organizational values/culture. Critical information is not surfaced and dealt with.

- *Depth is appropriate* – Engagement is at a real level and personal investment is high. People get into the process and share true feelings. Conflict is not avoided but dealt with openly and just resolution occurs. It fits developmental paths of interpersonal relationships.

- *Depth is too intense* – This takes people well beyond their skill levels and promotes too much risk-taking given organizational leadership and culture. Time has not been devoted to developing high-involvement work contracts that support values of interpersonality. (p. 811)

Thus, for an intervention to be adopted successfully by the organization, the OD professional, along with the organization itself and the internal steering team, must be cautious and calculating in determining the scope of the change. Returning to our earlier discussion, if the scope is broad, impacting multiple subsystems within the organization or even the entire organization, clear and specific goals must be established for the change to become fully institutionalized. Again, continuing feedback is necessary in order to adjust with needed changes along with the organization taking ownership of the change.

Reward Allocation.   To reward individuals for adopting and supporting the intervention within the organization, a reward system may be put in place to encourage members to take on and maintain new job functions, desired behaviors, and/or performance outcomes. These rewards may be either intrinsic (job/career development, challenging assignments, education, recognition, etc.) or extrinsic (e.g., financial rewards). However, as research studies have indicated (Herzberg, Mausner, & Block Snyderman's [1959] study is the classic, supported by many other studies since; Kohn's [1999] *Punished by Rewards* makes an interesting read on this topic), individuals respond more to intrinsic rewards on a long-term basis as opposed to monetary compensation.

Diffusion, Sensing, and Collaboration.   *Diffusing, sensing,* and *collaboration* describe the overall need for the organization to ensure that the newly implemented processes go as smoothly as possible to encourage continued commitment to change. ***Diffusion*** "refers to the process of transferring interventions from one system to another" (Cummings & Worley, 2005, p. 195). As such, an intervention reaches a broader base within the organization once it expands to new departments or subsystems within the organization. The positive aspect of diffusion is the ability to determine on a small-scale level (the intervention) the success that one might expect in the Adoption phase as successful interventions are institutionalized.

Sensing and *collaboration* refer to a feedback system to create awareness of what is and what is not going well during the adoption process. Are departments adopting the newly implemented changes? Are they committed to the long-term effort and taking on new values, behaviors, or norms? During the Adoption phase, organizations and individuals will be required to make adjustments based on continued feedback, whether from the internal steering team or management team.

If the OD professional along with the organization and the internal steering team have successfully focused on ensuring that these intervention factors are followed through to the institutionalization phase, we should expect the Adoption phase also to be successful. Cummings and

Worley (2005) also outlined five criteria to determine whether an organization has successfully adopted an OD intervention: knowledge, performance, preferences, normative consensus, and value consensus.

These criteria follow a chronological pattern, as individuals must first have the knowledge in order to perform the required work. Once employees have gained the knowledge and are able to perform, they can indicate preferences, or feedback, to improve the processes. Once individuals are committed to the change, normative consensus develops to create groupwide commitment to adoption of the processes. In turn—this is the final stage indicating successful adoption—also created is value consensus, the agreement among all members of the organization of the value of the change being instituted. Once value consensus is established among groups of individuals, the Adoption phase is fully integrated into the organization. Thus, one can postulate that knowledge, performance, preferences, and normative consensus have been reached for value consensus to be present.

For the Adoption phase to be successful, the organization must be both adaptable and flexible. Tan and Tiong (2005) expanded on Pegels's (1995) definitions of *adaptability* and *flexibility*. To them, *adaptability* is "defined as the ability of the organization to respond to external changes in the market," whereas *flexibility* is "defined as the ability of the organization to make changes to the internal structure of the organization in response to changes" (p. 52). Thus, when an intervention becomes adopted and successfully institutionalized in the organization, Lewin's (1947) Refreeze phase, discussed earlier in this chapter, does not mean that the organization becomes static and freezes per se. Rather, the organization must continue to be adaptable to the external environment in order to remain competitive. Furthermore, the organization must also maintain flexibility in order to adapt and respond to the implemented changes. Again, ongoing feedback is essential to support flexibility for the organization to commit to and adopt successful OD interventions.

RESISTANCE TO CHANGE

Folklore holds that people do not like change. While often accepted uncritically, simple logic shows that this belief is not true. Whether one accepts or rejects change is often based on an assessment, often unconscious, of the costs of the change relative to the benefits. Blanchard

(1989) demonstrated an interesting change exercise on videotape. He had workshop participants divide into pairs standing back to back. They were told to make five changes in their appearance and then see whether their partners could identify the changes. They were then asked to make an additional five changes. Having used this exercise a number of times, I can confirm Blanchard's conclusions:

- People will feel awkward, ill at ease, and self-conscious.
- People will think first about what they have to give up.
- People will feel alone, even if everyone is going through the change.
- People are at different levels of readiness for change.
- People will be concerned that they do not have enough resources.
- If you take the pressure off, people will revert back to old behavior.

The exception I have seen to this process has been with individuals who believed that the exercise gave them an excuse to experience gain (e.g., by taking off a tie or being able to be more informal than they might otherwise be). I often ask my classes whether they believe the folklore. Most of them do. Yet, if I offer to take them with me to Hawaii on vacation, all expenses paid, most of them—even though this was an unplanned activity requiring many changes in their lives—indicate that they would be thrilled to go. This point underscores, again, that it is not change per se that people react negatively to but only change in which they perceive the costs to be greater than the benefits.

Much has been made in the literature about resistance to change and, at the extreme, even of sabotage, and it is a common topic among OD professionals who believe that they have frequently experienced such resistance in their practice. Handling resistance to change begins from the first phase of the ODP model, Entry, and continues throughout all of the phases. By determining the possible sources of resistance to change and barriers to change, attention can be given to these factors right from the beginning. Gunn Partners (2000) suggested the following sources of resistance to change:

There is ingrained resistance to change in every organization.
Some of this resistance is human; some is structural. For example:
Thick layers of middle management and masses of red tape stifle

new thinking; independent "silos" operating in isolation from the rest of the organization do not collaborate; information used for power and influence coupled with decisions made in secret causes distrust and contempt; fragmented accountability generates confusion; low morale breeds low motivation; retribution for mistakes leads to low risk-taking; and conflict not dealt with in a healthy manner brings about stagnation. In organizations where such conditions exist, change comes slowly and often unsuccessfully. (p. 8)

Gliecher (cited in Beckhard & Harris, 1987) provided a classic *formula for change*: $D \times V \times F > R$, where R represents resistance to change, D is the dissatisfaction with the present situation, V is the clarity of the vision or positive picture of what is possible in the future, and F is the first real achievable steps people can take toward reaching the vision. If any one of D, V, or F is zero or approaches zero, then change will not occur because the resistance to change will not be overcome. Carrying this formula further, it is clear that adoption or institutionalization will occur only when the product of these three factors exceeds the strength of the resistance to change. Both the OD professional and the client organization, therefore, must pay attention to *all three* factors, keeping in mind that if any one of the factors is weak, resistance will prevail.

So, in simple terms, to overcome whatever resistance might be resident in the system, consider doing the following:

- Even when the intervention is at a level that is below organization-wide, keep in mind the big picture: the need, ultimately, to transform the whole system.
- Ensure that the benefits of the change are greater than the costs, to individuals and to subsystems.
- Be sure that top management is committed to the change processes.
- Be as explicit as possible about what the focus of the change is and the desired impact from the change.
- Communicate with employees on a continuing basis—about both what is being done and what is to be done. Do not assume that employees will hear the communication accurately the first time it is communicated.
- Communicate clearly what is expected from each employee during the adoption phase.

- Be clear about why the change is being institutionalized, which will generally require sharing the results of the evaluation phase broadly.

Force Field Analysis

A force field analysis is a problem solving tool used to identify the reasons ("forces") that support or oppose two positions to a question and the strength of each force. Kurt Lewin (1947) was the originator of the concept. In the context of this chapter, force field analysis could be used by to answer the question, "What factors affect the acceptance or resistance to a particular change?" The assumption of a force field analysis is that it is easier to reduce the factors that are resistant than to increase the strength of the driving (supporting) forces.

How Is a Force Field Analysis Conducted?

1. State the question to be answered; check that all agree. It needs to be worded so there are only two opposing responses.
2. Draw lines on a flipchart dividing the sheet in half; head each half with one of the two opposing responses.
3. Have the group brainstorm as many reasons ("forces") as possible for *each* option. Ignore no answer and permit no critique during brainstorming.
4. When responses are exhausted, review items for clarification, duplication, etc. Reword, where necessary, for clarification.
5. There are many ways to identify how strong a force each item is. One simple way is to treat each item with a 5-point Likert scale. "If you believe that this item is a very strong argument, hold up five fingers. If you believe that it is a very weak argument, hold up one finger. How strong an argument do you think the first item is?" The facilitator will then do a quick scan to identify the modal (average) response. This number is written next to that item.
6. Items that are perceived to be low (1, 2, and maybe 3) should be eliminated.
7. Given the arguments ("forces") that remain, participants would try to decide the question, OR, if the decision has already been made, the participants would work at weakening the arguments

that are barriers to the decision and, thus, are likely to lead to resistance to the change.

CHAPTER SUMMARY

If the Evaluation phase finds that the implementation was not successful, the Adoption phase is skipped, and the ODP cycle begins again. If the implementation of the intervention is deemed to be successful, then it needs to be reinforced so there is no regression to the prechange situation, and it then needs to be implemented across the organization.

There is some disagreement in whether the change can be set in the organizational culture, or whether the dynamism of the organizational environment is such that it will need to change continuously. As a result, the OD professional must be aware of the factors that improve the likelihood of institutionalizing successful interventions and that are those useful in overcoming institutionalized resistance to change. OD professionals must be skilled in working with those factors to ensure that the organization will successfully adopt the interventions.

QUESTIONS FOR DISCUSSION OR SELF-REFLECTION

1. What are some actions an OD professional and the organization leaders can take during the Adoption phase that can encourage an organization to institutionalize a desired change?

2. What are some advantages and disadvantages of an external OD professional being part of the adoption phase? Describe the same for an internal OD professional.

3. Who bears primary responsibility for institutionalizing desired change during the Adoption phase?

4. Discuss specific times when you have welcomed change and when you have resisted change. What were the factors present in each situation? When you resisted change, what could have been done to help you to accept the change?

5. Do you agree with the statement, "People don't like to change"? Discuss the reasons for your answer.

6. Do you think it is important to institutionalize successful change systemwide? Why or why not?

14

Reasons for Separation
from the Organization

CHAPTER OUTLINE

OVERVIEW Periodically, it is essential for clients and OD profession-als to explore their relationship to see whether there is still a need for the relationship on the part of the client, and to see whether the OD profes-sional still believes that value is being added to the organization through the relationship. This stage becomes difficult for internal OD pro-fessionals as they are gradually co-opted by the organization's culture. Both the organization and the OD professional must avoid overdepen-dency. How can a healthy relationship be maintained so that separation is not needed? How can it be determined that separation is appropriate and benefits both parties? How should separation be handled?

The final phase of the ODP model is Separation. This phase is not central to the ongoing flow of the model, as seen in Figure 14.1, because Separation ends the involvement of the client and the OD pro-fessional. A good ending is critical to support the work that has gone before it. In the ensuing conversation, it is important to discuss what each party learned from the process, suggest ways for each to improve working relationships in the future, and keep the door open for future work as circumstances change.

Unfortunately, separation does not always occur in a desirable way, for many reasons. Sometimes it is a case of personnel change. For example, an internal OD professional may receive a job offer that he or she finds attractive and choose to leave, despite unfinished projects. Or, the OD professional may leave because he or she has become frus-trated at the lack of commitment on the part of the organization to make any significant change. So separation occurs in these cases from decisions of the individuals rather than any planned intent on the part of the organization.

Such decisions of individuals can result in a separation that is detri-mental to the process and to others involved. An OD professional may be terminated because of budget cuts, dissatisfaction with the work, or a merger or acquisition that excludes the OD professional. Or the OD professional may never be told the real reason for the separation. The organization may simply not return phone calls or arrange for next steps in the process, leaving the OD professional wondering, "What happened?" Clearly, these are not good reasons for a separation, nor are the processes used in the separation the most desirable.

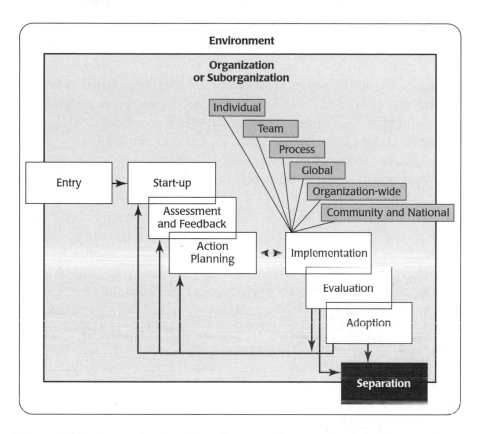

Figure 14.1 *Organization Development Process Model, Phase 8: Separation*

What follows is advice to both the OD professional and the organization about when separation becomes necessary and how it might best occur.

DEPENDENCY

As indicated in the first chapter, one of the distinctions between OD and traditional forms of consulting is that OD begins with interdependency, moving to independence, whereas traditional consulting is built on a dependency model. In spite of good intentions, however, instead of moving from interdependency to independence, on the part of both the organization and the OD professional, the move is sometimes toward dependency. When this occurs in an OD partnership, it is time to consider seriously whether it is time for the partnership between the OD professional and the organization to be severed. Separation is not the only solution, but it may become so if the organization and the OD professional do not understand reasons why dependency should be avoided and the signs of dependency, so that they can take steps to shift back to a path toward independence.

Dependency is not good for the organization for many reasons. First, as already discussed, the OD professional may lose objectivity, resulting in biased perspectives. Second, when dependency occurs, the skills of the OD professional are less likely to be transferred to the organization. Members of the organization also give up development opportunities when dependency develops because they do not get to practice the skills that the OD professional should rightly be transferring to them. Third, the desired change is more likely to be adopted into the organization when dependency is avoided. Fourth, external consultants can be expensive; dependency likely means that they will be paid more and longer than necessary than if independence had developed. Thus, there are real benefits for the organization in avoiding development of dependency.

Likewise, the problem for the consultant in developing dependency is that they cease marketing, relying too heavily on existing clients. As a result, when a client organization decides that it no longer needs an external consultant, then the external consultant may find that no work is available.

Dependency often goes unrecognized, in part because both parties find it easier to ignore the signs of dependency. To identify dependency more easily, the next section describes such signs.

Signs of Dependency

When an OD professional develops dependency on the organization, a few telltale signs begin to emerge. The OD professional would rather work with a particular client rather than other clients. All marketing efforts cease as the OD professional assumes that the relationship with this client will continue indefinitely.

Another sign of dependency may be the development of personal relationships among the people with whom the OD person is working.

This becomes a problem when boundaries are crossed, affecting the OD professional's ability to maintain a third party stance relative to the projects that are being undertaken in the organization. It may become difficult to give critical, honest feedback to someone with whom you are developing a friendship, especially if that friendship extends outside the workplace.

The OD professional may also want to hold onto information and expertise, rather than sharing the information with the organization and transferring the expertise into the organization, as an ethical OD professional is expected to do. This withholding may be a signal to the organization about how important it has become to the OD professional who is extending the relationship inappropriately for his or her own benefit.

An OD professional can become enamored of the power that is often ascribed to this role. As a result, rather than working with the organization to take on this power, dependency occurs, and the OD professional holds onto the power.

The organization can reflect a dependency in a number of ways as well. Numerous e-mails or telephone calls can be one such sign. Organizational members fail to make decisions without checking in with the OD professional. Clearly, these are important communication tools, and their use is not a problem per se. They signal a potential problem when they seem to contain unnecessary communications or when they become intrusive or overused.

Another signal of dependency may be the request for more of the OD professional's time than may be warranted by the needs of the organization as surfaced by the assessment process.

Just as during therapy, transference can occur between the OD professional and organizational members. This can lead to the desire to develop a personal relationship with the OD professional and vice versa. As suggested, moving from a professional to a personal relationship can have a negative impact on the ability of the two parties to function in an honest way together as the contractual agreement requires.

Failure of the organization to try to acquire the expertise that has been offered to the organization by the OD professional, requiring, instead, that the OD professional continue to be involved in the organization, can be another signal of dependency. Similarly, the OD professional can begin to anticipate what the client wants, rather than needs, and try to please the client organization rather than challenge it appropriately.

Dependency can also be reflected in the constant seeking for reassurance by either the organization or the OD professional that what they are doing is correct. It may even get to the point where, if the OD professional is external, the organization will try to hire the professional into the organization, or the OD professional will try to get hired by the organization. The organization may also give the OD professional sufficient work that the professional does not need to have other clients. And the professional may covertly or unknowingly allow or even encourage this to take place. While these practices are not always wrong, the OD professional must ask, "Whose needs are being taken care of here?" If it is the consultant's, then the boundary has probably been crossed. Furthermore, as many OD professionals come from the helping professions, they frequently have a need to be needed, fulfilling their own needs rather than those of the client.

What Should Be Done If Dependency Develops?

The signs of developing dependency should be addressed directly. By labeling the inappropriate behaviors and discussing them openly, it may be possible to turn things around and prevent the dependency from getting out of hand. If issues cannot be resolved, then the OD professional, whether internal or external, and the client organization may need to separate. Such separation, however, should likewise be intentional, with a clear understanding on the part of all parties involved of what happened and why the separation has become necessary.

Another alternative, as will be addressed more fully in the next chapter, is to participate in a social support system of other OD professionals with whom you can share concerns, vent feelings, reflect on your own motives, and so on.

. . . .

I once had a client with whom I had worked for a long time. It was a family business, and they needed a lot of OD help. However, the point came where I judged that dependency had developed and that separation was needed. I had developed a social relationship with the CEO and the sales manager, brothers who often saw things differently. And I saw the organization looking to me for answers rather than doing the difficult work that the organization needed to do itself. Once we talked about these issues and all involved agreed that we wanted the personal relationships to continue, we agreed that separation was needed. I saw my role at that point as helping the organization bring in another OD professional who could continue to work with them but who did not have the history of working with the organization or a history of personal relationships with senior management in the organization.

CO-OPTATION BY THE CULTURE

Somewhat associated with dependency is the concern that the OD professional may lose the third-party perspective about the client organization because he or she can no longer distinguish the culture of the organization. This is particularly a concern for internal OD professionals. Immersion may interfere with the ability of the internal person to see organizational cultures that are obvious to an external OD professional. Internal OD professionals may sometimes forget what is unique about their organization's culture. In this case, some of the very organizational issues that need to be challenged by the OD professional appear to be normative and, therefore, accepted by an internal person. This is not an indictment of internal OD professionals. Inside knowledge may be an advantage in some circumstances. However, no matter how skilled an OD professional is, familiarity can be a significant handicap.

There are a few things that can be done when an OD professional has been or is likely to become co-opted by the organization's culture. One, as stated earlier, is for the OD professional to meet regularly with other OD professionals for reflection sharing and support. Either in pairs or in a group, each person can challenge the other, reminding them of how unique the organizational culture is.

For external OD consultants, becoming co-opted may be a reminder of the importance of continuing to market to other organizations so a variety of organizational cultures are seen and being reminded, then, of the current client organization's uniqueness.

If this detachment and ability to see the organization clearly do not happen, then there may not be options other than for the OD professional to choose to leave the organization. For an internal OD professional, this may mean seeking another employer, though perhaps a transfer to another part of the organization is also a possibility. For the external OD professional, it may mean going through a separation process with the current client while moving on to other client organizations. Again, separation should be done clearly and intentionally, with an open understanding of why it is occurring.

TRANSFER OF SKILLS

Depending on the skill level, experience, and educational background of the OD professional, as well as the scope of the intervention, the length of time before separation will vary. When all of the expertise of the OD professional has been transferred, separation should occur naturally. Keep in mind that the primary task of the OD professional is to transfer his or her expertise to the client organization. If the OD professional has a limited skill set, then the Separation phase may occur relatively soon after Entry. An OD professional with a larger skill set may find that additional skills can be applied to the organization even after initial skills have been transferred to the organization. The danger, of course, is that the OD professional might end up selling services or products to the client to extend the contract, not because the client needs them.

The successful and complete transfer of skills by the OD professional to an organization can lead to a relatively easy separation process. When the need for this type of separation occurs, it is because the OD professional has been successful, as has the client organization. Both have fulfilled their roles by transferring and receiving the expertise of the OD professional. Again, the OD professional can be helpful in identifying other OD professionals who have the skill set necessary for the next step in the OD process. And the OD professional can then move on to another part of the organization or to another organization.

ADVERSARIAL RELATIONSHIPS OR DISSATISFACTION WITH WORK

At times the relationships between the OD professional and members of the client organization become so adversarial that there is little chance of successfully working together. Sometimes this development occurs because the OD professional is not competent in the skill areas required by the client organization. Sometimes OD professionals make mistakes that reduce the level of trust. Both of these outcomes can happen to any OD professional, but they are more likely to occur among OD professionals who do not have sufficient expertise or experience. Because there is no uniformly accepted method of confirming OD expertise, people who are unqualified may well find themselves in over their heads, reflecting not only their lack of specific skills but also their inability to read the organization accurately.

On the other hand, it is possible that a very experienced and competent OD professional may find that the client organization is unhappy because the assessment and feedback have pointed to difficult situations for which individuals within the client organization have to take ownership. As a result, personnel within the organization may be angry, embarrassed, or fearful.

OD professionals might also feel dissatisfied or frustrated with the responses of the client organization. Perhaps the OD professionals feel as if they are not being heard, that the organization really has no intent of making change, or that the organization refuses to receive the feedback provided.

In spite of any negative feelings that might exist on either side, or perhaps because of them, it is still important to discuss the nature of what is happening before the separation occurs. Many OD professionals, as part of their contract, include a guarantee of satisfaction. This provides an opportunity to talk about what has happened or is happening. It is possible that open conversation might salvage the project. And, even if it does not, there is then an opportunity and a responsibility to learn from the situation. Discussion will also clarify how the final invoice will be modified to meet the guarantee clause of the contract.

. . . .

I had been working off and on with a family owned business for almost ten years. I had been invited back to do a check-up assessment to see how things were going with the organization. Interviews were conducted, and many serious problems surfaced focused primarily on the perceived dictatorial style of the CEO, the daughter of the founder. As always, I had received a commitment from the CEO that results would be shared with the members of the organization. Because the results were so negative about her leadership, I met with the CEO and shared with her the results of the interviews. While she was unhappy with the results, she was not surprised and plans were made for the feedback and action planning session with the executive team.

During the session, it was clear that she was having difficulty with the feedback, especially as the executive team began to do the action planning in response to the feedback. During the break on the second day of action planning, she approached me to tell me how uncomfortable she was feeling about the process and thought that we should end the intervention. She then dismissed the executive team (and me). I tried several times to follow up with her to discuss what had happened, but she would not take my phone calls. This was not a separation done according to the theory.

BUDGET CUTS/DOWNSIZING

Internal OD professionals are always subject to the possibility of organizational downsizing. While, strategically, an organization might consider that during a time of downsizing an OD professional might deliver even more value, unfortunately, that is not always the way in which organizations make decisions. External OD professionals are even more vulnerable to organizational downsizing than are internal professionals. Clearly, there is less organizational commitment to an external OD professional, making it easier to discontinue an OD process.

In both cases, a deliberate and systematic conversation about the separation process and the status of the project should still take place, as difficult as that might be for both parties. This discussion serves to meet the psychological and business needs of both the client and the OD professional. As organizations tend to have economic cycles, it is very possible (even probable) that the economic fortunes of the organization will turn around in the future. Maintaining a positive relationship could well result in future employment or a future contract with the organization, especially if the separation has left both parties with good feelings in spite of the pain that is probably present.

MERGERS AND ACQUISITIONS

We live in a world that is marked by mergers and acquisitions. This trend can present wonderful opportunities for OD professionals, though, as mentioned earlier, it can also result in a separation. An external OD professional is actually likely to benefit from a merger or acquisition.

One of the most difficult aspects of a merger or acquisition is encountered in the process of trying to merge two organizational cultures that are often dramatically different from each other. Prior to their joining, organizations are certain to do a financial audit to ensure that the information shared about finances has been accurate. However, a cultural audit, which may be just as important as the financial audit, is seldom done. In fact, Schmidt (2002) reported that OD professionals were involved in fewer than half of the due diligence efforts to make sure that both parties were prepared to move forward with the merger or acquisition. When they were involved, it was most likely to be associated with doing a cultural audit.

- -

As an example, when Northwest Airlines merged with Republic Airlines, almost no attention was paid to merging the very different cultures of the two airlines. Insufficient attention was paid to the integration of the different processes and to the training of employees from the two airlines who would be working together using the merged processes. As a result, on the first day of operation under the merged process, almost everything went awry. Luggage was lost, passengers were frustrated over the slowness of the ticket clerks, and passenger satisfaction plummeted. It took more than 2 years for satisfaction to return to premerger levels. Where were the OD professionals in this process? So, if management is paying attention, a merger or an acquisition actually has the potential for reinforcing the value of the OD process.

- -

If two or more organizations that are in the process of joining are currently working with external OD professionals, or if each has its own OD professionals on staff, then there may, in fact, be an overlap that needs to be addressed. This situation could potentially lead to the canceling of the external OD professional's contract or the surplusing (or downsizing) of the number of internal OD positions.

As with the budget cut situation, it remains important to go through the separation process. Again, because the future is unknown, and because it is always important to learn what you can from the past, it is important to get feedback and provide feedback about your experiences together. Keep in mind the old saying, "Don't burn your bridges." From the organization's perspective, it is important to have this discussion so that there can be a smooth transition of in-process activities.

BETTER JOB OFFER

As an external OD professional, once you have signed a contract, you fulfill that contract whenever possible. To leave a client in the middle of a project because another client comes along is unethical and could be a disaster for your reputation. Don't do it!

On the other hand, an internal OD professional must always be aware of career development and career advancement opportunities. A person might consider moving to another organization for several reasons: an opportunity to apply a broader skill set, a better or simply different geographic location, better pay or benefits, greater supervisory opportunities, stronger chances for promotion, improved opportunity to be mentored or coached, improved job opportunities for a spouse, and on and on the list could go. All of these are legitimate reasons for moving to another organization.

There are still ethical considerations for the internal OD professional. Employment contracts sometimes have built-in specifications about how much lead time is required to give notice. At a minimum, in the United States, 2 weeks should be given; in other countries, organizations may expect 4 or even 6 weeks' notice. Even with that time frame, however, it is probably impossible for an organization to find a replacement before the OD professional's departure. So, if more lead time can be provided, consider giving it. Explore, as well, any contract that you might have signed at employment. Often professionals at this level are required to sign a noncompete clause that prohibits them from taking competitive work within a certain geographic area, in a similar industry, for a certain period of time. Working the separation out amicably may allow exceptions to be made to the agreement. The goal, as always, is to make the separation step as pleasant for all parties as possible.

END OF PROJECT

Sometimes an OD professional is contracted for a specific project rather than for the overall improvement of the organization. One example of a single-focus project might be facilitating a strategic planning process or conducting interviews for multirater feedback. Even though these approaches are not, of course, the most desirable way for an organization to interact with an OD professional, they are probably the most frequently used.

Separation in this situation may be more transitory in the sense that other projects will likely arise in the future, especially if the work was well received. This creates some challenge, however, because the temptation is greater to avoid a formal separation. However, if no future projects emerge, separation will not have happened, leaving both the client and the professional without a sense of closure. While the separation discussion may not be as detailed or lengthy as in the other situations described in this chapter, it is still important to have at least a brief conversation.

IMPORTANCE OF CLOSURE

As has been emphasized throughout this chapter, separation is an often ignored but very important phase in the organization development process model. When closure does not occur, feelings may remain unresolved and negatively color perceptions of those involved in the process. Important learnings may be left unaddressed and therefore not converted from implicit to explicit knowledge. The OD field is also relatively small, and stories are exchanged; when closure does not occur and stories are shared, people might feel uneasy or uncomfortable when they interact in the future with other professionals who have heard the stories.

Finally, from a business perspective, closure can also be the beginning of a new marketing endeavor. The organization you are leaving can well become a client again in the future, if separation is done correctly.

In each of the situations described, the formal separation can occur through a debriefing conversation on lessons learned, sometimes called *after-action review*. Such an approach is in keeping with a commitment toward continuous improvement or learning and can provide value for future projects for both the OD professional and the client organization.

CHAPTER SUMMARY

Separation, the final phase of the action research model, is initiated by a number of factors that can occur in the organization or within the OD professional. Some factors are clearly positive; others may be seen as negative. In every instance, however, there are major benefits to the organization and to the professional when closure occurs.

Closure usually involves an intentional conversation between the OD professional and the contact person within the client organization. In this conversation, it is important to discuss what each party learned from the process and to suggest ways for each to improve working relationships in the future. It is important to keep the door open for future work as circumstances change.

QUESTIONS FOR DISCUSSION OR SELF-REFLECTION

1. What are the most important factors to discuss in a separation conversation?

2. How would you see the conversation differing if the reason for the separation was organization initiated rather than professional initiated?

3. Under what circumstances do you think that it would be legitimate for an OD professional to separate from an organization?

4. Under what circumstances do you think that it would be legitimate for a client organization to separate from an OD professional?

5. Under what circumstances might a Separation phase actually lead back into the ARM cycle?

15

Ethics and Values Driving OD

CHAPTER OUTLINE

OVERVIEW   OD is a values-driven field. This quality is sometimes seen as one of its challenges. In determining what values should drive the field, there is the potential for conflict with the values of clients, especially those clients in the for-profit sector. In this chapter, areas that are particularly difficult ethically for OD practitioners will be presented and discussed, with suggestions of ways ethical decisions can be made. Reference will be made to the various professional ethics statements currently available. Values presented come heavily from my own practice and from the OD Principles and Practices on the OD Network Web site. The chapter includes a proposed flowchart for making ethical decisions.

Y ou may often have heard, "Just do the right thing!" If it were that easy, there would be relatively little to include in this chapter; I could simply refer you to one of the codes of ethics and be done. The reality, however, is that there are many times when determining the "right thing" to do is extremely difficult, especially when two or more desirable values come in conflict with each other. From my theological training comes this meaningful quote from Tillich (1963): "Life at every moment is ambiguous" (p. 32). A more down-to-earth way of stating this comes from Tom McLean, protagonist in the novel *China White*: "The world's a hell of a lot more gray than black and white" (Maas, 1994, p. 12). It is the gray area, the ambiguity, that makes ethical decision making difficult.

In this chapter, we will explore the nature of the tough decisions one must face to remain ethical in the field, suggest ways in which such decisions can be made ethically, and determine the value of the various codes of ethics that directly or tangentially relate to OD. A flowchart is presented near the end of the chapter, suggesting a process, but not the answer, to determining ethical practice.

WHAT ARE THE DIFFICULT ETHICAL DECISIONS TO BE MADE IN OD?

Perhaps not too surprisingly, in the complex and increasingly global business world in which we function as OD professionals, almost endless *ethical dilemmas* face the OD professional. The ones described in the following sections have been identified through research (DeVogel, 1992) and my personal practice.

Who Is My Client?

It is not always easy to identify who the client is. Is it the person who agrees to the project? Is it the person who signs the contract? Who is the person or parties to whom reports are to be sent? And what is the purpose of the intervention? Is it for the whole organization, for the board of directors, for the CEO, for the employees, for the stockholders?

The executive director of a not-for-profit organization asked a colleague and me to do an assessment of the organizational culture. It was his perception that the organization was not functioning well as a unit, preventing it from serving its clientele well. In addition, he felt some pressure from his board of directors to conduct the study. As with all such assessments, we received prior approval to share the information gained from the assessment process with employees. The assessment consisted of both interviews and written surveys.

The outcome of the assessment was that the executive director was the source of much of the disunity in the organization. His behaviors stemming from his active alcoholism and his relatively open extramarital affair with an employee were major contributing factors. Naturally, the executive director was not happy about us sharing this information with employees. He agreed, though, when we pointed out that the information was coming from the employees, and we reminded him of his preassessment agreement. He was adamant, however, that we could not share the information with the board, either in person, as we had requested, or in print. Because we had, in retrospect, contracted with the wrong client (the executive director rather than the board), we felt ethically bound not to share the information directly with the board. However, the board, as we assumed, demanded a report of the assessment from the executive director. And, eventually, the results were shared with them. About a year later, the front page of the paper announced that he had been fired.

We learned a lesson from this experience: the importance of contracting with the right client. Asking whether the purpose of the assessment was for the organization, the executive director, the employees, the board of directors, or the external stakeholders would also have been important.

Control over Flow of Information

Closely associated with the dilemma of identifying the client and the dilemma of confidentiality and anonymity that follows is the issue of what happens to the information gathered during the process of an intervention. At times, the client will use information collected for one stated purpose for an entirely different purpose. For example, the client may state that they want to collect information from employees about the processes they use in doing their jobs with the intent of improving the processes for quality and productivity. In fact, however, the client might want to use the information gathered to determine who should be released, especially during a downsizing, or who should be promoted. The parameters for the use of information must be firmly established by the OD professional before information is gathered. The ethical imperative for both the OD professional and the client is to ensure that, once information has been turned over to the client, the information is used as originally intended; the OD professional no longer has control over how the information is used.

Confidential and Anonymous Information

These two words, *confidential* and *anonymous*, are frequently confused and used as if they had the same meaning. They don't. *Confidential* means that information cannot be shared; *anonymous* means that the information can be shared but the source of the information cannot be shared. This principle has been explained in more detail in Chapter 4, along with a case story.

Ironically, my story of an ethical dilemma around confidentiality and anonymity is positioned around a consulting project in the headquarters of a religious denomination. Through the interviewing process, I learned about a problem related to possible embezzlement in one of the offices. If I had been doing the interviews under the condition of confidentiality, my struggle would have been about whether I could have said anything at all. Since the conditions were anonymity, I felt free to share the information, but not to specify who had told me or where the embezzlement was occurring. I believed that it would be relatively easy for the organization to identify the problem for itself if it chose to address the situation. Members of the organization did not agree, insisting that I tell them where it was occurring. I refused, citing the conditions of the contract. They continued to insist that I share the information with them, and my continued refusal ultimately led to the cancellation of my contract.

Conflict of Interest

It is not unusual for an external OD consultant to work for competitors within an industry, and internal OD consultants often move from one organization to another within the same industry. In fact, many clients prefer to hire someone who is experienced in a specific industry. Thus, many OD consultants work only in, for example, health care organizations. They often have information that could prove helpful for clients to have about their competitors. However, most contracts or memoranda of agreement address such *conflicts of interest*, prohibiting the sharing of any information about a client, either for a specific period of time or even indefinitely.

Fees and Billing

For any number of reasons, consultants often charge different fees to different clients. This procedure may be based on the client's ability to pay, the difficulty of the work, the nature of the organization (not-for-profit vs. for-profit), the location of the work, the extent of the OD professional's expertise, and so on. Furthermore, most codes of ethics for OD professionals (described later) require a certain amount of *pro bono* work (literally, "for the good," meaning that the work is not charged).

My goal is to do one pro bono consulting job a year, often associated with an organization working for the poor and disenfran-
chised (refugees, grassroots organizations, and others that match
my personal value system). I also try to do a couple of consultancies a year at a considerably reduced fee; given my theological
background, these are usually churches. I have a friend who
targets 10% to 20% of his work a year to being pro bono.

One of my clients provides a relatively steady amount of
work a year. They have negotiated a reduced fee based on a
commitment to a certain number of hours of work a year—sort
of a quantity discount. In addition, when I work with small
businesses, often family based, I charge less than I do with a
major corporation.

The question arises, Is it fair and ethical to charge different
amounts based on the client's ability to pay? I think it is, or I
wouldn't do so. But others disagree. There is also some question
about whether clients take the intervention as seriously when they
are not paying for it or are not paying "what it is worth."

Many other questions related to fees and billing raise ethical concerns. When the work is in another location where travel is involved,
how should the travel costs be handled? Although there should be no
question about the client paying for the actual expenses of the travel,
how should the time entailed in the travel be handled?

I regularly work for a client that is more than a 1-hour drive from
my home. If I travel down and back in one day, that's 3 hours
added to my workday. The way we have negotiated around this
matter is that I will be paid a certain minimum number of hours for
a day's worth of work. This arrangement partially recognizes the
value of my time traveling but also ensures that the length of time
that I work will be reasonable for the day.

Another client contacted me to help figure out how to add
value to an annual fishing trip to Canada for its senior executives.
This jaunt had become a ritual, but no work had been done
during the trip in the past. A number of women were now in

senior management roles, and they did not believe that it was cost-effective to take such a trip and not accomplish useful work. I worked with the manager of HR to construct what we both agreed would be useful activities to take up about 2 hours each day of the weeklong trip. The HR manager decided that he was not competent to facilitate the activities and asked me to join them for the week. Even though I would be working for just 2 hours a day, I would not be able to do other work for the rest of the day. I indicated that I was willing to do the work, but I would have to charge for five full days of work, including the travel time (by bus) to and from Canada. The organization was happy to do so; not only did I have an excellent experience working with the executives, but I also got in a lot of fishing and good fish eating! Was this appropriate? I think so!

Another billing question that surfaces when discussing ethics has to do with accounting for hours when the agreement calls for billing on an hourly basis. Because so much OD work is done off site, a trust level must exist so that the client perceives that the hours billed are accurate and not inflated. Agreement should also be reached as to how hours are going to be kept—to the nearest 10 minutes (as my lawyer does), to the nearest 15 minutes (as I do), only to half a day and a full day (as some of my colleagues do), and so on.

Working outside One's Areas of Expertise

As is evident from the content of this book, the field of OD is very large, and no one can be competent to work in every aspect of the field. Where this gets to be a dilemma is that no one is ever really an expert until that person has had a chance to do a particular type of work to develop that expertise. My solution to this dilemma, typically, is to charge much less when I am doing something for the first time and to be clear with the client that I am developing expertise in this particular area.

In the 1980s when the TQM field was developing in the United States, a colleague from a consulting firm specializing in TQM and I worked together with a high-tech organization that was interested in implementing TQM. We did not charge anything for our work with the firm because we saw it as a developmental opportunity. Not only did we learn from the experience and gain expertise, but the organization received the Baldrige Award (sponsored by the U.S. Congress and awarded in recognition of quality management after completing an extensive application and going through a detailed on-site visitation) and the Minnesota Quality Award (closely aligned with the Baldrige Award) for its excellence in applying quality processes.

The area in which the possibility of working outside one's area of expertise becomes the greatest concern is when the OD consultant begins to do work that comes dangerously close to therapy, with the accompanying possibility of actually doing harm to people. The risk comes from the rapid growth of *executive coaches* who are not trained therapists or who are not trained as coaches. Without appropriate training, these people often lack the qualifications to know the difference between coaching and therapy. An area of expertise required of every ethical OD person is knowing the limits of one's expertise and being able to make referrals to other professionals who are trained and competent in those areas.

Referrals to and from Other Professionals

As indicated, the ethical choice when confronted with work outside one's areas of expertise is to make a referral. How that referral is done, however, can sometimes create an ethical dilemma.

Early in my OD consulting work, I encountered a situation in which it became clear that it was time for me to leave a client because I had exhausted my level of expertise related to that client's needs. But the client still had OD work to be done. I made three referrals to the client, which selected one. Shortly thereafter, I received a check from the consultant who was hired. The check represented 10% of the first invoice, and the plan was that he would continue to send me 10% of all subsequent invoices. I had never heard of such an arrangement, so I began to do some research. It became clear that such a practice bordered on the unethical. It was a practice intended to increase the probability of similar referrals in the future, jeopardizing the basis on which referrals would be made. Instead of making referrals based on who would be best for the client, the temptation might be to make recommendations based on a potential commission. I returned the check and asked that no subsequent checks be sent.

Not everyone would agree with the decision I made. And the dilemma gets even trickier when consultants associate with one another. It is very common practice, for example, for small, independent consultants to work with other consultants when tasks become too large or outside one's level of expertise. One consultant (A) might contract with another consultant (B) to do OD work with a client who has contracted with consultant A. Consultant A would do the billing for all of the OD work and then pay consultant B. It is even probable that consultant A would pay consultant B less than what was received from the client to cover the costs of overhead and getting the contract in the first place. Is this ethical? Probably, even though the expectation is that consultant B would return the favor when he or she needs assistance with a project.

Giving and Receiving Bribes

Closely related to the prior issue, but a little more blatant, is the issue of bribes. Corruption is a major problem throughout the world, with some countries more notorious for this practice than others. In fact, bribery is so widespread that an organization has been established to provide rankings of which countries are "better" or "worse" on the issue of corruption. The *TI Corruption Perceptions Index 2004* (Transparency International, 2004) reveals that the United States is tied for 17th place, while the top three (indicating a perception of the least corruption) are Finland, New Zealand, and Denmark. Of the 147 countries listed, 106 scored less than 5 against a "clean" score of 10 in 2004.

If one is working in, say, Thailand (tied for 64th), where bribes are commonplace (Chat-uthai & McLean, 2003), the consultant is confronted with a decision about whether to participate and increase the opportunities for employment, or refuse to participate and find that getting and doing work is more difficult. Again, for those who live in the United States, it is illegal to make bribes, either domestically or internationally. And participating in bribery makes it more difficult for individual countries to combat their corruption.

There is no reason to accept a bribe, though determining the difference between a culturally appropriate gift and a bribe is often difficult. In many cultures, it is not only acceptable but expected that gifts will be exchanged based on a rather elaborate unwritten set of "rules." To refuse such a gift is to insult the person who has offered it. In general, the difference is one of magnitude—a bribe exceeds in value a culturally accepted gift. But that's the ethical dilemma: knowing what is acceptable and what is not is not easy.

Violating Copyright

A clear violation of copyright is really not an ethical dilemma. It is clearly against the law—and something that is illegal is no longer an ethical dilemma.

The law is not clear about how much of someone's work can be used before copyright is violated. Unfortunately, whether true or not, there is a perception that trainers frequently use others' material without permission and even without credit. Any time enough material is used to impact sales negatively, copyright has probably been violated. The use of any table, chart, or instrument, even if paraphrased, is probably a copyright violation. Perhaps one way to make this decision is to ask how you would feel if someone else used your material in a similar way without your permission.

Insider Knowledge of an Organization

Just as employees who work in a *publicly listed organization* are prohibited from using information that they learn on the job to their own financial gain, so, too, are consultants under the same prohibition. Thus, if an OD consultant learns that a particular organization is about to release information about a new product that is likely to increase the company's stock value considerably, the consultant is prohibited from sharing this information with any others and from purchasing stock personally.

This situation may pose an ethical dilemma because it is not always easy to tell what information is generally known to the public and learned through public means of communication, and what information has been gained from working with the organization.

Inappropriate Relationships

The potential exists for a number of inappropriate relationships for the consultant within the client organization. The most obvious is related to sexual harassment and sexual relationships. A consultant is subject to at least the same policies and regulations as exist for employees in the client organization. Ethical behavior calls for no romantic or sexual interaction with any member of the client organization during the term of the contract.

While romantic or sexual interactions are the most obvious inappropriate relationships, other relationships might also cause some ethical concerns.

One of my colleagues asked me to participate with her in a project with one of her long-term OD clients, a multinational company. We were to help prepare HR employees to do OD work by using training, needs assessments, career development, and coaching. There was potential for me to develop other business with them. Ethically, I needed to be very careful not to use my new connections with the HR people to get business and jeopardize the established relationship and business of my colleague.

Any relationship that affects the OD consultant's ability to work as a third party in an intervention will also raise ethical concerns. This is a particularly difficult situation for an internal OD professional who may work with the same people over a long period of time. Since many relationships develop in the workplace, an internal OD professional has to be particularly on guard to ensure that he or she is able to maintain an appropriate level of objectivity regarding the individuals involved in the organization.

Working across Cultures

We covered this topic in Chapter 11 on global interventions, but it is worth revisiting here. Transferring an intervention that has been developed in one country to another country, without modifying it for the peculiarities of that country's culture, creates an ethical dilemma. Because of the historical dominance of the United States in business, it is not unusual to see countries with very different cultures attempting to adopt practices that have become popular in the United Stated without considering the cultural implications.

I am often asked to do a workshop or make a presentation in a context other than the United States. The requesting organization often says, "Tell us about what is hot in the United States today. How do organizations in the United States do _____?" And the blank is almost always the latest fad that hasn't even proven its worth yet in the United States. It takes a lot of work to convince the contracting organization that we should at least take a critical look at the practice's value, both in the United States and in the country of focus.

I was contacted by an organization in Korea that wanted me to suggest how to use multirater feedback for performance appraisals. I responded that the research suggested that multirater appraisals raised many problems, though they were useful for employee development. Furthermore, the collectivist culture of Korea, in contrast with the individualistic culture of the United States, made this approach for the purpose of performance appraisals problematic. The issue of "loss of face" that is so critical in most Asian cultures also raises questions about the appropriateness of multirater feedback. Power distance (see Chapter 9), perhaps a contributor to loss of face, also makes multirater feedback inappropriate in Korea.

In spite of these concerns, many practices from the United States are finding a home in organizations around the world. Ethical considerations demand that such practices be thoroughly researched and modified to meet cultural and organizational needs.

Nature of the Industry

At times decisions are made not to accept employment or a contract with a specific organization because of the nature of the product or services in which the organization is involved.

A local corporation, a large conglomerate with a broad range of products, frequently asked me to work with it. However, one of its products was a particularly controversial weapons program. Many consultants did not find this product to be in conflict with their values. I was not comfortable with this production, however, so chose not to accept a contract. Likewise, I have personally chosen not to work with organizations that produce tobacco or alcohol products, and, so far, I have resisted opportunities to be involved in gambling-related organizations. Each consultant needs to be clear about his or her own values to know what kinds of industries to bypass—and each will make different decisions.

As with other dilemmas faced by OD professionals, there is no clear right or wrong choice about which industry to work in. For example, though I have indicated that I would not choose to work for an organization in an alcohol-related industry, I have worked for restaurants and hotels, both of which serve alcohol. So what makes the difference? It is not a clear-cut decision. Few decisions regarding industry are so obvious as to be easy.

Nature of the Work

Sometimes the OD professional has no problem with the industry of the potential client or employer but is uncomfortable, from a values perspective, with the nature of the work itself. I, for one, am not willing to take a contract when the objective is to find a reason to dismiss a specific individual, a request that is surprisingly frequent.

As another example, a consultant might be called in to help an organization with downsizing or with outsourcing work to another country, location, or organization. The consultant may be troubled by such disruptive changes and therefore uncomfortable accepting this assignment. These business moves, however, may be necessary for the organization's survival: if an organization goes bankrupt, no one will have employment. Moreover, in outsourcing to another country, work is being provided to the workers in that country, and that work may be more essential for life survival than for the workers who are temporarily displaced in the consultant's native country.

. . . .

I once worked for a safety equipment distribution company. One of its major sales items was safety gloves. When I began working for the company, it purchased all of its gloves from a U.S. manufacturer. However, the profit margins were extremely small, and, as the industry began to move to China for both the design and manufacture of gloves, so, too, did the client company feel the need to do the same to remain competitive. This move proved to be very effective. The company expanded its sales considerably, requiring that additional employees be added and warehouse and office facilities expanded. A close working relationship was established with a manufacturing facility in China that has since developed even more products.

. . . .

Again, it should be obvious that there are no clear answers about whether the kind of work that the consultant is being asked to do is ethical and appropriate.

Skipping Organizational Analysis

Is it unethical to skip steps in the ODP? Some would argue that many small interventions are appropriate without conducting a full-scale analysis, for example. If this is so, then the ethical dilemma emerges in trying to determine when it is essential to do an analysis, and, therefore, skipping this step becomes unethical.

Skipping the Evaluation Phase

Likewise, skipping the Evaluation phase may or may not be considered unethical. Why is this phase being bypassed? Is there concern that the findings might jeopardize the standing of the OD professional or management involved in the project? If so, it is probably unethical to skip this step. Is there, legitimately, not enough money available for the evaluation, or is there widespread belief in the effectiveness of the intervention? It might be more acceptable in these situations to skip the Evaluation phase.

Single-Tool Syndrome

The cliché for the *single-tool syndrome* is, "If all you have is a hammer, everything looks like a nail." Some OD professionals have developed expertise in a single area, such as six sigma. Then, no matter what the situation in a given organization, the temptation for such professionals is to search for a problem that can be solved by using six sigma. We see this syndrome happening with multirater feedback systems, coaching, leadership development, and so on. Many instruments require certification for their use (e.g., MBTI or DiSC). Professionals certified to use instruments often find a way to utilize such instruments in a consultation, whether or not the situation calls for their use. Such unsupported use probably borders on the unethical.

Nonsystems Work

A very common request is for a specified, limited intervention, such as conflict management, team building, team effectiveness and facilitation, or an educational workshop. An issue identified earlier is the request to do an intervention without conducting an organizational analysis. When a request for a specific, nonsystems intervention is made, probably no analysis has been conducted—but not always, which is what makes this a tempting offer for an OD professional. Yet, when there is no willingness to take a systems perspective, it is possible (and even probable) that other issues that arise during the intervention will not be addressed.

I received a telephone call from an assistant to the president of a university. The university had just initiated a new budgeting system that was causing intense competition between colleges. The assistant indicated that they were having severe conflict between deans. She asked whether I would be available to attend the August deans' retreat to do a workshop on team building. Naturally, I asked a few questions. The first question was how they knew that the right intervention was team building. She didn't have an answer to that one. I then asked whether it would be acceptable to pursue other issues that surfaced, such as the need to change the budgeting system that was causing the conflict. She replied that such an area would be out of bounds. Finally, I asked how much time I would have. "The agenda is very tight," the assistant responded, "so there is not much time available. We could probably give you an hour." Needless to say, I declined the contract. There was no way to succeed in making a difference in the system, and the client would clearly have been unhappy with the outcome.

From my perspective, it is never ethical to undertake a contract when it appears obvious that the intervention cannot have a positive outcome. When only a limited intervention is offered, the potential for impacting the entire system seldom exists. The exception to this, however, might be when the specific intervention seems to have value, and the potential exists for a greater systems impact later.

I was invited to do a full-day workshop with an organization in Saudi Arabia that had been very successful in its region in manufacturing and selling cement pipes. It was now interested in going global with its product. The workshop, for senior managers, was geared toward understanding what it would take to become global.

The workshop went well and was later repeated for employees at a supervisory level. Next, one-on-one meetings were held with senior management to help them develop a strategic plan for their functional areas for moving forward. Thus, the initial contract with a single intervention (workshop) expanded into a broader, strategic intervention.

Inappropriate Use of Information

As mentioned earlier, information collected for one purpose may be misused for another, unintended purpose. For example, many employee surveys ask questions about supervisors and managers. This information is often analyzed by department or function. Such surveys are intended to be used for the purpose of creating a baseline and identifying areas in which improvement can be made. Yet, they can be misused when their results are used for the purpose of performance appraisal and decisions about pay, promotion, transfers, and so on. This use is not appropriate, especially if employees are being told that the purpose is for improvement and benchmarking and not for personnel decision making.

Being Subsumed by the Organizational Culture

A particularly difficult ethical situation for internal OD professionals is the possibility of becoming subsumed by the organizational culture. The culture becomes so familiar that the third party nature of OD work disappears, and the OD professional can no longer see the culture objectively. Even external OD professionals who work with the same client over a long period of time run the same risk. Dysfunctional behavior can become "appropriate" only because it is familiar.

Delaying Separation

A temptation that faces both internal and external OD professionals is looking to extend the work and delaying the time of separation. Sometimes, this behavior is reflected in finding additional projects to work on, even though they are not critical or important to the organization. Sometimes, it means delaying the submission of a report, or extending the number of interviews being conducted, or increasing the number of observations made, and so on. Anything that is not useful for the client and that is designed with the sole purpose of extending the contract or employment is probably not ethical.

Failure to Transfer Skills

A primary commitment of the OD professional, in contrast perhaps, with other consulting professionals (as suggested in Chapter 2), is the commitment to transfer the OD professional's expertise into the client organization so that expertise is present in the organization when the consultant separates. I will often describe, during an intervention, the process that I am using along with its rationale so client members can acquire the skill. I will do mini–training sessions with internal members of the client organization for the same reason. This especially happens during coaching sessions. I may also create instruments (e.g., a team effectiveness instrument) that I leave in the client organization for its ongoing use. Many of my colleagues have questioned me about these practices, as they are concerned that this will decrease the number of opportunities for them to have work. Yet, this approach entails my belief about how ethical OD is done.

Putting Security before Forthrightness

A critical role for the OD professional is being able to "tell it like it is." Fear that such honesty or forthrightness will lead to dismissal, the cancellation of a contract, or a negative impact on one's reputation will inhibit the OD professional from being able to confront management with "the truth" as efforts are made to protect the work.

HOW DOES AN ETHICAL OD PROFESSIONAL MAKE AN ETHICAL DECISION?

One might think that the process of deciding what actions are ethical would be relatively easy in a field that is so well established, with a history of over 50 years. Such is not the case, however. Ethicists have developed a *taxonomy* of how people make ethical decisions, categorizing them into three approaches:

- **Deontology,** or values based on the past—laws, rules, standards, religious teachings, parental teachings, codes of conduct, values statements
- **Situational,** or values based on the present—what is the best decision to meet the needs of the present?
- **Teleology,** or values based on a vision for the future—what kind of society do we want to create (mission, vision, purpose, goals)?

Which approach one uses or sees as preferable will depend on that individual's value system. Thus, a religious person who believes that the sacred writings of his or her belief stance are immutable truths from the Supreme may make very different decisions than the religious individual who believes that sacred writings were appropriate for the time in which they were written but are not applicable in today's complex society. Moreover, some people may find others who share their faith conviction interpreting the rules or writings in very different ways.

Hall (1993) suggested a series of steps to take when confronted with a difficult ethical dilemma:

1. Define the problem.
2. Identify the stakeholders.
3. Identify the practical alternatives.
4. Determine the measurable economic impact of each alternative.
5. Identify the immeasurable economic impact of each alternative.
6. Arrive at a tentative decision.
7. Decide how to implement the decision.

Although these steps suggest a process, it is unlikely that two people who have different value sets will come up with the same decision. The point of all of this is that ethical decision making is very difficult. What follows in this section are suggestions of resources that that individuals can use in making ethical decisions. No one suggestion will likely suffice in every situation.

Codes of Ethics

Many professions believe that they can ensure ethical behavior of their members by providing them with a *code of ethics*, a list of statements about what is acceptable and what is unacceptable behavior. This approach seemingly assumes that ethical decision making is simple if people just know what decisions are "right." Because life is ambiguous, however, and because most dilemmas involve choices between positive values, such a list is not necessarily going to be very effective. In fact, DeVogel's (1992) research indicated that OD professionals seldom even know what the ethical statements of the profession are, and, even if they do know them, they seldom reference them when confronted with difficult ethical decisions. The existing codes in the field will be explored in greater detail in the next major section of this chapter.

Personal Values

A useful tool to assist in ethical decision making is to make a personal list of your values before you are confronted with an ethical dilemma.

Such an approach must be authentic, however, meaning that you must be committed to living by those values. To make a list of values to which you are not truly committed—in other words, they are just for "public consumption"—is likely to have more negative impact than positive. People will become cynical about the statements if they observe you behaving in a way that contradicts your statements.

. . . .

My consulting company colleagues (one of my sons and one of my daughters) and I developed a set of statements about the values we intend to apply in our consulting business:

Value Commitments of McLean Global Consulting, Inc.

- We strive always to operate ethically and with integrity. Whenever there is a question about integrity, we will discuss it openly with the client.
- We offer services only that are proven effective; we bridge theory to practice.
- Our goal is to partner with clients—to facilitate change, not to dictate it.
- We strive to transfer our skills and processes to client organizations.
- We seek long-term relationships that add value, while avoiding dependencies.
- We value *indigenization*—all of our work is customized to meet the culture of client organizations and the environmental context in which clients exist.
- We are firmly committed to upfront assessment to insure that the plans we develop with clients are appropriate for client needs and client cultures.
- We desire to conduct evaluation of all of our work to ensure that we mutually developed action plans that were effective.
- Generally, we will seek to work with an internal committee and an internal professional to ensure that our plans fit client needs and cultures.
- We are committed to inclusion and diversity.
- We strive to align our work with the client organization's mission, vision, strategies, and goals.

- We are process oriented; client contacts and client organizations will always know the content of their business better than we will.
- We encourage taking a systems perspective.
- We are driven by data, both quantitative and qualitative.

Accepted Practices in the Field

What is typically done when an ethical dilemma arises in the field? This question may be helpful in focusing on the issues involved in the situation in order to build options as to how the dilemma could be solved.

Let's go back to the issue about charging for travel time. Making such a decision need not be done in a vacuum. Benchmarking, or finding out what competitors do, is a good way to determine what typical practice is. What is normally done, however, is not necessarily the most ethical thing to do. Certainly any field has practices that are commonly found, but they need to be examined further to determine whether they are ethical. For example, it is common for people to stretch the truth (or lie) occasionally. But does common practice make lying ethical? It might, depending on the impact of the lie and the rationale for telling the lie. Some, however, would argue that it is always unethical to tell a lie, even though it is commonplace. So, this approach provides one approach to solving ethical dilemmas, but, in and of itself, it is not sufficient.

Reflection

Schein's (1994) *Reflective Practitioner* and Kidder's (1995) call for "energetic self-reflection" (p. 13) both suggested that taking time to reflect on past and future actions can help identify appropriate (ethical) actions. Some accomplish this self-reflection simply by setting aside regular time each day to think about one's practice. Some find meditation to be effective. What is important is to take the time regularly to consider one's actions.

Discussion with Professional Colleagues

Another way to explore options is to discuss ethical dilemmas with professional colleagues, being careful, of course, to protect confidentiality at all costs. For example, I make it a point to have lunch at least once a month with a professional colleague. In addition to building a community of practice, these informal meetings give us both an opportunity to share what is happening in our practices and to discuss alternative approaches, to help us see blind spots in our practices and to explore areas that might be bordering on the unethical. It is very difficult to share these observations with a professional colleague and then go ahead and act in an unethical way. Furthermore, something that you might see one way, your colleague might see in another way, helping you get a better sense of what is happening in the situation.

The Law

When considering whether what is being done is legal, we have probably moved past mere ethical considerations. If something is happening that could be regarded as illegal, that situation definitely calls for contacting your attorney to check its legality.

Some decisions are very difficult to determine whether they are unethical or illegal. Consider the case of Arthur Andersen's role in the shredding of Enron's documents. Although the Supreme Court has overturned the conviction of the firm for shredding documents when no charges had been made, declaring that such action was legal, a case may still be made for unethical behavior.

Would I Want This Action to Become Public Knowledge?

While perhaps simplistic, this question can still serve as a powerful tool for determining whether some action is ethical. What if the front page of the business section ran a story on this particular intervention? Would you be comfortable with this publicity? Would the community feel good about the reported actions? If the answer to any of these questions is no, then probably different decisions and actions are called for, even if some would argue that the actions are ethical.

Use a Decision-Making Model

Reflecting on my own process for deciding what I would or would not consider ethical in my practice, I have put together the model that appears in Figure 15.1. This illustration is not something a consultant would probably carry from project to project, but if it is studied and used as a point of reference, it can provide a basis for decision making that will be ethical and support the good faith in which decisions are made.

CODES OF ETHICS

In a desire to provide assistance to academics and practitioners, various professional organizations with an interest in OD have provided statements about values or guidelines for behavior. These materials are intended to help OD professionals facing ethical dilemmas make ethical decisions. They are sometimes called *statements of values* but, more often, *codes of ethics*.

What Is a Code of Ethics?

A *code of ethics* is a statement that has been approved and sanctioned by a professional organization for its members, specifying guidelines for ethical behavior and, in some cases, defining ethical and unethical behavior. There are two major distinctions among the various codes that exist. First, some codes of ethics, such as The OD Institute's, are really guidelines. That is, they are offered for the advice and counsel of its membership, but there is nothing that can be done if a member violates or deviates from the code. In contrast, other codes, such as that of the American Psychological Association (APA), are enforceable. That is, if a member is accused of violating the ethics code, he or she is taken before a group of peers, can lose membership, and, ultimately, have his or her license revoked if it is deemed that the member has violated the ethics of that profession. With the exception of the APA code, all of the other codes discussed in this chapter are advisory and not enforceable. Certainly, when a code is enforceable, it carries more weight than when it is simply advisory.

Another difference among codes is the relative emphasis on practice and academia. The code of the Academy of Human Resource Development, for example, is heavily oriented toward academia, whereas the code of The OD Institute is heavily oriented toward practice. Efforts have been made over the years to create a common set of ethics codes for those

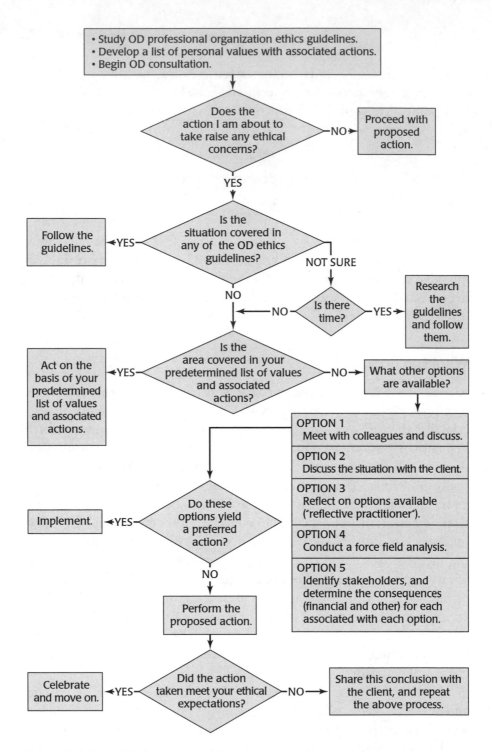

Figure 15.1 *Model for Ethical Decision Making in OD*

involved in OD, resulting in the *Organization and Human Systems Development Credo (July 1996)*, but, in fact, these efforts have not resulted in a common statement but, instead, one more in a long list of such statements.

What Are the Most Prevalent OD Codes of Ethics?

Each of the major professional organizations that have a focus on OD either has its own code of ethics or supports or endorses a statement made by another professional organization. It is not reasonable to reproduce all of the codes here. However, a brief statement is made about each of the codes, and a Web site where they can be found online is provided.

The Organization Development Institute.   The OD Institute (ODI) is a professional organization focusing primarily on practitioners. It is an international organization that also publishes one of the few journals focused specifically on OD, *The Organization Development Journal*. *The International Organization Development Code of Ethics* (1991) is found at members.aol.com/ODInst/ethic.htm and is one of the shorter statements (four pages). It is reproduced in the appendix to this chapter.

The ODI statement focuses on five broad categories of ethical decision making:

- Responsibility to Self
- Responsibility for Professional Development and Competence
- Responsibility to Clients and Significant Others
- Responsibility to the Profession
- Social Responsibility

It seems a little strange, with the rapid advances in technology in recent years, that this statement is now 15 years old. I am not aware of any efforts to update it. It is interesting, too, that ODI also endorses the *Organization and Human Systems Development Credo (July 1996)*.

Organization and Human System Development Credo (July 1996). This 1996 statement is endorsed by The ODI, along with its own statement, and it is the statement used by the OD Network, the largest of the practitioner OD organizations. This is also a four-page document developed by the Clearinghouse for Information about Values and Ethics in OD-HSD and is found at www.odnetwork.org/credo.html. This is clearly more of a statement of values that are intended to guide the field than a statement focused on specific activities. Thus, the ODI statement and the *O/HSD Credo* work very well together.

Academy of Human Resource Development.   The Academy of Human Resource Development published its first *Standards on Ethics and Integrity* in 1999 (www.ahrd.org). The document provides several general principles: competence, integrity, professional responsibility, respect for people's rights and dignity, concern for others' welfare, and social responsibility. Details are provided about standards, in addition to general standards, related specifically to

- research and evaluation,
- publication of work,
- privacy and confidentiality,
- teaching and facilitating, and
- resolution of ethical issues and violations.

While practice is covered in the statement, it is clear that the primary focus of these standards is on higher education. This statement, along with the statement of the APA, are the two most detailed and lengthy statements.

Academy of Management, Organization Development and Change Division.   The Web site of the ODC Division of the Academy of Management indicates that there is no specific ethics statement by the division, but it does provide a link to the statements of the ODI and the *O/HSD Credo*.

Society for Industrial and Organizational Psychology (SIOP).   Likewise, SIOP does not have its own ethics statement. Instead, it relies on and supports the *Ethical Principles of Psychologists and Code of Conduct* of the American Psychological Association (2002) (www.apa.org/ethics/code2002.pdf). Unlike the earlier statements that provide guidelines, this statement is an enforceable one that can lead to sanctions, loss of membership, and referral to other bodies that can revoke licenses.

The APA statement includes 5 general principles and 10 ethical standards, all in great detail. The general principles are listed here:

A. Beneficence and Nonmaleficence

B. Fidelity and Responsibility

C. Integrity

D. Justice

E. Respect for People's Rights and Dignity

The standards are the following:

1. Resolving Ethical Issues

2. Competence

3. Human Relations

4 Privacy and Confidentiality

5. Advertising and Other Public Statements

6. Record Keeping and Fees

7. Education and Training

8. Research and Publication

9. Assessment

10. Therapy

Although SIOP acknowledges that the APA does not always represent organizational emphasis well, it is important for members of SIOP to continue to have an association with APA and to make use of its statement of ethics.

Society for Human Resource Management.   The *SHRM Code of Ethical and Professional Standards in Human Resource Management* (undated at www.shrm.org//ethics/code-of-ethics.asp) is a relatively short document consisting of six principles:

1. Professional Responsibility

2. Professional Development

3. Ethical Leadership

4. Fairness and Justice

5. Conflicts of Interest

6. Use of Information

These principles, though generally similar to those in other statements, are not specific to the practice of OD but apply generally to those engaged in HRM activities.

International Society for Performance Improvement, and ASTD (formerly, American Society for Training and Development) Certified Performance Technologist.   This is an interesting example of a collaboration between two leading professional organizations—ASTD and ISPI (2002 found at www.certifiedpt.org/index.cfm?section=standards)—designed specifically for the jointly offered Certified Performance Technologist program. This code includes six principles:

1. Add Value

2. Validated Practice

3. Collaboration

4. Continuous Improvement

5. Integrity

6. Uphold Confidentiality

How Can a Code of Ethics Be Used Effectively?

The list of codes of ethics presented here is certainly not comprehensive. Several other statements of ethics might be tangentially or specifically related to the work of OD professionals. Nevertheless, we can see many similarities in the principles that are included in the published statements.

The bigger question, however, is what value the codes of ethics have and how they can be used most effectively in improving the ethical conduct of OD work. This is not an easy question to answer. First, most people's ethics come from values developed very early in life. These values are seldom impacted or even clearly recognized later in life unless some significant event occurs. This lack of recognition may be one more argument for suggesting that an individual use therapy as a way of clarifying his or her own values, perhaps even changing them if the person realizes that the values established earlier in life are inconsistent with those in the field. Furthermore, there is no evidence that a statement of ethics, especially one that provides guidelines only, makes any difference in how OD professionals behave. Even in those organizations with enforceable standards, only occasional application of the ethics results in sanctions.

So, do statements of ethical practice and values have any value? Yes, but only if they are subjected regularly and frequently to discourse within the profession. Only through such discourse do professionals have a forum to explore their own values and to understand how those values fit within the community of OD practice. Moreover, many people have a basic commitment to good practice, but they may not be clear about what integrity in the profession means. An ethics statement can serve as an educational tool to help those already committed to ethical practice understand the decisions that might be perceived as acceptable and those that might be perceived as unacceptable. The several statements that exist, however, have the potential of confusing OD professionals and discouraging them from reading any of the statements because of the sheer number from which to choose.

VALUES THAT DRIVE OD

In the first chapter, the statement of the OD Network as to the values that drive OD was presented. Many of the codes of ethics reviewed briefly here also present values that are prevalent in the OD field.

Worley and Feyerherm (2003) explored the issue of the values that support the OD field, concluding that

> OD was founded on humanistic values and ethical concerns like democracy and social justice; it was viewed by some as the organization's conscience. Most practitioners would agree that OD tends to emphasize human development, fairness, openness, choice, and balancing of autonomy and constraint. (p. 99)

Worley and Feyerherm's study of early leaders in the field highlights a dilemma currently facing OD practice. Some of the early leaders worry that this humanistic perspective present during the early days of the field is being set aside in response to the profit-making motive of organizations and OD professionals. Others, however, argue that, if

OD professionals do not address organizations' needs, they will not have work, and the OD field will have no impact on the field. My argument, given my view of the ambiguity of the field, is that creating a dichotomy is not necessary. By accepting/adopting an ambiguous approach to the field, we can affirm the historical humanistic values of the field while also supporting the for-profit and survival needs of organizations.

CHAPTER SUMMARY

Integrity is a common expectation in the codes of ethics, or statements of values, of all professional organizations representing the OD field. But how does an OD professional know when he or she is confronted with an ethical dilemma, and how does he or she decide what is an ethical response to such a dilemma? It is impossible to specify answers that apply to every time and every situation in which an OD professional might face an ethical dilemma.

Many examples of ethical dilemmas were suggested in this chapter, along with a number of approaches that individual OD professionals can use. Codes of ethics from several professional organizations were also explored briefly, though it is probable that such statements do not make a significant difference in the behavior of adults who formed their values as children. Open discourse is probably the most powerful tool for encouraging integrity in the field.

QUESTIONS FOR DISCUSSION
OR SELF-REFLECTION

1. Consider the dilemma stories presented in this chapter. How would you have decided or acted in the same situation? On what basis did you make that decision?

2. Think about a decision that you had to make that you found to be a difficult one from an ethical perspective. On what basis did you make your decision? In retrospect, would you have made a different decision? Why or why not?

3. Do you believe that there should be one common set of ethical statements for the field of OD, or is the field better served with multiple statements? Why?

4. Do you believe that codes of ethics should be guidelines or enforceable standards? What are the advantages and disadvantages of each approach?

5. One way to ensure that codes of ethics are enforceable is to require OD professionals to be licensed by the state, as psychologists are. Do you support this position or not? Why?

6. Is it more important for the OD field to continue to emphasize its historical humanistic values or to support the business needs and values of organizations? Why?

Our purposes in developing an International O.D. Code of Ethics are threefold: to increase professional and ethical consciousness among O.D. professionals and their sense of ethical responsibility; to guide O.D. professionals in making more informed ethical choices; and to help the O.D. profession itself function at the fullness of its potential.

We recognize that for us to exist as a profession, a substantial consensus is necessary among the members of our profession about what we profess, particularly our values and ethics. This statement represents a step toward such a consensus.

VALUES OF O.D. PROFESSIONALS

As an O.D. professional, I acknowledge the fundamental importance of the following values both for myself and my profession:

1. *quality of life* – people being satisfied with their whole life experience;
2. *health, human potential, empowerment, growth and excellence* – people being healthy, aware of the fullness of their potential, recognizing their power to bring that potential into being, growing into it, living it, and, generally, doing the best they can with it, individually and collectively;
3. *freedom and responsibility* – people being free and responsible in choosing how they will live their lives;
4. *justice* – people living lives whose results are fair and right for everyone;
5. *dignity, integrity, worth and fundamental rights of individuals, organizations, communities, societies, and other human systems;*
6. *all-win attitudes and cooperation* – people caring about one another and about working together to achieve results that work for everyone, individually and collectively;

7. *authenticity and openness in relationship;*

8. *effectiveness, efficiency and alignment* – people achieving the maximum of desired results, at minimum cost, in ways that coordinate their individual energies and purposes with those of the system-as-a-whole, the subsystems of which they are parts, and the larger system of which their system is a part;

9. *holistic, systemic view and stakeholder orientation* – understanding human behavior from the perspective of whole system(s) that influence and are influenced by that behavior; recognizing the interests that different people have in the system's results and valuing those interests fairly and justly;

10. *wide participation in system affairs, confrontation of issues leading to effective problem solving, and democratic decision-making.*

ETHICAL GUIDELINES FOR O.D. PROFESSIONALS

As an O.D. professional, I commit myself to supporting and acting in accordance with the following ethical guidelines:

I. **Responsibility to Self**
   A. Act with integrity; be authentic and true to myself
   B. Strive continually for self-knowledge and personal growth
   C. Recognize my personal needs and desires and, when they conflict with other responsibilities, seek all-win resolutions of those conflicts.
   D. Assert my own economic and financial interests in ways that are fair and equitable to me as well as to my clients and their stakeholders.

II. **Responsibility for Professional Development and Competence**
   A. Accept responsibility for the consequences of my acts and make reasonable efforts to ensure that my services are properly used; terminate my services if they are not properly used and do what I can to see that any abuses are corrected.
   B. Strive to achieve and maintain a professional level of competence for both myself and my profession by developing the

full range of my own competence and by establishing collegial and cooperative relations with other O.D. professionals.

C. Recognize my own personal needs and desires and deal with them responsibly in the performance of my professional roles.

D. Practice within the limits of my competence, culture, and experience in providing services and using techniques.

E. Practice in cultures different from my own only with consultation from people native to or knowledgeable about those specific cultures.

III. Responsibility to Clients and Significant Others

A. Serve the long-term well-being, interests and development of the client system and all its stakeholders, even when the work being done has a short-term focus.

B. Conduct any professional activity, program or relationship in ways that are honest, responsible, and appropriately open.

C. Establish mutual agreement on a contract covering services and remuneration.

D. Deal with conflicts constructively and avoid conflicts of interest as much as possible.

E. Define and protect the confidentiality of my client-professional relationships.

F. Make public statements of all kinds accurately, including promotion and advertising, and give service as advertised.

IV. Responsibility to the Profession

A. Contribute to continuing professional development for myself, other practitioners, and the profession.

B. Promote the sharing of O.D. knowledge and skill.

C. Work with other O.D. professionals in ways that exemplary what our profession says we stand for.

D. Work actively for ethical practice by individuals and organizations engaged in O.D. activities and, in case of questionable practice, use appropriate channels for dealing with it.

E. Act in ways that bring credit to the O.D. profession and with due regard for colleagues in other professions.

V. Social Responsibility

A. Act with sensitivity to the fact that my recommendations and actions may alter the lives and well-being of people within my client systems and the larger systems of which they are subsystems.

B. Act with awareness of the cultural filters which affect my view of the world, respect cultures different from my own, and be sensitive to cross-cultural and multicultural differences and their implications.

C. Promote justice and serve the well-being of all life on Earth.

D. Recognize that accepting this Statement as a guide for my behavior involves holding myself to a standard that may be more exacting than the laws of any countries in which I practice, the guidelines of any professional associations to which I belong, or the expectations of any of my clients.

NOTES

The process which has produced this statement (currently in its 22nd version) was begun in 1981. It has been supported by most O.D.-oriented professional organizations, associations, and networks in the United States. It was also supported unanimously by the participants at the 1984 O.D. World Congress in Southampton, England. To date, more than 200 people from more than 15 countries have participated in the process (Note: The endorsements are of the process and not the statement.) The process has included drafting a version, sending it out with a request for comments and suggestions, redrafting based on the responses, sending it out again and so on. Our aim has been to use the process to establish a substantial consensus including acknowledgment of the differences among us.

By providing a common reference for O.D. professionals throughout the world, we seek to enhance our sense of identity as a global professional community. Because this statement was initially developed within the United States, adapting it to other cultures has been necessary.

("The International OD Code of Ethics," 1991 Edition, was written by Dr. William Gellermann and published in *The International Registry of OD Professionals*, 2005 Edition, authored by Dr. Donald W. Cole, RODC, et al.)

16

Competencies for OD

CHAPTER OUTLINE

OVERVIEW   This chapter opens with a discussion of competencies—their definition and the reason for their use. Then, the following questions are addressed: What are the competencies required by OD professionals for working successfully? Does the professional need to have all of the competencies or only a subset? What competencies will be needed in the future? Several attempts to provide OD competencies have been undertaken. A list of competencies developed for The OD Institute has been adapted for this chapter, providing a self-check list for the individual considering entering the OD field. The instrument can also be used for colleagues to complete in a form of multirater feedback. Finally, the results of a Delphi study looking at the future competencies needed by OD professionals are presented.

This chapter focuses on competencies needed by professionals who wish to do OD work. *Competencies* are "a descriptive tool that identifies the skills, knowledge, personal characteristics, and behavior needed to effectively perform a role in the organization and help the business meet its strategic objectives" (Lucia & Lepsinger, 1999, p. 5). William M. Mercer, Inc. (2001, cited in Daniels, Erickson, & Dalik, 2001), defined *competencies* as

> personal attributes that contribute to and predict superior performance and success within a particular job, role, function, and/or organization. Competencies are what superior performers:
> - Possess as underlying attributes
> - Demonstrate in more situations
> - Apply with better results

Competencies are often captured in popular jargon as *KSAs*—knowledge, skills, and attitudes. In this chapter, the focus is on the competencies needed within one job classification—that of the OD professional.

WHY ARE COMPETENCIES USEFUL?

Competencies are useful for both the individual and the organization. Although this chapter is primarily directed toward the person considering entering the field of OD as a practitioner, the OD competencies suggested for both the present and the future are also useful to individual OD employees and to organizations seeking to hire or contract with an OD professional. This section, adapted from Gangani, McLean, and Braden (2004), outlines the importance of competencies and why they are useful.

For the Individual Contemplating Entry into the OD Field

Individuals contemplating entry into the OD field will find a list of desired competencies helpful to

- outline explicitly the KSAs an OD professional is expected to have or develop to determine what additional education or experience is needed to prepare for employment in the field;
- determine whether the competencies match self-assessment sufficiently to encourage the individual to enter the field rather than some other field.

For the Individual OD Employee

Just as individuals looking to enter the OD field can find competencies useful, so, too, can those who are currently in the field. Such people can find competencies useful to

- compare their self-assessment with the competencies needed for success in the field to determine a self-development plan, often referred to as an *IDP/PDP* (individual or personal development plan);
- support performance reviews, coaching, mentoring, and feedback sessions;
- set a target for promotion or development (career development).

For the Organization

Organizations also find competencies useful. They might use them to

- provide a measure of how well the company is doing in developing its OD employees;
- set a criterion goal for employee staffing and selection, as well as the selection of external OD consultants;

- provide managers and supervisors who work with OD professionals with useful development tools and assist in the coaching/mentoring process;
- focus on the organization's priorities;
- assist in budgeting for staffing and employee development;
- help in developing succession plans.

COMPETENCIES FOR OD PROFESSIONALS

Worley and Feyerherm (2003) reviewed past efforts to create competencies for OD professionals, concluding that such efforts had been undertaken by Head, Armstrong, and Preston (1996); Shepard and Raia (1981); Sullivan and Sullivan (1995); and Worley and Varney (1998). Worley and Varney (1998) listed seven foundational knowledge competency areas: organization behavior, individual psychology, group dynamics, management and organization theory, research methods (including statistics), comparative cultural perspectives, and a functional knowledge of business. They also identified five "core knowledge competencies":

- Organization design
- Organization research
- System dynamics
- History of organization development and change
- Theories and models for change

They cited as well six "core skill competencies":

- Managing the consulting process
- Analysis and diagnosis
- Designing and choosing appropriate interventions
- Facilitating and process consultation
- Developing client capability
- Evaluating organization change

For years, under the leadership of independent consultant Roland Sullivan and the auspices of The OD Institute, ongoing efforts have been made to create a list of OD competencies that had widespread approval among OD professionals. A formal process for such adoption has not taken place, but several editions of the list exist. The Worley, Rothwell, and Sullivan (2005) list, the 21st version, represents a synthesis of four of the most common competency models (see Appendix 16.1 for this list).

As you work with the list in the appendix, do not be discouraged. No one, including OD's founders and those who are now the most expert in the field, has mastered all of these competencies. And, as a beginner in the OD field, you will not be expected to have mastered even most of them. That said, this list can still be very useful as you plan your ongoing development and education in determining those areas that are of greatest interest and importance to you.

SUBSET OF OD COMPETENCIES

In spite of the comment in the previous section that no OD professional will have all of the competencies listed in the Appendix, the question remains, Can an OD professional practice with just a subset of the OD competencies? It is characteristic of our field that many OD professionals have only one subset of the competencies, and that is how they advertise their practice. Thus, there will be people who do nothing but conflict management, multirater feedback, executive coaching, and so on.

There is one major advantage to focusing on only one form of intervention—the OD professional becomes an expert in his or her field of practice. This is done through extensive esperience in that area and focusing professional development on that sole area. One's reputation also develops within that area as well, making the marketing process easier for the professional.

At the same time, as mentioned earlier, if the professional has only one set of competencies, the temptation for the OD professional is to propose his or her subset as the appropriate intervention, regardless of the situation. It is difficult, with only a subset of competencies, to have a systems view of the organization.

As with many other situations, it makes some sense to foster collaboration between those with a broad set of competencies with those who have a subset of competencies. Generalists and specialists working together are likely to complement each other, emphasizing the positive aspect of both approaches. It then makes the most sense for the generalist to be the lead professional, calling on specialists as needed based on the Assessment and Feedback phase, and Action Planning phase.

EMERGING AND FUTURE OD COMPETENCIES

According to Worley and Feyerherm (2003), "Most of these lists [of competencies] document what is [*sic*] currently accepted skills and competencies, but typically don't address what might be needed in the future" (p. 6). To overcome this deficiency, Eisen (2002) conducted a Web-based *Delphi process*, a research technique that uses questionnaires to gather consensus from individuals in different locations. The "participants generated 90 items about possible emerging competencies. There were 22 respondents in the multi-voting process for this stage. The following list reflects items that received 9 or more votes. There are 35 discrete competency statements, clustered into 12 themes." Eisen concluded that "organization developers will especially need the following competencies to implement these emerging intervention strategies and practice effectively in the first decade of the 21st century":

1. **Parallel interventions in complex human systems**
   - Knowledge and skills required to design and lead complex interventions, using multiple parallel techniques that work with individuals, teams, large-group stakeholder conferences, trans-organizational and trans-domain events, in fast-cycle sustained coherent change, and based on action, reflection, and learning at each of these levels.
   - Ability to design and implement individual and organizational interventions that build capacity to think, make decisions, and take action systemically, i.e. see the big picture; build in effective feedback loops; recognize or anticipate and adjust for unintended, delayed and counterintuitive long-term consequences.
   - Knowledge of societies, communities, and social system dynamics. The ability to convey the essence of "community" as a motivational concept. Deep understanding of the concept of "The Tragedy of the Commons" and how that is affected by factors such as mental models, structure, technology and globalization.
   - Ability to support effective decision-making: for individuals, groups, teams, organizations, inter-organizations, and communities. Skills for rapid time-to-value decision-making models, and methods.

- Strong program/project management methodology skills to manage complex business change initiatives that require firm attention to scope, cost, quality, and risk.

2. **Global, trans-domain and larger system work**
   - Ability to work ethically and courageously with inter-organization issues to create wider inclusive boundaries among stakeholders.
   - Skill in bridge-building and alliance management, including developing trust across a wide range of diverse constituents.
   - Awareness and skill related to working with the "larger" system, including contracting with the right person for the right scope of work.
   - Expanded knowledge of systems thinking to include a global perspective, how to build strategic alliances and use large group methods when appropriate.

3. **Culture work**
   - Deep understanding of culture: how it influences behavior, how it can be changed and developed, and the connection between culture and performance.
   - Understanding of culture as the core deep-structure organizing principle underlying all aspects of organizations—including hierarchies, reward systems, competitive strategies, technologies, work flow structures, and shared belief systems.
   - Ability to adapt to each unique cultural situation in applying our knowledge, skills, and strategies.
   - Ability to join organization participants in any change process as an intentional, evolving, collaborative reconstruction of shared ways of understanding and embodying meaning in their ways of working and being together.

4. **Self-as-instrument, continuous learning and innovation**
   - Effective continuous learning as needed to respond appropriately to emerging complex social needs and organizational dilemmas.
   - Commitment and skill for continuously reflecting on one's personal role as instrument of the work, and doing one's personal and professional homework as needed in order to be fully available for the job of catalyzing wisdom in organizations and communities.

- Ability to quickly scan a situation and produce innovative interventions that deal with that particular set of system dynamics.
- Skill in the use of action research to learn on the fly, and not just reapply techniques from another era.

5. **Use of technology and virtual interventions**
   - Proficiency in using virtual, on-line approaches or a blended on-line/on-site approach to address business challenges of geographically dispersed organizations through such means as conference calls, web-sites, and collaborative planning tools.
   - Knowledge of, and ability to use, practical and scalable (i.e. for any-sized groups) tools and systems that facilitate systemic thinking and action, and efficient communication and collaboration.
   - Cutting-edge knowledge and application ability regarding computer-based information management and communication facilitation; and, the ability to stay current with continuously and rapidly evolving technologies and best practices in those areas.

6. **Coaching for whole-systems leadership**
   - Coaching skills to work with top-level managers in reformulating their management philosophies and styles.
   - Ability to help leaders be congruent with emerging organizational forms that are self-organizing, and in which most operational processes and change are self-managed at the periphery rather than at the core.
   - Skills for developing transformational leaders who are capable of championing change, and transforming organizations.

7. **Dialogic reflection and action**
   - Ability to use and promote reflection, dialogue and exploration to understand issues, differences, values paradoxes and not rush to find a single problem solution.
   - Ability to facilitate conversations to create meaning and action—not only understanding.

8. **Accelerated methods and large group work**
   - Skills in facilitating collaboration, decision-making, problem-solving, planning for the future, networking, teamwork and

team building all with new methods that are faster and more effective; ability to train others throughout the organization to use these skills.

- Deep knowledge and skill in the design, management and facilitation of large group interventions.

9. **Purpose and strategic assessment**
   - Ability to identify and measure both strategic and tactical metrics to assess whether objectives are met.
   - Knowledge and skills to design and build measurement into contracts, and to build client appreciation and funding for this part of the work.

10. **Multidisciplinarity**
    - Multidisciplinary skills from areas such as future studies, economic analysis, public policy formulation, and systems thinking.
    - Awareness and acumen in business and finance, in addition to process skills.

11. **Knowledge management**
    - Understanding of the challenges of managing knowledge in an information-rich, fast-changing organizational environment.
    - Knowledge, skills and social technologies for designing and implementing effective methods for generating and disseminating valid relevant knowledge in organizations.

12. **Appreciative integral change**
    - Knowledge of the psychosocial dynamics of change, so as to awaken and build on people's natural disposition toward development; minimizing resistance by working on the positive side of the process.
    - Skills in building high performance organizations that are also a great place to work, and in articulating how this results in a win/win situation for the organization, the organization members, and customers; how a focus on both performance and people leads to competitive advantage.

(© 2002 Saul Eisen, Ph.D. Permission to use may be requested by contacting the author: saul.eisen@sonom.edu. From a Delphi study of global trends, implications for managers, emerging intervention strategies, and future competencies in OD, by Saul Eisen. Published online at www.Sonoma.edu/programs/od.)

Those interested in competencies for the future should also review references to Worley and Feyerherm (2003) in Chapter 17.

CHAPTER SUMMARY

To be a competent OD professional requires expertise in many different areas. *Competencies* are statements related to desired knowledge, skills, and attitudes, though authors often take a different perspective on how competencies are defined. Competencies in OD can be used by individuals exploring OD as a field of study and employment, as well as by internal and external OD professionals and those organizations that employ or contract with OD professionals. A comprehensive list of competencies for OD professionals is provided in the appendix to this chapter in a format that allows for self-assessment and priority setting for self-development. Finally, this chapter also explored future competencies through the results of Eisen's (2002) Delphi survey.

QUESTIONS FOR DISCUSSION OR SELF-REFLECTION

1. Why is it important to have competencies that address all three areas of knowledge, skills, and attitudes (KSAs)?

2. How might you personally use competency lists designed for OD professional?

3. Complete the self-assessment contained in Appendix 16.1. Discuss any competencies that you do not understand. Describe what you might do to close the gaps that are the largest for you between importance and level of expertise.

4. Compare the future competencies with the list of present competencies. What do you see as the major differences between these two lists? How might you begin to prepare for the future competencies?

APPENDIX 16.1
SELF-ASSESSMENT ON ESSENTIAL COMPETENCIES FOR OD PROFESSIONALS
(adopted from Worley et al., 2005)

No norms are provided for this self-assessment. As I have suggested several times in this book, it is not how you compare with others that is important but, rather, what is important for you as a priority for continuous improvement and as a beginning benchmark against which you can compare yourself 1, 3, 5, or more years in the future. In the spirit of ongoing improvement and lifelong learning, you should see a continuous rise in scores on these measures. If you do not see that result, then it is time to put your priorities back into self-development.

Be honest as you rate yourself on each of these competencies. No one else should see your results. This is a self-development exercise only. And it is also a way to review in some detail the competencies identified by others. Take time to read the competencies carefully, and use the opportunity to reflect on your own life goals, where you are today relative to the competencies, and where you want to put your energies first in self-development for the future.

In judging your level of expertise on each of the OD competencies described here, use the following scale:

5 = This is expert level—little improvement is needed.

4 = I feel quite comfortable in performing this competency, but I can still benefit from additional experience and understanding.

3 = I can perform this competency at a beginning level, but I require a coach or supervisor to assist me and give me frequent feedback.

2 = I can describe this competency, but I cannot perform it.

1 = I do not even know what this competency means.

To help you focus on the areas where you want to put emphasis on personal development, you will also be asked to rate the importance of each competency. Priority should then be given to the areas where there is the greatest discrepancy between your level of expertise and the importance level of that competency. At the extreme, an item ranked 5 in importance and 1 in level of competency should be given highest priority. Use the following scale for importance:

5 = This is an absolutely essential competency—cannot do OD work without it.

4 = While it might be possible to get by without this competency, the client organization would probably miss something quite important.

3 = Having this competency will help me with my OD work, and my client organization would benefit, but there would not be a huge loss if I do not have it.

2 = It might be nice to have this competency, but it really does not make a difference in doing OD work.

1 = I don't know enough about this competency to say whether it is important or not (go back and review that section of the book!) or whether it is not important at all for an OD professional to be competent in this area.

COMPETENCY CATEGORY	CURRENT LEVEL OF EXPERTISE	IMPORTANCE
Competency: Self-Mastery		
1. Be aware of how one's biases influence interaction	5 4 3 2 1	5 4 3 2 1
2. Consult driven by their personal values	5 4 3 2 1	5 4 3 2 1
3. Clarify personal boundaries	5 4 3 2 1	5 4 3 2 1
4. Manage personal biases	5 4 3 2 1	5 4 3 2 1
5. Manage personal defensiveness	5 4 3 2 1	5 4 3 2 1
6. Recognize when personal feelings have been aroused	5 4 3 2 1	5 4 3 2 1
7. Remain physically healthy while under stress	5 4 3 2 1	5 4 3 2 1
8. Resolve ethical issues with integrity	5 4 3 2 1	5 4 3 2 1
9. Avoid getting personal needs met at the expense of the client	5 4 3 2 1	5 4 3 2 1
10. Solicit feedback from others about your impact on them	5 4 3 2 1	5 4 3 2 1

COMPETENCY CATEGORY	CURRENT LEVEL OF EXPERTISE	IMPORTANCE

Competency: Ability to Measure Positive Change

11. Choose appropriate evaluation methods	5 4 3 2 1	5 4 3 2 1
12. Determine level of evaluation	5 4 3 2 1	5 4 3 2 1
13. Ensure evaluation method is valid	5 4 3 2 1	5 4 3 2 1
14. Ensure evaluation method is reliable	5 4 3 2 1	5 4 3 2 1
15. Ensure evaluation method is practical	5 4 3 2 1	5 4 3 2 1

Competency: Clarify Data Needs

16. Determine an appropriate data collection process	5 4 3 2 1	5 4 3 2 1
17. Determine the types of data needed	5 4 3 2 1	5 4 3 2 1
18. Determine the amount of data needed	5 4 3 2 1	5 4 3 2 1

Competency: Facilitating Transition and Adoption

19. Help manage impact to related systems	5 4 3 2 1	5 4 3 2 1
20. Use information to create positive change	5 4 3 2 1	5 4 3 2 1
21. Transfer change competencies to internal consultant or client so learning is continuous	5 4 3 2 1	5 4 3 2 1
22. Manage/increase change momentum	5 4 3 2 1	5 4 3 2 1
23. Mobilize additional internal resources to support the ongoing change process	5 4 3 2 1	5 4 3 2 1
24. Determine the parts of the organization that warrant a special focus of attention	5 4 3 2 1	5 4 3 2 1
25. Ensure that learning will continue	5 4 3 2 1	5 4 3 2 1

(continued)

COMPETENCY CATEGORY	CURRENT LEVEL OF EXPERTISE	IMPORTANCE

Competency: Integrate Theory and Practice

26. Present the theoretical foundations of change   5 4 3 2 1   5 4 3 2 1

27. Articulate an initial change process to use   5 4 3 2 1   5 4 3 2 1

28. Integrate research with theory and practice   5 4 3 2 1   5 4 3 2 1

29. Communicate implications of systems   5 4 3 2 1   5 4 3 2 1

30. Utilize a solid conceptual framework based on research   5 4 3 2 1   5 4 3 2 1

Competency: Stay Current in Technology

31. Use the latest technology effectively   5 4 3 2 1   5 4 3 2 1

32. Use the internet effectively   5 4 3 2 1   5 4 3 2 1

Competency: Ability to Work with Large Systems

33. Facilitate large-group (70–2,000 people) intervention   5 4 3 2 1   5 4 3 2 1

34. Apply the competencies of international OD effectively   5 4 3 2 1   5 4 3 2 1

35. Function effectively as internal consultant   5 4 3 2 1   5 4 3 2 1

36. Demonstrate ability to conduct trans-organization development   5 4 3 2 1   5 4 3 2 1

37. Demonstrate ability to conduct community change and development   5 4 3 2 1   5 4 3 2 1

38. Utilize a change model to guide whole-system change or transformation   5 4 3 2 1   5 4 3 2 1

Competency: Participative Create a Good Implementation Plan

39. Co-create an implementation plan that is (1) concrete; (2) simple; (3) clear; (4) measurable; (5) rewarded; and (6) consisting of logically sequenced activities   5 4 3 2 1   5 4 3 2 1

COMPETENCY CATEGORY	CURRENT LEVEL OF EXPERTISE	IMPORTANCE

Competency: Understand Research Methods

40. Utilize appropriate mix of methods to ensure (1) efficiency; and (2) objectivity; and (3) validity   5 4 3 2 1   5 4 3 2 1

41. Utilize appropriate mix of data collection technology   5 4 3 2 1   5 4 3 2 1

42. Use statistical methods when appropriate   5 4 3 2 1   5 4 3 2 1

Competency: Manage Diversity

43. Facilitate a participative decision-making process   5 4 3 2 1   5 4 3 2 1

44. Be aware of the influence of cultural dynamics on interactions with others   5 4 3 2 1   5 4 3 2 1

45. Interpret cross-cultural influences in a helpful manner   5 4 3 2 1   5 4 3 2 1

46. Handle diversity and diverse situations skillfully   5 4 3 2 1   5 4 3 2 1

Competency: Clarify Roles

47. Clarify the role of consultant   5 4 3 2 1   5 4 3 2 1

48. Clarify the role of client   5 4 3 2 1   5 4 3 2 1

Competency: Address Power

49. Identify and engage formal power   5 4 3 2 1   5 4 3 2 1

50. Identify and engage informal power   5 4 3 2 1   5 4 3 2 1

51. Deal effectively with resistance   5 4 3 2 1   5 4 3 2 1

Competency: Keep an Open Mind

52. Suspend judgement while gathering data   5 4 3 2 1   5 4 3 2 1

53. Suppress hurtful comments during data gathering   5 4 3 2 1   5 4 3 2 1

(continued)

COMPETENCY CATEGORY	CURRENT LEVEL OF EXPERTISE	IMPORTANCE
Competency: Helping Clients Own the Change Process		
54. Reduce dependency on consultant	5 4 3 2 1	5 4 3 2 1
55. Instill responsibility for follow through	5 4 3 2 1	5 4 3 2 1
56. Collaboratively design the change process	5 4 3 2 1	5 4 3 2 1
57. Involve participants so they begin to own the process	5 4 3 2 1	5 4 3 2 1
Competency: Be Comfortable with Ambiguity		
58. Perform effectively in an atmosphere of ambiguity	5 4 3 2 1	5 4 3 2 1
59. Perform effectively in the midst of chaos	5 4 3 2 1	5 4 3 2 1
Competency: Manage the Separation		
60. Be sure customers and stakeholders are satisfied with the intervention's results	5 4 3 2 1	5 4 3 2 1
61. Leave the client satisfied	5 4 3 2 1	5 4 3 2 1
62. Plan for post-consultation contact	5 4 3 2 1	5 4 3 2 1
63. Recognize when separation is desirable	5 4 3 2 1	5 4 3 2 1
Competency: Seeing the Whole Picture		
64. Can attend to the whole, parts and even the greater whole	5 4 3 2 1	5 4 3 2 1
65. Quickly grasp the nature of the system	5 4 3 2 1	5 4 3 2 1
66. Identify the boundary of systems to be changed	5 4 3 2 1	5 4 3 2 1
67. Identify critical success factors for the intervention	5 4 3 2 1	5 4 3 2 1
68. Further clarify real issues	5 4 3 2 1	5 4 3 2 1
69. Link change effort into ongoing processes of the enterprise	5 4 3 2 1	5 4 3 2 1

COMPETENCY CATEGORY	CURRENT LEVEL OF EXPERTISE	IMPORTANCE
70. Begin to lay out an evaluation model in the initial phases	5 4 3 2 1	5 4 3 2 1
71. Know how data from different parts of the system impact each other	5 4 3 2 1	5 4 3 2 1
72. Be aware of systems wanting to change	5 4 3 2 1	5 4 3 2 1

Competency: Set the Conditions for Positive Change

73. Clarify boundaries for confidentiality	5 4 3 2 1	5 4 3 2 1
74. Select a process that will facilitate openness	5 4 3 2 1	5 4 3 2 1
75. Create a non-threatening environment	5 4 3 2 1	5 4 3 2 1
76. Develop mutually trusting relationships with others	5 4 3 2 1	5 4 3 2 1
77. Use information to reinforce positive change	5 4 3 2 1	5 4 3 2 1

Competency: Focus on Relevance and Flexibility

78. Distill recommendations from the data	5 4 3 2 1	5 4 3 2 1
79. Pay attention to the timing of activities	5 4 3 2 1	5 4 3 2 1
80. Recognize what data are relevant	5 4 3 2 1	5 4 3 2 1
81. Stay focused on the purpose of the consultancy	5 4 3 2 1	5 4 3 2 1
82. Continuously assess the issues as they surface	5 4 3 2 1	5 4 3 2 1

Competency: Use Data to Adjust for Change

83. Use information to create positive change	5 4 3 2 1	5 4 3 2 1
84. Use intelligent information to take next steps	5 4 3 2 1	5 4 3 2 1
85. Establish a method to monitor change after the intervention	5 4 3 2 1	5 4 3 2 1

(continued)

COMPETENCY CATEGORY	CURRENT LEVEL OF EXPERTISE	IMPORTANCE
86. Use information to reinforce positive change	5 4 3 2 1	5 4 3 2 1
87. Gather data to identify initial first steps of transition	5 4 3 2 1	5 4 3 2 1

Competency: Be Available to Multiple Stakeholders

88. Collaborate with internal/ external OD professionals	5 4 3 2 1	5 4 3 2 1
89. Listen to others	5 4 3 2 1	5 4 3 2 1
90. Interpersonally relate to others	5 4 3 2 1	5 4 3 2 1
91. Use humor effectively	5 4 3 2 1	5 4 3 2 1
92. Pay attention to the spontaneous and informal	5 4 3 2 1	5 4 3 2 1

Competency: Build Realistic Relationships

93. Build realistic relationships	5 4 3 2 1	5 4 3 2 1
94. Explicate ethical boundaries	5 4 3 2 1	5 4 3 2 1
95. Build trusting relationships	5 4 3 2 1	5 4 3 2 1
96. Relate credibly, demonstrating business acumen and conversancy	5 4 3 2 1	5 4 3 2 1

Competency: Interventions

97. Convey confidence in one's intervention philosophy	5 4 3 2 1	5 4 3 2 1
98. Facilitate group processes	5 4 3 2 1	5 4 3 2 1
99. Intervene into the system at the right depth	5 4 3 2 1	5 4 3 2 1
100. Creatively customize tools and methods	5 4 3 2 1	5 4 3 2 1

("The Knowledge and Skill Necessary for Competence in OD," 2005 Edition, was written by Roland Sullivan, RODP, et al., and published in *The International Registry of OD Professionals*, 2005 Edition, authored by Dr. Donald W. Cole, RODC, et al.)

Issues Facing OD and Its Future

CHAPTER OUTLINE

OVERVIEW This chapter explores many of the issues and controversies that exist in OD. Consistent with the ambiguities addressed throughout the book, this chapter raises more questions than it answers. Next, the future of the field will be explored, including my vision for the future of OD. The book will conclude with a statement of the benefits of OD.

As I have often suggested throughout this book, there are multiple aspects of OD for which a consensus has not been reached. Competent practitioners and theoreticians have reached different conclusions about many critical aspects of OD practice. What follows is a balanced perspective of several of these issues, followed by a series of questions still facing OD. From there, varying perspectives of the future of OD are presented, followed by my personal vision for the field of OD.

ISSUES

An *issue* is a controversial aspect of a field for which more than one viable, often conflicting, response exists. The intent here is to suggest that these are questions that must be addressed by the field as a whole, not necessarily by each person working in OD. Some of the questions come from Provo, Tuttle, and Henderson (2003), as suggested at a preconference on OD at the Academy of Human Resource Development Conference. Questions have been clustered into larger themes.

Definition of OD

- Should there be a standard definition for *organization development*, given the myriad of definitions that currently exist? Should the definition be universal or country-, culture-, or company-specific?
- Is there such a thing as planned change as suggested in most definitions of OD, or is change beyond the scope of human control, as suggested, in part, by chaos theory?

OD Models

- What model of OD should be used—action research, organization development process, appreciative inquiry, or some other model?
- Is OD too problem focused, as claimed by appreciative inquiry? Does AI ignore aspects of the system by looking only at the positive, as claimed by some OD professionals?

OD as a Field of Study and Practice

- Should there be an OD field, or should good management incorporate OD principles and practices, thus eliminating the need for OD professionals?
- If there should be a field, should it be a separate field, or should it be viewed as a subset of human resource development, industrial and organizational psychology, organizational behavior, or some other field?
- What foundational fields should inform OD?
- Do the fields of OD and training and development relate to each other, are they the same field, or are they totally separate? What should the relationship be?
- What influences the development of the field of OD (e.g., the popular literature, interactions among OD professionals, the practice in organizations, research, etc.)?
- Should OD have a shared body of knowledge? If so, what should it be? Who should determine what it should be?
- Is OD's knowledge theory-based or practice-based, or a combination? What should it be?
- Who should pay attention to OD theory/research? Is there more interest in fads among practitioners and client organizations than in research findings and theory? If it should change, how will that happen?

Structure for Doing OD

- Should the preference for doing OD be with an internal or an external professional, or a combination of the two?

- How does OD differ from other forms of consulting?
- Should OD have an enforceable code of ethics? How can OD professionals help install integrity and combat corruption in organizations and governments when there are no consequences for unethical OD practices?
- Does OD look fundamentally different in profit organizations versus non-profit versus family businesses?
- How can OD encourage a greater presence among small enterprises (e.g., *jua kali* in Kenya, craftspersons in Kyrgyzstan and India)?
- What is the role of the internal OD professional (e.g., prophet, instigator, helper, covert operator, etc.)?
- What OD structure works best for internal OD professionals (e.g., reporting through HR, reporting through a strategic function, reporting directly to the CEO, etc.)?

Qualifications for Doing OD

- What competencies are needed to do OD? Is the list provided in the appendix of Chapter 16 comprehensive enough or too comprehensive? Can those with a subset of these competencies still be competent OD professionals?
- What background best prepares people to do OD? Many OD professionals have backgrounds in theology, business administration, counseling, psychology, HRD, and, specifically, OD. Does it make a difference in terms of OD outcomes?
- Should OD personnel be licensed (mandated by the state), certified (voluntary credential), both, or neither? If certified, who should do the certifying? On what basis should an OD person be licensed or certified, if they should be? Many certifications exist—some offered through universities, some offered through professional organizations (The OD Institute), and some through private organizations (e.g., NTL). Do they make any difference?
- Where should OD personnel be prepared? All of the options listed so far are possibilities. If prepared in universities, in what schools or departments should they be prepared?

- How should an OD professional continue to develop skills when experience is needed to have credibility to do the job but without harming individuals and organizations while acquiring the experience (e.g., mentoring, shadowing, or apprenticeship)?
- How should OD professionals develop their own competencies to meet the workplace needs of the future, when those needs are not yet known?

Outcomes of OD

- How should OD add to the value chain of an organization?
- What outcomes are desirable in OD? Should the priority for OD be higher profitability, greater productivity, improved employee or process performance, increased job satisfaction, better collaboration and teamwork, more innovation and creativity, or are all of these desirable outcomes?
- What should OD do to affect corporate social responsibility (CSR) to eradicate corporate corruption (e.g., Enron in the United States, chaebols [conglomerates] in Korea)?
- How should OD support the development of a rapid response strategic planning process?
- What should OD do to educate management to understand that solutions that may work in one organization/country may not work in other organizations/countries, requiring that leadership be positive, creative, and responsive to specific needs?
- How should OD create a link between activities/practices and outcomes?
- What role should OD play in helping organizations retain intellectual capital (by reducing employee turnover, minimizing the negative effects of employee retirements, etc.)?
- What role does OD have to play in helping an organization with its knowledge management?
- How can OD influence autocratic managers to change into listeners, coaches, mentors, and facilitators?
- How should OD be involved with layoffs and relocations in a humane way that does not destroy people and communities?

- How should OD help organizations close the gap between espoused theories/values and theories/values in use?
- How should OD help organizations to change from a short-term to a long-term perspective?

Fostering a More Humane Workplace

- What should OD do to challenge autocratic and power-hungry systems that exploit workers?
- What should be OD's role in removing violence from our work-places (as well as our communities and between countries)?
- What must OD do to develop systems in which workers have a degree of autonomy and share in the rewards of their labor?
- While moving to a workplace that relies on telecommuting, how should OD help retain interpersonal connectivity, motivate employees, and assure accountability?
- What should OD do to facilitate a better work–life balance for employees and managers?
- What should OD do to help organizations reduce the hierarchy to create a workplace that is more responsive to the rapidly changing environment?

Effectiveness of OD Interventions

- Can organizational cultures be changed? Although it is clear that changes can be made in the first level of culture (behaviors, artifacts), can they be made at the second (beliefs, values) and third (assumptions) levels? What interventions are the most successful in what circumstances for bringing about such changes?
- Can organizational culture be measured? If so, how?
- What is the efficacy of the many interventions suggested in this book and in what circumstances (e.g., large-scale interactive events, team building, T-groups, etc.)?
- How ethical or manipulative are the interventions typically used within OD? How should OD professionals react to employee refusal to participate (e.g., in values clarification on religious grounds, in team building on grounds of personal choice, etc.)?

- When do we define an intervention as a fad? How do we separate the fads from the truly effective and theoretically sound processes? Are things like balanced scorecard, 360-degree feedback, six sigma, total quality management, large-scale interactive events, scenario planning, reengineering, benchmarking, and learning organizations fads?

- Should OD have a role in the process of mergers and acquisitions? Should OD be pulled in automatically to do a culture audit just as the finance people do a financial audit?

- What is the role of OD in preparing organizations for the dynamic change that is overwhelming them today?

- What, if anything, can OD professionals do to help organizations renew and adapt to business cycles?

International or Cross-cultural OD

- Can OD be conducted in international settings given differences in country cultures in addition to organizational cultures? How does it differ from domestic efforts?

- Do OD professionals need to understand every culture in which they work, or can they have a global mindset or cultural literacy of learning in the moment?

Evaluating OD

- How should OD efforts be evaluated? Why do so few OD professionals and client organizations do so if it can be done?

- How should OD measure productivity in evaluating its effectiveness?

- How can we learn from analysis of others' failures, when it is rare that failures are published, or from our own failures if we do not acknowledge them?

Role of OD in the Development of Communities, Societies, Nations, and Regions

- What role, if any, should OD professionals have in the national HRD efforts being adopted by many nations and regions?

- What role, if any, should OD play in changing society at local, national, and international levels?
- How should OD influence government and quasi-governmental agencies' policies related to the workplace and workforce?
- What should OD do to develop greater intercountry collaboration (e.g., in the Middle East; in the five "stans" of Central Asia; between South and North Korea; between Taiwan and China)?
- What are OD's obligations to overcome infrastructure differentials among countries (e.g., telephones, televisions, computers, Internet connections, etc.)?
- What should OD's role be in changing the circumstances that support child labor?
- What should OD do to overcome illiteracy?
- What should OD do to develop acceptance and management of healthy conflict, so employees learn techniques of celebrating and managing conflict not only in their workplaces, but also in their families, their mosques/churches/temples/synagogues, their communities, and, ultimately, in the world community?
- What should OD do to strengthen its role in health-related areas (e.g., HIV/AIDS education, nutrition, infant care, smoking, drug and alcohol addiction)?
- What should OD do to eradicate corruption among public employees (e.g., customs officers, license officials, etc.)?
- What should OD do to create a climate for diversity, in which people of different races, ethnicities, religions, and gender can live together in harmonious peace (one world, one family)?
- What should OD do to minimize the gap between the haves and have nots, in technology, in finances, in literacy, in time?
- What role should OD have in encouraging corporations to take responsibility for the environment?
- What should OD do to strengthen educational systems to provide qualified workers for organizations?
- What should OD do to encourage corporate philanthropy for the development of the arts, sports, communities?
- What should OD's responsibility be in creating a balanced perspective of globalization, so individuals, organizations, and nations all benefit?

THE FUTURE OF OD

Depending on how the questions in the previous section are answered, OD may or may not have a future. Certainly, if one's perspective is that managers can take on the skills and processes of OD, then OD professionals per se may no longer be needed. Likewise, if OD professionals continue to operate based solely on fads or attempt to practice OD when they are insufficiently prepared and do not have the necessary competencies, then OD will lose its credibility and will not survive.

Although these scenarios are real possibilities, it is probable that OD will survive as a professional field well into the future. What it will look like is where we now turn our attention. Understanding the future and preparing for it have never been easy. Today, with the rapidity of change, predicting and preparing for the future is now nearly impossible. In spite of the difficulties, we will next consider what the future of OD might be. This future view will, of necessity, reflect the individual biases and world views of those looking to the future. All come from people involved in doing OD, creating probably a more positive view of its future than might occur if non-OD people were involved in this process.

Factors Affecting the Future Context for OD

Cummings and Worley (2005) described some key forces that are likely to affect the future of OD, including the economy, the workforce, technology, and organizations. According to them, the trends in the economy are toward more concentrated wealth, increased globalization, and greater ecological concern. The workforce in the United States is becoming more diverse, more educated, more contingent, and older with a diminished birthrate contributing fewer young people for the workforce. Technology is driving productivity within organizations, e-commerce exists in many forms, and, although not included in Cummins and Worley's discussion, this technology is allowing more and more outsourcing and telecommuting. Organizations are becoming more networked and knowledge based. According to Worley and Feyerherm (2003):

> These trends will affect organization development in several ways. OD practice will become more embedded in the organization's culture, more cross-cultural, and more diverse in its client organizations.

People practicing OD will need to be more technologically adept, and be ready to deliver on shorter cycle times. OD practitioners will need to be more focused on innovation and learning, more familiar with a wide array of disciplines and clearer about the values that guide their practice and behavior. (pp. 6–7)

AHRD Preconference

This section shares a perspective of OD's future from one of the presenters at the preconference referenced earlier (Provo et al., 2003). John Conbere, chair of the Department of Organization Learning and Development at the University of St. Thomas, posited the following as components of OD's future:

- The key to OD's future is to pronounce the truth and give hope.
- The relevance of OD is in question as some OD practitioners do not have the skills to do their work, some operate on fads, and many decision makers in organizations do not believe in OD.
- To be successful in the future, OD professionals will need to learn to succeed in organizations that operate as top-down, heavy-handed, fear-based entities.
- OD will need to learn better how to integrate systems thinking totally into our work (e.g., we put out fires but often don't change the system) and to work within the economic entity.

Early OD Leaders' View of the Future

Worley and Feyerherm (2003) discussed interviews with 21 OD thought leaders regarding the past, present, and future of OD, though the focus here will be limited to their views of the future. *Thought leaders* were defined as "practitioners and academics whose focus was strongly and clearly related to OD and who would be considered founders, or at least early contributors, of the field" (p. 98). They summarized their study by noting, "Our analysis of their answers confirmed some doubts about the field's current state but also provided hope by charting some paths to renewed rigor and relevance" (p. 114).

The thought leaders in the study identified 13 actions needed by the field of OD moving into the future (Worley & Feyerherm, 2003). No area garnered half of the responses; four were between 40% and 50%, in order as follows:

To rely a lot less on techniques and jumping on the latest fad.

To do more bridging among different stakeholders within the social sciences and a lot more working together.

Approaches to change that add value and are relevant to the organization and its members.

A lot more emphasis on individual and group related interventions OR a lot less emphasis on these. (p. 104)

The thought leaders' ideas of competencies that will be needed by OD practitioners in the future had even less agreement. Only one item exceeded 40%, and one item was between 30% and 40%:

Understand and work with large systems, including large organizations and large groups of people.

Have the mindset and ability to handle rejection and deliver tough messages to a client. (p. 105)

Not much that was found in this study really focuses on the future. Both the tasks identified that OD needs to do and future competencies are really presentations of how good OD should be done *today*, not in the future. Perhaps asking thought leaders who influenced the field 50 years or so ago is not the best way to look at the future.

MY VISION OF THE FUTURE OF OD

The perspectives presented so far, and those about future competencies in the preceding chapter, are not very bold and are tightly tied to the past. Perhaps, in our finite minds, that's the best we can do. What is easy in talking about the future of OD is that no one can say whether this vision is accurate—at least not until it is time to write the next edition!

Here are some ideas of where I think the OD field will go that will move it forward in dramatic ways. Whether the field is ready to take these steps, however, remains to be seen.

Identity of the Field

We should stop trying to isolate ourselves as is currently done by separating ourselves from the mainstream of the professional organizations of fields that have long been the foundations of OD. We do not need to have a separate Organization Development Network or OD Institute. Rather, we need to be actively involved in the Academy of Human Resource Development, the Society for Industrial and Organization Psychology, ASTD, the Society for Human Resource Management, the Academy of Management, and the many others that are relevant to our practice. We can continue to be a special interest group of these organizations (as with the Academy of Management), but only if the participants continue to be actively involved in the total organization and do not allow themselves to become segregated or isolated. OD professionals can only be successful in the future if they continue to collaborate with other functional areas in the organization. We should stop trying to create a boundary between ourselves and others but, rather, seek to bring our behavioral science expertise together to work collaboratively with the goal of improving the organization.

Focus of OD

While OD professionals with appropriate backgrounds will continue to work with individuals and teams, clearly the movement must be toward larger and more complex systems that require a high level of expertise. Increasingly, it will become essential for the field to figure out ways that we can become actively involved in megasystems, such as communities, nations, regions, and worldwide organizations, such as the World Bank, the United Nations, and the many NGOs (nongovernmental organizations) that function around the world. Even while we continue to work in organizations, the ambiguity of our field calls on us to work for the good of the broader society, which may, in many cases, be in direct conflict with the vision, mission, and goals of the organizations in which we are working.

Qualifications to Be an OD Professional

Something must be done to reverse the situation of the large-scale incompetence that many believe exists within the field. The call for certification and licensure is simply a call to replicate what does not work well in other settings. Yet, something must be done to help organizations become more competent at selecting both internal and external OD professionals. In other words, there must be consensus about what organizations should look for.

This goal will be difficult for many reasons, not the least of which is the turfism that exists within the field and the struggle over who will get to decide what will be communicated to organizations. My ideal approach would be to convene representatives from all of the professional organizations interested in OD (I estimate 35, with a membership approaching a half million) for a conference using the skills that OD professionals are supposed to have. The outcome of the conference would be to create a strong message to be communicated in many ways to organizations looking for OD help. Every organization might agree to post the consensus statement on its Web site, and every piece of communication sent out by a member of one of these organizations would have a reference to that site.

Ethical Behavior

The conference just envisioned could also develop a consensual ethics code that would be enforceable. The names of violators, after due process, would be listed on a Web site that would be available for anyone to consult. The code would require an ongoing self-development program and required activities to forward self-knowledge (including a possible requirement for ongoing therapy and supervised practice)

Learning from Failure

Academics have not acted on the concepts of the learning organization about the importance of learning from our mistakes or failures. It is extremely rare to find an article that admits to failure. Yet, interestingly, one of the articles on which I have received the most feedback was just such an article, in which we shared the results of a failed intervention in a school system and the lessons learned (Johansen & McLean, 1995). One of our professional organizations would do well with all of the award programs that they have in place to create an award for the best article that communicates a failed intervention as well as the lessons to be learned from the failure.

Reward Systems for Authors

One of the major problems within the OD field (as with many others) is the disconnect between theory and practice. Academics research topics of no or limited interest to practitioners, and practitioners pay little to no attention to the findings of researchers. This lack of a theory–practice bridge causes problems for both parties.

Several steps will be needed to solidify the bridge. First, a practitioner journal might be created that requires coauthorship between an academic and a practitioner. Professional organizations might provide seed money for research with the restriction that only partners representing both academia and practice are eligible to apply for the grant. Web sites might be set up by the professional organizations offering a small honorarium for having articles accepted and posted; to be eligible, the article must be based soundly on research and clearly communicate its impact on practice. The Academy of Human Resource Development is attempting to bridge this gap with a Theory-Practice Committee, practitioner preconferences, a practitioner track in its largely academic conference, and a theory-practice journal, *Advances in Developing Human Resources*.

Model the Values of the Field

We give lip service to being a value-based field, yet our practices often call these values into question. Effective OD professionals will live these values in such a way that they will stand out from the crowd. They will be sharing their knowledge (not copyrighting it, not protecting it, but sharing it freely), finding work–life balance, living with integrity, collaborating, challenging, taking risks, seeking deeper understanding of the self, volunteering—none of which will come easily to the field. Such outcomes will require a paradigm shift for OD professionals. I have been accused of seeing the half-full cup as three-quarters full. I am an optimist, an idealist—but I believe that the field is capable of such a shift. It will require, however, that the leaders in our professional organizations and in our academic programs begin to model such characteristics themselves and that they be explicit about the need and desire to make such a shift.

Creation of Indigenous Theories

OD is no longer restricted to the United States. Any review of the newsletter of The OD Institute or the letters in the *Organization Development Journal* will make clear how widespread OD now is in the world. But when you read about OD in these far-flung countries, it becomes clear that OD was simply transferred, almost untouched, from the United States to those countries. Where are the indigenous theories for OD? How has OD as practiced in the United States been impacted by OD theories developed elsewhere, with the notable exceptions of sociotechnical systems and the Tavistock Institute? It is time for researchers and practitioners alike to begin challenging the premises of OD that do not fit within a cultural paradigm and start to create and share theories and practices that are more appropriate for individual cultures. Perhaps a day will come when OD is seen as a worldwide practice developed from experiences around the world and open to modification based on specific cultural differences.

The End of the Solo Practitioner

Given the complexities that exist in organizations and the future probability that OD professionals will become much more involved in the strategic aspects of organizations, it is probable that the solo practitioner will become a thing of the past. No one person, no matter how competent and experienced, can do justice to what needs attention in these complex organizations. This will require, instead, collaboration—both among OD professionals and, as suggested elsewhere, among those with expertise in other aspects of organizational life.

CONCLUSION

Regardless of what the future holds for organization development, my hope is that you have found this book useful and that you now understand how important organization development is to those organizations that are important to us. OD, when correctly done by competent professionals, can benefit organizations in the following ways:

- OD forces us to use systems thinking that results in better and deeper answers to organizational challenges.
- OD's cyclical nature moves our organizations toward becoming a learning organization that seeks continuous improvement and lifelong education and training for all employees.
- OD empowers employees, those closest to the work.
- It provides management with the most meaningful benchmarks— internal rather than external.
- It focuses benchmarking on processes rather than only results, leading to long-term and continuous improvement in performance.
- Its holistic nature allows us to focus on both task/process and people outcomes.
- Because it is data driven, it moves us beyond assumptions of "what is" and forces us to confront "what *really* is."
- It provides feedback on whether our vision and values are embedded in the organization or simply a plaque on the wall.
- It moves the organization away from the use of expert consultants who hold onto their expertise to the use of facilitator consultants who transfer their expertise and affirm the expertise already resident in the organization.
- It can help us move from an ethnocentric, inward-looking organization to a geocentric, outward-looking organization.
- It can help replace fear in the workplace with joy in the workplace.
- The use of appropriate OD tools can stimulate innovation and creativity.
- OD helps us understand and set valid goals rather than no goals or wishful goals.
- It helps us identify inequitable practices and provide redress.
- It can strengthen all of those things we already do well.

But, for these things to occur, there must be

- commitment from the top,
- cooperation throughout the system,
- use of theoretically sound processes, not fads, and
- education and training to develop internal expertise.

With the principles and processes outlined in this book, you should be able to help your organization experience the performance outcomes that it desires. Good luck in the journey toward becoming a competent OD professional.

CHAPTER SUMMARY

Affirming once again the ambiguities that exist within the field of OD, I provided a comprehensive—though not complete—list of questions related to issues within the field in this chapter, without any attempt to provide answers or to direct the reader's thinking toward a given outcome. (The choice of the questions themselves, however, clearly reflects a bias on my part.) This chapter then explored what might be in store for the future of OD, drawing extensively from the work of Worley and Feyerherm (2003) and their report of the interviews of 21 thought leaders in OD. Finally, I shared my vision for the ideal future of OD, along with the reasons why OD will continue to thrive and contribute positively to all types of organizations and their stakeholders.

QUESTIONS FOR DISCUSSION
OR SELF-REFLECTION

1. Select several of the issues that intrigue you most. Discuss how you think the OD field should respond to the issues identified, along with your rationale.

2. Describe your vision for what you would like for the future of OD.

3. What is your realistic vision of what you think the future of OD is?

4. Compare your ideal and realistic visions for the future of OD. Are they different? If so, why? What will be required to match the two visions?

5. Discuss the list of advantages that OD offers to an organization. Do you think they are realistic? Why or why not? Suggest others that may be missing.

Glossary

360-degree feedback – (same as *multirater feedback* or *multirater appraisal*) is the process of receiving perceptions of one's performance from a variety of sources, typically supervisor(s), peers, direct reports, self, customers, and even suppliers.

3X approach – is a shorthand approach sometimes used to determine annual income needs for an OD consultant.

Action learning – is an approach to work with and develop people that uses work on an actual project or problem as the way to learn.

Action Planning – is the fourth step of the *organization development process model*; based on what was determined in the previous step, plans are mutually developed as to how the organization wishes to move forward.

Action research (AR) – is a distinguishing OD feature that posits that things change by simply looking at them.

Action research model (ARM) – is the dominant model in use in OD; it represents the activities involved in a change effort.

Adaptability – is the ability of an organization to respond to changes in the external environment.

Adoption – is the seventh step of the *organization development process model*; if the *evaluation* shows that the objectives of the *intervention* have been met, the change becomes a part of the way in which business is done in the organization.

Affinity diagram – is a process used to reduce a large number of items into a few categories.

Align (alignment) – is the process of ensuring that what is being done in a particular area or function is consistent with, and supports, the overall mission of the organization.

Alpha change (first-order change) – is change that is consistent with present processes, values, and understandings in the organization.

Ambiguity – occurs when there is no clear-cut or obvious answer.

Anecdotal research – is information relying on stories.

Anonymity – is when individuals are not identified or named.

Appreciative inquiry (AI) – is an OD approach that looks solely at the positive aspects of an organization or situation.

Assessment – is a process through which the actual situation of an organization is determined.

Balanced scorecard (BSC) – is an approach that bases *strategy* formulation and *evaluation* on four perspectives: financial, customer, internal business, and innovation/learning.

Benchmarking – is when management compares their processes (preferably) or results internally or relative to other organizations.

Best practices – are practices that are generally considered to produce high-quality results, often within the organization's industry.

Beta change (second-order change) – is a change in understanding of what matters with a stable measure.

Black Belt (or *Master Black Belt*) – is a designation for an employee who typically has mastered *six sigma* tools and methodology and teaches them to others.

Blending – is combining the best of local culture (indigenous) with specific elements from other cultures.

Brainstorming – is a common process used in teams to generate as many ideas as possible on a specific problem or issue.

Business process reengineering (BPR) – (same as *process reengineering*) is getting rid of existing processes and replacing them with new ones that are more effective and efficient.

Cause and effect – is when an action influences the result or outcome of another action.

Cause-effect diagram – (same as *fishbone diagram* and *Ishikawa diagram*) is designed to identify all of the causes of a specified problem, and then, from these possible causes, the one that is most likely to be the root cause.

Champion – is someone who oversees and supports a team's activities.

Change agent – is someone whose work in a given situation results in changes in that situation.

Change formula – (see *Formula for change*)

Change management – is expertise used to create predetermined differences or changes in an organization.

Change order – is a supplementary contract issued to a client to ensure there are no misunderstandings when it comes to budget and cost.

Change team – is a group of people who are "in charge" of directing predetermined actions to create change in an organization.

Chaos theory – is the belief that as much as we want to control the outputs of our *systems*, and as much as we think we are doing so, the systems themselves have a regenerating power that takes power away from individuals.

Check-up – is an organizational assessment.

Closed system – is a *system* that is interested neither in being influenced nor in influencing.

Coaching – is the process of equipping people with the tools, knowledge, and opportunities they need to develop and become more effective.

Code of ethics – is a formalized statement developed by a professional organization or official body that stipulates the behaviors that are acceptable and unacceptable for members of affected groups; such codes may also stipulate penalties for infractions.

Competence – is the knowledge and skills that a person has (or needs) in a specific area.

Complexity paradigm – is a way of thinking that sees the world as complex and chaotic because there are many interconnections and interdependencies; this concept is closely associated with *chaos theory*.

Concurrent validity – is when the instrument provides the same results as some other, proven instrument.

Confidentiality – is the act of keeping information private or secret.

Conflict of interest – is a situation in which the needs or desires of the client and the consultant, or of any two or more parties, are mutually unattainable, causing an *ethical dilemma*.

Confucian dynamism – is based on Confucian philosophy and refers to short- and long-term perspectives; the emphasis is on what one does, not what one believes.

Continuous change – is ongoing, evolving, and emergent.

Continuous process improvement (CPI) or **continuous quality improvement (CQI)** (same as *total quality management*) – is both a philosophy and a set of tools and techniques that enable managers to manage with data with a focus on continuously improving processes by reducing variation and improving effectiveness and efficiency.

Coopetition – is the simultaneous need for cooperation and competition.

Credibility – is providing proof that you are capable of successfully performing a task.

Cross-cultural team – is a group of individuals (usually from within the organization) representing different locations/cultures.

Cultural iceberg – is a model developed by Schein used to represent the key components of organizational culture: behaviors, norms, and artifacts; stated beliefs and values; and assumptions.

Cultural survey – is an organizational *assessment*.

Customize – is a process in which something is developed specifically for an organization.

Decision tree – is a tool used to plan how much time and financing is needed to accomplish a goal or objective .

Defect – is anything that does not meet a customer's expectations.

Delphi process – is used to gather consensus from individuals who are at different locations; it consists of a questionnaire that is completed multiple times with *feedback* about average perceptions between each response time, with the hope that respondents will move toward consensus.

Deontology – is an approach to ethics based on decision making that is consistent with a the past, such as rules, policies, religious writings, traditions, parental practices, and so on.

Diagnosis – is an organizational *assessment*.

Dialogue session – is a structured conversation designed to explore a topic that has potential for being conflictual, with the desired outcome of a deeper understanding rather than persuasion or resolution.

Diffusion – is the transfer of technology, skills, knowledge, and other aspects of one *system* or subsystem to another, whether internally or externally.

DiSC® – is an instrument using the constructs of dominance, influence, steadiness, and conscientiousness in personality identification.

Discipline – is a branch of knowledge.

Diversity – is the combination of people based on gender, age, ethnicity, race, religion, nationality, sexual orientation, geographic origin, and even ideas, politics, and ideologies.

Divisional structure – is an organizational structure organized around product lines or other common characteristic as determined by the organization.

Dominant company – is the acquiring company in an acquisition that absorbs the acquired company.

E change – is immediate and radical change driven by the economic needs of the organization.

Effectiveness – is doing the "right" thing.

Efficiency – is the greatest value at the least effort.

Emics – is the study of a culture by those who are part of that culture and that leads to consensus by those who are inside that culture.

Employee survey – is an organizational *assessment*.

Entropy – is a state of stagnation and even decline.

Entry – is the point at which a consultant begins to interact with an organization or process.

Environmental scanning – (same as *external scan*) is a method used to determine the marketplace competition and factors that are likely to impact the business.

Episodic change – is intentional, infrequent, discontinuous, and dramatic.

EPRG model – is the ethnocentric-polycentric-regiocentric-geocentric model that helps identify how organizations view their potential for global management potential.

Ethical dilemmas – are situations that confront individuals who must make a decision when there is no obviously correct or moral answer.

Ethnocentrism – is an approach to global business that assumes that the way in which things are done in the headquarters country are best; only people from the home country serve as managers.

Etics – is a study of a culture by those outside the culture, using scientific methods that must meet the scientific test of *validity* and *reliability*.

Evaluation – is the sixth step in the *organization development process model*; it allows the OD professional and the client organization to determine whether the change effort should be adopted, or whether the cycle needs to begin again to find a more effective intervention.

Executive coach – is a person who uses a specific application of coaching to focus on top levels of managers in an organization.

Executive committee – is a group of organization executives responsible for overseeing the project.

External consultant – is a person contracted from outside the organization.

External scan – (same as *environmental scanning*) is a method used to determine the marketplace competition and factors that are likely to impact the business.

Face validity – is a popular approach to establishing *validity* in which experts in the subject area indicate how well they think an instrument will measure what it is supposed to measure.

Feedback – is providing information back to individuals and groups from whom the information was obtained.

First-order change (alpha change) – is change that is consistent with present processes, values, and understandings in the organization.

Fishbone diagram – (same as *cause-effect diagram* and *Ishikawa diagram*) is designed to identify all of the causes of a specified problem and then, from these possible causes, the one that is most likely to be the root cause.

Fishbowl – is a process used to help individuals become aware of the impact of their interactions on team functioning by having a small group role-play while others observe and provide *feedback* on individual behaviors.

Flexibility – is an organization's ability to make changes in response to internal and external factors.

Force field analysis – is an OD tool used to identify the positive and negative factors (forces) influencing the question under consideration.

Formative evaluation – occurs during an *intervention* and enables rapid shifts to improve the intervention.

Formula for change – is $D \times V \times F > R$ by Gliecher, where D = dissatisfaction, V = vision, F = first achievable steps for change, and R = resistance; if D, V, or F equals or is close to zero, then there will be no change and resistance.

Functional area – is the part of an organization responsible for performing a specified function or types of tasks.

Functional structure – is an organizational structure based on functions.

Future search – is when a cross section of members of a *system* come together in a large-group planning meeting to explore the past, present, and future related to a specific, focused task.

Gamma change (third-order change) – occurs when there is a fundamental change in the importance of the measure itself that is applied.

Generalizations – are data based and are applied to the majority of members of different cultures.

Geocentrism – is an approach to global business in which *best practices* are chosen from any part of the organization, regardless of where it is located, and the best people are put in positions regardless of their country of origin.

GLBT – stands for *gay-lesbian-bisexual-transsexual*; it refers to various sexual orientations.

Global intervention – is an *intervention* designed to work across many cultures, ideally integrating the best from all of the cultures.

Green Belt – is a designation for an employee who typically has demonstrated proficiency in *six sigma* tools and methodology.

Ground rules – are a set of behavioral expectations agreed on by a team about how its members want to function.

High-context culture – is a culture that has implicit values that must be known for a person to communicate effectively within that culture.

Hipos – stands for *high-potentials*, or employees who have been identified as having strong potential to move into key positions in the organization.

Human resource accounting – is method that attempts to put all human resource inputs and outputs into financial terms for the purposes of evaluation.

Human resource development (HRD) – is any process or activity that has the potential to develop work-based knowledge, expertise, productivity and satisfaction, whether for personal or group/team gain, or for the benefit of an organization, community, nation, or, ultimately, the whole of humanity.

Human resource management – is a part of the human resource field that consists of activities linked to the personnel functions of an organization.

IDP – (same as *PDP*) is an individual development plan used to establish expectations and development needs of individual employees.

Implementation – is the fifth step of the *organization development process model* during which the plans that were made in the *Action Planning* step are implemented; in OD jargon, this is called an *intervention*.

Indigenization – is the process of customizing work, a model, a theory, or a concept to be culturally appropriate.

Infrastructure – is the foundation needed by a consultant to run the project successfully (having all the necessary supplies and support).

Interdependency – is the condition that prevails in a *system* when what happens in any one subsystem has varying degrees of impact on some or all of the other subsystems.

Internal consultant – is a person contracted from within the organization.

Internal scan – is part of the strategic planning process in which the organization gathers information on the internal context to understand how these factors will impact the organization.

Interval – is when the difference between all points is identical, but there is no absolute zero.

Intervention – is *implementation* of an action to create change.

Interview – is an *assessment* performed through asking questions and receiving responses.

Ishikawa diagram – (same as *cause-effect diagram* and *fishbone diagram*) is designed to identify all of the causes of a specified problem and then, from these possible causes, the one that is most likely to be the root cause.

Isolates – are those members of a team or group who are not involved or who do not actively participate; they are identified through the use of a *sociogram*.

Johari window – is a model for demonstrating the importance of self-awareness and *feedback* in communicating.

KSAs – is jargon for knowledge, skills, and attitudes competencies.

Laboratory training group – (same as *T-group*) is an unstructured group in which people participate as learners about themselves and how they are perceived by others.

Large-scale interactive events (LSIEs) – serve to get the whole organization together in one place and use small groups to interact on issues of importance to the entire organization, often to focus on mission and vision.

Learning organization – is an organization that has woven a continuous and enhanced capacity to learn, adapt, and change into its culture.

Letter of agreement – (or *memorandum of understanding*) is a written document outlining the understanding between the organization and the external professional about what is to be accomplished, by whom, when, and for what compensation.

Likert-type survey – is a questionnaire that requires a response from a choice of, usually, five or seven numbered options, e.g., 1 = strongly disagree, 5 = strongly agree.

Limited integration – is when two companies continue to operate as they did before a merger or acquisition.

Line management – provides leadership at the point where a product is produced or a service is delivered.

Longitudinal evaluation – is the measure of change in an organization over a long period.

Low-context culture – is a culture that has explicit values that can be relatively easily explained.

Management by objectives (MBOs) – is a method of performance management in which individuals develop or are given goals against which they will be assessed each year.

Master Black Belt – is a designation for an employee who typically has mastered *six sigma* tools and methodology and teaches them to others.

Matrix – is a diagram in which two or more variables or items are compared with each other.

Matrix structure – is an organizational structure in which each person reports to at least two managers, usually a functional manager and a product manager.

Max-mix – describes a group made up of representatives from all levels, all geographic locations, and all functional areas of the organization.

Mean – is the arithmetic average.

Memorandum of understanding – (or *letter of agreement*) is a written document outlining the understanding between the organization and the external professional about what is to be accomplished, by whom, when, and for what compensation.

Mentee – is a person who receives support and counsel from a more experienced individual in the organization, often someone (a *mentor*) in a position to help the individual advance in the organization.

Mentor – is a person, often in an influential position, who supports and counsels someone (a *mentee*) in an organization to assist that person in his or her development and advancement.

Mentoring – is a one-on-one relationship in which one individual (a *mentor*) supports and counsels another person (a *mentee*) to take advantage of opportunities for career and personal enhancement.

Mirroring process – is used to help two groups understand each other better.

Mission statements – are usually short, catchy statements that are easily remembered and communicate what the purpose of the organization is.

Mode – is the most common value in a set of observations.

Monochronic time culture – is a culture that is more linear and bases choices on "clock time."

Multirater appraisal – (same as *multirater* or *360-degree feedback*) is the process of receiving perceptions of one's performance from a variety of sources, typically supervisor(s), peers, direct reports, self, customers, and even suppliers.

Multirater feedback – (same as *360-degree feedback* or *multirater appraisal*) is the process of receiving perceptions of one's performance from a variety of sources, typically supervisor(s), peers, direct reports, self, customers, and even suppliers.

Mutual best of both – is an approach to mergers and acquisitions where a new company emerges as an integrated entity, drawing on the best from each of the two companies involved in the merger or acquisition.

Myers Briggs Type Indicator® (MBTI) – is an instrument used to assist people in identifying their personality type on four dimensions.

Needs assessment – is a process used to determine how people in that organization feel about the organization, specifically, what is and is not going well.

Newtonian paradigm – is a way of thinking that sees the world as linear and simple.

Nominal – is a scale in which the options or variables are named rather than given a value.

Nominal group technique (NGT) – is a form of brainstorming that ensures broad participation from members of the group.

O change – is evolutionary change consistent with OD principles.

Observation – is a record or description of something that has occurred and has been seen or heard.

Open-in system – is a *system* in which a group wants all of the information it can get (open in) but is not prepared to share it (closed out).

Open-out system – is a *system* in which a group wants to influence others (open out) but is not willing to be influenced (closed in).

Open space technology meeting – is a meeting based on the *dialogue* concept; it is used to address a wide range of topics within organizations, including strategic issues.

Open system – is where the desire is to gain knowledge (open in) and then to share it widely (open out).

Open systems mapping – is recording where the *system* currently is and what the organization wants the system to be in the future to help determine the steps needed to close the gap between what is and that which is desired.

Ordinal – is a scale in which items can be put in order, but there is no way to know whether the differences between two points are the same as between two other points.

Organizational analysis – is a process to determine how people in that organization feel about what is and what is not going well.

Organization development (OD) – is any process or activity that has the potential to develop in an organizational setting enhanced knowledge, expertise, productivity, satisfaction, income, interpersonal relationships, and other desired outcomes for the benefit of an organization, community, nation, region, or, ultimately, the whole of humanity.

Organization development process (ODP) model – is an OD model that consists of eight components or phases with interactivity among the phases.

Organizational learning – is the process through which an organization becomes a *learning organization*.

PDCA (plan/do/check/act) model – is a model to explain the necessity for ongoing organizational improvement and a process through which continuous improvement can occur.

PDP – (same as *IDP*) is a personal development plan used to establish expectations and development needs of individual employees.

PEST – which stands for *political/environmental/social/technological*, is one approach to *strategic planning*, looking at how these four factors affect the organization.

Penalty clause for nonperformance – is the penalty the external professional may be responsible for if the project is not successful or not completed on time.

Planned intervention – is an intentional action or set of actions designed to bring about specific and beneficial results for the organization

Plop – is a statement or a question that is ignored by other members of a team or group.

Polycentrism – is an approach to global business in which the organization allows the business in countries other than the headquarters country to function as they wish, with senior leadership from that country, so long as the company operates profitably.

Polychronic time culture – is a culture less concerned with "clock time" that bases choices more on the rhythm of relationships than on linear decision making.

Power distance – is the extent to which less powerful members of a society accept and expect the uneven distribution of power.

Power lab – is a group learning process developed by the Tavistock Institute in which some members are assigned certain roles to see how people react in a group setting.

Presenting problem – is what the client thinks the organization knows about a situation and labels as the problem; the organization may also have already determined how to address the identified problem.

Pro bono – (literally, "for the good") is work done at no cost, usually for a not-for-profit organization, consistent with expectations contained in most codes of ethics.

Process – a series of steps that starts by taking inputs and performing activities that produce outputs.

Process coach – acts as a consultant to the team and meeting process, providing *feedback* on the processes being used by the team or group.

Process consultation – is a primary OD process in which an OD consultant provides *feedback* to the organization.

Process intervention – is an *intervention* that is useful in improving organizational processes.

Process reengineering – (same as *business process reengineering [BPR]*) is getting rid of existing processes and replacing them with new ones that are more effective and efficient.

Process structure – is an organizational structure organized around common processes.

Project management system – is a method that allows an organization to track what is to be done, by whom, and when.

Project steering committee – (same as *steering team*) is a cross section of people with various demographics representing a range of areas from within the client organization formed to give direction to one or more projects.

Proportional random sampling – is the representation of employees proportionate to their presence in the organization based on selected demographics.

Psychometrics – is the general requirements for any measurement *system*, including *reliability* and *validity*.

Publicly listed organization – is a company listed on a stock exchange enabling individuals and organizations to purchase stocks or part ownership in the organization.

Purposive sampling – is the selection of employees because they fit prespecified criteria.

Qualitative data – are data that are textual in nature (as opposed to numerical) and usually gathered through *interviews* and focus groups.

Quality management – is the coordinated activities and philosophy used to improve an organization's quality.

Quantitative data – are data that are numerical in nature (as opposed to textual) and are usually gathered through *surveys* or observations.

Random sampling (random sample) occurs when every member of the organization has an equal chance of being selected.

Random selection (see *Random sample*)

Ratio – is a scale in which the differences between any two continguous points is identical, and there is an absolute zero base.

Regiocentrism – is an approach to global business that expects its suborganizations in countries in a region to operate similarly; managers are selected from the region.

Reliability – is an indicator of the consistency or stability of results obtained.

Requests for proposals (RFPs) – are requests from an organization for proposals to find the best-qualified external candidate or organization to perform a specific task.

Responsibility charting – is a formal process of clarifying ambiguous areas of responsibility in complex relationship situations in order to eliminate overlapping responsibilities and to ensure that there are no uncovered areas of responsibility.

Return-on-investment model – (ROI) is a method of *evaluation* that attempts to calculate, in financial terms, the relationship between inputs and outputs.

Sampling – is when a subset of the employee base is selected.

Scenario planning – considers all possible changes in the environment in the future and develops strategic responses for each before there is any way to know how the environment will actually change.

Scope of the project – defines the deliverables and boundaries of the project.

Scribe – is the person responsible for documenting activities at team meetings and future action steps.

Secondary data – are data that preexist entry into the organization.

Second-order change (beta change) – is a change in understanding of what matters with a stable measure.

Self-managed work teams – are teams that operate relatively autonomously, creating their own structure, mission, and processes.

Sensitivity training – is any process in which individuals become more aware (sensitive) of their own feelings and behaviors, as well as those of others; *T-groups* are an example of sensitivity training.

Separation – is the eighth step in the *organization development process model*; it occurs when the consultant withdraws from the organization, preferably having transferred his or her skills to the client organization.

Silos – describe a situation in which relationships in an organization are restricted to the boundaries of employees' own organizational unit, function, or department.

Single-tool syndrome – occurs when a professional knows how to use only one technique or instrument, leading to the recommendation, always, that that technique or instrument be used.

Situational – is an approach to ethics based on decision making that is consistent with the individual's present needs.

Six sigma – is both a statistical tool for improving productivity and a management philosophy.

Sociogram – is a visual representation that provides specific *feedback* on the way in which team members interact with each other.

Sociotechnical systems (STS) – is the focus on the interaction of humans, machines, and the environment; the concept is credited to Eric Trist.

Sponsorship – is provided to a project by someone who is in a position to provide financing, personnel, and support to that project.

Stakeholder – is any person and/organization with an interest in or attachment to an organization or situation and what happens to and within that organization or situation.

Standard deviation – is the statistical measure of the spread of results or variation.

Standardized – is doing something the same way from situation to situation, such as conducting a *survey* or performing a process.

Start-up – is the second phase of the *organization development process model* and begins during and immediately after the *Entry* phase.

Statistical process control (SPC) – refers to a number of statistical tools that are used to measure or report variation and performance in a process that helps determine whether and where an *intervention* may be needed.

Status reporting process – is the vehicle used for communicating with all key stakeholders the status of a project.

Steering team – (same as *project steering committee*) is a cross section of people with various demographics representing a range of areas from within the client organization formed to give direction to one or more projects.

Stereotype – is a way that people take information from their past and use it in future interactions with other people from different backgrounds.

Strategic alignment assessment – is a measure of how well the behavior of people and *systems* in organizations work together to support the goals, mission, and vision of the organization.

Strategic planning – is a process that typically looks into the future at 1-, 3-, and 5-year intervals and makes decisions on *strategy* and *tactics* based on what the organization believes the future will be.

Strategy – is a broad plan or approach used to achieve an organizational goal.

Succession planning – is the process of identifying, developing, and mentoring younger employees who will be able to move into management positions as employees retire, are promoted or transferred, or leave the organization.

Summative evaluation – is an *evaluation* performed at the end of the process.

Supplementary contract – is an additional contract issued by the client to ensure that there are no misunderstandings when it comes to budget and cost.

Survey – is a process of collecting data from an organization or suborganization for analysis, usually done through a questionnaire.

SWOT – stands for *strengths, weaknesses, opportunities*, and *threats*; it is one approach to *strategic planning* that looks at the strengths/weaknesses of the organization and the opportunities/threats in the environment.

Synergy – is the greater combined energy or influence of many combined as compared to that of a single entity or the total of the entities operating independently.

System – is contained by a boundary that separates it from the environment and consists of many subsystems; each system has inputs, processes, and outputs.

Systematic – describes a methodical approach in which the whole *system* is involved.

System cycle – is the ebb and flow of a *system*.

Systems perspective evaluation is an *evaluation* that recognizes that no one evaluation method can be sufficient and points to *triangulation*.

Systems theory – is a way of thinking about how the *system* is connected to everything else; nothing is truly isolated.

Systems thinking – is critical for organizational success; it is a framework for seeing interrelationships rather than things in isolation.

Tactics – are specific steps used to accomplish a *strategy*.

T-group (training group) – (same as *laboratory training group*) is an unstructured group in which people participate as learners about themselves and how they are perceived by others.

Tampering – occurs when changes are made to a process on the basis of little or no data, often leading to undesirable outcomes.

Taxonomy – is a list categorizing a construct into its component parts.

Teleology – is an approach to ethics based on decision making that is consistent with a person's vision for the future.

Third-order change (gamma change) – occurs when there is a fundamental change in the importance of the measure itself that is applied.

Thomas-Kilmann conflict mode instrument (TKI) – is a graphic indication of various types of conflict behaviors.

Three-step change model – is a model proposed by Lewin (1947) that suggests that organizations are changed through the process of unfreezing, moving, and refreezing.

Tickler file – is a file (or list) of things to be done.

Time line – is an outline of when specific portions of the project will be completed.

Total quality management – (same as *continuous process improvement [CPI]* or *continuous quality improvement [CQI]*) is both a philosophy and a set of tools and techniques that enable managers to manage with data with a focus on continuously improving processes by reducing variation and improving effectiveness and efficiency.

Transformation to new company – is an approach to mergers and acquisitions similar to the *mutual best of both* approach but adding the incorporation of totally new company practices and external *best practices* in creating the integrated new company.

Triangulation – is collecting data using two or more methods to increase the accuracy of the conclusions.

Validity – is measuring what you want to measure, all of what you want to measure, and nothing but what you want to measure.

Values clarification – is an exercise that helps individuals determine what their values are.

Values integration – is a process that helps individuals compare and align their values with those needed in the job and in their personal life.

Virtual teams – is a group of individuals within the organization representing different locations/cultures who are connected via cyberspace.

Vision statement – is a statement that captures and communicates what the organization wants to look like in its future; it is usually longer than a *mission statement*.

References

Academy of Human Resource Development. (1999). *Standards on ethics and integrity*. Retrieved May 31, 2005, at www.ahrd.org.

Academy of Management, Organization Development and Change Division. (2005). *ODC statement*. Retrieved February 5, 2005, at www.aom.pace .edu/odc/draftofvm.html.

Adler, N. J. (2002). *International dimensions of organizational behavior* (4th ed.). Cincinnati, OH: South-Western.

Albaeva, G., & McLean, G. N. (2004). Higher education reform in Kyrgyz-stan. *Journal of College Teaching and Learning, 1*(10), 47–54.

Alban, B. T., & Scherer, J. J. (2005). On the shoulders of giants: The origins of OD. In W. J. Rothwell & R. L. Sullivan (Eds.), *Practicing organization development: A guide for consultants* (2nd ed., pp. 81–105). San Francisco: Pfeiffer.

The American heritage dictionary of the English language (4th ed.). (2000). Boston: Houghton Mifflin. Retrieved December 26, 2004, at http:// dictionary.reference.com/search?q=organization.

American Psychological Association. (2001). *Publication manual of the American Psychological Association* (5th ed.). Washington, DC: Author.

American Psychological Association. (2002). *Ethical principles of psychologists and code of conduct*. Retrieved May 31, 2005, at www.apa.org/ ethics/code2002.pdf.

Bartlett, K. R., & Rodgers, J. (2004). HRD as national policy in the Pacific Islands. *Advances in Developing Human Resources, 6*(3), 307–314.

Bass, B. M. (1990). *Bass & Stogdill's handbook of leadership* (3rd ed.). New York: Free Press.

Becker, B. E., Huselid, M. A., & Ulrich, D. (2001). *The HR scorecard: Linking people, strategy, and performance*. Cambridge, MA: Harvard Business School Press.

Beckhard, R. (1969).*Organization development: Strategies and models*. Reading, MA: Addison-Wesley.

Beckhard, R., & Harris, R. T. (1977). *Organizational transitions: Managing complex change*. New York: Addison-Wesley.

Beckhard, R., & Harris, R. T. (1987). *Organizational transitions*. Reading, MA: Addison, Wesley.

Beer, M., & Nohria, N. (2000). Resolving the tension between theories E and O of change. In M. Beer & N. Nohria (Eds.), *Breaking the code of change* (pp. 1–33). Boston: Harvard Business School Press.

Bennis, W. (1969). *Organization development: Its nature, origins, and prospects*. Reading, MA: Addison-Wesley.

Bernardin, H. J., & Beatty, R. W. (1987). Can subordinate appraisals enhance managerial productivity? *Sloan Management Review, 28*, 421–439.

Berniker, E. (1992). *Some principles of sociotechnical systems analysis and design*. Retrieved December 23, 2004, at www.plu.edu/~bernike/SocioTech.htm.

Blanchard, K. (1989). *Managing the journey* [videotape]. Schaumburg, IL: Video Publishing House.

Bradford, D. L. (2005). Foreword. In W. J. Rothwell & R. L. Sullivan (Eds.), *Practicing organization development: A guide for consultants* (2nd ed., pp. xxiii–xxvii). San Francisco: Pfeiffer.

Briggs, Jr., V. M. (1987). Human resource development and the formulation of national economic policy. *Journal of Economic Issues, 21*(3), 1207–1240.

Budhwani, N., Wee, B., & McLean, G. N. (2004). Should child labor be eliminated? An HRD perspective. *Human Resource Development Quarterly, 15*(1), 107–116.

Burke, W. (1997). The new agenda for organization development. *Organization Dynamics, 25*(1), 7–21.

Burke, W. W. (2002). *Organization change: Theory and practice*. Thousand Oaks, CA: Sage.

Canadian Centre for Occupational Health and Safety. (2002). Job design. Retrieved on December 26, 2004, at www.ccohs.ca/oshanswers/hsprograms/job_design.html.

Carter, L., Giber, D., Goldsmith, M., & Bennis, W. G. (Eds.). (2000). *Linkage Inc.'s best practices in leadership development handbook: Case studies, instruments, training*. San Francisco: Pfeiffer.

Champy, J. (1995). *Reengineering management: The mandate for new leadership*. New York: HarperCollins.

Champy, J. (2002). *X-engineering the corporation: Reinventing your business in the digital age*. New York: Warner Business Books.

Chat-uthai, M., & McLean, G. N. (2003). Combating corruption in Thailand: A call to an end of the "white buffet." In J. B. Kidd & F.-J. Richter (Eds.), *Fighting corruption in Asia: Causes, effects and remedies* (pp. 317–348). Singapore: World Scientific.

Chermack, T. J. (2004). A theoretical model of scenario planning. *Human Resource Development Review, 3*(4), 301–325.

Cho, E. S., & McLean, G. N. (2002). National human resource development: Korean case. In U. Pareek, A. M. Osman-Gani, S. Ramnaravan, & T. V. Rao (Eds.), *Human resource development in Asia: Trends and challenges* (pp. 253–260). New Delhi: Oxford & IBH.

Cho, E. S., & McLean, G. N. (2004). What we discovered about NHRD and what it means for HRD. *Advances in Developing Human Resources, 6*(3), 382–393.

Chowdhury, S. (2001). *The power of six sigma.* Chicago: Dearborn Trade.

Clearinghouse for Information about Values and Ethics in OD-HSD. (1996). *Organization and human systems development credo.* Retrieved May 31, 2005, at www.odnetwork.org/credo.html.

Cooper, S. (2004). National governance and promising practices in workplace learning: A postindustrialist programmatic framework in Canada. *Advances in Developing Human Resources, 6*(3), 363–373.

Cooperrider, D., & Srivastva, S. (1987). Appreciative inquiry in organizational life. In R. Woodman & W. Pasmore (Eds.), *Organizational change and development: Vol. 1* (pp. 129–170). Greenwich, CT: JAI Press.

Corrigan, C. (2002). *What is open space technology?* Retrieved December 23, 2004, at www.chriscorragon.com/openspace/whatisos.html.

Crosby, P. (1984). *Quality without tears: The art of hassle-free management.* New York: McGraw-Hill.

Cummings, T. G., & Worley, C. G. (2005). *Organization development and change* (8th ed.). Mason, OH: South Western/Thomson.

Daniels, D. R., Erickson, M. L., & Dalik, A. (2001). Here to stay—taking competencies to the next level. *WorkatWork Journal, 10*(1), 70–77.

Dannemiller, K. D., & Jacobs, R. W. (1992). Changing the way organizations change: A revolution of common sense. *Journal of Applied Behavioral Science, 28*(4), 480–497.

Davenport, T. H. (1995). The fad that forgot people. *Fast Company, 1*(1), 70–74.

Deming, W. E. (1986). *Out of the crisis.* Boston: Massachusetts Institute of Technology.

DeVogel, S. H. (1992). *Ethical decision making in organization development: Current theory and practice.* Unpublished doctoral dissertation, University of Minnesota, St. Paul.

DeVogel, S. H., Sullivan, R., McLean, G. N., & Rothwell, W. J. (1995). Ethics in OD. In W. J. Rothwell, R. Sullivan, & G. N. McLean (Eds.). *Practicing organization development: A guide for consultants* (pp. 445–489). San Diego: Pfeiffer.

Dewey, J. D., & Carter, T. J. (2003). Exploring the future of HRD: The first future search conference for a profession. *Advances in Developing Human Resources, 5*(3), 245–256.

Dooley, K. J., Johnson, T. L., & Bush, D. H. (n.d.). *Total quality management and the revolution in management paradigm.* Unpublished manuscript available from senior author at Arizona State University.

Egan, T. M. (2002). Organization development: An examination of definitions and dependent variables. *Organization Development Journal, 20*(2), 59–70.

Egan, T. M., & Lancaster, C. M. (2005). Comparing appreciative inquiry and action research: OD practitioner perspectives. *Organization Development Journal, 23*(2), 29–49.

Eisen, S. (2002). *Top emerging competencies*. Results of a Delphi study distributed to participants. Retrieved February 13, 2005, at www.sonoma.edu/programs/od/.

Ellinger, A. D., Ellinger, A. E., Yang, B., & Howton, S. W. (2002). The relationship between the learning organization concept and firms' financial performance: An empirical assessment. *Human Resource Development Quarterly, 13*(1), 5–21.

Evered, R. D., & Selman, J. C. (1989). Coaching and the art of management. *Organizational Dynamics, 18*(2), 16–32.

Fitzpatrick, J. L., Sanders, J. R., & Worthen, B. R. (2004). *Program evaluation: Alternative approaches and practical guidelines* (3rd ed.). Boston: Pearson.

Freire, P. (1972). *Pedagogy of the oppressed*, Harmondsworth, U.K.: Penguin.

Friedman, T. L. (2000). *The Lexus and the olive tree*. New York: Anchor Books.

Friedman, T. L. (2005). *The world is flat: A brief history of the twenty-first century*. Waterville, ME: Thorndike Press.

Gangani, N. T., McLean, G. N., & Braden, R. A. (2004). Competency-based human resource development strategy. In T. M. Egan & M. L. Morris (Eds.), *Proceedings AHRD 2004 conference* (pp. 1114–1121). Bowling Green, OH: AHRD.

Gellerman, W. (1991). The international organization development code of ethics. In D. W. Cole (Ed.), *The international registry of O.D. professionals* (2005 ed.). Chesterland, OH: The Organization Development Institute. Retrieved on May 31, 2005, at members.aol.com/ODInst/ethics.htm.

Goldstein, T. L. (1993). *Training in organizations* (3rd ed.). Pacific Grove, CA: Brooks/Cole.

Goleman, D. (1995). *Emotional intelligence*. New York: Bantam.

Golembiewski, R. T., Billingsley, K., & Yeager, S. (1976). Measuring change and persistence in human affairs: Types of change generated by OD designs. *Journal of Applied Behavioral Science, 12*, 133–157.

Gray, B. (2005). *The experience of being a financial consultant and a person of color or Hispanic at ABC Financial Firm*. Unpublished doctoral dissertation, University of Minnesota, St. Paul.

Gundling, E. (2003). *Working GlobeSmart: 12 people skills for doing business across borders*. Palo Alto, CA: Davies-Black.

Gunn Partners. (2000). Change leadership, Part 1. *Horizons*, 1–16.

Hall, E. (1976). *Beyond culture*. Garden City, NY: Doubleday.

Hall, W. D. (1993). *Making the right decisions: Ethics for managers*. New York: Wiley.

Hammer, M., & Champy, J. (1993). *Reengineering the corporation: A manifesto for business*. New York: HarperCollins.

Harris, P. R., & Moran, R. T. (1979). *Managing cultural differences*. Houston, TX: Gulf.

Harrison, R. (1970). Choosing the depth of organizational intervention. *Journal of Applied Behavioral Science, 6*(2), 182–202.

Head, T., Armstrong, T., & Preston, J. (1996). The role of graduate education in becoming a competent organization development practitioner. *OD Practitioner, 28*(1 & 2), 52–60.

Headland, T. N., Pike, K. L., & Harris, M. (Eds.). (1990). *Emics and etics: The insider/outsider debate*. Newbury Park, CA: Sage.

Heap, N. (n.d.). *Open systems planning*. Retrieved December 23, 2004, at http://homepage.ntlworld.com/nick.heap/Opensystems.htm.

Hedge, J. W., & Borman, W. C. (1995). Changing conceptions and practices in performance appraisal. In A. Howard (Ed.), *The changing nature of work* (pp. 451–481). San Francisco: Jossey-Bass.

Heenan, D., & Perlmutter, H. (1979). *Multinational organization development*. New York: Addison-Wesley.

Herzberg, F., Mausner, B., & Block Snyderman, B. (1959). *Motivation to work*. New York: Wiley.

Hofstede, G. (2001). *Culture's consequences: Comparing values, behaviors, institutions, and organizations across nations*. San Francisco: Sage.

Holton, E. E., III. (1996). The flawed four-level evaluation model. *Human Resource Development Quarterly, 7*(1), 5–21.

Imai, M. (1986). *Kaizen: The key to Japan's competitive success*. Cambridge, MA: Productivity Press.

Inscape Publishing. (1996). *The DiSC classic research report*. Mount Prospect, IL: Author.

Inscape Publishing. (n.d.). *Personal Profile System® 2800 Series: Helping people work better together*. Chicago: Center for Internal Change. Retrieved August 15, 2005, at www.professionalchange.com/Inscape%20Brochures/E-Brochure%20for%20email/PPS.pdf.

International Society for Performance Improvement. (2002). *Code of ethics for Certified Performance Technologists*. Retrieved May 31, 2005, at www.certifiedpt.org/index.cfm?section=standards.

Johansen, B.-C. (1991). *Individual response to organizational change: A grounded model*. Publication No. 50. St. Paul: Training & Development Research Center, University of Minnesota.

Johansen, B.-C., & McLean, G. N. (1995). Team building in a public school system: An unsuccessful intervention. *Organization Development Journal, 13*(2), 1–12.

Juran, J. M. (1988). *Juran on planning for quality*. Cambridge, MA: Productivity Press.

Juran, J. M., & Godfrey, A. B. (Eds.). (1998). *Juran's quality handbook* (5th ed.) New York: McGraw-Hill.

Kamau, D. G., & McLean, G. N. (1999). A nine-month follow-up assessment of a large scale interactive event designed to implement organizational change in state government organization. In K. P. Kuchinke (Ed.), *Academy of Human Resource Development 1999 conference proceedings* (pp. 1148–1155). Baton Rouge, LA: Academy of Human Resource Development.

Kaneko, T. (2000). *Vision HR Plan 21*. St. Paul, MN: 3M.

Kaneko, T. (2003). *Inaugural message: Permeate the new corporate culture and promote continuous changes*. Tokyo: Sumitomo 3M Limited.

Kaplan, R. S., & Norton, D. P. (1996). *The balanced scorecard: Translating strategy into action*. Cambridge, MA: Harvard Business School Press.

Karpiak, I. (2005). *Taken-from-life: The tasks of autobiography in adult education*. In *2005 Hawaii International Conference in Education* (pp. 2111–2120). Honolulu: East-West Council for Education.

Katzenbach, J., & Smith, D. (1993). *The wisdom of teams*. Boston: Harvard Business School Press.

Kidder, R. M. (1995). *Good people make tough choices: Resolving the dilemmas of ethical living*. New York: Morrow.

Kirkpatrick, D. L. (1998). *Evaluating training programs: The four levels* (2nd ed.). San Francisco: Berrett-Koehler.

Kluckhohn, F. R., & Strodtbeck, F. L. (1961). *Variations in value orientations*. Evanston, IL: Row, Peterson.

Kohn, A. (1999). *Punished by rewards: The trouble with gold stars, incentive plans, A's, praise, and other bribes*. Boston: Mariner Books.

Konopaske, R., & Ivancevich, J. M. (2004). *Global management and organizational behavior: Text, readings, cases, and exercises*. New York: McGraw-Hill Irwin.

Landis, D., & Bhagat, R. S. (Eds.). (1996). *Handbook of intercultural training* (2nd ed.). Thousand Oaks, CA: Sage.

Lee, M. (2004). National human resource development in the United Kingdom. *Advances in Developing Human Resources, 6*(3), 334–345.

Lewin, K. (1947). *Frontiers in group dynamics*. Washington, DC: Psychological Association.

Lewin, K. (1951). *Field theory in social science*. New York: Harper & Row.

Lim, M. B. (2005). Philippine experience—Promoting a culture of peace through community-based learning in conflict affected areas. In *Proceedings of the 2005 Hawaii International Conference on Education* (pp. 2444–2445). Honolulu: East-West Council for Education.

Lindahl, K. (1996). *What is the dialogue process?* Retrieved December 23, 2004, at www.asc-spiritualcommunity.org/Process.html.

Lucia, A. D., & Lepsinger, R. (2002). *The art and science of competency models: Pinpointing critical success factors in an organization*. San Francisco: Jossey-Bass/Pfeiffer.

Luft, J., & Ingham, H. (1955). *The Johari-Window: A graphic model for interpersonal relations*. Los Angeles: University of California Western Training Lab.

Lutta-Mukhebi, M. C. (2004). National human resource development policy in Kenya. *Advances in Developing Human Resources, 6*(3), 326–334.

Lynham, S. A., & Cunningham, P. W. (2004). Human resource development: The South African case. *Advances in Developing Human Resources, 6*(3), 315–325.

Maas, P. (1994). *China white*. Rockland, MA: Wheeler.

Marquardt, M., Berger, N., & Loan, P. (2004). *HRD in the age of globalization: A practical guide to workplace learning in the third millennium*. New York: Basic Books.

Marquardt, M., & Reynolds, A. (1994). *The global learning organization: Gaining competitive advantage through continuous learning*. Burr Ridge, IL: Irwin.

Marshall, R. (1986, April 6). *The role of apprenticeship in an internationalized information world*. Paper presented at the Conference on *Learning by Doing* sponsored by the International Union of Operating Engineers, the U.S. Department of Labor, and Cornell University, Albany, NY.

McCauley, C. D., & van Velsor, E. (2003). *The Center for Creative Leadership handbook of leadership development* (2nd ed.). San Francisco: Jossey-Bass.

McKenzie-Mohr, D., & Smith, W. (1999). *Fostering sustainable behavior: An introduction to community-based social marketing*. Gabriola Island, BC, Canada: New Society.

McLagan, P. (1989). *Models for HRD practice*. Alexandria, VA: American Society for Training and Development.

McLagan, P., & Suhadolnik, D. (1989). *Models for HRD practice: The research report*. Alexandria, VA: American Society for Training and Development.

McLean, G. N. (1997). Multirater 360 feedback. In L. J. Bassi & D. Russ-Eft (Eds.), *What works: Assessment, development, and measurement* (pp. 87–108). Alexandria, VA: American Society for Training and Development.

McLean, G. N. (2001). Human resource development as a factor in the inevitable move to globalization. In O. Aliaga (Ed.), *Academy of Human Resource Development 2001 conference proceedings* (pp. 731–738). Baton Rouge, LA: Academy of Human Resource Development.

McLean, G. N. (2004). Lifelong learning in the context of changing organizational cultures. In *Lifelong learning and new learning culture 2004 international conference proceedings* (pp. 170–179). Chia-Yi, Taiwan: National Chung Cheng University.

McLean, G. N. (2004). National human resource development: What in the world is it? *Advances in Developing Human Resources, 6*(3), 269–275.

McLean, G. N. (2005). Examining approaches to HR evaluation: The strengths and weaknesses of popular measurement methods. *Strategic Human Resources, 4*(2), 24–27.

McLean, G. N., Bartlett, K., & Cho, E. S. (2003). Human resource development as national policy: Republic of Korea and New Zealand. *Pacific-Asian Education, 15*(1), 41–59.

McLean, G. N., Damme, S. R., & Swanson, R. A. (Eds.). (1990). *Performance appraisal: Perspectives on a quality management approach*. Alexandria, VA: American Society for Training and Development.

McLean, G. N., & Kamau, D. G. (1998). A case study using a large-scale interactive event to implement organizational change in a nonprofit government organization. In R. Torraco (Ed.), *Academy of Human Resource Development 1998 conference proceedings* (pp. 404–411). Baton Rouge, LA: Academy of Human Resource Development.

McLean, G. N., Kaneko, T., & van Dijk, M. S. (2003). Changing corporate culture across countries: A case study of Sumitomo 3M Limited (Japan). In C. T. Akaraborworn, A. M. Osman-Gani, & G. N. McLean (Eds.), *Human resource development in Asia: National policy perspectives* (pp. 1-1–1-9). Bangkok, Thailand, and Bowling Green, OH: National Institute of Development Administration and Academy of Human Resource Development.

McLean, G. N., & Karimov, M. (2005, April). *Final report: Developing and strengthening education leadership for the future: Kyrgyzstan.* Partnership Agreement under Bureau of Educational and Cultural Affairs FY2001 NIS College and University Partnerships Program of the U.S. State Department, Washington, DC.

McLean, G. N., & McLean, L. D. (2001). If we can't define HRD in one country, how can we define it in an international context? *Human Resource Development International, 4*(3), 313–326.

McLean, G. N., Osman-Gani, A., & Cho, E. (Eds.). (2004). Human resource development as national policy. *Advances in Developing Human Resources, 6*(3).

McLean, G. N., & Sullivan, R. (1989). *Essential competencies of internal and external OD consultants.* In W. J. Rothwell, R. Sullivan, & G. N. McLean (Eds.) (1995), *Practicing organization development: A guide for consultants* (p. 51). San Francisco: Jossey-Bass/Pfeiffer.

McLean, G. N., Sytsma, M., & Kerwin-Ryberg, K. (1995, March). Using 360-degree feedback to evaluate management development: New data, new insights. In E. F. Holton III (Ed.), *Academy of Human Resource Development 1995 conference proceedings* (Section 4-4). Austin, TX: Academy of Human Resource Development.

McLean, G. N., Yang, B., Kuo, C., Tolbert, A., & Larkin, C. (2005). Development and initial validation of an instrument measuring coaching behavior. *Human Resource Development Quarterly, 16*(2), 157–178.

Moon, Y. L., & McLean, G. N. (2003). The nature of corruption hidden in culture: The case of Korea. In J. B. Kidd & F.-J. Richter (Eds.), *Fighting corruption in Asia: Causes, effects and remedies* (pp. 297–315). Singapore: World Scientific.

Murrel, K. L. (2000). Organizational change as applied art: Blending pace, magnitude, and depth. In R. T. Golembiewski (Ed.), *Handbook of organizational consultation* (2nd ed., pp. 807–813). New York: Dekker.

na Chiangmi, C. (1998, October 1). *Current outlook and trends of HRD in Thailand.* Handout distributed in International HRD course, University of Minnesota, St. Paul.

Nadler, L., & Nadler, Z. (1989). *Developing human resources: Concepts and a model* (3rd ed.). San Francisco: Jossey-Bass.

Nevis, E. C., DeBella, A. J., & Gould, J. (1995). Understanding organizations as learning systems. *Sloan Management Review, 36*(2), 73–85.

Noe, R. A., Hollenbeck, J., Gerhart, B., & Wright, P. (1997). *Human resource management: Gaining a competitive advantage* (2nd ed.). Homewood, IL: Irwin.

OD Network. (2003). *OD principles of practice*. Retrieved February 5, 2005, at www.odnetwork.org/principlesofpractice.html.

Organization and human systems development credo (July 1996). (1996). Retrieved August 7, 2005, at www.odnetwork.org/credo.html.

Organization development: A straightforward reference guide for executives seeking to improve their organizations. (1991). Chesterland, OH: The Organization Development Institute.

Osman-Gani, A. M. (2004). Human capital development in Singapore: An analysis of national policy perspectives. *Advances in Developing Human Resources, 6*(3), 276–287.

Osman-Gani, A. M., & Tan, W. L. (1998). Human resource development: The key to sustainable growth and competitiveness of Singapore. *Human Resource Development International, 1*(4), 417–432.

Osman-Gani, A. M., & Tan, W. L. (2000). International briefing: Training & development in Singapore. *International Journal of Training & Development, 4*(4), 305–323.

Patten, M. L. (2001). *Questionnaire research: A practical guide*. Los Angeles: Pyrczak.

Pegels, C. C. (1995). *Total quality management: A survey of its important aspects*. New York: Boyd & Fraser.

Persico, J., Jr., & McLean, G. N. (1994). Manage with valid rather than invalid goals. *Quality Progress, 27*(4), 49–53.

Perspective: The exigencies of globalization. (1998, April). Retrieved September 15, 2002, at www.pagecreator.com/~newsroom/page5.html.

Peterson, D. B., & Hicks, M. D. (1996). *Leader as coach: Strategies for coaching and developing others*. Minneapolis: Personnel Decisions International.

Pfeiffer, J. W., & Jones, J. E. (1978). OD readiness. In J. W. Pfeiffer & J. E. Jones (Eds.), *The 1978 annual handbook for group facilitators* (pp. 219–226). La Jolla, CA: University Associates.

Pipal, T. (2001, March). *My Worldcom and welcome to it*. Keynote presentation at the Annual Conference of the Academy of Human Resource Development, Tulsa, OK.

Provo, J., Tuttle, M., & Henderson, G. (2003, February 26–27). Notes from a preconference of the Academy of Human Resource Development, Minneapolis, MN: "OD in a Changing World: Emerging Dynamics of Organization Development." (Available from authors or from Gary McLean.)

Rangel, E. (2004). Policies for employment and higher education in Mexico: An approach to human resource development as policy. *Advances in Developing Human Resources, 6*(3), 374–381.

Rao, T. V. (2004). Human resource development as national policy in India. *Advances in Developing Human Resources, 6*(3), 288–296.

Reinhold, C. R. (n.d.). *Introduction to Myers-Briggs personality type and the MBTI.* Retrieved December 26, 2004, at www.personalitypathways.com/MBTI_intro.html.

Schaffer, R. H., & Thomson, H. A. (1992). Successful change programs begin with results. *Harvard Business Review, 70*(1), 80–89.

Schein, E. (1980). *Organizational psychology* (3rd ed.). Englewood Cliffs, NJ: Prentice Hall.

Schein, E. (1985). *Organizational culture and leadership.* San Francisco: Jossey-Bass.

Schmidt, A. (2002). *Making mergers work: The strategic importance of people.* Alexandria, VA: Society for Human Resource Management.

Scholtes, P. R. (1988). *The team handbook: How to use teams to improve quality.* Madison, WI: Joiner Associates.

Schön, D. (1983). *The reflective practitioner: How professionals think in action.* London: Temple Smith.

Schön, D. (1987). *Educating the reflective practitioner.* Washington, DC: American Educational Research Association. Retrieved December 26, 2004, at http://educ.queensu.ca/~ar/schon87.htm.

Scotland, M. (2004). National human resource development in St. Lucia. *Advances in Developing Human Resources, 6*(3), 355–362.

Semler, S. W. (2000). Exploring alignment: A comparative case study of alignment in two organizations. In K. P. Kuchinke (Ed.), *Proceedings of the Academy of Human Resource Development Annual Conference* (pp. 757–764). Baton Rouge, LA: Academy of Human Resource Development.

Senge, P. M. (1990). *The fifth discipline: The art and practice of the learning organization.* New York: Doubleday.

Shepard, K., & Raia, A. (1981). The OD training challenge. *Training and Development Journal, 35,* 90–96.

Shirts, G. (1977). *Bafa-bafa.* Del Mar, CA: Simulation Training System.

Shtogren, J. A. (1999). *Skyhooks for leadership: A new framework that brings together five decades of thought—from Maslow to Senge.* New York: AMACOM.

Smith, P. A. C., & Peters, V. J. (1997). Action learning: Worth a closer look. *Ivey Business Quarterly, 62*(1), 63–69.

Society for Human Resource Development. (n.d.). *SHRM code of ethics and professional standards in human resource management.* Retrieved May 31, 2005, at www.shrm.org//ethics/code-of-ethics.asp.

Sorenson, P. F. (1996). An interview with the Sullivan's [*sic*]: Roland and Kristine. *Organization Development Journal, 14*(4), 4–17.

Sorensen, P. F., Gironda, L. A., Head, T. C., & Larsen, H. H. (1996). Global organization development: Lessons from Scandinavia. *Organization Development Journal, 14*(4), 46–52.

Stolovitch, H. D., & Keeps, E. J. (Eds.). (1992). *Handbook of human performance technology: A comprehensive guide for analyzing and solving performance problems in organizations.* San Francisco: Jossey-Bass.

Sullivan, K. (1997). Quickening transformation: Three efforts: Community, organization, and self. *Organization Development Journal, 15*(1), 53–61.

Sullivan, R., & Sullivan, K. (1995). Essential competencies for internal and external OD consultants (15th ed.). In W. Rothwell, R. Sullivan, & G. N. McLean (Eds.), *Practicing organization development: A guide for consultants* (pp. 535–549). San Diego: Pfeiffer.

Sussman, L., & Finnegan, R. (1998). Coaching the star: Rationale and strategies. *Business Horizons, 41*(2), 47–54.

Swanson, R. A. (1994). *Analysis for improving performance: Tools for diagnosing organizations and documenting workplace expertise.* San Francisco: Berrett-Koehler.

Szalkowski, A., & Jankowicz, D. (2004). The development of human resources during the process of economic and structural transformation in Poland. *Advances in Developing Human Resources, 6*(3), 346–354.

Tan, V., & Tiong, T. N. (2005). Change management in times of economic uncertainty. *Singapore Management Review, 27*(1), 49–68.

Tavistock Institute. (2004, July 1). *Authority, leadership and organization* Retrieved December 26, 2004, at www.tavinstitute.org.

Tillich, P. (1963). *Systematic theology, Vol. III: Life and the spirit, history and the Kingdom of God.* Chicago: University of Chicago Press.

Tippins, N. T. (2002). Organization development and IT: Practicing OD in the virtual world. In J. Waclawski & A. H. Church (Eds.), *Organization development: A data-driven approach to organizational change* (pp. 245–265). San Francisco: Jossey-Bass.

Tolbert, A., Larkin, C., & McLean, G. N. (2002). *Coaching for the gold: Instrument and technical manual.* Minneapolis: Larkin International. (Sample is available at http://eccointernational.com/organizationdevelopment/ organizationdevelopment_tools_coachingprofiledescription.html.)

Tolbert, A., & McLean, G. N. (1995). Venezuelan culture assimilator for training United States professionals conducting business in Venezuela. *International Journal of Intercultural Relations, 19*(1), 111–125.

Tolbert, A. S., McLean, G. N., & Myers, R. C. (2002). Creating the global learning organization (GLO). *International Journal of Intercultural Relations, 26,* 463–472.

Trompenaars, F. (1994). *Riding the waves of culture: Understanding cultural diversity in business.* New York: McGraw-Hill.

Transparency International. (2004). *TI Corruption Perceptions Index 2004.* Retrieved May 30, 2005, at www.transparency.org/cpi/2004/cpi2004.en .html#cpi2004.

Tuckman, B. W. (1965). Development sequence in small groups. *Psychological Bulletin, 63*(6), 384–399.

Uttal, B. (1983). The corporate culture vultures. *Fortune, 108,* 66–72.

Virakul, B., & McLean, G. N. (2000). AIDS in the workplace: Experiences and HR practices in Thai business organizations. *Thai Journal of Development Administration, 40*(3), 27–46.

Watkins, K. E., & Marsick, V. J. (Eds.). (1996). *In action: Creating the learning organization.* Alexandria, VA: American Society for Training and Development.

Weick, K. E., & Quinn, R. E. (1999). Organizational change and development. *Annual Review of Psychology, 50,* 361–386.

Weisbord, M., & Janoff, S. (2000). *Future search: An action guide to finding common ground in organizations and communities.* San Francisco: Berrett-Koehler.

Wheatley, M. J. (2001). *Leadership and the new science: Discovering order in a chaotic world.* San Francisco: Berrett-Koehler.

Worley, C. G., & Feyerherm, A. E. (2003). Reflections on the future of organization development. *Journal of Applied Behavioral Science, 39,* 97–115.

Worley, C. G., Rothwell, W. J., & Sullivan, R. (2005). Organization development competencies (Version 21). In D. W. Cole (Ed.), *The international registry of organization development professionals and organization development handbook* (pp. 43–46). Chesterland, OH: The Organization Development Institute.

Worley, C., & Varney, G. (1998, Winter). A search for a common body of knowledge for master's level organization development and change programs. *Academy of Management ODC Newsletter,* 1–4.

Yamnill, S., & McLean, G. N. (in press). Human resource development in a religious institution: The case of Wat (Temple) Panyanantaram, Thailand. *Human Resource Development International.*

Yang, B., Zhang, D., & Zhang, M. (2004). National human resource development in the People's Republic of China. *Advances in Developing Human Resources, 6*(3), 297–306.

York, L., O'Neil, J., & Marsick, V. (Eds.). (1999). *Action learning: Successful strategies for individual, team and organizational development.* San Francisco: Berrett-Koehler.

Zanko, M., & Ngui, M. (2003). The implications of supra-national regionalism for human resource management in the Asia–Pacific region. In M. Zanko & M. Ngui (Eds.), *The handbook of human resource management policies and practices in Asia–Pacific economies (Vol. I & II)* (pp. 5–22). Cheltenham, U.K.: Elgar.

Name Index

Subject Index

451

About the Author

Dr. Gary N. McLean

A Canadian by birth, Gary N. McLean was raised in London in Ontario, Canada. Attending the University of Western Ontario, after 1 year at Graceland College in Lamoni, Iowa, he received an honors B.A. in business administration and office administration. At Teachers College, Columbia University, where he met and married his wife, McLean earned a master's and doctorate, both in business education. From United Theological Seminary in Minnesota, he received a master's of divinity degree. Though he considers himself a global citizen, he actually holds dual citizenship with the United States and Canada.

McLean has been involved in higher education for 40 years, 36 of them at the University of Minnesota, and has worked as an OD consultant for 35 years, with more than 50 clients (many repeats). A son and a daughter have joined him now, in McLean Global Consulting, Inc. In addition, he is a part owner of HRConnection, an HR company that provides support for small-group sharing among HR professionals, as well as contract and placement services for HR professionals.

As an OD professional, McLean has worked in more than 40 countries; published in excess of 200 articles and book chapters; and authored, coauthored, or edited 22 books. His scholarship has resulted in the awarding of Outstanding Scholar by the Academy of Human Resource Development. His excellence in teaching has been recognized by both the College of Education and Human Development and the University of Minnesota through the awarding of the designation as Morse Alumni Distinguished Teaching Professor. McLean has been awarded lifetime membership in the Minnesota OD Network in recognition of his service to OD.

Active in many professional organizations, McLean has served as president of the International Management Development Association and as president of the Academy of Human Resource Development. He has also been an editor of four refereed journals.

Family is extremely important in McLean's life. His six children, only five and a half years apart in age as a result of adopting four Korean children, are now adults. They, along with three grandchildren (and one on the way), form the base of a wonderful, diverse, and expanding family. All of his children and their families live within 15 minutes of his home, meaning, happily, that he sees a lot of them.

About Berrett-Koehler Publishers

Berrett-Koehler is an independent publisher dedicated to an ambitious mission: Creating a World that Works for All.

We believe that to truly create a better world, action is needed at all levels—individual, organizational, and societal. At the individual level, our publications help people align their lives and work with their deepest values. At the organizational level, our publications promote progressive leadership and management practices, socially responsible approaches to business, and humane and effective organizations. At the societal level, our publications advance social and economic justice, shared prosperity, sustainable development, and new solutions to national and global issues.

We publish groundbreaking books focused on each of these levels. To further advance our commitment to positive change at the societal level, we have recently expanded our line of books in this area and are calling this expanded line "BK Currents."

A major theme of our publications is "Opening Up New Space." They challenge conventional thinking, introduce new points of view, and offer new alternatives for change. Their common quest is changing the underlying beliefs, mindsets, institutions, and structures that keep generating the same cycles of problems, no matter who our leaders are or what improvement programs we adopt.

We strive to practice what we preach—to operate our publishing company in line with the ideas in our books. At the core of our approach is *stewardship*, which we define as a deep sense of responsibility to administer the company for the benefit of all of our "stakeholder" groups: authors, customers, employees, investors, service providers, and the communities and environment around us. We seek to establish a partnering relationship with each stakeholder that is open, equitable, and collaborative.

We are gratified that thousands of readers, authors, and other friends of the company consider themselves to be part of the "BK Community." We hope that you, too, will join our community and connect with us through the ways described on our website at www.bkconnection.com.

BE CONNECTED

Visit Our Website

Go to www.bkconnection.com to read exclusive previews and excerpts of new books, find detailed information on all Berrett-Koehler titles and authors, browse subject-area libraries of books, and get special discounts.

Subscribe to Our Free E-Newsletter

Be the first to hear about new publications, special discount offers, exclusive articles, news about bestsellers, and more! Get on the list for our free e-newsletter by going to www.bkconnection.com.

Participate in the Discussion

To see what others are saying about our books and post your own thoughts, check out our blogs at www.bkblogs.com.

Get Quantity Discounts

Berrett-Koehler books are available at quantity discounts for orders of ten or more copies. Please call us toll-free at (800) 929-2929 or email us at bkp.orders@aidcvt.com.

Host a Reading Group

For tips on how to form and carry on a book reading group in your workplace or community, see our website at www.bkconnection.com.

Join the BK Community

Thousands of readers of our books have become part of the "BK Community" by participating in events featuring our authors, reviewing draft manuscripts of forthcoming books, spreading the word about their favorite books, and supporting our publishing program in other ways. If you would like to join the BK Community, please contact us at bkcommunity@bkpub.com.